Forgotten Voices

Forgotten Voices

The Expulsion of the Germans from
Eastern Europe after World War II

Ulrich Merten

Transaction Publishers
New Brunswick (U.S.A.) and London (U.K.)

Library of Congress Catalog Number: 2011029450
ISBN: 978-1-4128-4302-7
Printed in the United States of America

Library of Congress Cataloging-in-Publication Data

Merten, Ulrich, 1930-
   Forgotten voices : the expulsion of the Germans from Eastern Europe after World War II / Ulrich Merten.
      p. cm.
      ISBN 978-1-4128-4302-7 (alk. paper)
   1. World War, 1939-1945—Refugees—Europe, Eastern. 2. World War, 1939-1945—Forced repatriation. 3. World War, 1939-1945—Atrocities—Europe, Eastern. 4. Population transfers—Germans. 5. Germans—Europe, Eastern—History—20th centruy. I. Title.
      D809.G3M47 2012
      940.53'14—dc23
                        2011029450

To Carole Merten Lockerbie, indefatigable companion
and editor, and Margit Merten Wagner source of
my love for German history and culture.

Contents

Preface

This book offers a multifaceted and, in the English language, largely unknown history of the expulsions of Germans from Eastern Europe written by one who himself lost his home. Ulrich Merten, born in 1930 in Berlin, fled Nazi Germany for the United States as a child together with his parents, who actively opposed the Nazi regime. His father, Dr. Georg Muhle Merten, was a member of the German Democratic Party and *Regierungsrat* (Councilor) in the Prussian Ministry of the Interior during the Weimar Republic, which he actively supported. In fact, during the mid-1920s, he became head of a government intelligence organization that was in charge of prosecuting antidemocratic activities and thus opposed the Nazi party early on. Once the Nazis were firmly ensconced in power, he was charged with high treason and incarcerated in the notorious Oranienburg concentration camp north of Berlin in 1934–1935. The years before their emigration to the United States in 1938/1939, when Georg Muhle Merten remained active in the anti-Nazi resistance, were extremely difficult for the family. Yet, once he was settled in New York, the elder Merten resumed his anti-Nazi activities and worked for British and American intelligence, in which capacity he helped unveil Nazi commercial and financial activities in the United States and South America.

Ulrich Merten, the author of this study, has held a life-long interest in the fate of the German population in the former German provinces of East and West Prussia, Pomerania, Silesia, Eastern Brandenburg, and the Sudetenland, as well as the destiny of the large German minorities in Poland, Hungary, Yugoslavia, and Rumania that were expelled from their native territories after 1945. After attending universities in Switzerland and Spain, Ulrich Merten graduated from Columbia and Pennsylvania's Wharton School before embarking on a distinguished career in banking. It was during his extended stays in central Europe in the immediate postwar period that he witnessed first-hand the plight and misery of millions of ethnic German refugees. Now more than six decades later, retirement has finally afforded him the time to investigate these problems in depth and acquaint the American reader with one of the corollaries of the most destructive war in human history with which even the educated public on this side of the Atlantic is wholly unfamiliar.

Before World War II, well over eighteen million Germans lived in what was generally referred to as Eastern Europe during the Cold War, that is, in East Prussia, Pomerania, the eastern Part of Brandenburg, Silesia, the free city of Danzig, as well as in territories outside the-then German Reich, in Czechoslovakia, notably the Sudetenland, in the Baltic States, in interwar Poland, Hungary, Rumania, Yugoslavia, and in parts of the Soviet Union.[1] Beginning in the late summer months of 1944, of those who had survived the war up until then, more than fourteen million were expelled. Between the end of 1944 and 1948, about two million were killed or died of starvation or suicide. And even though no reliable figures exist, there is a basic consensus that the overall number of those who perished was in the neighborhood of two million.[2]

Of the millions of refugees who survived, more than eight million made it to one of the three Western zones of occupation that became West Germany in 1949; more than four million found a temporary home in the Soviet zone, the latter-day East Germany, from whence many subsequently fled to the West; while about half a million, mostly from the Sudetenland, Yugoslavia, and Rumania, found a home in Austria.[3] Since Germany's war-torn and bombed-out cities could barely support their own indigenous populations, refugees were generally settled in rural parts of Germany, such as Mecklenburg-Vorpommern in the East, or Bavaria, Schleswig-Holstein and Niedersachsen in the West, to the point that in the late 1940s, the populations of Schleswig Holstein and Niedersachsen had risen by more than 50 percent.

In what was the Soviet zone of occupation that became East Germany in 1949, the East German regime denied, for political reasons, that any wrongs had been committed against the expellees. This was reflected in semantic changes, so that politically charged terms such as "expellees" or "refugees" were changed to "Umsiedler" (re-settlers) or "new citizens." In West Germany the problems of the expellees and refugees soon receded from public consciousness by the late 1950s and 1960s in spite of the enormous numbers involved. There had been little interest in their fate from the beginning, since indigenous local populations were faced with seemingly insurmountable problems of their own after 1945. In the gloomy postwar years, starvation was widespread, and before the Marshall Plan and the full onset of the Cold War, it seemed quite likely that the destroyed German cities would never be fully rebuilt. No wonder then that refugees were made to feel unwelcome and undesired, though until the 1950s their sheer numbers constituted a formidable presence at the polls that had to be taken seriously by politicians. In both parts of Germany they quickly came to be associated with extreme nationalism and Nazism and were disproportionately blamed for Hitler's rise to power. It is a fact that in the elections of the early 1930s, Prussia's eastern provinces—East Prussia, Pomerania, and parts of Silesia—were strongholds of the National Socialist German Workers Party (NSDAP), which won over 50 percent of the vote in some districts in the 1932 parliamentary elections. And it is also true that the ethnic German population in the Sudetenland rallied around Konrad Henlein's nationalistic Sudetendeutsche Party—partly as a reaction to the repression of the Sudeten German minority by the Czechoslovak government ever since 1919. But millions of those expelled from East Prussia, Pomerania, and Silesia had voted for the SPD, the Center Party, or other Weimar democratic parties before Hitler came to power in 1933. The blanket condemnations refugees encountered were thus wholly unjustified.

That the actual process of the expulsions was a far cry from "the orderly and humane way" in which they were supposed to be conducted according to Article Thirteen of the Potsdam Agreement, signed on August 2, 1945, by the American President Truman, Soviet leader Stalin, and the British Prime Minister Attlee, was well known at the time. In fact, Western democracies were fully aware of the nature of the expulsions of the ethnic German population from what had been their homeland for more than 800 years and of the human cost involved, as is borne out by a letter from Bertrand Russell to the London *Times* of October 23, 1945, in which he wrote: "In eastern Europe now mass deportations are being carried out by our allies on an unprecedented scale, and an apparently deliberate attempt is being made to exterminate many millions of Germans, not by gas but by depriving them of their homes and of food, leaving them to die by slow and agonized starvation."[4] Yet, in the immediate postwar period the mental climate, even in the West, was understandably such that after all the crimes committed by Hitler's henchmen in the name of Germany, any reprisals visited upon German refugees, regardless of their involvement with the regime, seemed justified. All Germans were implicated in this charged atmosphere and few asked whether particular individuals had supported the Nazis or opposed them.

The strengths of Ulrich Merten's detailed and careful study are manifold. He aptly contrasts the authenticated and verified eyewitness accounts assembled by the West German government in the 1950s, which attest to the suffering and inhumane treatment of the expelled German population, with accounts of German atrocities, such as concentration camp death marches, and the participation of ethnic Germans in Waffen SS units, such as the "Prinz Eugen Division" in Yugoslavia. He also makes it very clear that in those days the dividing line between good and evil was fluid. The same Red Army that committed savage atrocities against the civilian population in the East also liberated the annihilation camps and brought the Nazi death factories of Auschwitz, Sobibor, and elsewhere to a standstill. Merten also offers us here a very comprehensive account that covers expulsions of ethnic Germans not just from the former German provinces of East Prussia, Silesia, eastern Pomerania, and Eastern Brandenburg, but also from Poland, Czechoslovakia, Hungary, Yugoslavia, and Rumania. Throughout the book, the author provides clear explanations needed to elucidate the historical context for the American reader, such as brief histories of German settlements in countries that, in the case of Rumania, for example, reach back into the Middle Ages. And he throws light on the motivations of governments by providing official justifications of the expulsions put forth, for example, by Poland, Czechoslovakia, and Hungary.

To understand the ferocity of the expulsions and the atrocities committed in their wake, it is important to remember that Hitler's war of extermination in the East and the mass murders committed by his regime, had just preceded them. Merten does an exemplary job of elucidating this vital connection. In postwar Germany, the political Left has tended to ignore the topic of the expulsions of the German population from the east. Some have accused those who write about the expulsions and *Vertreibungsverbrechen*—the crimes accompanying them—as serving the interests of the political Right or seeking to lessen German culpability for the outrages of the Nazi period. This is manifestly not the case here. Ulrich Merten provides us with a balanced account of this emotionally charged issue. Based on his own eyewitness experience and understanding, as well as his mastery of the relevant literature, the author approaches this topic with both a cool intellect and an informed heart.

Hermann Beck
University of Miami
Miami, July 2011

Notes

1. Gerhard Reichling, *Die deutschen Vertriebenen in Zahlen*. Teil I: *Umsiedler, Verschleppte, Vertriebene, Aussiedler 1940-1985* (Bonn: Kulturstiftung der deutschen Vertriebenen, 1995), 17; Andreas Kossert, *Kalte Heimat. Die Geschichte der deutschen Vertriebenen nach 1945* (Berlin: Siedler, 2008), 22–23.

2. Kossert, *Kalte Heimat*, 41; Jörg Echternkamp, *Nach dem Krieg. Alltagsnot, Neuorientierung und die Last der Vergangenheit 1945-1949* (Zürich: Pendo, 2003), 47, speaks of "over two million," while Manfred Görtemaker, *Geschichte der Bundesrepublik Deutschland. Von der Gründung bis zur Gegenwart* (Frankfurt/M: Fischer Taschenbuch, 2004), 169, mentions the figure of "about 2.1 million."

3. Echternkamp, *Nach dem Krieg*, 50; Kossert, *Kalte Heimat*, 10.

4. Quoted in Kossert, *Kalte Heimat*, note 14, 359.

Acknowledgments

I wish to recognize the invaluable assistance given to me by Dr. Hermann Beck, a leading modern German historian as well as by Dr. John Flynn who shares these honors. Both read the manuscript and their comments were much appreciated. Thanks should also be extended to Robert Ross, the first to read the manuscript; to my son, Philip, for having created the book's Web site; Dr. Henry Hamman for his advice on the arduous task of writing and publishing a book; Attorney Margarita Muiña for her help on legal matters, particularly relating to copyright issues; and Dr. Walter Weinberger who reviewed the chapter on the expulsions from Czechoslovakia. Special mention should also be given to Dipl.-Ing.Herbert Prokle, Director of the Donauschwäbische Kulturstiftung, of Munich for permission to use many of the personal, eyewitness reports of the victims of communist repression in the former Yugoslavia and to Klaus Mohr, M.A., of the Sudetendeutsche Stiftung, Munich, for permission to use several photographs from their archives. Last, but certainly not least, a special thanks must be extended to Dr. Irving Louis Horowitz without whose guidance this book would never have appeared.

Foreword

They have sown the wind, and they shall reap the whirlwind.
—Hosea 8:7

In January of 2009, the international news agency Reuters reported that a mass grave containing 1,800 bodies was found in Malbork, Poland, the previous Marienburg, West Prussia. Polish authorities suspect that they were German civilians. They were probably killed by advancing Soviet forces or in their subsequent flight. "We are dealing with a mass grave of civilians, probably of German origin. The presence of children....suggests they were civilians" reported Zbigniew Sawicki, a Polish archeologist supervising the exhumation. "It is very puzzling that no personal belongings have been found among the remains.... We have few clues as to how these people died, though there is a high probability that they were war victims" Sawicki said. It was reported that some one hundred bodies were found with bullet holes in their skulls, though the probable cause of death for many was hunger and cold. According to the Associated Press, town official Piotr Szwedowski said, "These people died in such an inhuman way, were dumped so inhumanely, that we need to bury them in dignity and respect."

More than sixty years ago the German Nazi regime committed great crimes against innocent civilian victims: Jews, Poles, Russians, Serbs, and other people of Central and Eastern Europe. At war's end, however, innocent German civilians in turn became victims of crimes against humanity. This book proposes to let these German victims of ethnic cleansing tell their story in their own words so that they, and what happened are not forgotten. Likewise, it is just as important to record the voices of the victims of the Nazis in order to also keep the memory of their suffering alive.

It is not the purpose of this book to promote the equivalency of the crimes against German civilians in the East vis-a-vis German crimes against the people of Eastern Europe. That is impossible, as the root cause of this tragedy was the Nazi German regime that caused this war and the genocide of Jews, Poles, and Russians.

As a leading German historian, Hans-Ulrich Wehler, said, Germany should avoid creating a cult of victimization, and thus forgetting Auschwitz and the mass killing of Russians. It should also be remembered that the 1945 Potsdam Agreement between the three powers sanctioned these expulsions, although it was stipulated that it be done in an "orderly and humane" manner.

Nevertheless, applying collective punishment to an entire people, no matter what the circumstances, is a crime against humanity. It should also be recognized that this was a European catastrophe, and not only a German one, because of its magnitude and the broad violation of human rights on European soil.

Note: Please refer to http://www.forgottenvoices.net, for all maps and photographs.

I

Background

I am particularly concerned at this moment, with the reports reaching us of the conditions under which the expulsion and exodus of Germans from the new Poland are being carried out. Between eight and nine million persons dwelt in those regions before the war. The Polish Government say that there are still 1,500,000 of these, not yet expelled, within their new frontiers. Other millions must have taken refuge behind the British and American lines, thus increasing the food stringency in our sector. But enormous numbers are utterly unaccounted for. Where are they gone, and what has been their fate? The same conditions may reproduce themselves in a modified form in the expulsion of great numbers of Sudeten and other Germans from Czechoslovakia. Sparse and guarded accounts of what has happened and is happening have filtered through, but it is not impossible that tragedy on a prodigious scale is unfolding itself behind the iron curtain which at the moment divides Europe in twain. I should welcome any statement which the Prime Minister can make which would relieve, or at least inform us upon this very anxious and grievous matter.
—Former Prime Minister Winston Churchill's statement to
Parliament on August 16, 1945

It was the greatest expulsion of a people from their ancestral homelands in the history of modern Europe. More than fourteen million Germans either fled or were forced to leave their homes in Eastern Europe after World War II. As such it can be considered the most egregious case of ethnic cleansing ever to have occurred in Europe. Although it is impossible to accurately calculate how many died or went missing in this flight and expulsion, the German government estimates that more than 2,100,000 Germans were victims of these actions. (It is very difficult to find consistent figures for the number of German expellees or the loss in lives. One of the reasons is that there were many Germans living in this area who were evacuated from the West to escape allied bombing attacks. One German government source states

1

that the total refugees and expellees from Central/Eastern Europe amounted to 16.5 million with total casualties at 2.23 million.)[1]

The expulsions originated in two areas in Eastern Europe, the first from provinces that were a part of the German state prior to World War II. (See map 1) They were awarded to Poland as a result of the Yalta agreement in February 1945 between the three great powers, and the subsequent Potsdam Conference in July–August of the same year. The Potsdam agreement ratified these boundaries, subject to an eventual peace treaty with Poland. These German states were East Prussia, south of Königsberg (the northern portion was awarded to the Soviet Union), East Pomerania, East Brandenburg, and Silesia. The Germans who lived in this area are known as "Reichsdeutsche," or national Germans. (See map 2)

The German population was also expelled from regions in Eastern Europe where they had lived as minorities as a result of the Treaties of Versailles and St. Germain (with Austria). These treaties, together with the Trianon Treaty (with Hungary), rearranged the boundaries of Central and Eastern Europe after World War I, based in great part on Wilson's fourteen points (reflecting the idea of national states based on the dominant ethnic group but with cultural and political rights for the minorities). The principal communities were in Czechoslovakia, Bohemia, and Moravia, known as the Sudetenland. In Western Poland they were in the Polish Corridor, West Prussia (Pomorze), the province of Posen (Poznan), and Upper Silesia (Gorny Slask). Germans had colonized and lived in these areas for more than 800 years. There were also large German minorities in Rumania, Transylvania, and in the Banat, of the Danubian Swabians, located in the Danube basin in present-day Romania, Hungary and in the Vojvodina, Serbia. (For example, the Hungarian king Geza II, 1141–1162, invited German colonists to Transylvania to defend the borders against Mongolian incursions.) Most of these ethnic Germans lived in former Habsburg lands, except for those in Poland, who, prior to World War I, were Prussian. These Germans are known as "Volksdeutsche," or ethnic Germans. (See map 3 of German settlements in the former Austro-Hungarian Empire)

The Reasons for Ethnic Cleansing

Reasons for the ethnic cleansing of Germans are many, varied, and complex. Most obviously, it was motivated by a desire for revenge and the settlement of old scores for the mass murders committed by Nazi Germany in these Eastern European lands and in the Soviet Union. The Nazi regime committed horrendous crimes in the name of Germany. Not only were almost six million Jews killed, originating primarily from Eastern Europe, but also about three million non-Jewish Poles were the victims of executions, death camps, forced labor, and starvation.[2] According to the Holocaust Museum in Washington, DC, 12.4 million Russian civilians were killed or starved to death by German forces, including about one million Jews.[3] As the former German President, Richard von Weizsäcker, said in a speech to the German parliament on May 8, 1985, "The genocide of the Jews is... unparalleled in history."

It should be pointed out that on May 13, 1941, one month before the German attack on the Soviet Union, Hitler authorized German soldiers to kill Russian civilians in the course of the conflict, without fear of any punishment.[4] To control the occupied eastern lands, he also ordered that "The troops available for securing the conquered Eastern Territories will, in view of the size of this area, be sufficient for their duties only if any resistance is met, not by legal punishment of the guilty, but by striking such terror into the population that it loses all will to resist ... The Commanders concerned are to be held responsible ... they will contrive to contain order, not by requesting reinforcements, but by employing suitably draconian methods."[5] In September 1941, Field Marshall Wilhelm Keitel, Supreme Commander of the Wehrmacht, ordered that German troops in Yugoslavia take harsh measures against partisans. Reprisals against partisans were to be that for every German soldier killed, one hundred captured partisans be shot.[6]

As a further example: in Yugoslavia the desire for revenge stemmed, in part, from the massacres committed by the Waffen-SS. They recruited very energetically in the German communities in the Yugoslav Banat region, in today's Vojvodina. Over 15,000 men served in the SS Volunteer Mountain Division "Prinz Eugen." Early in the war, these were mostly volunteers, but later, as the war began turning against Germany, the SS had to resort to forced recruitments. This Division was principally engaged in fighting Tito's partisans, mostly Serbs. It gained notoriety by conducting a series of massacres of Serbian and Croatian civilians in Dalmatia in March of 1944. Thus it came as no surprise that the Yugoslav Partisan government after the war considered the German community collectively responsible for these war crimes. It interned many ethnic Germans in concentration camps (about 55,000 died), and sent many, some 27,000–37,000, as slave labor to the Soviet Union, of whom few survived. The rest fled or were expelled to Austria and Germany.[7]

Perhaps the most significant reason for the expulsion of the Germans from Poland was Stalin's major war goal of moving his frontiers westward, in order to create a new "cordon sanitaire" for the protection of the Soviet Union. Poland was to receive German territories in the west in compensation. The German population was to be transferred to the remaining Germany. By moving the Soviet western border to the Curzon Line (see map 4) in Eastern Poland (Western Byelorussia and Western Ukraine), first achieved by the infamous Molotov–Ribbentrop Pact of August 1939, the country was divided between Germany and the Soviet Union. As early as November 1943, at the Tehran conference, Roosevelt, Churchill, and Stalin agreed, in principle, that the Western boundaries of the Soviet Union would be at the Curzon Line, without delineating, however, Poland's boundaries with Germany. (The Curzon Line was the demarcation line proposed by the Allies during the Soviet–Polish War of 1919–1920. Neither the Poles nor the Soviets accepted the Allied plan. One of the Allied mediators was Lord Curzon. The Polish victory gave much of Western White Russia and the Ukraine to Poland.) At the Yalta "Big Three" conference, in February 1945, it was agreed again that the Curzon Line would be the Western boundary of the Soviet Union. Poland would be compensated by lands ceded by Germany, east of the Oder and Neisse Rivers. The Potsdam Conference ratified these agreements with the understanding that final German/Polish borders would be settled by a peace treaty. The German population of these regions was to be expelled and replaced by Poles resettled from Eastern Poland. After the Conference was over, Soviet Deputy Foreign Minister Vishinsky noted with satisfaction that the "U.S. delegation left Potsdam realizing Eastern Europe has been permanently lost to Russia by the Anglo-Americans."[8] (Vishinsky's conversation with the Bulgarian representative in Moscow on August 18, 1945).

The ethnic cleansing of the Germans was also instrumental in consolidating the communist governments in Eastern Europe and ensuring Soviet hegemony over this territory. Stalin advocated this shift in boundaries because it would, he calculated, ensure eternal enmity between Poland and Germany. According to this hypothesis, its purpose was to make the population of these countries dependent on their communist rulers and the Soviet Union, as they were the only ones who could protect them against German revenge for taking their land.[9] They were told that once Germany revives, there will again be a "Drang nach Osten" for the recuperation of lost territories. Only the Red Army and the communist governments could stand in the way of this new German imperialism. Thus, the people had no choice but to support their government, no matter how unpopular it later became. For this reason, the Polish government in exile in London did not support the annexation of the Eastern German regions precisely because they foresaw that it would force Poland to seek the protection of the Soviet Union. It was widely thought that the main beneficiary of the expulsion of the Germans was the communist parties of Eastern Europe.

In the case of Czechoslovakia, the postwar political leadership, particularly the communists, justified the expulsion of the Germans in terms of their social revolution to create a peoples' democracy by eliminating German private ownership of factories and farms. As such, it was a harbinger of the subsequent illegal acts of confiscation by the communist regime, which seized power in 1948. Indeed, it has been said that the radicalization of the Czech people, in their hatred of their German minority, helped to create the conditions for a communist totalitarian regime.[10]

Adding to the perceived need for the expulsions was the consensus reached during and after the war in a number of occupied countries, especially in Poland and Czechoslovakia, that the old paradigm of multiethnic states—set by Wilson's fourteen points—was no longer viable. For example, it is reported that Edvard Benes and his exile government in Great Britain came to the conclusion that the first Czechoslovak state had failed because large numbers of its citizens did not have any loyalty to the state. These minorities, especially the Germans, were considered basically disloyal and incapable of assimilation into the dominant culture. Based on their recent war experience, they were considered a fifth column and traitors who could not be a part of the new Czechoslovakia or Poland.[11]

Undoubtedly, the German minorities in these countries were used as pawns by the Nazi regime in order to foster its imperial designs on its neighbors. In trying to maintain their national identity, they asked for financial and political help from the German government. They received the assistance requested, but were used, in turn, by the Nazi government to promote its expansionist objectives. In both Poland and Czechoslovakia, however, large elements of the German population, particularly the older generations, were prepared to accommodate themselves to their country of residence. Their major aim, however, was to maintain their German culture, including language and way of life. Nevertheless, successful Nazi propaganda directed especially to the younger generations, estranged them from their homeland and made them look to Germany for their future. On the other hand, the assimilation policies of Poland and Czechoslovakia, often forced, alienated many Germans.[12] They had divided loyalties, between the state they lived in and Germany, which remained their cultural motherland. After the war, former Czechoslovakian President Benes said "Our Germans ...have betrayed our state, betrayed our democracy, betrayed us, betrayed humaneness, and betrayed human kind."[13] And the postwar Polish communist leader, Vladyslaw Gomulka, said, "We must expel all the Germans because countries are built on national lines and not on multinational ones."[14]

The treatment of the German minorities in Hungary and Romania was substantially different from that in the other countries. Although the Potsdam Agreement called for the expulsion of all ethnic Germans from Hungary, this was carried out in a more orderly manner and there was little of the violence and hatred witnessed in Poland, Czechoslovakia, and Yugoslavia. The motivation for the expulsion of the Germans from Hungary was not the creation of a homogeneous Magyar state (since they had been generally well assimilated in the dominant culture), but rather the opportunity to seize their lands in a reform sponsored by the communists and allied parties. In Romania, instead of expelling the German communities, large numbers were sent to the Soviet Union as slave laborers. On their release, many were not permitted to return to their homes but sent instead to East Germany. Their lands were confiscated in the communist land reform, destroying their means of economic support. In the 1970s, the Romanian dictator, Nicolae Ceaucescu, permitted the emigration of ethnic Germans to the German Federal Republic in exchange for substantial financial assistance. In time, most Germans in Romania voluntarily left for West Germany.

Thus, from the mosaic of cultures and different ethnic groups that characterized Eastern Europe and the Balkans, national states emerged after the war with homogeneous populations, achieved principally by expelling Germans. (Shortly after the war, some Hungarians were also resettled from Slovakia at the request of the Benes government, but the numbers were never large because the Soviet military authorities in Hungary and the Hungarian Communist Party strongly opposed it. The most important non-German population transfer after the war was that of Poles from Eastern Poland after it was annexed by the USSR. In this process, about 2.1 million Poles moved from the Ukraine, Byelorussia, and Lithuania.[15] Most were settled in former German provinces given to Poland in exchange for lands lost in the East. Although, according to contemporary reports, this move was voluntary,[16] their fear of living in the Soviet Union was, undoubtedly, a strong inducement to leave).

Lastly, simple greed must surely have played an important part in motivating the populace to support the expulsion of the Germans, as authorities permitted looting and illegal confiscation of their property. Basically, it became for many a struggle for the confiscation of German homes and property. Many Germans were well off, compared to the local population. German peasants were generally efficient farmers and often excited the jealousy of their neighbors. Hungarian land reform, instituted at the end of the War, was a justification for the seizure of all lands held by German peasants, even if their farms were below the minimum size for expropriation. The confiscation of German farms and property was also a prelude to the subsequent communist nationalization of land and other productive enterprises. Once there was a precedent for the arbitrary seizure of property, it was difficult for the Polish or Czech farmers and the middle class to protest the state's subsequent seizure of their properties.

The Expulsions

The expulsions began with great brutality in May/June 1945. They were first characterized as "wild" expulsions, done on an ad hoc basis not only by the military but also by ordinary Czechs or Poles. In the Sudetenland, for example, Czech militia, partisans, and revolutionary guards attacked German residents without mercy, shot them indiscriminately, and forced them into humiliating tasks so that even Soviet troops were often shocked. In fact, ironically, Germans frequently saw them as their savior from Czech excesses.

No. 26 [17]

Report of the experiences of A. L., once a member of the German Women's Signals Corps in Prague. Original, dated 17 April 1952, handwritten, 4 pages.

Excesses of Czechs against Germans employed in removing barricades in Prague; removal of sick civilians and wounded soldiers from Prague to Sorau in Silesia.

As a member of the Women's Signals Corps, I was transferred to Prague in April 1945. During the first days of May, having handed in my resignation from the armed forces earlier, I received my discharge papers. On the day after I had got them, I intended to return home to Schleswig-Holstein. I was just at the hairdresser's, when I heard noise and shouting from the street outside. Everywhere, Czech and red flags had been hoisted. A change had come about so suddenly that there was no time to think and to comprehend clearly what was happening. I tried to reach the railway station as quickly as possible and boarded a tram in order to get there. But everything seemed to be upset and the traffic dislocated, and when I inquired in German whether the tram was traveling to the station, I was immediately pushed from the moving tram. Fortunately, it happened in front of a German hospital. German soldiers who had watched the incident from a window, took me to safety. Many Germans—soldiers, men and women—who had been unable to reach their homes, were already assembled in a hall.

On 9 May, all women without children had to assemble in the courtyard. The oldest woman present was 75 years of age. I also belonged to this group. We were divided up into working teams and then chased across the town right down to the Moldau. All the time we had to keep our hands up. If anyone of us dropped her arms, the guards maltreated her with the butts of their revolvers. The mob in the streets behaved even worse. Especially the older women excelled themselves and had armed themselves for this purpose with iron rods, truncheons, dog leashes, etc. Some of us were beaten so badly that they collapsed and were unable to get up again. The rest, including myself, had to remove barricades at the bridge. Czech police cordoned off the place where we worked, but the mob broke through and we were again exposed to their maltreatment without any protection. Some of my fellow sufferers jumped into the Moldau in their desperation, they were immediately fired at. We were sup- posed to carry heavy iron pipes which we were completely unable even to lift. For this we received again terrible blows. Then we were ordered to carry large paving stones, always putting five on top of one another. The blows had weakened our arms so much that we kept on dropping these stones. One of the Czechs had a pair of large scis- sors, and one after another of us had her hair cut off. Another Czech poured red paint over our heads. I myself had four teeth knocked out. Rings were torn by force from our swollen fingers. Others were interested in our shoes and clothes, so that we ended up by being almost naked—even pieces of underwear had been torn from our bodies. Young lads and men kicked us in the abdomen. In complete desperation, I also tried to jump into the river. But I was snatched back and received another beating. I can also remember that one of the Czechs recorded the whole scene with a film camera, I still fail to understand for what purpose...

When the barricades had been cleared, we were ordered to sit down in a line on the bridge. Panic seized us... With our hands up, we were chased back to the field hospital. The German doctors who were still present there, wept when they saw us in our condition.

I broke down completely, all my strength had left me. When I recovered consciousness, I could not see anything because my face was swollen so badly. Apart from the external injuries, I had also received internal ones. For several weeks I was in bed in this hospital, there were no medicines available and the food consisted of watery soups and some occasional bread. There was no milk available for the babies. But the Czech caretaker proved to be a human being, secretly he brought us rolls and white bread, although this could be no more than a drop in the ocean. Whilst helping us, he was very anxious lest someone betray or denounce him.

A few weeks later, we were pushed into cattle trucks and taken to Sorau in Silesia. Men and women were squashed into these trucks, no blankets or straw were provided. The bandages of the wounded could not be renewed and maggots could be seen crawling in them. Nearly all of us suffered from dysentery. Many died during the journey. A special detachment had the job of removing the dead at the larger stations, but the relatives of the dead were not given permission to leave the trucks. An ordinary tin had to be used as a lavatory. When we passed through Dresden, the population brought us bandages and provisions, but it was not nearly enough. Some members of our transport who were able to walk, managed to make their escape here.

We disembarked at Sorau. Already on the following day, however, the Germans of this town were driven out of their homes by the Poles. So I dragged myself again to the station, slowly and on two sticks, in order to try and re-cross the Oder-Neisse-Line. A Russian helped me. He spoke some German and hid me in the brake box of a goods wagon. He even brought me some food, a man's shirt and the jacket of an overall. Yet I was terrified. He behaved very decently, however, throughout the whole journey. I left this train in Kottbus in order to reach Berlin. On the roof of another train I reached Berlin. In July 1945, after a great deal of difficulties, I arrived in the Western zone.

In March of 1945, the Polish military command declared that the entire German people shared the blame for a criminal war.[18] Over 105,000 Germans were sent to labor camps in Poland, awaiting expulsion. The Polish authorities converted concentration camps, such as Auschwitz-Birkenau and others, into internment and labor camps where the Germans suffered from mistreatment, malnutrition, and disease.[19]

9

Subsequently, the conduct of the expulsions was ameliorated by decisions taken at the Potsdam Conference in August of 1945, which called for the expulsions "to be effected in an orderly and humane manner." (By this time, however, about 5,100,000 Germans had already fled or were expelled from Poland and Czechoslovakia.)[20] Antifascist Germans, those who helped their national governments during the war years as well as those who considered themselves assimilated to the dominant ethnic group, were to be exempted from transfer to Germany. As a practical matter, however, with very few exceptions, they were all expelled.

The Potsdam Conference, of the heads of state of the United States, Great Britain, and the Soviet Union (France was not invited), was called to plan the peace and occupation of Germany and the disposition of Germans living in former German lands ceded to Poland as well as in other East European lands. Thus the decision to expel the Germans from Poland, Czechoslovakia, and Hungary was confirmed. There was never a question, however, of not expelling the Germans. This was previously decided at Yalta as well as by the individual governments involved. Churchill, Roosevelt, and Stalin all concluded that the expulsion of Germans from these territories was a prerequisite for a stable postwar order.[21]

On December 15, 1944, Prime Minister Churchill stated before the House of Commons, "A clean sweep will be made. I am not alarmed by the prospect of the disentanglement of populations, nor even by the large transferences, which are more possible in modern conditions than they were before. The disentanglement of populations which took place between Greece and Turkey after the last war … was in many ways a success, and produced friendly relations between Greece and Turkey ever since."[22] This forced exchange of populations, resulting from the Treaty of Lausanne of 1923, led to the expulsion of more than one million Greeks from their homes in Asia Minor, and about 400,000 Turks from Greece.[23]

Therefore, the issue really was how to do it, because the Allied Powers, especially the United States and Great Britain, did not wish their zones of occupation to be overwhelmed with destitute refugees. They already had to deal with severe housing and food shortages. Thus, not only did the Western Allies insist on humane and orderly transfer, to avoid the existing chaos, but they also wanted an agreement on the distribution of these expellees among the different occupation zones of Germany.

There was a point of disagreement, however, between the Western Allies and the Soviet Union on the location of Poland's Western border at the Neisse River. Churchill, particularly, was concerned that it would give Poland too much of the available arable land, making it more difficult to feed the Germans and thus place too heavy a burden on the Allied powers. Proposals were made to locate the Western boundary at the upper Oder River. This was firmly rejected by the Soviets. The Western Allies did not insist because they did not want to endanger relations with the Soviet Union at this stage for the sake of Poland's German border and, in any event, there was very little they could do about it as the land was occupied by the Red Army. (Also a compromise was made rejecting Soviet demands for reparations from the Western zones of occupation, with each occupying power looking to its own zone for reparations.)[24] An agreement was eventually reached, later that year, on Poland's Western borders and to resettle 6.65 million Germans in the three allied zones of occupation, to be accomplished between December 1945 and July 1946.[25] This figure was an estimate of the German population still remaining in the East.

The Flight from the Red Army

The flight from terror first began in the East Prussian village of Nemmersdorf (County of Gumbinen, see map 5), which was taken briefly by Soviet troops in October of 1944. When German troops counter-attacked and reoccupied the village, they found scenes of utmost horror. The former chief of the general staff of the XXXXI Panzer Corps, Erich Dethleffsen, testified before an American Army Court in July 1946 that when the German Army retook the town, they found that a large part of the civilian population had been shot by Soviet troops. Many were nailed to barn doors and then killed. The Soviets raped a large number of women, prior to shooting them. (After the war, historians calculated that soldiers of the Red Army raped approximately two million German women.)[26] The murdered also included fifty French prisoners of war.[27] These atrocities confirmed the worst fears of the German people, echoing Propaganda Minister Goebbels' most dire warnings of Soviet terror and revenge, and undoubtedly helped to explain the fierce and tenacious resistance by the Wehrmacht to the Russian onslaught in the last years of the war.

Please refer to http://www.forgottenvoices.net, for a photograph (#1) of German civilians murdered by Soviet Forces, Nemmersdorf, October 20, 1944.

No. 8

Eyewitness report of the medical student Josefine Schleiter of Osterode in East Prussia. Attested copy, 20 November 1951, 20 pages. Printed in part.

Experiences on the flight and among the advancing Russians in the area of Osterode

We continued on our way to Elbing for hours through the white snow which kept getting deeper. We were plastered all over with snow and had cold feet, and with our numbed fingers we had to spread the bread which was eaten with the cold milk which we had brought in a can. We spent the night on a farm. The people of the farm were on the flight, and strangers had found quarters there for a few hours. In the rooms there was straw and we slept on it for a few hours. The kitchen was crowded out. All the women wanted to cook on one stove and it was a long time before we also could make our soup.

The next morning we went further. The roads were full of refugees, of carts and people on foot. Now and then motorcars full of people and baggage drove past us and were followed by the envious looks of those walking...

Then there was a cry "The Russians are in the neighborhood" and all of us were seized with panic... Suddenly a man arrived on horseback and shouted in a loud voice: "Everyone for himself. The Russians will be here in half an hour." A paralyzing fear came over us.

Suddenly the panzer shot over us. The little town of Preussisch Holland before us was being bombarded. We lay down on the earth near a thick tree, and the projectiles flew over us...

Suddenly the shooting stopped, the panzer rolled up and on all sides there were Russian soldiers in snowshirts. The confusion was so great that one at first did not know whether they were German or Russian soldiers, but then we saw German soldiers with their hands up. They had come from a hospital train and were standing before the Russian soldiers. They were collected together and led away.

The panzer rushed through the rows of carts. Carts were hurled into the ditches where there were entrails of horses, and men, women and children were fighting with death. Wounded people were screaming for help. Next to me was a woman bandaging her husband who was losing blood from a big wound.

Behind me a young girl said to her father: "Father shoot me," "Yes father," said her brother who was about sixteen years old, "I have no more chance" The father looked at his children, the tears streaming down his cheeks and he said in a quiet tone: "Wait still a little while children."

Then came an officer on horseback. Some German soldiers were brought to him. He took his revolver; I shut my eyes, shots fell, and the poor fellows lay in front of us shot in the head, an expression of horror on their faces. The corpses remained there, no one dared to touch them...

We stood on the edge of the road looking at the panzer rolling past and at the soldiers... They waved to us and shouted out: "Hitler ka-putt." Some of them jumped off the panzer, when they moved more slowly, and came towards us: "Urr, Urr," they shouted hoarsely... In a second, numbers of people had been relieved of their watches and rings...There was then a search for arms. It was some hours, before the Russians had passed by...

It was already getting dark and we thought over what we should do. We were helpless on the road and no one worried about us. The Poles, who had worked on the farms as laborers and were on the flight with us, quickly became friends with the Russian soldiers, because they could understand one another, and said to us: "Go home, eat and drink. The Russian is good, nothing will happen to you." The road echoed with the passing panzer. We went further with our carts. The Frenchmen had left us. They collected together and thought they would be at once discharged and sent home... We decided to go by a bye-way to the next farmhouse. This was, however, full of Poles and we went to the nearby house of a farm laborer. It was barricaded, and we had to break the door open with a hatchet which we had found in the barn. There were two pigs there in front of empty troughs. Fowls were on the perches, but there was no food to be seen. We made a fire in the kitchen, ate a little and sat the whole night on the chairs in terror. We did not dare to move...

The next morning we found the other rooms and a furnished bed-room with a stove. We made a fire, and a young man fetched milk from the farm. The warmth, thank God, made us feel better. Then steps were heard, the blood froze in our veins, and this I could see in the faces of the others. Several officers and soldiers came in. One of them could speak some German, again they shouted: "Hitler kaputt. We are going to Berlin." They brought meat which I was to cook... When I had cooked the meat, they ate it with bread, the bones were thrown on the table or on the ground, then they drank from the vodka they had brought with them, smoked and tried to talk to us. Time and again groups of soldiers and officers came in, who warmed themselves and ate the meat and bread they had brought with them.

In the night we had lain down on the beds. There were again steps, an officer came in, flashed an electric torch in our faces and asked: "Germanski?" We answered in the affirmative. Thank God he left the room again. We lay in silence on the beds and waited for the dawn to come. Mr. N. was quite broken-hearted and kept saying: "Where can my wife be with the children?"

We remained here four days. The third night five officers came with revolvers and said: "Get out, we are going to sleep here." Where were we to go? In the next room sixteen Frenchmen had taken up their quarters. We went to them and asked if we could remain the rest of the night there. They agreed, and we sat the whole night freezing there. The following afternoon I had prepared potatoes for the evening and was frying them in the pan, when some drunken young officers came into the room. One of them could speak some German and said: "Your lives are in danger. Run away at once." We put our coats on and went into the yard, where our carts were standing. In the morning everything had still been in the carts. But by now both carts had been plundered. Linen, victuals and trunks had disappeared; there were bits of linen lying torn to pieces on the ground. The horses were quickly harnessed, but the Russians continued to stand near us with their machine-pistols, and observed us threateningly... We set out on our way, in order to go again to the farm of Mr. N. On the way we walked on both sides of the carts, in order to relieve the horses. Occasionally Russian motor cars drove past us.

Suddenly a motor car stopped and three very tall fellows surrounded and seized hold of me, and threw me into their car. My cries could not be heard in the snow-storm. The car started off and I was standing in it, being gazed at by one of the Russians. I was ice-cold. Since midday I had been without food and had nothing but what was on my body. One of the fellows, who was covered up in rugs, grinned at me and asked cynically: "Cold?" The car slowed down and I sprang out, it stopped immediately and I was again thrown back. There then followed the most dishonoring moments of my life which I cannot describe. The car stopped again suddenly. I jumped out and driven by a terrible fear ran as quickly as I could into the winter darkness. It must have been about ten o'clock, and no house was to be seen anywhere. Under my feet was deep snow, I had military boots on, which one of the Frenchmen had given me as my own were wet through and through. The hard leather, however, pressed into my muscles. I ran without stopping until I came to a little bridge. Here I took refuge and would have liked best to lie down in the snow, in order not to wake up again. What will now happen I thought? If a Russian finds me here that will be the end, or if I come into the headlights of a car I shall be carried off. All over my body I was icecold, for I was standing up to my calves in soft snow... Then I heard carts and people passing quietly by. Thank God they were also refugees on their way to Osterode. They still had all their property in the carts; I joined them and we proceeded for about another 8 to 10 kilometers. We came to a big farm. Here we were stopped by Russians, who had seized the farm. We were searched and told that we would not be able to proceed on our way before the next morning.

We were brought into the big cow-shed. The cows were running about outside in the snow. There were more than a hundred people here. People were sitting on the stone-troughs. Some of the men had fetched wood and were making a little fire. If one stood near it one could warm one's self a little. Terrible hours followed, particularly for the women. From time to time soldiers came in, also officers, and fetched girls and young women. No shrieking, no begging, nothing helped. With revolvers in their hands they gripped the women round their wrists and dragged them away. A father who wanted to protect his daughter, was brought out into the yard and shot. The girl was all the more the prey of these wild creatures. Towards morning she came back, terror in her child-like eyes, she had become years older during the night. She sank down into the straw, because her body was no longer capable of giving expression to her feelings. We were all over-come by sadness and desperation. We waited. No more soldiers came, thank God. Around the farm soldiers were standing with the familiar fur caps on their heads and their machine-pistols at their belts.

The next morning all carts were searched for arms. Women and children could pass through. I joined a group and passed alright through the control. The highway was full of refugees. We went on foot beside the carts. The ditches were full up with oats which had been thrown into them, with beds, linen and bits of clothing. People had thrown their things away, in order to make their carts lighter, so that they could move more quickly forwards, for all of them had taken too much with them. They had taken with them household utensils, victuals, beds, clothing, as they had thought they would be able to live somewhere as evacuees in the Reich, until the war was over. But things had turned out otherwise. Very valuable things were strewn about here and must get ruined in the wet. One continually saw the corpses of German soldiers, men, women and children which, however, had now been brought into the fields and at least covered up... In the evening we came to a farm, where we wanted to stay the night.

Here some Frenchmen had already taken up their quarters and were just slaughtering a pig. The owner of the house lay in the yard shot. The moon was shining on his face, which was full of terror... We went into a big room and fetched straw and pushed it into the broken windows. We chopped up wood and made a fire. The room became slowly full, and men, women and children made themselves beds of straw. Coffee was made in the kitchen, and soon everything was still, as everyone was eating his supper. They were mostly farmers, who had large stocks of bread, butter and meat.

I had to look for a place after I had bandaged a sick person who had been brought in. She had a wound as big as a fist in her back, and was also wounded in the leg and in the arms. She had been severely hit during the shooting... I had sat down on a washing bag.

Since the previous midday, I had nothing to eat. I wondered if anyone would have pity on me... It is terrible to have to beg for a piece of bread. The mother of the wounded girl, to whom I first applied, refused, saying that they were a large family and themselves hadn't got much. At last a young country woman gave me a slice of bread with dripping, which I hungrily devoured. In the kitchen the Frenchmen gave me even a cup of milk and peeled potatoes. On the next day I went to a farm which was quite near. Here I was destined to remain some weeks. The young farmer's wife was very kind and put me up as her guest.

There follows a detailed description of the experiences of the authoress in Osterode until September 1945.

Please refer to http://www.forgottenvoices.net, for a photograph (#2) of a grief-stricken German woman. An aged German woman, overcome by the worry of trying to find a home, breaks down and cries, head in hand. In her other hand she holds the shafts of a small hand-barrow containing her few, scant belongings.

It is estimated that three to four million Germans fled the Red Army prior to the end of the war.[28] The flight began in Romania, in August of 1944, when that country changed sides. It extended to the German settlements in the Baltic, principally Memel (now Klaipeda in Lithuania), in the early winter of 1944, and subsequently to East Prussia. As the Soviet Armies reached the southeastern border of Germany in Silesia, the exodus began there as well. When the Russians reached the border of Hungary in early 1945, the Danubian Swabians from the Banat in Hungary and Yugoslavia began to take flight. Once peace was declared in May 1945, however, there developed a counter movement of Germans returning to their homes in the East. It is estimated that over one million inhabitants of these regions then returned to a very-uncertain future.[29] Many, ironically, were ordered to return by Soviet and even by American occupation troops.

A problem common to all those fleeing from the Soviets was whether to leave or not to leave. The regional Nazi political authorities, the Gauleiters, forbade the population from leaving, and when they had no choice but to order an evacuation of the towns and villages, it was often too late as the Red Army rolled in, with often devastating results for the refugees. Frequently it was the German army that facilitated their flight, despite the Nazi Party's prohibition. In other cases the

Wehrmacht hindered refugee flight because they needed the roads for their own retreat from the Russians. It has to be realized that total confusion reigned, as there were no plans for the orderly evacuation of the civilian population. The Nazi Party was in denial about the danger presented to the civilians by the Russian winter offensive and considered any talk about evacuation treason.

With the Soviet occupation came deportation to slave labor camps in the Soviet Union. Trainloads of German civilians were sent East to the Ukraine, the Urals, Central Asia, and Siberia. They never knew their destination. It is estimated that 750,000 ethnic German civilians were sent to the Soviet Union as slave labor. Many never returned.[30] The lucky ones returned after four to five years. They worked twelve to fourteen hours a day in labor camps, collective farms, factories, and mines under harsh conditions. The mortality rates were reported to have been immense.[31]

The expulsion was a particularly great shock to the inhabitants of the provinces that were a part of pre-1939 Germany. Many had returned to their farms and villages after their flight from the war front. They hoped to restart their lives once peace was declared. This was not to be and they were expelled West of the Oder river. "We proceed with the Germans, as they did with us." "It was necessary to carry out the task in so harsh and decisive a manner, that the German vermin do not hide in houses, but will flee from us." These quotes are from the command of the Second Polish Army.[32]

After the Potsdam Agreement, the expulsions slowed until the end of 1945, but then accelerated again in 1946. In that year about two million Germans were expelled from Poland, mostly from the former German provinces. By November of 1946, more than 1.4 million Germans were expelled from the Sudetenland into the U.S. occupation zone, mostly to Bavaria. Three-quarter million were sent in June 1946 to the Soviet zone of occupation.[33] It should be noted that prior to that time, the borders of the Soviet zone of occupation were closed for a time to German refugees from Poland and Czechoslovakia, due to lack of shelter and food.

No. 330

Eyewitness report of the clergyman Erwin Seehaber of Gross-Wittenberg, district of Deutsch-Krone in Pomerania. Photo-copy, 7 December 1949, 7 pages. Printed in part.

Experiences on an expulsion transport at the end of February 1946

In the first part of his report the author describes the flight, the running down by the Russians, and the sufferings under the Russian and later under the Polish occupation.

The news came like a thunder-bolt to us, that the Germans were being driven out of the territories east of the Oder. On the 26 February 1946 a group of militia appeared in the monastery; they were headed by the second mayor, and had a list of all the Germans, who were to go with the first transport, my name was at the top of the list. We had to pack and get out of the place within 10 minutes... I succeeded in putting warm clothes on the children, and in packing some victuals. My wife was at work, but was not on the list. It was only when I energetically protested, that she was put on the list and informed, that she was to be expelled.

We were then brought severely guarded into a large building, and my wife appeared towards the evening. In the course of the day and the night about 400 persons were driven together here from the surrounding villages. All of them reported, that they had had to evacuate their dwellings within10 minutes, and that they only had been able to bring a few things with them. Many of them had had to tramp as much as10 kilometers, and as the snow was deep, they could only get along with great difficulty. Many women had to throw away their baggage, as they had to carry their little children, who otherwise would have collapsed of exhaustion in the deep snow. For they were mercilessly driven on by the militia, who proceeded in reliefs by sledges. Most of these people arrived at the camp completely exhausted.

The building was overcrowded, and there were about 36-42 people forced into a room of 30 square meters. We could not rest, and had only a very small amount of straw. We had to lie or sit on the bare floor, and the sanitation was utterly inadequate. There was no food, and no-one was allowed to leave the building. The transport was supposed to depart on the 27 February, but it was delayed... On the 28 February 1946 there was at last some food, at midday we received an indefinable warm soup, and in the evening 2 slices of dry bread and coffee. We received this diet every day, until the transport departed on the 3 March 1946...

There were goods wagons there, and 37 persons were put into each wagon. Most of the wagons were defective, and had no stoves. Our food on the way consisted of one loaf for 4 persons, and a tablespoon of dried milk. The train at last moved off on the 3 March 1946 at about 17 o'clock, after a second transport had arrived from Treptow-Rega, and to which our train was coupled. We reached Stettin towards the evening on the 4 March, after having made long detours, because many bridges had been destroyed, and were not repaired.

We were again put into a camp, which was about 3 kilometers from the railway station at Tornay. The camp consisted of some blocks of houses, which were surrounded by barbed wire. The camp was much too small for the number of people, as another transport had arrived before us. The people were then simply driven like cattle into the next-door houses, until it was impossible to get anymore in. A sentry was posted there, and that was the end of the matter.

The scenes, which we witnessed, were simply shocking: children screamed for hunger and cold, most of the windows were broken, women cried and collapsed of exhaustion. In the room, into which we had been forced, a woman with 5 children went mad... The next morning we were brought into the actual camp, and were first registered. Everyone received a card with his name and occupation; this card indicated the different stages, which one had to pass through, before being transported further. We had to go to be deloused, and then to the customs, that is to say to have one's baggage searched. What seemed to be of use was stolen, and the searching was very thorough. Anyone, who was found with jewelry, had to undress until he was naked. Children, who were a year old and still lying in a perambulator, had to be taken out of it; the perambulators were stolen. As I had no more valuables, my savings bank book was taken from me, but I managed to save my family book.

The customs office was like a warehouse, all kinds of things were lying about, such as cloaks, dresses, shoes, bacon, sausage, perambulators, furs, trunks, beds, etc., all had been stolen. The stay in this camp was more horrible than in Greifenberg; the people literally had to lean on one another. Food was to be distributed, and even milk for children, but when one had been queuing up for 4-5 hours, and it was finally one's turn, there was then nothing more left.

On the 9 March 1946 in the morning we at last went to the station. There was a truck for aged and sick people...We were then put into goods and passenger wagons. Some of the wagons had no windows nor stoves. On the way to the station we again received dry bread for the journey. We at last departed in the afternoon for the west. There was more plundering on the way by Poles, who jumped into the slow moving train and threw out all that they could lay hands on. The train guard, which was in the first wagon behind the engine, did not trouble itself about this.

We all breathed freely, when we arrived in Lübeck, and saw that there were no Russians in the station.

The expulsions after the Potsdam Meeting were more organized and relatively less brutal than the "wild" expulsions, but for the inhabitants of these areas they were devastating. Not only did they lose all their possessions and homes where they had lived for many generations, but they had to leave in overcrowded open carriage trains, or on foot in long treks. For example, in December of 1946, fifteen hundred refugees were crammed into a nineteen-car train. Death from disease and starvation was rampant. The expellees were usually only allowed to take with them one small suitcase and often not even that. They were harassed all the way to the railway station or transit camps by the local population, police, or militias.[34] Representatives of the Western Powers who oversaw the reception of these refugees in their zones of occupation were horrified by the inhuman conditions under which the transfers were made. By the end of 1949 most expulsions were finished. Among the last transported to the West were some of the inhabitants of Königsberg, in East Prussia, now Kaliningrad, who were expelled by the Soviet authorities. (See map 5) With that almost symbolic occurrence, 800 years of German culture in East Europe came to an end.[35]

Please refer to http://www.forgottenvoices.net, for a photograph (#3) of refugees escaping from East Prussia, Winter 1945.

Notes

1. Alfred Theissen, *Die Vertreibung der Deutschen-unbewälltigte Vergangenheit Europas* [The Expulsion of the Germans – Unresolved Past] (Bonn, 1995), 1; Andreas Kossert, *Kalte Heimat* [Cold Homeland] (Munich, 2008), 9. It should be mentioned that some sources give the total number of expellees at fifteen million; Gerhard Reichling, *Die Deutschen Vertriebenen in Zahlen* [The German Expellees in Numbers] (Bonn, 1986), 28–36; also Heinz Nawratil, *Die Deutsche Nachkriegsverluste* [German Losses after the War] (Graz, 2008), 35.

2. Richard C. Lukas, *The Forgotten Holocaust: The Poles under German Occupation 1939-1944* (Lexington, KY, 1986), 38, 39.

3. United States Holocaust Memorial Museum, Holocaust Encyclopedia, *The German Army and the Racial Nature of the War against the Soviet Union* (Washington, DC, 2011).

4. Guido Knopp, *Die Wehrmacht, Eine Bilanz* [The Wehrmacht, an Assessment] (Munich, 2007), 143.

5. Terry Goldsworthy, *Valhalla's Warriors, A History of the Waffen SS on the Eastern Front 1941-1945* (Indianapolis, IN, 2007), 81.

6. Karl H. Theile, *Beyond "Monsters" and "Clowns"; the Combat SS: Demythologizing Five Decades of German Elite Formations* (Lanham, MD, 1997), 294.

7. Charles Ingrao and Franz A. J. Szabo, eds., *The Germans and the East* (West Lafayette, IN, 2008), 357.

8. Laszlo Bohri, *Hungary in the Cold War 1945-1956* (Budapest, 2004), 72.

9. Richard Blanke, *Orphans of Versailles, the Germans in Western Poland 1918-1939* (Lexington, KY, 1993), 241.

10. Tomas Stanek, *Verfolgung, 1945* [Persecution, 1945] (Vienna, 2002), 17.

11. Eva Schmidt-Hartmann, *Menschen oder Nationen? Die Vertreibung der Deutschen aus tschechischer Sicht, Die Vertreibung der Deutschen aus dem Osten* [People or Nations? The Expulsion of the Germans from Czechoslovakia: The Expulsion of the Germans from the East] (Frankfurt/Main, 1995), 190.

12. Anthony Komjathy and Rebecca Stockwell, *German Minorities and the Third Reich* (New York, 1980), ix, x, xi.

13. Heinz Nawratil, *Vertreibungs Verbrechen an Deutschen* [The Crime of the Expulsion of the Germans] (Frankfurt/Main, 1986) as cited in Norman M. Naimark, *Fires of Hatred, Ethnic Cleansing in Twentieth-Century Europe* (Cambridge, MA, 2001), 112.

14. As quoted in Norman M. Naimark, *The Russians in Germany* (Cambridge, MA, 1995), 146.

15. Naimark, *Fires of Hatred*, 132.

16. Benjamin Lieberman, *Terrible Fate; Ethnic Cleansing in the Making of Modern Europe* (Chicago, 2006), 245.

17. This and subsequent eyewitness accounts in this book were all taken from a series of books published in the period 1954–1961 by the Federal Ministry for Expellees, Refugees and War Victims, of the German Federal Republic, Bonn. This series, comprising five volumes, covers the expulsion of Germans from East of the Oder-Neisse Line in Poland, Czechoslovakia, Romania, Hungary, and Yugoslavia. Its purpose was to leave a permanent historical record of what occurred in the words of the victims. It was edited by Theodor Schieder, of the University of Cologne, and four other scholars from various German universities as well as from the Federal German archives. Professor Schieder was a nationalist and a conservative who was professor of history in Königsberg, East Prussia, during the Nazi period. After the war, he was head of the Association of Historians in Germany. Another member of this editorial board was Hans Rothfels, who was expelled from his teaching position by the Nazis and went into exile in the United States, teaching at Brown University and the University of Chicago. After the war he became a professor at the University of Tübingen. These works in the words of the editors were to ensure careful "authentication and verification" that all accounts were completely historically accurate. In reading these stories, it must be emphasized that they were all from victims of expulsion and violence, and generally did not reflect on the violence done by the Nazi German regime on the people of the East.

18. Lieberman, *Terrible Fate*, 233.

19. Naimark, *Fires of Hatred*, 129.

20. Ibid., 111.

21. Jerry Z. Muller, "Us and Them; The Enduring Power of Ethnic Nationalism," *Foreign Affairs* 87, no. 2 (March/April 2008): 27.

22. Alfred M. de Zayas, as quoted in *Nemesis at Potsdam* (London, 1977), 11.

23. Klaus-Dietmar Henke, *Der Weg nach Potsdam-Die Allierten und die Vertreibung, Die Vertreibung der Deutschen aus dem Osten* [The Way to Potsdam; the Allies and the Expulsion; the Expulsion of the Germans from the East] (Frankfurt/Main, 1995), 59.

24. Debra J. Allen, *The Oder-Neisse Line, The United States, Poland and Germany in the Cold War* (Westport, CT, 2003), 29.

25. Lieberman, *Terrible Fate*, 239.

26. Norman M. Naimark, *Russians in Germany* (Cambridge, MA, 1995), 80.

27. Werner Arndt, *Die Flucht und Vertreibung* (The Flight and Expulsion) (Wölfersheim-Berstadt, 2004), 21.

28. Lieberman, *Terrible Fate*, 223.

29. Thomas Darnstädt and Klaus Wiegrefe, *Die Rache der Sieger* (The Revenge of the Victors) (Munich, 2005), 94.

30. Robert G. Moeller, *War Stories, The Search for a Usable Past in the Federal Republic of Germany* (Berkeley, 2001), 40.

31. Lieberman, *Terrible Fate*, 229.

32. Ibid., 234.

33. Ibid., 243.

34. Ibid.

35. Henke, *Der Weg nach Potsdam*, 82.

II

The Flight and Expulsion of the German Population from East of the Oder-Neisse Line (Poland)

As a people which suffered from the war, we experienced the tragedy of forced resettlement as well as its associated violence and crimes. We remember also that innumerable individuals from the German population were victims of forced resettlement and that Poles were often the offenders...

I want to state it openly. We lament the individual fate and suffering of the innocent Germans, who lost their homeland as a result of the war...

—From the speech of Professor Wladyslaw Bartoszewski, Foreign Minister of Poland, to the German Parliament on April 28, 1995, on the occasion of the fiftieth anniversary of the end of World War II.

The Soviet Attack on East Germany and the Flight of the Civilian Population

The Soviet conquest of Eastern Germany, in the winter and spring of 1944/1945, can be best characterized as an army aggressively pillaging, murdering, burning, and raping its way across a defeated land.

Ambassador George F. Kennan made the following observation in his book, *Memoirs, 1925–1950*:

> The disaster that befell this area with the entry of the Soviet forces has no parallel in modern European experience. There were considerable sections of it where, to judge by all existing evidence, scarcely a man, woman or child of the indigenous population was left alive after the initial passage of Soviet forces; and one cannot believe that

they all succeeded in fleeing to the West ... The Russians ... swept the native population clean in a manner that had no parallel since the days of the Asiatic hordes.

Undoubtedly these atrocities were in revenge for Hitler's declared war of annihilation against the Soviet Union and its people. But it was more than that. It was the specific strategy of the leadership of the Red Army to incite these war crimes and permit acts of violence against the civilian population. The purpose was to arouse the Soviet soldiers to fight more fiercely against the German enemy and to counteract four years of war weariness. Soviet war-time writers, particularly I. Ehrenburg and K. M. Simonov, broadly disseminated their propaganda of hate to the troops to incite them to revenge.

Major Lev Kopelev, a writer and scholar of German literature, was present during these battles in East Germany. The author of *No Jail for Thought*, he was arrested by Stalin for anti-Soviet behavior and bourgeois humanism. He quotes his superior in the Political Administration of the fiftieth Army as saying:

> Zabashtansky had called me in for a heart-to-heart talk. 'You can understand,' he said; 'we're all sick and tired of this war, and the front-line soldiers most of all. When we were fighting on our own soil, everything was simple: we were fighting for our homes, to drive the enemy away. But now we're on their soil, and the soldier who's been under fire for four years now, and has been wounded—and knows that his wife and kids are hungry back home—he's got to go on fighting, on and on! Forward, always forward!
>
> 'Now, we're materialists, aren't we? So what's needed now? First, for the soldier to go on hating, so he'll want his revenge. And second, for the soldier to have a personal interest in going on fighting, to know why he should climb out of that trench and face that machine gun once again. So now, with this order, everything is clear: he'll get to Germany, and there everything is his—goods, women, do what you want! Hammer away! So their grandchildren and great-grandchildren will remember and be afraid!'
>
> 'Does that mean killing women and children?'
>
> 'Don't be silly. Why bring in children? Who's going to start killing children? You? Me? But if you want to know the truth, if there are any who will do it, let them kill the little Fritzes in the heat of the moment, until they get sick of it themselves'...[1]

The worst excesses were committed in the first months of the Soviet advance into Germany, from January and February 1945, to April and the armistice at the beginning of May. By this time, however, the Soviet command became very concerned about the increasing indiscipline of the soldiers and their destruction of German property which was destined to be taken to the Soviet Union. In late June 1945, with the replacement of the military commanders, a concerted effort was made to contain the pillage and rape by the Soviet soldiers, but with only partial success.[2]

There was one further consequence from the Soviet terror against the German population. It facilitated the later expulsion of the Germans from the lands that were to be annexed to Poland and the Soviet Union, because a portion of the population had already fled the Soviet Army. Stalin told the Polish communist leader, Wladyslaw Gomulka, how to get the Germans to leave: "You should create such conditions for the Germans that they want to escape themselves." At the Potsdam Conference of the "Big Three" in July 1945, Stalin is reported to have said that the area to the east of the Oder-Neisse line was already clear of Germans, as many had been killed in the war and the rest had run away from the Red Army. He said that not one German lived in the territory to be transferred to Poland.[3] (See map 11)

The Soviet Attack on East Prussia

On January 13, 1945, the Soviets opened their offensive against East Prussia with a drive to Königsberg (Kaliningrad). (See map 5) German troops at first resisted fiercely, but by January 27, the city was mostly surrounded. By that time, however, the Nazi party chief, the Gauleiter Erich Koch, had already fled to the West in his special train, with the other members of the Nazi hierarchy. Indescribable confusion reigned in Königsberg; there were no evacuation plans, the hospitals were overflowing with wounded, the City was overrun with refugees from the surrounding countryside, and German soldiers were milling around aimlessly, trying to leave the city. The Party left instructions that in case of a Russian breakthrough, the civilian population was to escape to the seaport of Pillau (see map 6). However, as there was no coordination with the army, total chaos resulted because the area was already a combat zone.[4]

With the aid of reinforcements, the German army was subsequently able to stabilize the front around Königsberg for a short time. In a coordinated attack with German forces from Samland, the garrison temporarily broke the Soviet encirclement. This permitted about 100,000 civilian refugees to reach the port of Pillau, where they were taken by ship to the West.[5] In the long run, however, German army strength was insufficient to prevent another Russian encirclement. A last breakout of Wehrmacht units and civilians was attempted on April 9. The result was a slaughter of German soldiers and civilians by superior Russian forces. The surrender of Königsberg on April 10 and the retreat by remaining German forces from Samland, via Pillau and the Nehrung, ended any hope of rescuing the German civilian population from the Soviet forces.

One of the last great crimes of the SS was committed at night on the beaches near Pillau. On January 30 they shot 3,000 inmates of the concentration camp Stutthof, mostly women. They had been promised evacuation from the port to the West. The SS also led to the West long columns of prisoners from the closed camps in East Prussia, in order to hide evidence of their murderous regime.[6]

Stutthof Concentration Camp

The Stutthof camp was opened in September 1939 near the city of Danzig (Gdansk) as a civilian internment camp for Polish intelligentsia and Jews. (See map 7) Following the precedent of most concentration camps, it became a labor re-education camp and finally in 1942 a regular concentration camp. A crematory and gas chamber were added in 1943. Those prisoners too weak or sick to work, were gassed. Originally, it was primarily a camp for non-Jewish Poles, but with the approach of the Soviet Army, in July–August 1944, Jewish prisoners arrived in large numbers from the evacuated concentration camps in the Baltic countries. Forced labor for the German armaments industry became increasingly important in 1944, resulting in the establishment of forty subcamps in the area of West Prussia. Of the total prisoner population estimated at 110,000, more than 85,000 died. The camp was liberated by Soviet forces on May 10, 1945.[7]

The author of the eyewitness account below grew up in Vilnius, Poland (now Lithuania). She was from an upper-middle-class family owning a clothing store in that city. As Jews, she and her family were forced to relocate to the Vilnius ghetto when the German Army attacked the Soviet Union in June 1941. When the ghetto was liquidated by the Nazis, all women capable of working were sent to the Kaiserwald concentration camp near Riga, Latvia. With the approach of the Russian Army in late 1944, they were evacuated to the Stutthof concentration camp. (Source: *Thanks to My Mother*, Schoschana Rabinovici, New York: Dial Books, 1998.)

Credit Line: from *Thanks to My Mother* by Schoschana Rabinovici. Translated from Hebrew to German by Miriam Pressler, and from German to English by James Skofield. Copyright © 1991 by Schoschana Rabinovici, Tel Aviv and Vienna. German translation © 1994 by Alibaba Verlag Gmbh. English translation © 1998 by Dial Books. Used by permission of Dial Books for Young Readers, A Division of Penguin Young Readers Group, A Member of Penguin Group (USA) Inc. All rights reserved.
(See map 7)

...The prisoners at Stutthof made up an international camp. Men in particular were held prisoner there. In the second half of 1944 the Stutthof camp became one of the camps involved in the "final solution," that is, the extermination of the Jews. Then the conditions in the camp, which were already terrible, grew even worse. The camp was simply unprepared to accommodate—even temporarily—all the people who were taken there by the huge transports.

At that time they also began transporting Jewish women there. The new camp was big. There were twelve Jewish blockhouses in its domain.... Originally, each had been designed to hold five hundred people; fifteen hundred to two thousand were now being housed in each blockhouse.

On October 1, 1944, we stepped out in orderly rows along the street between the canals...We stood on the roll call ground, the big square of the "old camp," which was hemmed in on two sides by blockhouses. To our left were the entrance gates and the rear of the headquarters; to our right a double barbed-wire fence with electric wires. All about the area stood watchtowers.

We had to stand there a long time as the officer and the kapos walked between the rows among us, considering us and seeking out the weak and the sick. Those were immediately led away in the direction of the chimney...

Our part of the camp served as a transit camp: the women there didn't work. For that reason, each day you had to stand for hours of roll call, out in the open, in rain and snow, in heat and cold. A German doctor sometimes came and scrutinized the women. He went along the rows, considering the legs of each one and deciding from their appearance whether the women were worth keeping alive or not.

Day after day several dozen of the "sick" would be sorted out from among the rows of women and sent to the gas chambers, or they would be killed by injection.... We got only half food rations, because we weren't working. Hunger tormented us...

27

The time dragged on. We did nothing, but it was forbidden to remain in the blockhouse during the day. We moved about the square between the blockhouses, stood for roll call, or sat leaning against the blockhouse walls... The men weren't working either, and we were terribly worried about them; from experience, we knew that only those who worked had a chance to stay alive...

At the end of October a group of officers from the German army appeared in the camp. They set themselves up in the middle of the square. We were ordered to leave the blockhouses and go to the square. All at once one of the officers ordered all the seamstresses to step forward... The officer chose fifteen women. We were not among them. Then the officer announced he needed upholsterers, and furriers. Raja (the author's mother) seized the opportunity.... She was skilled in working with furs, she said, and I was her chief assistant...But the officer needed still more furriers. Raja encouraged all her friends to sign up for this work....

The skilled workers—about forty—chosen by the officer for work in a shop lined up in three rows and left the Jewish women's camp under guard. We went to work. Our workshops were in heated barracks, and our work involved repairing fur coats for the German army. We set out each morning. We got our midday meal in the workshop: a thicker soup than you got in camp, and an extra ration of bread...At night we went back to the camp to sleep...

The winter of 1944-45 was especially severe. It snowed a lot, and the cold reached minus thirty degrees centigrade... Typhus spread through the camp. Each day there were dozens of dead. Morning after morning the women carried the night's dead out of the block-houses and laid them down next to the wall. From there they were taken away on wagons beyond the fence. Since the crematoriums were no longer sufficient, they began burning the dead on a pyre. The pyre burned not far from the fence of the Jewish women's camp, and we could see it...

And then, all of a sudden, the liquidation of the Stutthof camp began. At the evening roll call of January 25, 1945, the evacuation of the camp was announced, and convoys were arranged for transportation.

The Death March (See map 8)

Snow, frost, ice, biting cold—none of these words even comes close to expressing what I experienced when I stood outside, naked, on the night of January 25-26, 1945.

An hour earlier we had been hustled from the showers with cries of, "Out, out!" Using their clubs, they had thrashed us out of the warm, damp room in which we had just showered... the door was suddenly thrown open; snow and ice swirled in and brought freez-ing cold with them...

Wet, naked, and barefoot as we were, we soon pushed tightly together, and the frost enveloped us... I was no longer smaller and thinner than everyone else, for all the women were small and thin, with sunken breasts; nothing more than skin and bone...

My skin was transparent, my legs were gaunt, crooked, and long, and my arms looked as if a heavy weight had pulled them down and elongated them. My body, too, was only skin and bones; a small body compared to its limbs, with the shoulder bones sticking out starkly, and ribs that you could count. On my thin neck, which looked as if it could break at any moment, sat a much-too-large head, with a small face and overlarge eyes...

I found myself in the midst of a cluster of women who were trying to warm one another by rubbing their naked bodies against each other. The cold had enveloped us, but the worst cold came from below.

We were standing on snow and ice; our feet were naked and we couldn't stand still; the cold burned our soles. And so we hopped from one foot to another; in the crush, we often stepped on the feet of others.... The air was frozen and so stiff it seemed you could cut it with a knife. It was minus twenty-five degrees centigrade.... One woman crumpled to the ground and could no longer rise. Another broke down. Hands stretched out to haul them back up, but it was too late; they could no longer be helped. Finished.

In the early-morning hours, after the unendingly long night, our clothes arrived from being disinfected. Petrified, our bodies glazed by a thin layer of ice, we went to the cart where our clothes were being distributed. One after another, each got her bundle. A couple of women, a couple of "lucky ones," also took the bundles of the women who would no longer need them... we found a pair of big, beat-up boots—men's boots, soldier's boots—that no one laid claim to. I stuck my stiff feet into those boots; I simply shoved them in. Given the circumstances, it was impossible for me to put shoes on any other way. And although our thin clothes were insufficient protection against the cold, we still felt more secure now.

A hot drink was distributed—thin tea, but at least it was hot. We drank, and warmed our hands and fingers on the tin bowls. Our noses and foreheads were also somewhat warmed by the hot steam...

Suddenly a motorcycle appeared, and behind it a black automobile with the commanders of the camp and the officers. We got the order to line up in rows of four and to begin moving in the direction of the main gates.

Thus began the death march...

All in all, over eleven thousand people set out marching in columns. A further eleven thousand from Stutthof and the surrounding camps were assigned transportation by small ships. It was the last ride for most of them: Anyone who didn't die of hunger and thirst went down with the ships, which were bombed not only by the Allies but also by the Germans.

We left Stutthof on the twenty-sixth of January, but the liquidation of the camp had already begun about four A.M. on the morning of January 25, with a roll call for the entire camp...The roll call had lasted a very long time: in the course of it, those slated for evacuation had been singled out.

After disinfections the people were arranged in rows, and the columns set out on the march: Polish men, Lithuanians, Letts, French, Russians, and Germans from Blockhouses I and II, numbering over sixteen hundred people, went as the first column. These were considered privileged, and they were joined by prisoners who had worked in the Jewish hospital.

The second column was comprised of men from Blockhouses III and IV; most of them were Polish and Russian prisoners of war; all together thirteen hundred fifty men.

The third column was men from Blockhouses V and VII: Poles, Russians, Danes, Czechs, Germans, and Norwegians, numbering fourteen hundred prisoners.

The fourth column was composed of Poles and Russians from Blockhouses VIII and X, totaling twelve hundred fifty men—all weak prisoners and sick people.

In the fifth column were Polish, Russian, Italian, and German Jews from Blockhouses IX and XIII, all together eleven hundred men...

The sixth column, from Blockhouses XII and XV contained mostly Polish prisoners and a few Russians.

The seventh column (and the last to get underway on the night of January 25) was made up of women from the first blockhouse of the old non-Jewish camp. There were nine hundred women prisoners from all the diverse nations in the camp.

The next day, January 26, at three A.M., eight hundred twenty men got underway: Norwegians, Poles, Russians, and Frenchmen. On the same day, at about six in the morning, yet another column set out. This was the ninth, and it had thirteen hundred women from the new camp, most of them Jewish—Raja and I were in that column.

I learned this tally only much later. On that day, January 26, 1945, I didn't know how many people had left the camp. It seemed to me the whole camp was marching; the whole world was marching; all of humanity was marching...

Beyond the gates each of us got a blanket, a half kilo of bread, and a half packet of margarine. Most of the prisoners were so starved that they immediately ate up their ration...

The march had been planned by the Germans for an earlier date—for the beginning of January. But because of the approaching front and the big Soviet offensive that had begun in the area on January 12, the appointed day had been postponed. On the day of our departure the Soviets were thirty kilometers away from us.

The commander of the march was SS Captain Theodor Mayer. He commanded forty soldiers with revolvers, and SS men armed with machine guns.

Fifteen soldiers accompanied the two final columns on January 26, the second day of the march. Additionally, there was a protective force comprised of twenty-five German soldiers with large German shepherd dogs that constantly ran back and forth. According to the plan, each column would put twenty-five to thirty kilometers behind them each day; their distance from one another would measure about two kilometers.

The route passed through villages and small "Kaschuben" (Germans of Slavic origin) towns. The prisoners were to sleep in empty barns or stables, and warm food was also to be ready and waiting for them...

The going was tough for us. We walked more slowly than expected. The roads were covered in snow; in many places the snow was so deep, we sank into it. Many times the snow had to be removed before we could go on. The trek was hard and exhausting. Even those who were healthy when we set out became weak and dragged their feet along behind them. Along with that, the cold was unbearable—minus twenty to twenty-five degrees centigrade. The cold wind off the ocean blew frozen snow into our faces... The roads were clogged by fleeing German civilians. Each commander of a prisoners' column was trying to find a route along side streets, in order to bypass the civilian populations. And so it happened that we fell behind and didn't reach the village assigned for our overnight rest. The guards broke into farmers' barns and stables so that we would have quarters for the night.

There was also no food for us. The supplies didn't arrive. We got absolutely nothing to eat the first days of the march...On the third and fourth days of the march, the weather became even worse; it began to snow heavily. We moved forward, covered in snow like mummies... in the snowy, desolate fields, all sounds carried loudly.

When we heard a gunshot, we knew once more that someone hadn't made it; that someone had stumbled; that someone had fallen down, or had simply gone too slowly and had fallen behind the column...

On both sides of the road, we saw the dead bodies of prisoners from the columns that were marching ahead of us. You could see that some

31

of the dead had broken down and died from hunger and exhaustion; others had been shot, and the blood that flowed from their wounds stained the snow red...

The call "Stutthof is marching" was spreading like wildfire among the natives. The train of shadows was attracting the attention of the people. They were gathering at the edge of the road, waiting in the cold and snow for hours. They had come from the farthest villages; they now stood there in silence, despite the attempts of our armed guards to drive them away.

In those days most of the civilians no longer had any fear of the SS. They stood there, angry, silent, and reproachful; a gray mass. That same evening the natives brought big buckets of hot, thick soup to the church in which we had stopped for the night. It was a bean soup, with meat and bacon...

After an eleven-day march, after about one hundred twenty kilometers, what remained of our column—reached Tauentzien (Tawecin) Camp. Tauentzien. a small town to the north of Lauenburg (Lebork) lay on a hill. Almost the entire area belonged to a wealthy German landowner, who was also mayor of the town. The forest behind his house belonged to him as well.

There in the forest the SS had built a work camp that was supposed to be used only in the summer, at harvest time. Several small wooden barracks stood in the camp, which was fenced in with barbed wire. We were taken there. Besides us women who were still alive after eleven days of the death march, there were also members of the fascist regime of Lithuania, who had been arrested toward the end of the war. They had turned against the Germans so as not to be pulled down into the coming ruin. In addition to these there were Norwegians, Letts, Finns, French, and Poles. Their columns had arrived before us and had occupied the best barracks at the site.

Because of the composition of the prisoners, "classes" sprang up here at the end of the world. Besides the Norwegians and Finns, the most privileged were the former members of the Latvian and Lithuanian regimes. These prisoners got water to wash in, and large rations of bread, bean soup, and cabbage.

The second group, the French, also got good soup, and were given the opportunity to work in the cattle stalls of the surrounding farmsteads. The Poles were isolated in the camp and got only one ration of bread and soup per day. We Jewish women had the worst of it...

When our six hundred women arrived, they stuck us into the two small barracks that stood by the road on the other side of the square. The winds were especially strong there. Our barracks was bare; there were neither bunks nor anything to cover ourselves with. Only fresh straw had been thrown into it.

All amenities were lacking in that part of the camp. Our barracks, the one on the road, had been erected in haste from old planks, with broad cracks between the individual boards. There was no floor; the straw covered the damp earth.

We had neither a well nor any other water supply. Drinking water was scarce, and we didn't even dare think of washing ourselves. There was also no sewer system in the camp, and the one latrine that was at our disposal was in the forest, behind the men's barracks. We could go there only as a group, under the supervision of the blitz maidens who guarded us...

Day by day the food rations got smaller; there were no regular supplies to the camp, and the camp leaders soon were only looking after themselves. The prisoners had to satisfy themselves with the kitchen garbage...

Because the hunger was becoming ever greater, the camp authorities brought in sick animals and dead horses and cows; soup was cooked from their flesh. Out of sheer hunger, the prisoners fell on the remains of the food that had been thrown out of the kitchen and fought over it. They even quarreled over the intestines of the dead animals.

Almost all the prisoners suffered from intestinal diseases and diarrhea with heavy bleeding; they began relieving themselves in every corner of the camp. Spotted typhus led to intestinal typhus and that led to a highly dangerous pathology. But there was neither a doctor nor any medicine in the whole camp.

The death toll climbed from day to day; first there were a few deaths, then, dozens. The dead were hauled out of the barracks each morning, taken to the forest, and thrown into a deep ditch. Quicklime was strewn over the corpses. There was no work in the camp, except cleaning the toilet of the camp authorities or disposing of the dead...

February brought rain, and most of the women were coughing and running fevers. Dreadful weeks passed by. On March 7, in the late hours of the evening, we were called to an extra roll call. "Hurry up, hurry up, out, out!" The cries sounded very nervous, and at first we didn't know what was up. In the darkness we could hear shouting, dogs barking, and orders from all sides...

Raja was pushing me, but no reproaches helped her this time. I couldn't stir myself; I wanted to sleep. Raja began scolding, but she suddenly sensed I was burning with fever. At a loss, she began to dress me herself...

We could hear the horrible shouting of the blitz maidens. They were already approaching to hit us when Raja succeeded in getting me up. She supported me so I didn't fall down...and took me outside onto the square.

The whole camp was assembled there. In the dark, under a light rain, the roll call began. We were divided into groups, men and women separated. Raja saw that the groups were slowly beginning to move forward, but when she tried to lead me and get into line, I couldn't walk... my legs wouldn't obey me; it was as if I were crippled...

Raja feverishly considered what she could do. She knew from experience that I would fall behind the group after the first few steps, and then ... She didn't even dare think about it. Her wounded leg pained her greatly; the wound wasn't healing and had entirely festered...

In that moment she reached a decision. Convinced she was doing the right thing, she plucked up her courage and turned to one of the blitz maidens. She said the two of us, she and I, were sick and wanted to remain in the camp. The blitz maiden was surprised by her determined request. She tried to explain that a horse wagon had already been ordered for the sick, so that everyone could leave the camp. But Raja, as well as the woman, knew what any exaggerated concern of the Nazis for the sick meant: death. When another blitz maiden passed by, Raja turned to her and demanded that we be left behind. This one agreed. She ordered us to return to the barracks as quickly as possible.

The train of prisoners began to move...We stayed alone on the roll call ground. Raja supported me, and slowly, very slowly, we returned to the barracks. The whole room was now at our disposal, and there was enough space to lie down. We lay down on the straw. I was burning with fever and took almost no notice of my surroundings anymore. The guard who had been left behind to watch over the camp looked through the open door. Before she lay down, I heard Raja ask the guard, "When will we be shot?"

The young German answered, "I haven't any orders yet. When I get the order to shoot you, then I'll do it." With these words he closed the door. A few blankets had been left behind. Raja covered me up well and stopped up the cracks in the wall next to me before she lay down beside me. I fell asleep.

The next morning I was somewhat better. The guard brought us a good breakfast from the farmers in the neighborhood: bread, margarine, jam, and tea. At noon we got hot chicken soup with meat, and that evening hot porridge, along with bread and tea again. We ate until we were full...

But the next day passed quietly, too. We got food and were permitted to rest in the barracks all day long. I slept, woke up sometimes, ate something, and slept again.

A few times Raja went out to the square to see what was going on outside. But other than our guard, nobody appeared to be there any longer. Once, when Raja returned, I was awake. She told me that all the camp inmates had gone. It seemed the two of us were alone. She tried to prepare me for "the end." I was barely reachable; only the good food interested me.

In the evening we heard the roar of cannons and rocket launchers from the front. That night we were wakened by the noise of heavy engines driving on the nearby street, passing our barracks. Raja looked out through the cracks and saw tanks driving through Tauentzien to Lauenburg, in the direction of Danzig (Gdansk). The earth trembled; the noise was deafening, and gunshots and explosions could be heard from time to time.

When it grew light, Raja recognized the insignias on the military vehicles. They were red stars, and on the caps of the soldiers who sat on the vehicles there were red stars.

It was the Soviet army—our liberators!

A number of prisoners were also evacuated by ship. The following report describes their ordeal.

This eyewitness account of a prisoner at Stutthof, written by Trudi Birger, recounts the flight by ship from Stuffhof until liberated by an English warship. (See map 8) She was born in Frankfurt, Germany, but the Jewish family fled to Memel, (Klaipeda), Lithuania, in 1933. When Nazi Germany absorbed Memel into the Reich in 1939, the family fled again to Kovno, Lithuania. There she experienced the Soviet annexation of Lithuania in 1939, and when the Nazis captured the city in their attack on the Soviet Union in June 1941, the family was transferred to the Kovno ghetto. In 1944, with the approach of Soviet Forces, the ghetto was liquidated. She and her mother were then shipped to the Stutthof concentration camp located near Danzig (Gdansk) on the Baltic. The author was injured in a work-place accident while digging antitank ditches in West Prussia. She and her mother had to return to Stuffhof because of her injury and as she could no longer work she was destined for the gas chamber. She was saved at the last moment by the German secretary of the SS camp commander who took pity on her and her mother. (Source: *A Daughter's Gift of Love: A Holocaust Memoir* by Trudi Birger, Philadelphia, PA: The Jewish Publication Society, 1992.)

Reprinted from *A Daughter's Gift of Love*, © 1992, by Trudi Birger published by The Jewish Publication Society, with the permission of the publisher.

...Meanwhile, things were changing in the camp. After January 1945 they stopped using the gas chamber. If we didn't die by ourselves, the Nazis weren't going to process us in their death factory anymore. Of course, we were all so weak, hungry, and ill that many of us died every day without the help of poison gas. The gas chamber may have been retired, but the crematorium worked overtime...

By early 1945 the Russians started to shell the camp sporadically... The first evacuations from Stutthof took place in late January. During the last months of the war, the Nazi concentration camp empire started falling apart. Apparently they wanted to destroy the evidence. In long columns they marched off all the prisoners who were able to walk, about twenty-five thousand people. These were the infamous death marches...

About ten thousand inmates, including my mother and me, were left in Stutthof; the ones who were too sick or weak to leave on foot. At that time my mother came down with typhus... When my mother was moved to the typhus ward, I was placed out in the hallway where there were six wooden platforms, three on each side, with two patients in each platform...

People were dying of typhus at a tremendous rate. The camp fell into disarray. The crematorium couldn't cope with the volume of corpses, so they built a huge pyre to take care of the excess... Meanwhile, the Russians continued to shell the camp from time to time, but they didn't come...The inspections and selections had stopped, and the Germans left us more or less alone. In the disorder I was able to hobble over to the quarantine section to find out how my mother was...

At that moment a Russian shell landed on the hospital barrack. Just the noise of the explosion knocked me down. When I had pulled myself to my feet again, I saw there was blood beneath my mother's bed. We both felt our bodies to see whether we were wounded. No, we were intact. Then we saw that shrapnel had ripped through the walls and killed some of the people in the beds at the end of the room. People were screaming in pain and fright. Smoke was coming from the corridor where I had just been lying. I hopped back to my place, but it was gone. The shell had fallen right there, and all my friends were dead. Everyone in the room had been ripped to shreds by shrapnel.

Incredibly, my mother recovered from typhus. I don't understand how she managed. Once the fever left her she nearly starved to death... After marching off most of the prisoners in late January 1945, the highest officers among the Germans also abandoned the camp, and we remained with a lot fewer guards. Of course, there was no possibility of escaping or rebelling. We were all too sick to walk more than a few steps; otherwise we would have been sent away with the other prisoners. The Kapos didn't behave quite as savagely as before. There was less torture and indiscriminate killing. We knew the Red Army was on its way...

Finally, in late April, they began the final evacuation from the Stutthof concentration camp. Weak as we were, they made us trudge along the seacoast on foot, without giving us any food. It was a six-hour march. We were surrounded by panic and disorder. The guards kept shouting, "Schnell! Schnell!" (Fast! Fast!). My bad leg suffered terribly on the march. It could barely support my tiny weight, but I had to walk by myself. I bit my lip and kept on. Mother was too weak from typhus to help me. Actually, I was afraid she would die any minute. ...

They marched us along the Baltic sea coast. A brisk wind blew in off the water and chilled us to the bone. At last we got to the three big cattle barges they had prepared for us... They were good-sized boats with large, deep holds and no railing around the narrow deck. A metal ladder led down into the hold. They sent about a hundred women down that ladder, making us lie down in filthy straw.

The barges put out to sea, and we had no idea where they were headed. All we heard was the roar of the engines and the pounding of waves against the sides. When it rained, the rain poured down on us and wet the straw. When the water was rough, the barges rolled so wildly we were sure they would capsize. Many of the women were seasick, and we were all petrified...

Women kept dying. They gave us no food, not even drinking water. We had to drink the filthy liquid, rain mixed with seawater, that lay on the bottom of the hold beneath the straw. We chewed on the straw like animals, just to fool our stomachs. German crewmen leaned over the hatch opening and jeered at us every once in a while:

"You cows! You pigs! Let's see you die like swine!"

Aside from the Germans who were running the boat, there were Polish and Ukrainian prisoners down in the hold with us, the criminals who had done all the manual labor at Stutthof. Among ourselves we called them cavemen. They were barbaric, and we were petrified of them. Their main job was to throw our corpses into the sea...

Often however, they didn't wait until a woman was dead. They threw a few of the older women and the ones who got very sick into the water just to be rid of them. I was afraid they would notice my mother and throw her overboard, too, so I lay on top of her and hid her in the straw beneath me. That also kept us warm...

The voyage dragged on for ten days. Then on May 4, nearly the last day of the war, a British bomb exploded near our barge and damaged it. Luckily it wasn't a direct hit, but a fire started somewhere on board. The barge sprang a leak and the stern began to sink. All of us were in a panic, but hardly any of us had the strength to move.

I reacted first, instinctively, like a horse in a burning barn. I jumped to my feet and forced my mother to get up, too. Then I leaped over to the iron ladder. I was the first to reach it. My mother followed close behind me. The ladder was hot in my hands. I quickly climbed up to the narrow deck and then turned around to pull my mother up after me... and the two of us ran toward the highest place on the deck, right near the edge.

For the first time I had a chance to look out at the sea... It was a brisk, clear day. A few other ships and barges full of prisoners were in sight. Some of them seemed to have been hit by shells as well. British warships were also visible, approaching us. The German vessels had hoisted white flags. They were surrendering. These were flags of peace...

Meanwhile, however, our barge was burning and sinking. More and more of the surviving prisoners from Stutthof kept emerging up the hot metal ladder from the hold. They were crowded on the narrow deck now, struggling toward the high side of the listing ship...

For some reason the German cook was in charge, giving orders to everyone. There were hardly any other Germans left on the barge... He looked around in panic, trying to think of something to do to save the sinking barge. Suddenly he screamed, "Das Schiff ist zu schwer!" (The ship is too heavy!). "Die Juden ins Wasser!" (Jews in the water!). He wanted to lighten the load. For a moment, nobody moved. I looked around the deck and saw all sorts of heavy things they could throw overboard: big crates of ammunition, machinery, even a bicycle. Why the Jews?

He shouted again, hysterically, "Die Juden ins Wasser!!" The Polish and Ukrainian prisoners began to move forward to obey his orders. They started pushing us toward the edge of the deck.

Things happened very slowly. A British vessel was drawing closer, but that didn't stop the Polish and Ukrainian prisoners from pushing us toward the edge of the deck. There was no railing. We would fall in, one by one, if no one stopped them...

From where did the strength and inspiration come to me then? I remembered my father's stories of martyrs dying with the words Shema Yisraelon on their lips ("Hear, o Israel" [the Lord our God, the Lord is One]). I was not going to die without crying out once more to God...

"What's that!" Suddenly the German cook who was giving orders stopped everything. "What are you shouting?" "I'm praying to my God!" I answered proudly.

"You can forget about your God. In a moment you'll be down in the cold water, and the fish will eat you." "No, they won't," I screamed at him defiantly in German. "God has saved me until now, and He is not going to let me die at the last minute. You Germans will go in the freezing water, not us Jews." I pointed down at the water. "You've lost the war, don't you know? Now the British are coming to get you." I pointed out toward the British warship that was heading toward us, close enough now that we could see the sailors on deck.

Something convinced him to relent. He called out, "Die Juden bleiben hier!" (The Jews stay here!). He ordered the Polish and Ukrainian prisoners to stop pushing us, and so none of the thirty surviving women was thrown into the water...

A grotesque band of people stood on the tilting deck of the sinking, burning barge on that early May afternoon in 1945, shivering in the chill as the evening approached: eight German crewmen, some of whom were wounded; four Polish and Ukrainian thugs; and about thirty Jewish women, nightmarishly thin and exhausted. The British warship approached warily, training its guns on us, perhaps expecting a sinister German trick masked by the white flags of surrender.

At last, the British ship drew alongside, towering above us. Over a loudspeaker, in English-accented German, they ordered us all to raise our hands. A sailor cast a heavy line down to our barge, and the interpreter ordered one of the sailors on board to make it fast. Soon they rigged up a rope ladder, and we had to climb up. This was very difficult for us. The distance between the two vessels was considerable, but the knowledge that the Germans had finally lost the war gave us the energy to make it...

Everything happened very calmly. The English sailors worked fast and efficiently. They helped us with a will, but there were no smiles on their faces. Perhaps it's hard to smile at people who look the way we did. They didn't separate the Jews and the Germans on the ship. Suddenly we were clustered with our enemies and former masters, waiting for mugs of hot English tea with sugar and milk. As weak and exhausted as we were, we started fighting with each other to get served first. We had been so degraded by our treatment that we could no longer act like civilized human beings...

The British sailors felt sorry for us and wanted to give us piles of food, but the ship's doctor stopped them. He ordered them to give us small portions of soup and bread, saving us from our wild hunger and their goodwill. It had been so long since we had eaten decent food in normal quantities that we could easily have killed ourselves by overeating.

Night had fallen by the time they took us ashore at Kiel and brought us to a school dormitory.... Looking back on it, I see that during the first weeks of May, the British didn't have any clear idea of what to do with us or how to treat us. They sent us to a hospital staffed by Germans who behaved very badly toward us. They still hated us and tried to humiliate us as though we were prisoners, guilty of some crime. But we weren't at their absolute mercy anymore...

Once the fighting was completely over, the British were no longer preoccupied with winning the war. Gradually, as it became clearer to them just who we were and what we had undergone, our treatment improved...

When we climbed up that rope ladder from the sinking German cattle barge to the British warship, we made a momentous transition from the status of slaves or less than slaves to that of human beings who deserved care and medical treatment. We experienced a sudden restoration of the most basic human rights that had been taken away from us, equally suddenly, by the Nazis in 1941.

The Flight of the Population from East Prussia

The lack of preparedness for the rescue of the civilian population from the Soviet assault was due, first and foremost, to having placed the state and economy under Nazi party control. Hitler had lost all confidence in the Wehrmacht after the July 20th assassination attempt on him by German army officers. The German army realized full well that the military situation in the autumn of 1944 was hopeless due to serious losses in the East, and the advance of the allies to Germany's western frontier. Hitler gave the authority to the regional party leaders, the Gauleiters, to prepare the defenses in the East, as well as to raise a militia, the Volkssturm, of very young and over-age men. All men between the ages of sixteen and sixty-five had to report for duty, even though they were previously exempted from military service because of being physically unfit or for their work in occupations critical to the war effort.

The Nazi party chiefs received authority to build fortifications in the eastern provinces, although they had no military experience. In July 1944, the male population of East Prussia had to build a line of fortifications near the former Polish–German border. During the summer and fall of 1944, they were sent for three or four weeks to the eastern frontier of East Prussia to make antitank trenches, dig fox holes, and build bunkers—called the Ostwall. In the Wartheland district (Province of Poznan), German and Polish workers and slave labor built two lines of fortifications, one reaching from Leslau, Kutno to Wielau, and the other between Kolmar, Posen, and Lissa. In Silesia, the Barthold Enterprise line was built along the old frontier between Poland and Germany, and in West Prussia, a line of fortifications was erected along the eastern borders of Pomerania and Brandenburg.[8] (See maps 9, 10, and 12)

In the construction of these fortifications, the military commanders of these regions had only advisory and not command functions. They were therefore viewed by the German army as useless and unsustainable and troops were even lacking to man these defensive lines. They were considered desperate measures having more of a political objective to maintain civilian morale than a military one. As it turned out, and as expected, they were totally unable to stop the Soviet advance. It was said in East Prussia that the Russians would only need three hours to pass the Ostwall, the first two and a half hours to laugh over it and then half an hour to destroy it.[9]

Please refer to: http://www.forgottenvoices.net, for a photograph (#4) of members of the Civilian Labor Corps constructing antitank trenches in East Prussia.

The performance of the Volkssturm was not much better. Although the young ones, the Hitlerjugend, often stood their ground against the enemy, the older ones usually retreated in disorganized mobs when confronted with fierce Soviet attacks. The induction of all men into the Volkssturm also brought with it a serious collateral problem of a lack of able-bodied men to lead the civilian treks escaping the Russians. They were therefore primarily made up of children, women, and old men who could not do the hard work of leading the columns on bad roads in freezing weather.

The Nazi party provincial leaders were victims of their own illusions and did not consider it necessary to plan for the orderly evacuation of civilians, despite the frequent pleas of the army to make timely preparations. Some plans were made but with delay, because the party completely underestimated the force of the Soviet attacks. When evacuation was ordered it was usually at the last minute, often resulting in the refugee columns being overtaken by Soviet forces with tragic results.

While the Soviet attack on Königsberg was under way, the Soviet army under Marshall Rokossovskii attacked west-north-west in the direction of the lower Vistula river. On January 23, advance units reached the city of Elbing (see map 9) just as the mayor was telling the population that the military situation had stabilized. A day later, the

Soviets reached the Frisches Haff and East Prussia was cut off from the rest of Germany. Many Wehrmacht divisions were now caught in a giant pocket.

As all road and railway connections to the rest of Germany were severed, the treks of refugees were forced to cross the frozen Frisches Haff to the Nehrung, a land spit that led to the city of Danzig (Gdansk) and the possibility of evacuation by sea from there to the West (see map 9). Hundreds of thousands of refugees streamed across this frozen sea at great danger not only from the constant Soviet shelling and air attacks, but also because the ice gave way frequently under the weight of the wagons and people. Added to the hardship of the refugees, the winter of 1944/1945 was one of the severest on record. Temperatures dropped to −20 to −30 degrees Celsius. All roads were ice and snow-bound, leading to many deaths from freezing, particularly among older people and young children.

Please refer to: http://www.forgottenvoices.net, for a photograph (#5) of the flight over the ice of the Frisches Haff in East Prussia, Winter 1945.

No. 20

Eyewitness report of the High School Graduate M. M. of Lyck in East Prussia. Original, 9 November 1951.

Flight over the Haff to the west of the Reich

On the 21 January 1945 Lyck had to be evacuated. My mother, my sister and I took a sad farewell from my father, who had been called up to the Volkssturm, and also from my grandparents. My grandfather intended to take as much as possible of our movable goods with him and set off with his trek in the direction of Arys.

We reached Rastenburg with one of the last trains and spent the night there with relatives. The broadcasting reports which we heard made it clear that East Prussia was in a hopeless situation. Meanwhile there came the fateful news, that no more trains were running to the Reich. Now, our one thought was to leave Rastenburg as quickly as possible. My grandmother remained behind with her maid-servant, as she was absolutely determined to wait for her husband. We were never to see her or my grandfather again.

At the goods-station at Rastenburg we found refuge in a covered box car of a train, which was taking soldiers in the direction of Konigsberg. In Korschen we had to get out but had the luck of catching another goods train, which was overcrowded with refugees. Infants died of hunger on the way.

On the 26 January 1945 we reached Bartenstein. In their fear of falling into the hands of the advancing Russians numerous refugees, in spite of the bitter cold, had gone so far as to get into open goods-wagons of the transport. When we reached Bartenstein many of them were already frozen to death.

We remained the night in our wagon. At dawn we left the goods-train and looked for quarters in Bartenstein. A lady of Lyck, whom we knew, joined us with her son. He had been overtaken by the flight during his sick-leave. The cold had reached a temperature of 25 centigrade below zero. While we were on our way we heard the dull rumbling of artillery in the distance.

We found quarters and rested two days. Then the artillery fire, which was getting nearer, forced us to leave the town of Bartenstein. During the ceaseless explosions of the army installations, which were being blown up by our own troops, we made our way in the midst of a wave of desperate refugees out of the town. We soon saw that it would be impossible to get ahead on the highways. We, therefore, returned to the goods-station and again had the enormous luck of finding a wagon which was only moderately full. Our acquaintance got hold of some railway men, who, after a lot of talking to, coupled our wagon onto a hospital train which was going in the direction of Braunsberg. The railway men looked after the refugees in a touching manner and brought us food and drink.

On the 1 February 1945 we reached Braunsberg. Here we heard the latest bad news: Allenstein fallen. Elbing occupied by the Russians. We were in a huge pocket.

Russian airplanes plastered the town of Braunsberg incessantly with bombs and machine-gun fire. A friend of my mother's took us into her house. Many refugees had to stay in cellars. We remained in Braunsberg until the 10 February 1945. Every day we had to queue up for hours waiting for food and coal. The rumbling of the multiple Stalin rocket-guns got nearer every day. There was no more light and gas. Ten of us were living in one room. We decided to leave the town. With a few other companions in misery we quitted our abode and groped through a pitch-dark night along a highway covered with corpses, and carcasses of animals. Behind us was Braunsberg in flames, to the left of us there was raging a violent battle for Frauenburg. At about midnight, entirely covered in dirt and mud, we reached the little town of Passarge on the Frisches Haff. We awaited the dawn in a barn... In the meanwhile the bitter cold had changed to continuous rain. We reached the shore of the Frisches Haff, took a breathing space of a few minutes and then proceeded on our march to the Nehrung on the other side.

The ice was breaking and at some places we had to drag ourselves with pains through water 25 centimeters deep. We continually tried the surface with sticks. Bomb-craters compelled us to make detours. We often slipped and thought we were already lost. With our clothes wet through and through movement was difficult. But deadly fear drove us on in spite of our shivering bodies.

I saw women do superhuman things. As leaders of treks they instinctively found the safest way for their carts. House utensils were lying scattered all over the ice, wounded people crept up to us with imploring gestures, dragged themselves along on sticks and were pushed forward by friends on little sledges.

Six hours long we passed through this valley of death. Then tired to death we reached the Frische Nehrung. We lay down in a small fowl pen and slept for a short while. Our stomachs rumbled with hunger. On the next day we proceeded further in the direction of Danzig. On the way we witnessed shocking scenes. Demented mothers threw their children into the sea, people hanged themselves; others fell upon dead horses, cut flesh out of them and fried the pieces over open fires; women gave birth to children in carts...

In Kahlberg we put ourselves at the disposal of the Red Cross and looked after wounded people in the hall on the strand. On the 13 February 1945 we went on board a hospital ship, as nursing personnel. The next day we reached Danzig-Neufahrwasser and left the ship.

On the 15 February 1945 we were allotted quarters in Zoppot. My mother, sister and myself were hardly able to stand up on our feet. Nevertheless, we dragged ourselves to the goods-station in Gotenhafen and here for the third time we had a miraculous piece of luck and were taken in an army-post goods wagon to Stolp in Pomerania. On the 19 February 1945 we came as nursing personnel with a hospital train by way of Hannover to Gera in Thuringia, and here we stayed with relatives. This was the 28 February 1945 and on this day our flight from East Prussia ended.

The first stages of the flight from East Prussia began on the 18–20th of January, and lasted until the encirclement of the province by the Red Army at the city of Elbing on January 24. The flight was from East to West. People attempted to cross the Vistula River in West Prussia with only limited success. A small portion of the population of the Eastern Districts were also able to leave by railway before the Province was encircled. All railway traffic to the West ceased after January 22, and as described previously, the only path of flight was over the Frisches Haff to the land spit, the Nehrung. Hundreds of thousands of refugees took this way, hoping to reach the port of Danzig for ships to the western part of Germany or Denmark. By the end of February, the ice over the Haff began to thaw, and this escape route was also eliminated.

Of the total East Prussian population in 1944 of 2,350,000, about 75 percent were able to escape from the Russian offensive. This included those from the city of Memel (Klaipeda), in former Lithuania, annexed by the Third Reich. Of these, about 500,000 left in the autumn of 1944, coinciding with the first Soviet attack on East Prussia. In January of 1945, about 250,000 were able to reach the west via train or trek, before the encirclement of East Prussia. What is most notable is that about 450,000 were able to trek over the ice to the Nehrung and further to Danzig. From the port of Pillau, in the Königsberg district, 450,000 escaped by ship to the West and those (about 200,000) that could not get on to a ship, trekked over the Nehrung to Danzig. It is estimated that 500,000 were not able to escape the Soviets, and were expelled later that year and in 1946 to Germany.[10]

"Operation Hannibal" was the name given by the German navy to the mass evacuation of civilians and military from East and West Prussia. All available German ships were sent to East Prussia, including many prewar passenger ships. The main ports were Pillau in Samland, near Königsberg, Gotenhaven (Gdynia), near Danzig (see map 9), and the last to surrender on May 5, Hela, on a spit north of Danzig. Over two million people succeeded in reaching the West, a sea evacuation considered history's largest.[11] In the process, however, there were numerous tragedies. Passenger ships full of refugees, mostly women, children, older people and wounded soldiers, were sunk as a result of enemy action. Most notable was the sinking of the passenger ships Goya, General von Steuben, and the famous case of the Wilhelm Gustloff, a former Nazi cruise liner.

No one really knows precisely how many people were on the Gustloff on her last voyage, because refugees streamed on board in panic and no precise count was ever made. It is now estimated that about 9,000 of the approximate 10,000 people on board drowned, including 4,000 children. As such it was one of the greatest maritime disasters of all time, exceeding the Titanic's toll of 1,500 lives lost. After the war, efforts were made in Germany to classify the sinking of the Gustloff as a war crime. This was unsuccessful as the ship was not marked as a red cross ship, it carried navy personnel, and it was lightly armed. Understandably, nothing ever came of these endeavors. All in all, some 33,000 people died on the Baltic on the way to West Germany and Denmark.[12]

No. 33

Eyewitness report of the school-master Otto Fritsch of Königsberg in East Prussia. Original, 26 May 1952.

Sinking of the "Karlsruhe" while transporting refugees

After being pensioned in April 1938 I lived with my wife in Königsberg (East Prussia). My only daughter was married to the school-master Koytek in Bischofsburg (East Prussia);... On the 27 August 1944 I was bombed out in Königsberg and then moved with my wife to my daughter in Bischofsburg. When the flight began in January 1945 I went with my wife, my daughter and her three little children on the 22 January in a salvage train from Ortelsburg in the direction of Königsberg. On the 22 February my daughter with two children and myself arrived in Fischhausen in East Prussia. The youngest child of my daughter and my wife had already died. As no one was allowed to leave the town it was impossible for us to go further. On the 7 April the town was violently bombed and the attacks began to get worse; the result was that an order was issued on the 10 April to immediately evacuate the town. On the 10 April a train brought us to the Port of Pillau, where we were put on board the freighter "Karlsruhe," and in the evening steamed away at about 8 o'clock.

Early the next day we reached the promontory of Hela where the ship docked. Here a large convoy was assembled and our ship had to join it. Just before the departure of the convoy the leading ship came to us and enquired about our load, our speed and the number of persons on board. These were made up as follows: 888 East Prussian refugees, 25 railway men and half a company from the Hermann Goering Regiment, that is to say altogether a thousand people. As our ship could only do 7 nautical miles an hour, but the convoy wanted to sail at a speed of 9 nautical miles, we were to be taken in tow by another steamer; this, however, was not done, because there was no tow-line available. At 9 o'clock the convoy set out from Hela, but there was a fairly strong counter-wind.

For this reason, and as our ship could not keep up the pace, the convoy had the next morning, that is to say the 13 April, not traveled as far as had been laid down. The captain of the leading ship, therefore, offered to take our ship in tow, in order that the convoy could move more quickly. In order to fix the tow-line, both our ships had to halt for a time, and they were both a good distance behind the convoy. This was a favorable opportunity for the Russian airmen to attack both ships; for they did not venture to attack the main convoy, as it was strongly equipped with anti-aircraft guns.

At 9.15 o'clock there was air-raid alarm on our ship. A wave of hostile aircraft arrived but their bombs did not hit us and the machine-gun fire was about 30 meters out of line. One hostile plane was hit by our two anti-aircraft guns, fell about 50 meters away from our ship into the sea and sank. There immediately came a second wave of hostile planes. These sank our ship. One bomb hit the engine-room, which would perhaps not have caused the ship to sink, but one air torpedo hit the side of the ship, so that it broke into two parts and in 3 or 4 minutes had sunk in the sea. It was terrible to hear the screams of those drowning and of those wounded by machine-gun fire and the torpedo.

My daughter with her two children and myself were standing on the deck. Then this broke in two under my feet, and I was thrown into the ice-cold water; when I came again to the surface I was able to catch hold of a beam floating in the water, and thus to save myself from drowning. After a short time there came near to me a square sheet-metal tin, apparently a kind of lifeboat with a cable around it. I gripped hold of this and held fast, until I was saved by the mine-sweeper No. 243. I had no idea where my daughter and her two children were. It was only four to five hours later, that I met my grandchild, who was 2½ years old, in a cabin of the ship. According-ing to what the sailors told me, he had been sitting astride a short beam holding on with his two little hands and crying bitterly. My daughter and the other grandchild were drowned, for they were not on the ship where I was, and they were not on the list of those saved which the second ship had drawn up. The number of those saved on my ship were 72, whereas the other ship which had come to our rescue had taken on board about 80 people. Therefore, of the 1,000 people who had been on the Karlsruhe about 150 were saved and 850 drowned. The ship which had saved us brought us to Denmark, where I remained with my little grandchild until 30 October 1947.

There follow some conclusive remarks of the author about the fate of his son-in-law.

The Flight of the Population from West Prussia and Pomerania

The area in the lower Vistula River and Danzig became a great reception and transit area for refugees from East and West Prussia, especially after the Red Army had cut off East Prussia from the rest of Germany, when it reached the coast at Elbing (Elblag) in January 1945. About 800,000 East Prussians sought refuge there, plus about 200,000 refugees from West Prussia and Eastern Pomerania. The East Prussians arrived via the land spit, the Nehrung, and flooded the area around Danzig looking for a way out to the West. Apart from these refugees, the local German population totaled almost three million people, 1.6 million in East Pomerania, 404,000 in the city of Danzig, 310,000 in West Prussia, and 307,000 in Posen (Poznan) province.[13]

The land route, including railways, were still functioning in January and February 1945 as the Soviets had not reached the Baltic in Pomerania. Many refugees, however, made the mistake of remaining in Danzig and Pomerania due to the relatively peaceful conditions prevailing there. Additionally, as elsewhere, the Nazi party had forbidden the population, including the refugees, in Pomerania and West Prussia to flee. Thus, when the Soviets launched their attack on East Pomerania and Danzig at the beginning of March, there were still 2.5 million Germans living in this area, of which about 25 percent were refugees. Only a small portion were able to cross the Oder river and escape to the West, after the offensive began.[14]

On March 1, the Soviets launched three armies against the German defenders in Pomerania. By March 3 they had already broken through to the Baltic at the city of Kolberg (Kolobrzeg), Pomerania, and smashed the German army into fragments. The Germans to the East had to fall back on West Prussia and Danzig, and the forces to the West were forced back to the Oder River and Stettin. The result was that the Eastern forces were caught in a pocket centered on the lower Vistula River. At the same time the Soviets, under Marshall Rokossovskii, launched a major attack against Danzig and West Prussia taking Stolp in East Pomerania on the Baltic coast on March 8.[15] (See map 12)

Refugees from East and West Prussia and Eastern Pomerania on the way West had to turn around and head east to the Danzig pocket. Their only way to safety was to reach one of the harbors, Gdynia or Danzig. Huge numbers of refugees were wandering around aimlessly, trying to find a safe haven, and many treks were overtaken by the advancing Russians. Because of the rapid Soviet advance, a large part of the urban and rural population of Eastern Pomerania did not have a chance to flee, especially as the Nazi party prohibited flight or delayed it too long. When they did finally give the authorization, on March 10, most of Pomerania east of the Oder River was in the hands of the Red Army.

Please refer to: http://www.forgottenvoices.net for a photograph (#6) of a German refugee trek through the City of Danzig (Gdansk) fleeing the Red Army, February 1945.

The German navy sent all available shipping to the ports in the bay of Danzig. Large numbers of refugees were taken out of the pocket, but this became increasingly difficult as both Danzig and Gotenhafen (Gdynia) were rapidly surrounded by Russian troops. The only other port was Hela on a spit of land to the north of Danzig. (See map 9) People had to be ferried there from these ports which shortly thereafter fell to the Soviets. Over 365,000 refugees crowded into this tiny port, surviving under the most desperate of circumstances. Nevertheless, more than 387,000 people were evacuated from Hela in the month of February 1945. The port itself held out until the end of the war. The last ship left Hela on May 6 with more than 50,000 refugees and soldiers. Over 900,000 people were brought out by sea from ports in the Bay of Danzig and Eastern Pomerania, but 1.5–2 million Germans were left behind under Russian occupation.[16]

No. 69

Report of Mrs. E. H. of Luggewiese, district of Lauenburg in Pomerania.

Original, 13 June 1951.

An experience during the Russian invasion

According to orders from the mayor we had to evacuate our village of Luggewiese on 9 March 1945 and go to the neighboring village of Gross Damerkow, which was only 4 kilometers away, but lay in the middle of a forest. I, therefore, set out with my two children, my mother and my sister Kate, who was 25 years old, and stayed with my parents-in-law who lived in Gross Damerkow. Many of our relatives and acquaintances had already fled there. On the next day, the 10 March the Russians stormed this place also. In the course of the day, many other refugees had come from the other neighboring villages, and we were at least 30 persons in one room. The first Russians who came into the houses, demanded watches, rings and other valuables. What was not voluntarily given was torn away from the people by violence. From us they also took our trunk with victuals. This went on for about two hours...

Suddenly a female neighbor came in screaming out that the Russians wanted to take her with them. There then came two Russians into our room:

"Woman come," and seized two women by the hands. These women screamed and begged so much, that the Russians let them go and then went away.

Thereupon, a big Russian came in. He did not utter a single word, but looked around the room and then went to the back where all the young girls and women were sitting. He beckoned once with his finger to my sister.

As she did not stand up at once, he went close up to her and held his machine pistol against her chin. Everyone screamed aloud, but my sister sat mutely there and was incapable of moving. Then a shot resounded. Her head fell to the side and the blood streamed out. She was dead instantly, without uttering a single sound…

The Flight of the Population from the Warthegau (Province of Poznan) and East Brandenburg

The great Soviet offensive on the Central Front, whose destination was Berlin, began in January 1945. Already, on January 25, the capital of the Warthegau, Posen (Poznan), was encircled. Within eighteen days, the offensive swept over 400 kilometers from the great bend of the Vistula River to the middle course of the Oder River in East Brandenburg, which the Soviets reached on February 2. Due to the speed of the Soviet advance, the treks of refugees lasted only two weeks, compared to months in East and West Prussia and Pomerania. (See map 12)

The German population in this area was approximately 1.4 million. East Brandenburg had 640,000 people, and the Reichsgau Wartheland, 670,000 (Prior to the War, this was the Polish Province of Poznan and was incorporated into the German Reich. In 1939 and 1940, the Nazi government also settled German immigrants in the Warthegau from areas incorporated into the Soviet Union by prewar treaty with Nazi Germany, from the Baltic, and Bessarabia and Bukovina in the Balkans. It is estimated that only 30 percent of the population in this Province was German.) There were also about 90,000 Germans living in German-occupied Poland, the General Government.[17] (See maps 13 and 14)

The flight of the population from the Eastern Wartheland began on January 16. But by that time it was already too late to avoid being overtaken by the Red Army as the Nazi Party authorities ordered the evacuations at the last minute. As in other districts, the Party completely underestimated the force and the swiftness of the Soviet attack.

There was also a lack of transportation, trains were mostly not running, and the majority of the people had to organize and travel in treks in bitter cold weather.

Germans from Western Wartheland and the city of Posen had more luck in reaching the Oder River and the West as the distance was shorter. It is estimated, however, that less than one half of the people setting out reached the safety of the Oder River. The people of East Brandenburg, the territory to the east of the Oder River, suffered very substantial losses as they did not flee in time. Although refugees were constantly passing through their territory from the east, they thought they were protected by the series of fortifications built in late 1944 along the old German–Polish border. Additionally, the party leaders forbade flight and when the Soviet troops suddenly appeared, evacuation orders were given too late. For example, a train full of refugees going to the city of Küstrin on the Oder was surprised and destroyed by Russian tanks. At the appearance of Soviet troops, the country population fled in panic, but very few were able to reach the West. Generally, not more than 30–40 percent were able to escape and cross the Oder River.[18] The loss of life in this flight was very high, due to combat, the intense cold, and exhaustion, particularly amongst the children and old people.

Please refer to: http://www.forgottenvoices.net, for a photograph (#7) of a refugee trek with fleeing German soldiers in East Prussia in the vicinity of Braunsberg, February 1945.

The Flight of the Population from Silesia

When the great Soviet offensive began on the Eastern Front in January of 1945, Marshall Konev's First Ukrainian Front concentrated its attacks on the Upper Silesian industrial region (East Upper Silesia was in prewar Poland). This region was of great strategic importance to Germany, as it was one of the last remaining major German industrial areas not destroyed by bombings, such as the Ruhr or regions already occupied by the Allies, like the Saar. Its coal mines produced 95 million tons a year, and its steel mills 2.4 million tons. Important factories producing German armaments were located in the city of Kattowitz.[19] Through a series of aggressive flanking moves, the German army was forced to evacuate this industrial region. By January 22, the Soviet forces reached the Oder River and began establishing beachheads on the opposite shore. The encirclement and siege of the Silesian capital, Breslau (now Wroclaw), began at this time. (See map 12)

The population of Silesia prior to the war was about 4.6 million, but as a result of the Allied air offensive over Germany, an additional 450,000 people were evacuated to this province.[20] Because of its distance from

Allied air bases, it did not suffer the heavy bombardments of West Germany. The flight of the population from the Soviet attack was less onerous than from East Prussia or Pomerania as they generally were not overtaken by the advancing Russians or forced into encircled pockets. The evacuation moved mainly from east to west, in waves, determined by the speed of the advances of the Soviet offensive. Many refugees also fled over the mountains to Bohemia and Moravia in Czechoslovakia, a road that was still under the control of the German army. Once there, however, at war's end, they suffered again, this time from harassment and expulsion by Czech forces.

Only women and children were permitted to leave from the Upper Silesian territories. Industrial workers were forbidden to evacuate in order to maintain industrial production to the very last. Evacuees in nonpriority jobs were taken by train to the West, whereas those that did not leave in time had to escape via Czechoslovakia. Nevertheless, most of those engaged in industry and mining did not manage to leave. They included many Poles or Germans who considered themselves integrated Poles. About one-half million Germans remained after the Russian occupation and were subsequently expelled by the Polish government.

The evacuation of Lower Silesia did not begin until the 19th of January on the insistence of the army, which wanted a twenty-kilometer civilian free zone west of the Oder River. When, by the middle of February the Red Army finally encircled Breslau, there were still 200,000 civilians caught in the city. Hitler had declared it a fortress, meaning that it was defended bitterly by remaining German army units, who did not surrender until the date of Germany's capitulation on May 6. Civilians suffered terribly during this period with more than 40,000 dead.[21] The civilian population in the Breslau rural area, however, were generally able to leave in time by rail, motor transport, or treks to Saxony. Only a minority remained behind.

During the months of February and March, fighting in Lower Silesia was limited, but refugees continued to pour out of the region going either to Saxony or Bohemia/Moravia.

One problem faced by the refugees was lack of horses for use in the treks as Silesia was not as agricultural as Pomerania or East Prussia. Trains, buses, and other motor transport were always over-crowded, explaining why so much of the population was unable to escape. As happened so frequently in this campaign, many were caught and over-run by the rapidly advancing Soviet forces.

Due to the fact that the German army was able to mount a successful defense along the Oder River in February and March, 1945, many of the inhabitants of this region lost their fear of the Soviets and remained in their homes. Some even who had previously evacuated returned to their homes. Thus, when the Red Army attacked again in force, and quickly penetrated the German defensive lines, the population had to flee at the last moment. About 300,000–400,000 succeeded in escaping from Lower Silesia, but tens of thousands were not so fortunate and were overtaken by the Russians with great loss of life.

After the war, the German government estimated that of the 4.7 million people living in Silesia in 1945, about 3.2 million were able to escape, one-half each to Saxony and Czechoslovakia. Some1.5 million remained behind.[22]

No. 109

Report of the District Chief Inspector Gustav Zolker of Namslau in Lower Silesia. Original, 27 November 1952.

Incidents when evacuating: Evacuation of the people to the district of Landeshut and further to the western part of the Sudeten country. The conditions there after the capitulation and the removal of the refugees to Saxony.

In the autumn of 1944 the work on the frontier fortification known as "The Barthold Enterprise" began. The people were called up for this work in the highest proportion possible. During the last months of the year 1944 the eastern front kept getting continually nearer to the Silesian frontiers. The population was not informed about the danger which would result. Indeed the District Party Organization deliberately prevented any information getting out. It was only on the insistence of the deputy Landrat Frauenholz, that in the middle of January 1945 a meeting of the mayors of the district and of the political leaders was summoned to Stojan's Inn in Namslau: this inn was also called the Hotel Towngate. At this meeting the Kreisleiter pointed out, that the military situation gave no reason for anxiety, but all the same the plan for evacuation, should things become serious, was made known...

On the 19 January 1945, 15 o'clock the Kreisleiter spoke publicly to the population of the town of Namslau, who were anxious because of the refugee treks from the eastern districts of Silesia and from the southern part of the Warthe area, and also because of the retreating columns of the army. He stated, that there was no reason for anxiety, as he had received information from higher authority, according to which the military situation was satisfactorily clarified. It was, however, no longer possible to put the people at ease, as Russian panzer spearheads had been already sighted at a distance of about 15 kilometres from Namslau. Two hours after the speech of the Kreisleiter, that is to say at about 17 o'clock his office published the order for evacuation, which had been issued by Gauleiter Hanke who was Reich Defense Commissioner for the area.

The farmers from the different villages were to take the population of the town with them. This, however, was a failure as the order had been issued too late. The town population waited in vain for the horses and carts. Some of the people, however, were taken away by retreating military vehicles. The trek from the village of Glausche could not start, although it had been got ready, because in the meanwhile the Russian panzers had reached the railway station of Glausche (route Namslau to Gross Wartenburg), and were blocking the road to Namslau. On the 20 January 1945 in the morning the panzers had disappeared, and the evacuation was able to be carried out as ordered. During this night many inhabitants and Russian, Polish and civilian workers employed on the Barthold Defense position were killed or wounded by machine-gun fire. In the village of Ordenstal the commander of the Volkssturm battalion of Landeshut, Silesia, was killed. He had taken the Russian for German panzers. The panzers shooting around in all directions passed very swiftly through the neighboring place of Hennersdorf. Here there were also killed and wounded.

Dr. Heinrich, the Landrat of the district of Namslau was serving with the army. On the 19 January 1945 he arrived back in Namslau from a military course. This was a great piece of luck for the population of Namslau. Dr. Heinrich did not come officially, in order to do service in Namslau, but on his own initiative, in order to help, as the news which he had received gave rise to the very greatest anxiety. Owing to his intervention with higher authority of the government and with the Reich railway, trains were supplied for removing the population. These trains left the town at short intervals. Great numbers of the population were thus brought away from Namslau and the neighboring villages...

The population remained about three weeks in Landeshut, and then an order was issued for strangers to be evacuated from the district of Landeshut. The population of the district of Namslau had to go to the district of Luditz in the Sudeten area, which was near to Karlsbad...

The people of Namslau, were accommodated, when they arrived, in the refugee camp in the secondary school, and had to remain there for weeks. The rationing and sanitary conditions in this camp were indescribably bad.

The people of Namslau were not billeted in private houses, until Chief Inspector König, chief of the administrative office in Namslau, and the District Farmers' Leader Seidel, and also the Landrat of Luditz, had made repeated complaints and applications to the competent authorities.

There were really friendly relations with the population of the town and district of Luditz. Unfortunately, however, victuals began to get short, as there were no supplies coming in.

After the capitulation a jeep arrived with five American soldiers and one officer. These, however, only remained a few hours in the town, and for a short time kept coming every day again. A few days later, a Russian detachment came to Luditz as occupation. The sufferings of the population now began, and there was no distinction made between natives and refugees. Both night and day the Russian soldiers left the people no peace. Young girls and women had to be careful not to be seen in the streets and remained in hiding, as they were also not safe in their homes.

Meanwhile, Czech gendarmes, militia and civilian administrative officials arrived. There were endless searching of houses and arrests of persons. In this regard the refugees got off comparatively better. Those arrested received for the most part, after being interrogated, a large swastika on their backs, and were then brought to the Czech school near the Landrat's office, in which I was then working.

These people were brought in and guarded by militia, which was clad in uniforms of the German Africa Corps.

The treatment in this prison was terrible, I worked 50 meters away and could still hear the screams. I also often met men, who had been beaten until they were blue all over, and who could only move if helped to do so.

Here the author gives an example.

When the Czechs took over the Sudeten country, the towns and villages were cleared of the refugees in them. Relying on the announcements of the victorious Powers, according to which the administrative frontiers of Germany should remain those of 1937, the expellees made their way home. In June 1945 I joined a trek of about 300 persons with 60 horses and carts.

The Czech office organizing the trek, had ordered that this was to appear before the town, in order to receive the trek identity cards. When we arrived there, we were driven together to a square, which was in the neighborhood, and we were then surrounded by the militia… The leader of the militia shot in the air with his pistol, in order to make us listen. He announced, that only so much baggage could be taken as each could carry with his hands, and that all the rest had to be left behind. Only one horse and cart might be taken for little children and sick persons. After negotiating with the Czech Landrat, we were ultimately allowed to take five horses and carts with us. After waiting for five hours the trek started, and proceeded in the direction of the Reich frontier towards Saxony. After having gone a short way, the column was attacked by Russian soldiers, and the end of the column, which was straggling a little behind, was robbed of its few goods and chattels.

A few days later, the trek was stopped by two Czech gendarmes, and two horses and carts were taken from us. These gendarmes did not only beat the trek leader but also several other persons, because the papers produced had not been properly stamped by the Czech authorities in Luditz.

About the middle of June 1945 we arrived at the frontier between Czechoslovakia and Saxony in the neighborhood of Annaberg in Saxony. In the course of the Czech frontier control, all persons including small children were thoroughly searched by the militia. The controlling officials threw everything away, which they did not think to be necessary, with the result that we only kept, what we had on our backs. It must be mentioned, that in the course of this procedure people were ill-treated...

The members of the trek were gradually distributed by the refugee office in Kamenz to different parts of the Soviet zone of occupation. At the present time, there are only a few people from Namslau in one place. A part reached West Germany after many wanderings.

The Return of the German Population to Their Homes East of the Oder-Neisse Line

At the time of the Yalta Conference of the heads of state of the United States, Great Britain, and the Soviet Union, in February 1945, Stalin pressed for the acceptance of Poland's new western borders, at the Oder-Neisse line. One justification for this annexation of Germany's eastern provinces, he stated, was that its German population had already fled the advancing Red Army. There were no Germans left in the area, Stalin maintained.[23] This was not correct. Even though about 7.5 million Germans did flee from both the former national territory plus lands that were in prewar Poland and Danzig, about 4.4 million Germans remained behind at the time of the German capitulation.[24]

After every war, refugees from fighting have always been allowed to return to their homes even if these were destroyed. This has been confirmed by international law, rules of war, and general humane treatment of noncombatants. In the spring of 1945 none of the refugees from the East ever thought that they would never see their homes again. Germans from the Reich provinces of Pomerania, Silesia, East Prussia, and East

Brandenburg just waited for the end to hostilities in order to make their way back home. In June 1945, however, the Polish government stationed five divisions of the new Polish army on the Oder and Neisse rivers to block their return. Even though the Polish authorities prevented the homebound refugees from crossing the Oder-Neiss line in June/July of 1945, nevertheless it is estimated that over one million refugees were able to return to their homes. Even 10,000 inhabitants of Breslau (Wroclaw), the capital of Silesia, returned to their destroyed city.[25]

As early as January 1945, refugees in the lands already occupied by the Soviet Armies began their return to their homes in East and West Prussia and East Brandenburg. Another wave of refugees followed in March of that year, when residents of East and West Prussia returned from Pomerania where they had been overtaken by advancing Russian forces. Also, many inhabitants of Pomerania, who were not able to reach the West ahead of the advancing Soviet forces, began to return home. The Silesian population that escaped from the Soviets by crossing the mountains into Bohemia and Moravia in Czechoslovakia were the least hindered in returning to Silesia. The Czechs did not want them under any circumstance and expelled them, and the Polish government could not prevent their crossing the border of a "friendly" country. About 400,000 Silesians were able to return in this fashion, and it was reported that the towns and villages regained about 50 percent of their original population. All in all approximately one million Silesians were able to return from their flight.[26]

The attitude of the Soviet authorities to this stream of refugees was contradictory and uncertain. In many cases they left them where they were or let them go home again. In many cases they ordered them to return to their homes, even though they knew that this land would eventually be absorbed by Poland. They were undoubtedly motivated by concerns of a humanitarian crisis in their zone of occupation. The trek home began on the West bank of the Oder River. Once the Polish government closed the border in June 1944 to returning refugees on the Oder and Neisse rivers, huge crowds of displaced and homeless Germans gathered on the West bank.

It was really amazing that any refugees were able to return at all. They were totally impoverished and usually hungry. They had no animals left for the treks, and suffered many hardships from Soviet and Polish troops. For many, it took months to reach their homes and the difficulties often surpassed those encountered in their flight.

Once they arrived home, many were then shipped as slave labor to the Soviet Union.

As a result of the return of many of the inhabitants of the Eastern provinces, the German population increased by about 1.5 million to a total of 5,650,000, distributed as follows: East Prussia 800,000, Pomerania 1 million, East Brandenburg 350,000, Silesia 2.5 million, the prewar Polish territories of West Prussia and Posnan 800,000, and Danzig 200,000.[27] These people were all eventually expelled to the West.

Deportation of German Civilians as Forced Labor to the Soviet Union

For the Soviet Union, the legal basis for the deportation of German civilians in the occupied areas of Eastern Germany arose from an agreement at the Yalta Conference, in February 1945. Stalin was able to secure acquiescence of the Western Powers to bring German workers to the Soviet Union as a form of war reparation. This had been planned by the Soviet Supreme Command even before Germany's surrender and was centrally directed and organized. It not only applied to Germans living east of the Oder-Neisse line, but also to the ethnic German population in Czechoslovakia, Hungary, Romania, and Yugoslavia. It did not apply, evidently, to Germans in the Soviet occupation zone in Germany.[28]

The deportations had already begun in January 1945, before the Yalta agreement, and lasted to the end of April of that year. Most people were sent to the Donets Basin in the Ukraine, to the Urals and the Caucasus. The German civilians were literally herded together by the commands of the various Soviet army groups, depending on the quotas that they were given. Prior to their deportation, they were placed in assembly camps, barracks, or prisons. Silesia proved to be the easiest province to gather able-bodied men up to the age of sixty to fill the Soviet deportation quotas. Miners and industrial workers were forbidden by the Nazi authorities to leave their work, so many ended up in the Soviet Union as slave labor. The Russians had great difficulty in fulfilling their quotas in East and West Prussia and Pomerania due to the lack of able-bodied men. Consequently, many women and girls were seized to meet these quotas.

No. 160

Eyewitness report of Ilse Lau of Zandersielde, district of Marienwerder in West Prussia. Original, without date.

Forced deportation by way of Soldau to the South Ural. Conditions of life and work in coal mining.

The 31 December 1944 was the last New-Year's Eve, which we had at home. The whole family was together. On the 22 January 1945 our flight began by way of Weissenberg and Dirschau to Polish territory. In Schoneck we had three beautiful weeks, on the flight, which I shall never forget. I worked as receptionist with the ear specialist, in the military hospital in charge of Dr. Gramsch.

Our first meeting with the Russians was on the 11 March in Schonwalch close to the Baltic. Daddy was led away, and is said to have been shot the same day. We remained free for two days, kept in hiding and were not raped.

On the 13 March 1945 our fate overtook us in Krussen, in the district of Stolp. After endless cross-examination Mummy was allowed to go home, Gert and I remained imprisoned. After six long marches we reached Konitz, where we were at first quartered in the penitentiary. From there we went to Soldau.

On the 7 April 1945 we were put in the train for Russia...

On the 28 April 1945 I was detrained at the camp of Korken in the South Ural. We were all of us ill and weak, for the food on the journey had been utterly inadequate. On the 9 May the Russian captain told us, that the war was at an end. What difference would that make to us prisoners? Would we return home sooner, or should we have to do years of forced labour? The latter is what happened.

On the 13 May 1945 I was sent to work on a collective farm. There life was more bearable than in the large camp of Korken, where there were about 3,000 prisoners. We worked in the potato-fields from sunrise to sunset... The food on the collective farm was comparatively good, and we were well treated. We got rid of vermin, because we could keep ourselves clean. We began to feel like human beings, but this was not to last long.

On the 6 July 1945 at 9 o'clock in the evening we had to pack all our things.

A truck appeared and went with us the whole night through the locality. We had been told, that we were going home. We landed, however, at the colliery near Tscheljabinsk, in the South Ural. As a result of the official medical examination, I was put into category 1, and could, therefore, be put on underground work in the mines.

On the 12 July I went for the first time into the pit. It is a strange feeling to be suddenly 120 metres beneath the earth. Around us everything was dark, there was only one electric bulb for lighting the lift. We lit our miners lamps, and then began working. All the pits had their numbers. The pit, in which I had my baptism of fire was pit N 42 bis." It was by far the worst pit. There was water everywhere on the ground of the mine gallery...Our food consisted of soup and gruel three times a day and of 1,200 grames of bread. The bread alone kept us going, that is the reason that those, who worked on the surface, gradually broke down, because they only received 500 grames of bread a day. I shall never forget in my life; how I liked eating dry bread.

I worked for two months in this pit. Then typhoid broke out in the camp and we were quarantined, that is to say, we were not allowed to go out to work, and every day were given a horribly painful injection. Further, we were every third day deloused... When the commission discovered anyone with lice, the person in question immediately had his hair shorn. I not only had to thank my cleanliness but also my luck for the fact, that I never lost my hair. In October the medical commission released us for work. There were considerably fewer of us, and we had to be distributed among five pits in the neighborhood.

My new place of work was in pit 43. The pit was far more modern than the other one, but demanded much more of us workers... One was only allowed to leave the dark hole after finishing one's "norm." It happened, that we sometimes had to remain as much as 16 hours down in the pit. When we had finally finished our work by summoning up our last strength, we were not allowed to go up in the lift, but had to climb up the ladders (138 meters).

We were often near to desperation. We were never able to sleep enough, and we were always hungry...We earned no money, and our clothes were falling to pieces. Practically no one had received post from home, and we were getting tired of life....

In January 1947 things had got so far, that we could no longer master our work. It was then my job to fill the coal trucks, and push them a short distance to the gallery, from where they were dragged away by the electric bus. I had no more strength, and I was beginning to calculate, how long it would be before my hour had come.

Then the order was issued, that the money we earned was no longer to be paid to the officers of the camp, but that the pit-workers were to receive their money personally. Every month 140 rubles were paid in taxes to the camp. One could not expect to be given gratis the glorious wooden bunk, the straw sack and the light. The Russians hoped, that by paying out in cash more work would be done. And this actually happened. The more I worked, the more I earned and the more I could eat. Unfortunately we soon earned too much for the Russians, and the rate of pay was reduced. From 1947 we were able to buy bread, potatoes, butter, meat and everything. Bread and potatoes were within our means...

I then became friends with a girl named Margot. All my friends up to now, Ilse Kohtz of Zandersfelde, Jutta Krause, who was a high school girl of Mohrungen, and Klarchen Struck of Stolp, had died. Since I was together with Margot, my standard of life rose. We did our housekeeping together, the one of us who worked at nights was the manageress and cook...

When we had fed ourselves up a little, we began to buy blouses, a woolen skirt, stockings and such like things. We did not want to be beggars forever.

Margot worked as mate of the driver of the electric bus, and I had become a carrier of pit-props. A comrade and myself had to fetch the wood, which the miners needed for supporting the galleries. It was often very hard work, and it was not so simple to drag poles 2 1/2 meters long and which were very thick through a tunnel, which was low and 100 meters or more long, the tunnel itself being only 1 meter high. It was impossible to get the Russian women to do this work. The German girls were, of course, not asked, and if the work was not done well, this was reported to the camp. The result: sabotage and prison.

In the course of time I had so accustomed myself to the dragging of wood, that I did not want to do any other kind of work, more especially so as the pay was not bad. I received about 500 rubles a month in cash. I could have lived very well from the money, if I had earned it every month. But I was very ill: inflammation of the lungs, malaria and contusions, while working often caused me to have to go into hospital. Then I received no money and had to live from my small savings. Margot always remained well and, if she had not looked after me so faithfully, my lot would have been a sorry one. If one was ill for any length of time, one did indeed get some food from the camp, but this was too much to die of and too little to live on.

On the 21 July 1949 I had my last accident in the pit. Through the contusions I developed an inflammation of the cellular tissues, and this kept me in bed for 4 months.

On the 19 November 1949 I was then really ripe for going home, and was put into a transport of soldiers from Tscheljabinsk. On the 16 December 1949 our transport arrived in Friedland. Then I had to pass through the hospitals of Göttingen, Bahlburg and Juist. 4 wonderful weeks in Wangerooge followed. Everywhere everyone did all they could for me. It is really lovely to be free again and back home.

About 218,000 civilians were deported to Russia, with most coming from Silesia, about 62,000, and the fewest from East Prussia, about 44,000.[29] Ironically, the Soviets often came into conflict with the Polish authorities, who were also putting able-bodied Germans in internment and penal camps for use as forced labor. It is reported that in those cases the Soviets prevailed in selecting the workers they wanted.

The workers were transported to Russia in cattle cars, about 2,000 people per train. The journey lasted an average of three to six weeks, with insufficient food, and for the earlier deportees, in freezing cold. The mortality rate often reached 10 percent.[30]

Once in the camps, the deportees had to do the most difficult physical labor such as working underground in the coal mines, forestry, and excavation work. In the spring and summer many also worked on collective farms. Work conditions were terrible, usually with twelve-hour days. Norms were set based on their age and health condition. If they exceeded their norms, in order to receive some benefits, then their norms were increased, a typical modus operandi of the system. The greatest mortality rate was in the spring and autumn of 1945, when more than 50 percent of the inmates of the camps died due to hard work, insufficient rations, and unhygienic conditions.

Subsequently, conditions improved somewhat and later in 1945, the sick and those unable to work were sent back to Germany. After that, the forced labor camps were gradually broken up and the deportees returned to Germany from 1946 to 1948. The last slave labor transport back to Germany occurred in 1949. It is now estimated that about one-half of those sent to the Soviet Union as forced labor died in the course of those deportations.[31]

> No. 140
>
> Eyewitness report of F. K. of Burgkampen (Jentkutkampen) district of Ebenrode (Stallupönen} in East Prussia. Original, November 1951.
>
> **Treatment of German deportees on the way to forced labor in the Ural.**
>
> I was taken prisoner by the Russians on the 1 February 1945 along with my family and many other companions in misery, when we were trekking from East Prussia. We were driven together in hundreds into the area of Rastenburg. More and more refugees kept joining us. We were then loaded onto trucks, women, old and sick men, and children closely packed together, so that we could only stand jammed together. No one could turn or move... 30 kilometers behind the Lithuanian frontier we stopped and were dragged out of the trucks. Children up to 10 years of age were dragged from their mothers...
>
> We were then locked up in a barracks. There was no room for us all there, but the Russians drove us together with rifle-butts, until the rooms were so overcrowded, that we were standing packed together like sardines. This we had to endure three days. Once a day we got a thin water soup. Boards had been so closely nailed across the win-

dows, that no fresh air came in. There was one room still free, into this room the men were driven, had to strip naked there, in order that our clothes could be separately searched. Valuables, such as documents, photographs and wedding rings were stolen...

During the third night, that is to say on the 5 February 1945, we were again loaded onto trucks and taken to a railway station. There was a long goods train there, and 120 people were forced into each wagon, women and men separately. From now on our sufferings grew worse. The wagons were filthy from top to bottom, and there was not a blade of straw. When the last man had been driven in by blows with rifle-butts, we could only stand packed together like sardines. This was the way, in which we departed for the Ural... A bucket of water and crumbs of bread, served up to us on a filthy piece of tent canvas, were our daily food.

The worst part were the nights. Our legs got weak from the continual standing, and the one leant against the other. The state of affairs was impossible, for the journey lasted 28 days. When the train stopped, mostly for the night, we were not left in peace. The guards came to the wagons, and hammered on them from all sides... 10 to 15 men had already died during the first eight days. We others had to carry out the corpses naked under guard, and they were piled up at the end of the train like wood in empty wagons. Every day more and more died...

Thirst was worse than hunger. The iron fittings of the wagons were damp through the vapor and breath. Most of the people scratched this off with their dirty fingers and sucked it: many of them got ill in this way. The mortality increased from day to day, and the corpse wagons, behind the train, continually increased in number.

About the 2 March we arrived at the Ural, there were then 30% to 40% less men in each wagon than when we started. The rest of us poor wretches looked like a crowd of walking corpses. After we had stumbled out of the train, we had to parade in front of it, and kneel for two hours in deep snow. Many of them froze to death, for the temperature was 45° below zero centigrade. We were covered from head to foot with a crust of dirt and filth, and looked terrible. The Russians led us in this state stumbling or rather creeping through the roads of the Ural. The Russian population stood on the edge of the road with terror in their faces, and watched the procession of all these miserable people. Those, who could not walk any further, were driven on, step-by-step, by being struck with rifle-butts.

We now stopped in front of a sauna-bath. This was fatal for most of us.

For everyone was thirsty and rushed to the basins, which were full of dirty water, and each drank until he was full. This immediately caused the awful dysentery illness. Here we were again plundered. When we finally came to camps, more than a half of what remained of us poor wretches already had typhoid. In a few days many died of this illness. Those, who recovered, were dragged from camp to camp, and had to do the hardest kind of work. The majority of us were farmers from Stallupönen, Gumbinnen and many from the district of Rastenburg. A small remainder was sent back home after two years.

What I have here reported, I have been through with my own family. My poor wife died, as a result of this catastrophe.

The Expulsion of the German Population from East of the Oder–Neisse Line

The Treatment of German Civilians in the Former Reich Territories

On February 5, 1945, even before the war was over, Boleslav Bierut, Premier of the Provisional Polish government, stated that Poland had taken over the civil administration of all German territories to the east of the Oder–Neisse Line. Polish government departments were already administering extensive Eastern German territories long before the Potsdam heads of state meeting.[32] Although the Soviet military were ostensibly still in command of the administration of these recently conquered German territories, by the autumn of 1945, they had relinquished authority to the Polish government.

In May of 1945, the Polish government issued a decree entitled "Concerning the Administration of the Regained Territories." (The Polish government referred to the lands it annexed east of the Oder–Neisse Line as "regained." It considered these lands historically Polish.) It established, unilaterally, that these territories were henceforth Polish and Polish law and administration would prevail. Although the U.S. government protested these actions, ultimately the Western Allies had to accept the Soviet "fait accompli" at the subsequent Potsdam peace conference.

When this occurred, these former German territories came under the security control of the Polish army and Militia. In the autumn of 1945, the Polish Zloty was introduced, Polish became the obligatory language, German place names were changed to Polish, and education and even church services became exclusively Polish. Every effort was made to obliterate any remnant of this region's historical German past. As for the remaining German population in these territories, they suffered from the application of collective punishment for their attributed collective guilt for the war crimes perpetrated against Poland by the Nazi government and German army.

A purge of German civilians began immediately to determine who belonged to the Nazi party and its organizations. Criminal Courts were established, but generally accepted legal practices were not followed. Numerous prison camps were established or reopened, including Auschwitz, Birkenau, Lamsdorf, and others, and many Germans, including women and children, were incarcerated there. Sometimes even whole villages were made prisoners. Arbitrary arrests were commonplace, with most everyone labeled a Nazi. These camps normally held between 3,000 and 5,000 people. When they were finally closed in the summer of 1946, it is estimated that 50 percent of the inmates, preponderantly women and children, had died from malnourishment, ill-treatment, and diseases.[33]

Additionally, many civilians were forced to work as slave labor in industry and coal mines, especially in Upper Silesia, and above all on farms. Due to the lack of food, ironically, working on farms for the new Polish owners, even for no wages, was often sought after by the impoverished and hungry population. Polish settlers also began to arrive from Eastern and Central Poland and were placed in German homes and farms by the Militia. Large estates, however, were directly taken over by the Polish government and were managed as state farms, with the German peasants now working for the Polish State, temporarily, until they were expelled. By the end of 1946, all privately owned German farms were in Polish hands. In this fashion, the inhabitants of the eastern provinces were deprived of their property before they were expelled. At the end of 1948, the "Ministry of Regained Territories" was dissolved and the German lands east of the Oder and Neisse were incorporated into the administrative structure of the Polish State.[34]

In general, as reported by the German victims, the Poles were considered much more relentless in their persecution of the German population than the Soviets, which is surprising considering the brutalities of the Soviet troops in their onslaught on Germany. This is explained by the economic needs of the Soviet armed forces who did not wish to drive the Germans out of their factories and farms. A report to Moscow by the Political Section of the Red Army on August 30, 1945 states, "The German population is starving in many places, in other areas they are under the immediate threat of starvation in the near future. Not only does the plundering of the Germans on the part of the Poles not stop, but it gets stronger all the time. There are more and more frequent cases of unprovoked murder of German inhabitants, unfounded arrests, long prison confinements with purposeful humiliations." The report continues that matters were so dire, that the Red Army had to intervene sometimes to control the Poles, leading to conflict between Soviet soldiers and the Poles.[35]

No. 206

Eyewitness report of the farmer K. S. of Bulgrin, district of Belgard in Pomerania. Original, 18 December 1947, 8 pages. Printed in part.

The Polish settlers come in and the German population is deprived of their property. Conditions of life and work in villages which had become Polish and on Russian administered estates.

The author begins by observing, that he was wounded, and returned from a prisoner of war camp to his farm in Bulgrin in summer 1945, which is 12.75 hectares in area.

A short time after I had come home, Poles arrived in our village; first they came separately. They sized up the place, and settled on farms which they liked. We Germans had to give them first a room, with all the furniture, linen, etc., which was in it.

First of all the Poles behaved in a quite friendly way to us, which they, of course, did, in order to learn something about managing the farm. We thought, and the Poles confirmed this by what they said in this belief, that they would only be having asylum with us for a short time, as everything in Poland had been destroyed by the war. As we had no newspapers in our village, we were at the mercy of reports and rumors which the Poles circulated. Furthermore, our wireless sets had been destroyed by the Russians.

None of us had an idea at that time, that we should for the time being be allowed to remain in our native village, in order to work for these intruders, and manage the farms for them. For they had no idea of how to do this themselves...

There was soon a Polish police or militia organized in the village, consisting of young Poles, who had worked for German farmers during the war, and had generally been well treated. These. young men, therefore, knew the conditions in the village very well, and subjected the Germans to chicanery, and plundered them.

Under the protection of this militia, the Poles ventured to commit more and more excesses against Germans. They drove us out of our beds at night, beat us, and took us away for days at a time, and locked us up...The Pole took over the dwelling of the German family with all the furniture, clothing, etc. in it....

Thus our conditions of life steadily got worse. The Pole on my farm gave me 12 Pounds of rye a month, which he exactly weighed for my family of six persons. This we ground ourselves, and baked or made bread from it, and this, although we in the same year had harvested 40 hundred weight of rye from my farm...

As there was a lack of bread, we were chiefly dependent on potatoes. There was scarcely any other kind of food for us Germans, as the Poles took the meat, fat and eggs for themselves.

With the exception of one cow per family the Russians had driven away all the cattle, when they marched in. However, the Russians and Poles consumed the milk and butter from this one cow, and especially so, as the Polish family was a large one, which continually received "visitors." The result was, that we had to work all the harder. We were got out of our beds during the winter at 6 o'clock in the morning, and also father, who was 70 years old, had to chop up fire-wood in the dark stable.

The Russians had already taken away most of the agricultural machines and the work was, therefore, much harder for us, we had to do most of it with our hands. The machines and apparatus, however, which were still there, had been made unusable by the Poles in a very short time, as they did not know how to work them...

In the autumn of 1945 the Poles took possession of our old village church, in which our ancestors had been baptized and married. Everything inside the church, which reminded one of us Germans, amongst such things also the old memorial slabs for those who were killed in the wars of 1866, 1870/71 and 1914/18, were torn out and destroyed....

As our conditions of life kept getting worse, and it was clear, that we were confronted with famine, we moved in February 1946 to the neighboring village, where there was a Russian command headquarters. The farming villages had been chiefly taken over by the Poles, whereas the Russians ran the big estates, the products of which they used for their troops.

Our move had to take place under cover of darkness, for if the Poles had noticed anything, they would have beaten, ill-treated and completely plundered us... Conditions under the Russians were somewhat better, especially where there was a commandant, who was to some degree friendlily disposed to the Germans, and we would in this way be able to bridge over the time better, until the final decision in regard to the frontiers of Eastern Germany was reached. We hoped and believed, that this would not be long. For we still hoped, that our home would not be separated from Germany; however, if we were with the Poles, we must expect to be expelled from one day to the other, if this suited them.

With the Russians, everyone who worked received the following victuals: 650 grams of bread, 10 grams of meal, 140 grams of oats, 10 grams of noodles, 25 grams of meat, 10 grams of bacon or substitute fat, 10 grams of oil, 35 grams of sugar, 30 grams of fish, 30 grams of salt, 4 grams of coffee, and 920 grams of potatoes and vegetables. These were the rations laid down, of which some were often not distributed, particularly such as oil, sugar, meat, bacon and noodles.

There was never fresh meat and fish. The meat consisted only of bones. Each one received, for instance, a pig's bone, or an ox' bone or a bone from game, a general mix up and only offal, such as feet, heads, etc. The meat had been lying about for days unsalted, when we received it. Particularly in the hot season it already stank and it was impossible to eat it. The victuals were distributed for 5 days. Old people, sick ones and children, that is to say all those who could not work, received no rations, and one had to get them something to eat by stealing. As the estate had a German administrator, and Germans were also in charge of the granary, we often received from these people "a special rationing." As there was a lack of stuff for washing, it was inevitable, that many of us got lice, which it was extremely difficult to get rid of, in these circumstances.

In July I got typhus, although the Russians had inoculated us several times. I was sent to a hospital in Koslin, which was installed in a municipal building... For the Germans there was also a lack of medical attendance and medicaments. The medicaments, which had been left to the hospital by the Poles, were very expensive. For instance, an injection cost 150 zlotys. But we only got 10-20 zlotys, apart from our food, from the Russians monthly for our work.

The food in the hospital was very bad. Soup was made for the patients from offal such as fish bones, which were fetched from a Russian kitchen. I was discharged from the hospital after 3 months, but as I had rheumatism, as a result of the typhus, and had to hobble with a stick, I was utterly incapable of working. On the 1st October my wife was discharged from her work, as the Russians, after the work in the fields had been finished, ruthlessly discharged all workers, whom they did not want for looking after the cattle, and for the work necessary on the farm. Thus winter was at hand, and we had nothing, and were without food, for we received no more rations from the Russians, as we did not work.

When we were discharged, the Russians told us, that they would bring us across the Oder, that is to say, that they would expel us, for the Poles would in any case soon do so. The Russians also said, that, as we had worked during the summer for them, they would see, that we got away, in order that we should not be totally plundered by the Poles. On the 14 November, the Russians put us into two tractor trailers. There were about 180 people, old and sick persons,, women and children. We were brought to Koslin. Here the Russians saw that we departed the same day with a transport train, which was waiting. We were thus saved from having to remain for weeks in the camp at Koslin.

The author then describes how his expulsion proceeded, until he reached West Germany.

The Treatment of Volksdeutsche in Poland and in the Soviet Enclave of East Prussia

The treatment of those Germans living in prewar Poland, the Volksdeutsche, was considerably harsher. Basically, the German population was considered to be traitors to Poland, even though their communities had been there for centuries. (See map 13 of German settlements in prewar Poland) By a decree of February 1945, their properties were confiscated without indemnification. Many were tried for treason. After their trials, mostly in 1946/1947, they were sentenced to at least three years in prison. After they were released, many were required to do forced labor, before eventually being expelled from Poland. The Polish government attempted to differentiate between those Polish citizens who declared themselves German, and those of German origin who were assimilated to Polish culture. The former were considered "hostile" elements to be eliminated from Polish society, by a government decree of September 1946. The latter, if they demonstrated by their conduct that they belonged to the Polish Nation, and declared their loyalty, could be rehabilitated and remain in Poland.[36]

To complicate matters, in the fall of 1939 and the beginning of 1940, hundreds of thousands of Poles were expelled or transferred from the Provinces of Posen (Poznan) and West Prussia (Pomorze), to the German-occupied zone of Poland, known as the General Government by the Nazi government. (Some reports state that the number of expellees or those sent as forced labor to Germany reached 1.2 million.)[37] (See map 14 of the German division of Poland) These territories were incorporated into the German Reich as Reichsgauen Wartheland and Danzig-Westpreussen. The Polish farms, homes, and stores were confiscated by the German authorities to make room for the transfer, by the Nazi government, of about 800,000 ethnic German settlers from Bessarabia (present day Moldavia), Bukovina (Romania), and the Baltic lands.[38] (This figure is contested; however, some say only 350,000 ethnic Germans were transferred there, with the balance coming from the old Reich.)[39] These Balkan and Baltic lands had been incorporated into the Soviet Union as a result of prewar treaties and agreements with Nazi Germany. The irony is that this precedent provided a ready example to the Poles that the forced resettlement of an ethnic group was a solution to their national problem of a minority that did not want to assimilate.

Much of the ethnic German able-bodied population was placed in central labor camps. From there many were sent to the industrial area of Upper Silesia or to Warsaw to clear war ruins. Most of the camp inmates, however, were sent to work on private or state farms. The old, the sick, and children stayed in the camps and suffered undernourishment, sickness, and harassment. Typhoid epidemics raged in the camps in the summer and autumn of 1945, resulting in a high death toll. Conditions improved somewhat thereafter until their expulsion from Poland.

There were about 250,000–300,000 Germans still living in that portion of East Prussia which was annexed by the Soviet Union. Many were deported to Russia, and those that were not, were subject to forced labor, either cleaning up Königsberg or working on state farms, especially in the depopulated eastern parts of East Prussia. The population suffered from food shortages and only those that worked received any rations. Epidemics of typhoid and dysentery were widespread and the mortality rate was very high. The availability of food supplies improved somewhat by 1947. The German rural population, however, continued to live on the land, working on collective farms. They were not immediately expelled to Germany as happened in Poland. The expulsions, nevertheless, started in the summer of 1947 and were completed by 1949.[40]

No. 176

Eyewitness report of the gardener A. Riemann of Ludwigsort, district of Heiligenbeil in East Prussia. Original, January 1953, 8 pages. Printed in part.

Conditions of life and work of the German inhabitants of the district of Heiligenbeil, under Russian methods of administration, and the principles of Russian economy from 1945 to 1948.

The author reports first of all on his experiences during the flight, and when he met the Russians in Samland, up to his return to Ludwigsort in May 1945.

In the course of the summer of 1945 German families kept returning to Ludwigsort. Many had already been in Pomerania or even further to the west. They returned to East Prussia, in order to die there. In autumn there were about 400 inhabitants there, I was temporarily nominated mayor, and had to draw up lists of the inhabitants and register the deaths. The chief thing was to supply workers for all possible and impossible purposes. There were, of course, no wages paid, and the food was moreover inadequate. No one liked going to this work. In the spring of 1946 the Russian Secret Service took over the whole administration.

In the autumn of 1945 our winter seed was ripe for harvesting. Although most of the grain remained in the fields, it saved many thousands of people their lives during the winter months. The great mortality began the next year, for there were neither bread nor potatoes, as nothing had been planted in the province. For miles the fields were covered with thorns and thistles. In our district about 20,000 morgen were scantily tilled. All the rest lay fallow, and became in the course of time wooded.

This was chiefly due to the system of "norms," which was also introduced into agriculture. All work was reckoned, and paid according to "norms." It was generally impossible to achieve these "norms," especially considering how physically exhausted the people were. In order to earn the merest necessities of life the work was, therefore, done badly and superficially. For every 30 workers there was a supervisor, who received wages, and had to reckon the work done in square meters with a measuring instrument.

For every kind of work there was a special "norm," for instance, for hoeing onions three different grades, first, second and third hoeing. The whole method of working is so complicated, that an army of officials is necessary for running a farm of 2,000 morgen. The system of piecework so jeered at by Communists has been substituted by a cunning form of exploitation.

Until the end of June we were allowed to do the farm work in our own way. Then everything was changed. Administrative officers were attached to the different command officers, and decided what was to be done. Every locality, where Germans lived, was allotted an area, which had to be harvested. The crop was to serve exclusively to feed the Germans. Machines were brought, chiefly bundling machines. The army supplied the horses. In the course of the summer the population of Ludwigsort harvested about 300 cartloads of rye and wheat. They were put dry in stacks and in barns. Nevertheless, a great amount remained in the fields, because there were not enough workers and machines.

The summer grain, as far as the Russians had sown any at all, all remained standing. As soon as the crop was brought in, the threshing

71

began. However, not for the Germans, but every military authority and all troops passing through, etc., who cared to do so, procured threshing machines, set the Germans to do the work, and, of course, took the threshed grain away with them. What was not threshed lay where it was, and got drenched with the rain. Civilians came even from as far as White Russia, and threshed the corn with sticks, in order to get alcohol from it. They earned their living by selling this to the soldiers...

After the harvest there were new orders issued. The fields had to be prepared for the winter sowing. Men and women had to dig the fields, 200 square meters being the "norm" per day. Owing to their physical weakness the majority scarcely achieved the half. A plough with two emaciated horses had to do a hectare every day. It is no wonder that instead of plowing, the ground was only scraped, and that, instead of being dug, it was only a little rummaged. Further, the seed was put much too late into the soil. It was a pity, that the grain was so senselessly wasted. But the command was, "norm" according to plan! No one could do anything against this.

Conditions continued to get worse. First of all the Russians dissolved their local command office in October 1945. An administrative officer came from Heiligenbeil occasionally to Ludwigsort. Apart from this, the colonel of an infantry regiment had to decide everything, that was to be done in Ludwigsort: it had become a garrison. Young Lithuanians were called up for service and trained there. Shooting ranges were laid out, and also places for bomb dropping. The rattling of machine-guns scarcely stopped during the day. As soon as 1945 the Russians were arming at high pressure. We were out of contact with the rest of the world, and we lost all hope of there coming an early change in our desperate situation...

Meanwhile the frontiers were severely guarded, and closed by high barbed wire. No one was allowed to go to Poland or Lithuania, and we were veritable prisoners in our own country... Excesses and violence increased. Shooting on our farm was not rare. If in the evening the doors were bolted, and could not be at once opened, when Russians were outside and knocking, then they immediately shot through the windows or doors. These evening visits were mostly directed at the women. Anyone, who wanted to save himself, had to spring through the window on the other side of the house, whether he was clothed or unclothed, and whether it was raining or ice-cold. The only way of saving one's self was by running away in the darkness into the wood. The women did not dare to return, until everything seemed to have quieted down again.

One evening we heard excited voices before the door of our house, which were quickly followed by a shot. We rushed out in all directions, and found a Russian soldier writhing on the ground. The police were called, and appeared at once, and took the wounded man to a doctor. Fortunately he survived, and was able to state, that he had been shot by a Russian captain who, of course, had run away. The shot had not been meant for him, but for a German night watchman, who wanted to prevent the two Russians from breaking into the house to look for women. If the Russian had not been able to give evidence, the blame would, of course, have been put on to the Germans, and we might be no longer alive.

In this way the autumn passed, and Christmas was almost there. Then the order was issued, that Ludwigsort must be evacuated by the Germans...

On Christmas Eve itself the dwellings, as far as there were any, had to be given up. Only a few craftsmen were allowed to remain, because they were specialists. We had to get out of our house, but were allowed to move to my brother Franz, because he was working as a tailor for the Russians, and was allowed to continue living in his own house. All the others had to move to places in the neighborhood, such as Schwanis, Rippen, Wendelau, Laukitten, Gross Klingbeck, etc. Of course, no provision had been made for quarters. Everyone had to look out for himself, and see where he could stay...

The spirits of the people naturally sank, particularly so, as there were no news from the rest of Germany. In the course of the winter a state farm was established in Rippen, and had to deliver all its products to the military authorities. The director lived with his staff in Rippen, and all the officers were there.... The dairy and the nursery garden were established in Schwanis. My brother Paul, who was also a gardener, went in the winter of 1945-1946 to Rippen, and lived there with the Russian administrative captain.

As the conditions got continually worse in Ludwigsort, and meanwhile the military had been relieved by civilians, I moved in the summer of 1946 with my wife to Schwanis, in order to manage a nursery garden there for the state farm on the land of Diester. My own hothouse in Ludwigsort had been already dismantled in September 1945 and sent to Russia.

Almost all Germans got work on the state farm, or with other administrative authorities, such as the post, the municipality, the school, etc. The workers also received food coupons. Those, who could not work, such as old people, sick people, etc., received no food coupons. If these unhappy people had no relatives, who could perhaps help them with food, then they were doomed to die of hunger...The wages, as far as any were paid at all, were very bad, as a result of the "norm" system; all the same one managed somehow or other to live.

There were on an average 40-50 women occupied in the nursery garden in Schwanis. I remained there, until I came with a transport to Germany in 1948.

As already mentioned, the military personnel was transferred in June 1946 to Lithuania, and was replaced by a civilian one. We heard from the soldiers, that we need expect nothing good of this, and this proved to be right. It was not until the managers of the administration had been several times changed, that things got a little better in 1947. This administration first of all had its seat in the district court in Heiligenbeil. Two months later it moved to Ludwigsort, and took up its quarters in the house of the master sweep Steinau. Ludwigsort thus became in a certain sense the district town, and was in the future called Ladushkin.

During the first days after the civilian administration had been established, all the mayors were summoned to Heiligenbeil... After a short interrogation, work was at once assigned to us. In Ludwigsort 750 tons of hay were to be harvested, by the end of July 1946. I mentioned the difficulties, because it would be impossible in the circumstances. "Siberia" was the only answer. If we had no horses, then we must collect the hay by carrying it ourselves...

The Russian civilians came with the administration to Ludwigsort, so that there were generally only barns and stables left, as quarters for the Germans... The administrative buildings of Schmidt's farm, which had been repaired by the military administration, were for the most part dismantled, and used as fuel. When there was nothing more available in Ludwigsort, it was the turn of the other localities to pass through this process of destruction. If a dwelling house anywhere was repaired, two new ones had to be dismantled elsewhere, in order to provide the material.

It was the same thing, in regard to the fields. Meadows became swamps, fields became wooded land. In some places the young plants reached a height of 3 meters. Malaria raged among the German population.

In 1947 and 1948 the first transports of Russians arrived. They came from the remotest parts of Asia. They had been sent on their way, with magnificent promises; they were to receive 2,000 rubles, a cow, a sheep and a few fowl. They were also promised a nice house. Their disappointment, however, was great, when they found out, that they had got to work on collective farms. Many of them secretly sold their cattle, and went back to Russia.

At the end of 1947 the conditions of life became slowly more bearable for those of the German population, who had survived the worst time; and this was in spite of the fact, that the Russian economic and administrative methods had not changed in principle. Gradually wages began to be paid for work done, and it was possible to obtain victuals for rubles on the free market and in stores. It is true, that the supply was very irregular, as there was often embezzlements on the part of the Russians, but the famishing period seemed to be at an end. Furthermore, a reform of the currency increased the purchasing power of the ruble. Of course, the Russians first of all received supplies, and it often happened, that the Germans, after having queued up for hours, had to go away again with empty stomachs.

It should also be mentioned, that during the winter months of 1946 to 1947 an orphanage was founded for children without parents; German women worked there under the supervision of Russians. At the end of 1947 these children came with a transport to Germany...

The cemeteries, frequently a measure for judging the standard of civilization in a country, were completely neglected during the occupation time. Grave stones in particular were used for erecting Russian monuments, and for repairing the roads. There were cinemas and stores in the churches, which were not dismantled.

Not all Russians are convinced of the infallibility of the Communist doctrine and principles. On the contrary the elder generation is mostly opposed to the system of terror. Such persons helped the Germans as far as they could, and often secretly made them presents...

Our one object, therefore, was to be free again, and live among Germans.

Considering the speed of sovietization in East Prussia, our notion, that the Germans had become slowly a nuisance to the Russians, was confirmed, particularly with regard to the military fortifying of the district of Kaliningrad(Königsberg). The first reports, that people would be sent to Germany, were spreading. Finally things got so far, and on the 27 November 1947 the first 1,100 Germans left East Prussia by way of Allenstein for Erfurt. We were with the second transport on the 7 April 1948. The rest of our relatives, who had remained behind, followed with the third transport in October 1948.

The Expulsions

The expulsions of the German population started in earnest in June 1945, even before the Potsdam Conference. The greater part of the population of the former German provinces of East Brandenburg, Pomerania, and Silesia were assembled in transit camps, received departure cards, and sent by trains over the Oder to the West. Those Volksdeutsche who remained in Danzig and West Prussia, and who were not deported to the Soviet Union or placed in Polish labor camps, also were sent to the West. Polish action was comprehensive, rigorous, and often accompanied by brutality against a pauperized civilian population.

A journalist for the *New York Times*, Anne O'Hare McCormick, reported on the "nightmarish conditions" of the refugees in February 1946. In the fall of that year, she reportedly labeled the transfer a "crime against humanity for which history will exact a terrible retribution."[41]

By the middle of July, however, this exodus was slowed due to the protests of the Soviet Army, who were faced with huge masses of refugees concentrated on the West Bank of the Oder river, in Soviet-occupied Germany. The people were all in wretched condition, and the Soviet occupying authorities could not cope with this human disaster.

The Polish government was required by the terms of the Potsdam Agreement to stop the expulsions until the Allied Control Council had drawn up a plan to determine the capacity of each occupation zone to absorb these expellees. However, the government ignored this agreement and continued to expel Germans to the Soviet zone of occupation. These expulsions went on without interruption until the late autumn of 1946.

Certain Germans were exempted, temporarily, from this forced resettlement. They were those working for the Russians as well as individuals in critical positions, especially in the mining and metallurgical industries. Poles who had acquired German citizenship, but felt themselves to be Poles by reason of language and heritage, were also exempt. Additionally, the Polish government exempted "autochthonous" residents of these German lands. These ethnic groups were the Masurians in East Prussia, and the Kashubians in West Prussia and Pomerania, as well as many inhabitants of Upper Silesia. They were originally Slavic peoples whom the Polish government considered to be Poles, but over the generations had become thoroughly Germanized. By 1951, however, Polish policy toward those Germans still remaining in Poland began to change. Workers in specialized industries and critical occupations were forced to accept Polish citizenship. This was strongly resisted by the ethnic minority, and by 1960 the vast majority had opted for emigration to West Germany.[42]

No. 372

Letter of E. B. of the village of A., district of Sensburg in East Prussia. Certified copy, May 1949.

Compulsory option for the Polish state enforced by ill-treatment and violence on the part of the Polish administration in February 1949.

I shall never forget the month of February in this year. Up to then there were still more than 12,000 of us Germans in the district of Sensburg. Then canvassing meetings were held, at which we were severely prohibited to make purchases or sales or to leave the places, where we were living, unless we exercised our option for Poland. Also the Poles and Masurians were threatened with punishment, if they bought anything from or for us Germans. The police carried out checks in the businesses and at the market, and took the few people, who had dared to come to the town without a Masurian identity card to the Police station. But even this measure did not bring the desired success.

Then the canvassers went with armed policemen to the different villages, and all Germans from 14–100 years of age were urgently ordered to appear, in order to sign. If anyone was ill in bed, they came to his house, and anyone who hid himself was hunted out, and brought to the authorities. All the inhabitants of our village refused to exercise their option for Poland. Therefore, 28 of us were put into a truck, and taken to Sensburg. I was among these people: Furthermore, there were men and women of different ages, even a mother of 8 small children, of whom the youngest was five years old. Those, who remained behind, were ordered to report themselves after 2 days to the mayor, or else they would be arrested.

We were taken out of the truck in Sensburg, half of us being handed over to the political police, and the rest being brought provisionally to the militia. First of all we were shut up in a concrete cellar. At short intervals a policeman came, and asked who had already thought things over. Later he brought us to a room next to the guardroom...Here we were at least able to sit on the wooden floor, but we received no food.

The second evening an official said to us, that we ought to be reasonable and to sign, for, as he said, there had in January been a conference in Warsaw, at which there were representatives of the Russian, Polish, American and British governments, who had decided, that not a single German was to be allowed to cross the Oder, as there was famine there, and not enough houses. Indeed all those must come back from the Reich, who were from these parts, for it was at last time, that families should be reunited.

As, however, these parts were now Poland, and we as Germans were not allowed to live in Poland, we had got to exercise our option. Then we should have the same rights as the Poles, and within 4 days to 4 weeks our men would be back from the Reich, and would be with their families.

Many women said that, if they exercised their option, they would never be reunited with their husbands, as the latter would get a divorce, and the women would have toiled all these years in vain to maintain their children. They were then told, that the men would be called upon to come, and that, if they refused, the women would have a reason for divorce, and could marry Poles. They were also told, that permits from outside to go to the Reich, would not save them from signing... I had to go the next day to the political police, and was put into a brick cell, with other companions in misery. There they took everything away from us: rugs, sheets, shawls, belts, bags, handkerchiefs and towels, soap and combs and even shoe-laces. The men had to hand over their caps and braces. Those who signed received the things back. We were given nothing to wash and comb ourselves with during the whole week... We received sufficient food...

We were asked again and again, why we did not want to sign. Our answers were convincing and well founded, but all the same, no one left the building without being compelled to sign. We were repeatedly told, that this land had been Polish 700 years ago, and that the people living here now must be reunited with the Poles, who were their ancestral forefathers. The Germans were only on the other side of the Oder.

When I was asked, I said that I could not sign, as I had been born in the Reich.

Then they hesitated a moment, and asked me where my parents and grandparents were born, and I replied that these also came from the Reich, and that I had never had relatives here. First they looked at me in doubt, but then said to me, that I must sign, and I should then get my passport and could go away. I, thereupon, replied that, if I could not go back home as a German, I was not going to do so as a Pole. I was then told, that I should be put into the forced labor camp. I was ready for this, and likewise all the others, who were put to the test...

Then my ears were boxed... When I still did not sign, I was ordered to take off my cloak and clothes, and the door was shut. Then I had to bend over a chair, and was beaten with a truncheon; I was continually cynically asked at intervals, if it hurt. I clenched my teeth, and did not utter a sound. There were two other officials in the room, but all three were wearing civilian dress. One of them sat opposite to me, who watched the whole proceeding with a malicious grin.

They would have continued to ill-treat me, but someone wanted to come into the room. I had to dress myself again, and was led back into the cell with 5 other women, who had been treated in about the same way. There were now about 21 of us women in the cell. The next night one was fetched out every quarter of an hour; the next morning there were only 8 of us left in the cell, as all the others had already yielded to the violence. Some of them came back tottering, in order to tell their relatives that they had signed. As the sentry might have heard, we did not dare to put any questions to them, but we saw what they had been through.

The 8 of us remaining were shouted at, that, if we did not soon come on our own, we should see after 3 hours what would happen. We saw how hopeless the situation was, but all the same waited, until we were called. We then put our names underneath a form, on which were printed the words: "I request to be given Polish citizenship, and promise to be faithful and obedient to the Polish State." We felt, as if we had signed our own death sentence.

The men were treated even worse. They were shut up in a room, in which lime-dust had been strewn thickly. Here the poor fellows had to walk about day and night with their trousers in their hands as their braces had been taken away from them. They were forbidden to lie down or sit down, and were closely watched. They were only allowed to go out, in order to relieve themselves once in 24 hours, and this without considering whether they were old or sick. Many men and women had either heart, kidney or bladder complaints, or suffered from rheumatism, and had great pains to endure. Women were allowed to relieve themselves 3 times a day. During the cross-examinations those questioned were punched, received upper-cuts in the chin and kicks.

My foster father was 60 years old, and on one occasion he received "treatment" from 7 o'clock to 11 o'clock in the morning, and in the course of this he was continually thrust with his head against the wall; when he said, it would be better if they shot him, they gave him a cord to hang himself up, and told him otherwise to jump out of a window on the third floor, for a bullet was too good for him. Finally he had to bare the lower part of his body and to bend over a chair. He fainted, however, before he began to feel the truncheon, for he had disease of the heart. These fellows did not even hesitate to beat women and girls on their bare bodies.

We had suffered very much, but now they had violated us in the very worst way. We had now only one wish, and that was to escape from such a condition of affairs, and to get to our fellow Germans in the Reich.

In the summer of 1946 certain improvements occurred in the system of expulsions. The previous winter, the Allied Control Commission had devised a plan for the orderly transfer of Germans from Poland. Of the estimated 3.5 million Germans then residing in the former German eastern provinces and in Poland, two million were to be transferred to the Russian zone of occupation, and 1.5 million to the British zone. This transfer was to end in 1946.[43]

In the year 1946, about two million Germans were expelled to the West. Most went to the British zone, whereas in the previous year, they went mostly to the Soviet zone of occupation. In the year 1947, the transfers became more orderly. At this point many skilled workers, who had been retained in Poland, were forced to leave or allowed to leave. Also going were many who had opted for Polish citizenship as well as Germans considered "autochthonous" by the Poles. After all the hardships of the East German population in these postwar years, they now welcomed expulsion because it meant for them an end to their suffering. The last comprehensive expulsion was in 1949. In 1950/1951 the German Red Cross and British authorities organized the "Link Action" whose purpose was to reunite families. In this last transfer, about 44,000 Germans came across the Oder River, [44] which brought to a finish the expulsion of Germans from Poland.

There are reports that over half a million Germans remained in Poland after the expulsions. (Several sources stated that there were up to two million ethnic Germans who were able to stay in Poland, though precise figures are difficult to find.) These are former Germans who considered themselves Polish by culture and language. It also includes the "autochthonous," namely Mazurs, Kashubes, or Silesians. With the fall of the communist regime in Poland, and with the assistance of the Federal German government, they have organized themselves into an "Association of German Friendship Circles in Poland" (Verband der deutschen sozial-kulturellen Gesellschaften in Polen). It promotes German cultural activities, including language schools. It is said to have 420,000 members.[45]

A Summary of the Different Stages of the Expulsions

Taken from Documents on the Expulsion of the Germans from Eastern-Central Europe, Vol. I; Prof. Theodor Schieder, Editor; Federal Ministry for Expellees, Refugees and War Victims, Bonn, Germany.

Number of expellees:

Before the Potsdam Agreement (June to July 1945) particularly out of East Brandenburg, East Pomerania, and Lower Silesia:	250,000

From late in summer until late in autumn 1945. from all East German territories with the exception of that part of East Prussia administered by the Russians:	400,000
During the year 1946 particularly out of Silesia, East Pomerania, and the part of East Prussia administered by the Poles:	2,000,000
During the year 1947 from all the territories of East Germany administered by the Poles and from that part of East Prussia administered by the Russians:	500,000
During the year 1948 from the part of East Prussia administered by the Russians and from Poland:	150,000
During the year 1949 from that part of East Prussia administered by the Russians and from Poland:	150,000
During the years 1950/1951 in accordance with the "Link action":	50,000
Total:	3,500,000

T. David Curp, in his book, *A Clean Sweep? The Politics of Ethnic Cleansing in Western Poland, 1945-1960,* states that there was a tremendous human and economic cost to Poland as well as cultural impoverishment by the expulsion of the Germans. This national revolution not only facilitated the consolidation of Poland's communist government, but made possible Soviet control over the country. The intolerance that the ethnic cleansing of the Germans generated permitted the Poles to remember Germany's many crimes, while forgetting those of the Soviet Union and Stalin. The former first secretary of the Polish communist party, Wladyslaw Gomulka stated this very clearly when he said that anti-German hatred was the force binding Poles to the communist system.[46]

No. 325

Eyewitness report of Mrs. Maria Popp of Labenz, district of Dramburg in Pomerania. Attested copy, 4 July 1949.

Driving out of the German people unfit for work out of Labenz and other places in the district of Dramburg during December 1945; plundering during the journey to Scheune.

The memorable 15 December 1945 began like all other days, and there were all kinds of rumors. We, of course, believed it when we heard, that there would be a great searching of houses during the next days, and with much plundering. On Wednesday, the 15 December, all the Poles were concentrated into the village, and all of them had already been armed. We went on with our work, but naturally asked ourselves what this meant.

At midday the first people were driven out of our village, and were given 20 minutes to pack. The driving out continued the whole afternoon, until 8 o'clock in the evening. The last were only given a minute to leave the house, and there was no consideration shown to aged and sick people. First we were all driven into the church, and there we had to pass a night... On Sunday during the forenoon, it was made clear to us, that we were not going on a pleasant journey, but that we had to suffer for what the SS had done...

At 3 o'clock in the afternoon we were ordered to line up before the church.

Then the Russians came up and selected workers from our midst. After this our column consisted mostly of sick people, aged people, cripples, women and children. It was really a helpless column, which started off, and went in farmcarts as far as the railway station in Janikow. A goods train was already waiting there for us. The people were being driven out from the whole district, and it took a whole day, before they all arrived at the station. The plundering began, before the first batch got into the train, and on Monday evening the journey began.

The worst part was not that most of the people had no food, but that the plundering on a large scale now began. Whole bands of fellows attacked every wagon, and when 2 left it 3 got in. The train kept stopping to help the plundering, and no one was left in peace. There were about 70-80 persons in each wagon, and each one was separately searched for valuables or money. Anyone, who was wearing good clothes, had to take them off, even shoes if the plunderers liked them. If anyone refused, he was beaten until he yielded...

In this way we traveled to Scheune, and I think that everyone of us shudders, when he hears this name again. Every kind of cruelty, which it was possible to think of, was committed against us. We were all in a shocking condition, owing to hunger, cold and the great agitation. Very few of us were able to think clearly, and no-one dared to help the cripples and the dying. Many disappeared, and many were brought on a stretcher to a room, where they were again plundered by the Poles, and left there to slowly freeze to death.

We stood a day and a night on the platform, and then suddenly it was announced late in the evening, while we were seeking refuge from the cold behind a shed, that the train would start in 5 minutes. Perhaps our predicament had become known to higher authorities? The Russians now took over the train, and there was peace. The plundering stopped, and this seemed uncanny to us at first.

On Friday we arrived in Mecklenburg, and had to leave the train at Woldegk, totally exhausted. There we were given food for the first time, and were assigned to the villages from the camp.

When I today think of this expulsion, I am surprised how people found the strength to survive it. I always see the cripples before my eyes, when I think of it. The crutches were snatched out of their hands, and one of them was literally kicked to death. I shall never forget his screams in my life. The most sad part was, that the healthy people remained behind, and that those, who were in need of care, were sent on the journey...

The Polish Government's Justification for the Expulsion of the German Population

The Polish justification for the annexation of German lands and the expulsion of its inhabitants basically rests on two propositions; first, it was compensation for the losses of the Polish nation due to the German occupation. The Germans undoubtedly committed unspeakable atrocities against the Poles. Second, these territories were historically Polish, and therefore were labeled "regained territories"; it was only just that they be returned to Poland. For this reason, the Polish government never spoke of the expulsion of the indigenous German population, but of the "transfer" or "resettlement" back to their ancestral home in Germany.

There was also one other argument for the annexation of Germany's eastern provinces. That was to straighten and shorten the Polish–German frontier in order to make it more defensible in case of future German aggression. This was first expressed by General Sikorski, the head of the Polish exile government in London. After his war-time death, however, this argument was never emphasized.[47]

The justification for the annexation of the Eastern German provinces as compensation for the lost territories in the east to the Soviet Union, was never put forward by the Polish government, although it was by the Western Allies. The Poles could not have done so because it would have implied that the Soviet annexation was arbitrary, and contrary to the will of the Polish people. Although this was the rationale of the Western Powers who acquiesced to this annexation when faced with a Soviet "fait accompli," it was impossible for a Polish communist government to acknowledge it. This position was confirmed by Soviet Foreign Minister Molotov at the April 1947 Moscow Foreign Ministers' Conference, when he said, "the question discussed at Potsdam was not merely of compensation for Poland for the territories she ceded to the Soviet Union in the east. Such an explanation would be simplifying things. Only territories inhabited by Ukrainians and White Russians have been joined to the Soviet Union and these people should naturally be united with their brothers in the Soviet Ukraine and in the Soviet Byelorussia. In the west Poland has returned to her ancient territories which were once the cradle of Poland. Her present territory coincides with the historic territory of the Poland of the Piasts" (Poland's first royal house).[48]

The Destruction of the Polish Nation

The Soviet-German Non-Aggression Pact of August 1939 gave Hitler a free hand against Poland. The resultant Nazi subjugation of Poland was based on their racial theories that Slavs are subhuman and destined for extermination, or enslavement in the case of the able-bodied. Prior to the invasion of Poland in September 1939, Hitler is reported to have said, "The destruction of Poland is our primary task. The aim is not the arrival at a certain line, but the annihilation of living forces.... Be merciless! Be brutal.... It is necessary to proceed with maximum severity.... The war is to be a war of annihilation." Heinrich Himmler, the head of the SS, echoed these words when he said, "the Slavs are to work for us. Insofar as we don't need them, they may die.[49]

After the German conquest of Poland, the western provinces, which were part of the Reich prior to 1918, were absorbed again into the Reich as Reichsgau Danzig-Westpreussen and Reichsgau Wartheland. The balance of occupied Poland was the General Government, originally under military control and then under Nazi civilian control. (See map 14) At the time of the incorporation of the western provinces into Germany, this area had a population of 10.1 million, of whom 8.9 million were Poles and the rest ethnic Germans. This relationship changed subsequently with the Nazi colonization programs and the expulsion of a part of the Polish population, judged to have been about one million inhabitants. Most were sent to the territory of the General Government.[50]

To permit the destruction of the Polish nation and culture, Nazi policy first and foremost aimed at eliminating the Polish elite. Hitler entrusted this job to Himmler's SS, including the police. The Governor General, Hans Frank, stated, "The Führer told me, 'What we have now recognized in Poland to be the elite must be liquidated; we must watch out for the seeds that begin to sprout again, so as to stamp them out again in good time.'"[51] The elite included the professional sectors of Polish society, teachers, doctors, businessmen, clergy, writers, artists: in other words, the intelligentsia. Members of the Polish aristocracy, many of whom served in the armed forces, were also targeted. For example, one of the first acts of the occupation authorities in late 1939 was to arrest and send to Sachsenhausen concentration camp in Germany 200 professors of the University of Cracow. In early 1940 a mass roundup by the occupation authorities, entitled "Extraordinary Pacification Action," resulted in the murder of at least 6,000 members of the intelligentsia, with several thousand more being sent to Auschwitz, where most of them subsequently died.[52]

After the war, Polish sources report that the country lost 45 percent of its doctors, 57 percent of its lawyers, more than 15 percent of its teachers, 40 percent of its professors, 30 percent of its engineers, and more than 18 percent of its clergy.[53] The Polish educational system was particularly hard hit. In the General Government, secondary schools and universities were closed. Even attendance at elementary schools was only 50 percent of prewar totals. This reflected the aims of the Nazi regime, whose Governor, Hans Frank, said, "The Poles do not need universities or secondary schools; the Polish lands are to be changed into an intellectual desert." The occupation authorities also closed all scientific, artistic, and literary institutions, including libraries.[54]

Polish workers and farmers were deported en masse to the Reich to work in factories and farms. Initially, the German government attempted to recruit these workers but with little success. Subsequently, the authorities resorted to forced roundups. By late 1943, this coerced conscription resulted in more than 1.6 million Poles working as slave labor in the German armaments industry and on farms. Additionally, 300,000 Polish prisoners of war were subject to forced labor in Germany.[55]

The statement has even been made that the Polish nation was saved from total destruction by Nazi Germany's need for Polish labor because of the labor shortage in Germany. This labor shortage had begun already in 1940. Polish labor became more important with the German attack on the Soviet Union in the summer of 1941, and the need became acute after the battle of Stalingrad in early 1943. The Germans even considered recruiting the Poles to fight the Soviets.[56]

Some six million Poles were killed in World War II, of which about one half were Polish Jews. This represented 22 percent of the country's prewar population, which is said to have been the highest rate of loss of any country in Europe. They, Jewish and non-Jewish, died in extermination camps, prisons, and mass executions, as well as from epidemics, starvation, hard labor, and general ill-treatment. The first non-German prisoners of Auschwitz were Poles. They were the largest ethnic group until 1942, when Jews became the largest group. In the Stutthof concentration camp in East Prussia, until 1942, 90 percent of the inmates were Poles.[57]

The great German novelist, playwright, and Nobel Prize winner, Gerhart Hauptmann, a native of Silesia, recorded in his diary on December 30,1939, "After waking up, the terror of the war pressed in my chest: Poland! How much hate has been released there. We destroyed Poland, delivered up half of it to the Russians, calling forth all the spirits of revenge on us for a century. Why is it that this pitiless nationalism has been aroused everywhere and in everything?"[58]

The Historical Justification for the Expulsion

The history of the interaction between the German and Polish nations in the German eastern provinces began in the year 966 AD, when German missionaries baptized Poland's King, Miesko I, who founded Poland's first royal house, the Piast Dynasty. In 1000 AD, the German King of Saxony and Holy Roman Emperor, Otto III, met with the son of Miesko I, Boleslaw I Chrobry, at Gnesen (Gniezno), and named him "frater et cooperator Imperii" (brother and partner of the Empire). This freed the Polish crown from paying tribute to the Holy Roman Empire. The German emperor then made Gniezno into an archbishopric and named three new bishops for Cracow, Kolberg (Kolobrzeg), and Breslau (Wroclaw). This made the new Kingdom of Poland ecclesiastically independent of the German hierarchy and established Polish political and religious influence in Silesia and Pomerania. In subsequent years, Poland's kings and nobility invited German colonists to help settle and develop the economic and urban life in these territories,[59] whose original inhabitants were western Slavic tribes that had moved in from the east.

In 1181, the Holy Roman Emperor Friedrich Barbarossa made the Duke of Pomerania, Bogislaw I, a prince of the Empire. In the thirteenth century, the colonization of Pomerania by German settlers began, invited by the Dukes of Pomerania. Most of the major towns were founded at this time. Pomerania became fully a part of the Empire in 1338. In 1648, Western Pomerania was ceded to Sweden as a result of the Treaties of Westphalia, ending the Thirty Years' War. At the same time, Eastern Pomerania was given to Brandenburg-Prussia. The last vestiges of Swedish rule ended in 1814. The kingdom of Prussia subsequently governed all of Pomerania after the end of Swedish rule until the Prussian state was formally dissolved in 1945.

Silesia became an independent principality within the Polish realm of the Piasts in 1138. The Silesian ruling Duke, Henry I, in the period 1201–1238, began a systematic colonization of his principality by bringing in settlers from Germany and Wallonia (the French-speaking region of Belgium). In this period, 120 towns and 1,200 villages were founded.[60] A combined Silesian army of Polish and German knights was defeated by Mongolian hordes at the battle of Liegnitz in 1241, but Silesia was not occupied. In 1250, Breslau (Wroclaw), the capital of Silesia, was refounded by German settlers and became an important commercial center. By 1335, Silesia left Polish sovereignty and became a part of the Holy Roman Empire of the German Nation. This occurred when Poland ceded Silesia to the Bohemian crown, a member and elector of the Empire. In 1526 the province became an inheritance of the House of Habsburg, the ruling family of Austria and the Holy Roman Empire. In the three Silesian wars in the period 1740–1763 between Prussia and the Austrian house of Habsburg, Prussia annexed most of the province of Silesia. It was a part of the Prussian state, within Germany, until the end of World War II.

Due to the strong desire of the important Polish minority in Upper Silesia to belong to the reconstituted Polish nation after World War I, a plebiscite was held in March 1921, under the auspices of the League of Nations, to determine the future national status of Upper Silesia. Sixty percent of the population voted to remain German (707,393 for Germany to 479,365 for Poland), but the League decided, nevertheless, to count the votes by the communes, and a portion of Upper Silesia was therefore granted to Poland.[61]

The early history of East and West Prussia is basically that of the Order of the Teutonic Knights and of the Hanseatic League. The Order was founded at the time of the Fourth Crusade in 1190 in Acre (today Akko in Israel) as a monastic order of knights to help poor and sick German pilgrims in the Holy Land. They were supported by a group of merchants from Lübeck and Bremen. The Knights founded the hospital of St. Mary of the Germans in Jerusalem. As such, it was the third knightly religious order in the Holy Land with the Knights of the Temple of Solomon (Templars) and the Order of the Hospital of St. John in Jerusalem (Hospitallers). Pope Celestine II formally recognized the Order in 1192 as an independent monastic order. The Holy Roman Emperor, Frederick II, made the Grand Master and his successors Princes of the Empire. After the Christian forces were defeated in the Holy Land by the Muslim Saracens, King Andrew of Hungary asked the Order in 1210 to defend Transylvania (in today's Romania) from marauding bands of Cumans, a Turkic people from Central Asia. After having pacified the province, the Order was expelled, however, by the Hungarian King as it was creating its own state within his kingdom.

The Polish Prince Konrad of Masovia called the Order to East Prussia in 1225 to Christianize and colonize the land. The original settlers were the Prussians, a tribe related to the Baltic people. The following year, the Holy Roman Emperor granted the lands of the lower Vistula river (West Prussia) and East Prussian lands to the Order in the Golden Bull of Rimini. They created an independent monastic feudal state bringing peasants, craftsmen, and merchants from Germany as well as some from Flanders and Holland. At this time they founded the major towns of Thorn (Torun), Kulm (Chelmno), Elbing (Elblag), and Königsberg (today Russian Kaliningrad)., the latter founded in 1255.

In their conquest of Prussia, the Knights were assisted by and gave protection to the Hanseatic League, an early medieval association of merchants trading in the Baltic. The League was founded in Lübeck in the thirteenth century, and all major ports and cities of the Baltic were either founded by the League or were members such as Danzig, Elbing, Kulm, Thorn, and Königsberg in former East and West Prussia, as well as Riga in today's Latvia and Tallin (formerly Reval) in Estonia, and Visby, County of Gotland, in Sweden.

For the next fifty years the Knights fought continuous battles to convert the Prussians and develop their lands. Once this was accomplished, the pagan Lithuanians were the target of their ongoing warfare of conversion. This continued until 1386, when the Grand Duke of Lithuania, Jogaila, was baptized and married Queen Jadwiga of Poland and became the joint king of Poland and Lithuania. With the Christianization of Lithuania, the crusading rationale for the Order's existence ended. In 1410 a combined Polish and Lithuanian army defeated the Knights at Tannenberg in East Prussia. As a result the Knights ceded the western half of its territory to the Polish crown, which became known as Royal Prussia, and their remaining state in East Prussia (Ducal Prussia) became a vassal of the Polish King.

Please refer to: http://www.forgottenvoices.net, for a photograph (#8) of the medieval palace of the Grand Master of the Order of the Teutonic Knights in Marienburg (Malbork) in former West Prussia.

The last Grand Master, Albert of Brandenburg of the Hohenzollern family, converted to Lutheranism in 1525, secularized the Order's Prussian territories, and received from the Polish crown the hereditary rights to the Duchy of Prussia. The Protestant Duchy of Prussia therefore became a fief of Catholic Poland. With the assistance of the Swedish King, Charles X Gustav, after the Thirty Years' War, Prussia proclaimed its independence from Poland (at the Treaty of Oliva with Poland in 1660) and with the help of the Swedes recovered a part of its territory in West Prussia. Ducal Prussia then became the Kingdom of Prussia in 1701, ruling Brandenburg-Prussia. In 1772, as a result of the first partition of Poland, the remaining lands in West and South Prussia were annexed by the Kingdom of Prussia.[62]

In the nineteenth century, increasing nationalism, both German and Polish, heightened tensions and conflicts between these two peoples in the Prussian provinces of Posen (Poznan), West Prussia (Pomorze), and Upper Silesia (Gorny Slask). Bismark launched his attack on the Catholic Church (the Kulturkampf), which affected particularly the Polish Catholic minority in these Provinces. In 1887 he forbade the teaching of Polish.[63] Although these restrictions were ameliorated somewhat under subsequent governments, the pressure to assimilate to the dominant German culture was very great.

As a result of the Versailles Peace Treaty, the first two of these Provinces, as well as a portion of Upper Silesia (Gorny Slask), became Polish. The City of Danzig (Gdansk) was excepted and became a free city under the supervision of the League of Nations. Although by the terms of the Peace Treaty, Poland was required to respect the rights of minorities; the new Polish government did everything in its power to de-Germanize those ethnic Poles who adopted German culture and pressured the German inhabitants to assimilate, even dispossessing them of their lands. This was done in the guise of a land reform which affected German-owned lands more than Polish. In the Polish census of 1921, the German community in Poland totaled 1,059,000 or 3.9 percent of the total Polish population.[64] As a result, however, of these Polish national assimilation policies, many Germans emigrated to Germany, particularly those in the professions, so that by the time the Nazi regime attacked Poland in 1939, the German population numbered only 800,000–1,000,000.[65]

Please refer to: http://www.forgottenvoices.net, for a photograph (#9) of the town hall in Breslau (Wroclaw), Silesia, built in the fourteenth century. This is a good example of the North German/Baltic brick gothic style.

Finally, it should be stated that in recent times historians have de-emphasized or even ignored the argument justifying the annexation of the German eastern states; that is, they were originally Polish in the early Middle Ages, and therefore "recovered" territories. Today's argument is much simpler, and one can say much more honest: Nazi Germany started the war and attacked Poland. The country was devastated. Poland, as one of the Allies, won the war and Germany lost.

Notes

1. Lev Kopelev, *No Jail for Thought* (London, 1975), 52.
2. Norman A. Naimark, *The Russians in Germany: A History of the Soviet Zone of Occupation 1945-1949* (Cambridge, MA, 1995), 90.
3. Alfred Maurice de Zayas, *A Terrible Revenge, the Ethnic Cleansing of the East European Germans, 1944-1950* (New York, 1986), 82.
4. Christopher Duffy, *Red Storm on the Reich* (New York, 2002), 160.
5. Ibid., 208.
6. Thomas Darnstädt and Klaus Wiegrefe, *Die Flucht, Der Treck nach Westen* [The Flight, the Trek to the West] (Munich, 2005), 35.
7. *Stutthof, the first Nazi concentration camp outside Germany*, http://www.jewishgen.org; Stutthof National Museum, Poland.
8. Prof. Theodor Schieder, ed., *Documents on the Expulsion of the Germans from Eastern-Central Europe, The Expulsion of the German Population from the Territories East of the Oder-Neisse Line*, Vol. I (Bonn, 1954), 8.
9. Ellizabeth Wiskemann, As told in, *Germany's Eastern Neighbours; Problems Relating to the Oder-Neisse Line and the Czech Frontier Regions* (London, 1956), 88.
10. Ibid., 121.
11. Clemens Höges and others, *Die Flucht; Die verdrängte Tragödie* [The Flight; the Suppressed Tragedy] (Munich, 2005), 55.
12. Rudolf Augstein, *Die Flucht, Rückwärts krebsen um voranzukommen* (The Flight; Going Backwards in order to go Forwards] (Munich, 2005), 48.
13. Schieder, *Documents on the Expulsion of the Germans from Eastern-Central Europe*, 34.
14. Ibid., 37.
15. Duffy, *Red Storm on the Reich*, 192.

16. Schieder, *Documents on the Expulsion of the Germans from Eastern-Central Europe*, 41.
17. Ibid., 23.
18. Ibid., 27.
19. Duffy, *Red Storm on the Reich*, 89.
20. Schieder, *Documents on the Expulsion of the Germans from Eastern-Central Europe*, 41b.
21. Ibid., 44.
22. Ibid., 47.
23. Alfred Maurice de Zayas, *Nemesis at Potsdam, the Expulsion of the Germans from the East* (London, 1977), 85.
24. Schieder, *Documents on the Expulsion of the Germans from Eastern-Central Europe*, 62.
25. Andrea Kossert, *Kalte Heimat, Die Geschichte der Deutschen Vertriebenen Nach 1945* [Cold Homeland; the Story of the German Expelees after 1945] (Munich, 2008), 30.
26. Schieder, *Documents on the Expulsion of the Germans from Eastern-Central Europe*, 60.
27. Ibid., 62.
28. Ibid.
29. Ibid., 65.
30. Ibid., 66.
31. Ibid., 67.
32. Ibid., 83.
33. Ibid., 86.
34. Ibid., 94.
35. Norman A. Naimark, *Fires of Hatred, Ethnic Cleansing in Twentieth Century Europe* (Cambridge, MA, 2001), 127.
36. Ibid., 131.
37. Wolfgang Benz, *Fünfzig Jahre nach der Vertreibung, Die Vertreibung der Deutschen aus dem Osten* [Fifty Years after the Expulsion. The Expulsion of Germans from the East] (Frankfurt/Main, 1995), 46.
38. Karl Schlögel, *Bugwelle des Krieges, Die Flucht* [Bow Wave of the War: The Flight] (Munich, 2005), 180.
39. Benz, *Fünfzig Jahre nach der Vertreibung, Die Vertreibung der Deutchen aus dem Osten*, 46.
40. Schieder, *Documents on the Expulsion of the Germans from Eastern-Central Europe*, 74.
41. Debra J. Allen, *The Oder-Neisse Line, the United States, Poland and Germany in the Cold War* (Westport, CT, 2003), 43
42. Stefan Wolff, ed., *German Minorities in Europe* (New York, 2000), 80.
43. Schieder, *Documents on the Expulsion of the Germans from Eastern-Central Europe*, 113.
44. Ibid., 119.
45. Wolff, *German Minorities in Europe*, 86.
46. T. David Curp, *A Clean Sweep? The Politics of Ethnic Cleansing in Western Poland, 1945-1960* (Rochester, NY, 2006), 11, 12.

47. Wiskemann, *Germany's Eastern Neighbours*, 71.
48. Jozef Kokot, *The Logic of the Oder-Neisse Frontier* (Warsaw, 1959), 13.
49. Richard C. Lukas, *The Forgotten Holocaust, the Poles under German Occupation 1939-1944* (Lexington, KY, 1986), 4.
50. Ibid., 6, 18.
51. Ibid., 8.
52. Ibid., 9.
53. Ibid.
54. Ibid., 10, 11.
55. Ibid., 33.
56. Wiskemann, *Germany's Eastern Neighbours*, 57, 58.
57. Lukas, *Forgotten Holocaust*, 38.
58. Naimark, as quoted in *Fires of Hatred*, 125.
59. Curp, *Clean Sweep?* 14.
60. Ulrich March, *Die Deutsche Ostsiedlung* [The German Settlement of the East] (Bonn, 1998), 11.
61. Wiskemann, *Germany's Eastern Neighbours*, 29.
62. March, *Die Deutsche Oastsiedlung*, 10.
63. Wiskemann, *Germany's Eastern Neighbours*, 11.
64. Anthony Komjathy and Rebecca Stockwell, *German Minorities and the Third Reich* (New York, 1980), 65.
65. Wiskemann, *Germany's Eastern Neighbours*, 121.

III

The Expulsion of the Ethnic German Population from the Former Czechoslovakia

Czechs and Germans on the Way to a Good Neighborship

Address by President Vaclav Havel to the Charles University, Prague, February 17, 1995

...Our relationship to Germany and the Germans has been more than merely one of the many themes of our diplomacy. It has been a part of our destiny, even a part of our identity. Germany has been our inspiration as well as our pain; a source of understandable traumas, of many prejudices and misconceptions, as well as of standards to which we turn; some regard Germany as our greatest hope, others as our greatest peril. It can be said that the attitude they take toward Germany and the Germans has been a factor through which the Czechs define themselves, both politically and philosophically, and that it is through the type of that attitude that they determine not only their relationship to their own history but also the type of their conception of themselves as a nation and a state...

...It would be a dangerous oversimplification if the transfer of the Germans from our country after the war were to be perceived as the only item in the tragic coming to an end of the thousand years of Czech-German coexistence here. Physically, the transfer undoubtedly was the end of our life together in a common state, because it was with the transfer that that coexistence was actually terminated. But the lethal blow that caused its death was struck by something else: the fatal failing of a great part of our country's German-born citizens who gave preference to the dictatorship, confrontation and violence embodied in Hitler's national socialism over democracy, dialogue and tolerance, and while they were claiming their right to their homeland, they in fact renounced their home country. In so doing, they negated the outstanding accomplishments of the many German democrats who had helped build Czechoslovakia as their home. Whatever the deficiencies of the solution of the nationalities

93

issue in pre-war Czechoslovakia may have been, they can never justify that failing. Those who committed it turned not only against their fellow citizens, against Czechoslovakia as a state and their own status as citizens of that state; they turned against the very foundations of humanity itself. They embraced a perverted racist ideology and began immediately to apply it in practice. It is marvelous that many descendants of our former German fellow citizens have understood that and are now working selflessly and patiently for a reconciliation between our peoples...

...I have already stated more than once in the past that evil is of an infectious nature and that the evil of the transfer was only a sad consequence of the evil which preceded it. There can be no dispute about who was the first to let the genie of national hatred out of the bottle. And if we, that is, the Czechs are to recognize our share of responsibility for the end of the Czech-German coexistence in the Czech lands, we have to say, for the sake of truth, that we let ourselves become infected by the insidious virus of the ethnic concept of guilt and punishment but that it was not us who brought that virus, at least not its modern destructive form, into this country.

My third remark on the end of the Czech-German coexistence concerns the Munich Agreement. I am not sure whether certain people, especially on the German side, are sufficiently aware of the fact that Munich was not simply an unjust solution of a disputable minority issue but the last and, in a way, crucial confrontation between democracy and the Nazi dictatorship. At that time, democracy capitulated and thus paved the way for the dictatorship to launch its inconceivable assault on all the fundamental values of civilization and on the very essence of human coexistence, possibly the most severe such assault ever made in human history. To Hitler, Munich was the final test of democracy and its ability to defend itself; he took the Munich capitulation of the democrats as a sign that he was free to unleash a war. His calculation proved to be wrong and democracy prevailed in the end, but only at a great sacrifice that could most probably have been avoided if democracy had not given in to the delusion of appeasement and had resisted Hitler at the time of the Munich crisis. Again, two different aspects of the matter should be distinguished: while in military terms World War II began with the attack on Poland, there is no doubt that the Munich dictate was its political beginning. Did a great German politician not say many years ago that Munich meant the moment from which everything plunged into the abyss? The part that many of our German-born fellow citizens played in the preparations for Munich and in its aftermath cannot be narrowed to a struggle for their minority rights. The issue then was not the Germans from the Czech lands, nor merely the dismemberment of Czechoslovakia as a prelude to its subsequent occupation. At that time, war was declared, in no uncertain terms and at the international level, upon human freedom and dignity. Were not the German opponents of Nazism the first victims of Nazi vengeance in the Czech lands? Even now, admitting this may not be easy for many Germans, especially for those who were affected by the population transfer, just as it is not easy for many Czechs, handicapped by the decades without freedom when this subject was taboo, to admit the damage they did to democracy and thus to themselves by adopting after the war the idea of expelling the Germans from their home....

The History of German Settlements in Czechoslovakia

According to the 1910 Austrian census, the number of German-speaking inhabitants of the historic provinces of Bohemia, Moravia, and former Austrian Silesia was 3,747,000.[1] These provinces formed part of the Austro-Hungarian Empire (see map 3) and were under direct Austrian rule. They constituted principally solid language blocks close to the frontiers of Austria and Germany, among the majority Czechs. The German minority lived mostly in cities and towns while the Czech population in this region was predominantly rural. German Bohemia was characterized by light, export-oriented industry, whereas in the Czech lands heavy industry dominated. After the formation of Czechoslovakia, the 1930 census showed that the Germans were the largest minority group in the nation, totaling 3,150,000 or 23.6 percent of the total Czech population.[2]

The Germans began to settle in the Bohemian lands in the middle of the twelfth century, with the peak of the first wave of colonization in the thirteenth century. This movement eastward of peoples from central Europe had begun already in the Carolingian period when the area between the Elbe and the Oder rivers was settled. Not only peasants, merchants, and artisans came from Germany, but religious orders came to settle as well and colonize the area. These were mainly Cistercians, but also Benedictine and Premonstrant monks. Already in the year 1004 Bohemia became a vassal of the Holy Roman Empire but kept its right of self-government. In 1029, Moravia became a part of the Bohemian Duchy.[3]

The medieval ruling family in Bohemia, the Premyslids, encouraged this settlement in order to exploit new agricultural lands, open mines, and create new towns. From this there developed a mixture of German and Czech communities. The Slavic place names reflect this cultural and economic interaction between the two peoples. The peasants, both German and Slav, who settled on the manors of the lay and ecclesiastical lords in this area became a part of the reigning

95

feudal system. Most of the towns in Bohemia and Moravia established in the early middle ages owe their origin to this colonization. The exception was the Hussite city of Tabor. German law from the cities of Nuremberg and Magdeburg was introduced for the towns.[4] (See map 16 of German settlements in Bohemia and Moravia)

In 1198, the Holy Roman Emperor raised the Premyslid Duke, Ottokar I, to king of Bohemia, and shortly thereafter, the king of Bohemia became an elector of the Holy Roman Empire. In the early fourteenth century, Charles I of the house of Luxemburg became German king, and in 1355, as Charles IV, became Holy Roman Emperor. He came to the Bohemian throne through his grandmother, who was a princess of the Premyslid house, and established his capital in Prague. German became a court language, in addition to Czech. The first German university was established in 1348 in Prague. At that time Prague was considered the heart of the Holy Roman Empire of the German Nation. The close political union with their German neighbors brought the Czechs into cultural, economic, and ecclesiastical association with contemporary Western Europe.

Please refer to: http://www.forgottenvoices.net, for a photograph (#10) of Prague Cathedral, constructed by Peter Parler and his workshop in the fourteenth century. The Parlers were a renowned family of architects from the Rhineland responsible for many churches and cathedrals in Southern Germany and Austria. It was built mostly in the German late gothic style.

In the early fifteenth century, Jan Hus, professor and founder of the Czech faculty at Prague University—of which he later became rector—preached the reformation of the Catholic Church. Aside from its theological aspects, his purpose was also to create an ethnic-based Czech nationalism founded on the beauty and dignity of the Czech language and its people. After the execution of Jan Hus as a heretic at the Church council of Konstanz in 1415, a populist-nationalist war broke out, lasting from 1419 to 1438, with devastating results. In 1526 the lands of the Bohemian crown fell to the Habsburgs, who were both kings of Germany and emperors of the Holy Roman Empire. Prague and Bohemia had a leading role in the outbreak of the Thirty Years' War, when in 1618 the Protestant Estates of Bohemia, both German and Czech, came into conflict with the Catholic Habsburgs by supporting a Protestant German elector as King of Bohemia.[5] Bohemia and Moravia remained a part of the Austro-Hungarian Empire until the end of World War I.

The ethnic German settlements in the Carpathian Mountains, in today's Slovakia, had their origin in the thirteenth century, when King Bela IV of Hungary (Slovakia formed part of the Hungarian kingdom) invited Germans to colonize the land. Their settlements were concentrated around Pressburg (Bratislava—the capital today of Slovakia), in Central Slovakia, and the Zipser region near the city of Kaschau (Kosice in Eastern Slovakia).[6] (See map 17 of German settlements in Slovakia) Aside from settling peasants on their lands, the Hungarian kings invited many experienced German miners to develop the mining resources of the Carpathian Mountains. As was the case in the other German Eastern settlements, the colonizers received many privileges, including tax exemptions, for a number of years. Apparently, these privileges did not cause conflicts with the local population because some of them, such as the election of their own local officers and councils, were also extended to the indigenous people.[7] As a result of increasing Hungarian nationalism in subsequent centuries, particularly the nineteenth century, the Magyarization of the German population caused an emigration, including many who went to the United States.[8] By 1938, the ethnic German population of Slovakia was between 150,000 and 200,000, making up about 4.7 percent of the total Slovakian population.[9]

The nineteenth century also saw an increase in German–Czech tensions. On the one hand, the growth of capitalism had increased German dominance in the Habsburg Empire, as German capital was the main source of industrial growth. This had the effect of fostering immigration of Czech workers from the countryside to the cities. In 1880, the Czech population in the Sudetenland was 8 percent; by 1930, it had grown to 35 percent.[10] They were subject to German assimilation pressures, which led to a great deal of friction. On the other hand, the Czech middle class, as a result of the industrial development in Bohemia and Moravia, became quite prosperous. They began to push back against this forced assimilation, and their elites established close relations with their Western European liberal and democratic counterparts. Czech political leaders became spokesmen for the democratization of the Austro-Hungarian Empire—in conflict with the militarist and authoritarian views of the German and Hungarian power structure. Their efforts were concentrated on the defense of the Czech language to avoid being submerged by the dominant German culture.

One of the consequences of the Austrian defeat by Prussia in 1866 was the Compromise with Hungary made the following year, in effect giving the Hungarian government full national autonomy and equal rule with the Austrian Germans in the Empire. In 1897, however, when the Austrian Prime Minister, Count Kasimir Felix Badeni, attempted to secure equality for the Czech language with German and to introduce a bilingual administration in Bohemia, he met with violent resistance from the German community. Subsequently, he had to rescind his decrees. The one bright spot in German–Czech relations was the Moravian Compromise of 1906. This was an agreement for equal Czech and German representation in the Moravian Diet, to which the Czechs agreed even though they formed 70 percent of the population. Also, each national group was to have its own schools in districts where it formed at least 20 percent of the population. In Bohemia, however, the ethnic conflict remained unresolved.[11]

Please refer to: http://www.forgottenvoices.net, for a photograph (#11) of a view of the town of Böhmisch Krummau (today Cesky Krumlov) showing the palace of the princely House of Schwarzenberg. It is the second largest palace in the Czech Republic constructed from the fourteenth to the eighteenth century.

The peace treaty of St. Germaine in 1919, between the Allies and the Austro-Hungarian Empire, created the Czechoslovak Republic, based on President Wilson's right of self-determination for Eastern Europe's major ethnic groups. The German population in Bohemia and Moravia voted overwhelmingly to be incorporated into the new Austrian Republic, but the Allies rejected this proposal. What was previously a Czech problem in the Bohemian and Moravian lands now became a German problem, that of an ethnic group that refused to assimilate. Their over-riding goal was to maintain their German identity and nationality. The leaders of the new Czechoslovakia, confirmed democrats and liberals, Tomas Masaryk and Edvard Benes, proposed that the new Czechoslovakia solve the minority problems by creating a new Switzerland of federal regions. Despite being accorded benefits such as local self-government, and authority over their German language schools, what the Germans really wanted was full self-government within Czechoslovakia. Tensions were exacerbated by the world depression of 1930, which hit the German areas of Bohemia hardest due to the export orientation of their light industry. Unemployment there was three times higher than in the Czech areas.[12]

Memorandum No. 3, Chapter VI, Submitted to the Paris Peace Conference by the Czechoslovak Delegation in 1919

Memorandum No. 3.

The Problem of the Germans in Bohemia

VI. The Position of the Germans in the Czechoslovak Republic

It is absolutely necessary to know how the German population will be dealt (with) within the Czechoslovak State. The Czechoslovak Republic is not only willing to accept—if occasion arises—any international legal regulation laid down by the Peace Conference in favor of the minorities, but is moreover willing to go beyond such regulation and to grant the Germans all the rights due to them.

The Czechoslovak Republic will be an absolutely democratic State; all elections will be by universal and direct suffrage; all offices will be open to all citizens; the right to their own schools, judges and courts will never be denied to any minority. It must be added here that the Czechs, although conscious of the fact that the Germans were specially favored by the previous regime, have no intentions of suppressing, for example, the German schools, universities, schools of technology, notwithstanding the fact that these have not recently been well attended.

To sum up: the Germans in Bohemia would possess the same rights as the Czechoslovaks. The German language would be the second language of the country and measures of oppression would under no circumstances be used against the German part of the population. The constitution would be similar to the constitution of Switzerland.

This constitution will be established not only because the Czechs have always had a profound feeling for democracy, right and justice and would justly admit those rights even to their enemies, but also because the Czechs are of the opinion that the aforesaid arrangement, favorable to the Germans, would also be advantageous to the political interests of their own country.

They (the Czechs) proved during the 19th century that they had a practical, but above all a political sense. They are much too "realistic" and have too much commonsense not to see that violence and injustice were the causes of the decline of Austro-Hungary and that any similar policy would harm their own country. These historical facts are admitted by the Germans themselves. The German press was filled with descriptions of the revolution, which took place in Prague in November 1918. The reports state unanimously that the Czechs guaranteed freedom to all Germans and respected their personal security and property as well as their rights as free citizens.

Resume:

1. The traditions of Czechoslovakia guarantee that the new Republic will in no way oppress the Germans; on the contrary, they will have the benefit of a regime of freedom and justice.
2. In the course of the recent revolution in Bohemia the Czechs demonstrated this by guaranteeing to the Germans complete security.

Quoted from: *Documents on the Expulsion of the Sudeten Germans*, Wilhelm K. Turnward, editor.

Despite the rise in tensions, much of the German population, particularly the older people, came to terms with being a minority in the Czechoslovak Republic. They were represented in the Czech parliament. The Sudetendeutsche Social Democratic Party was the strongest German party until the 1935 elections.[13] With the rise of the Nazi party in Germany, however, these conditions changed radically and a new far-right nationalist party, the Sudeten German Party, led by Konrad Henlein, demanded complete autonomy. The Nazi German government fully supported and used this movement to achieve its own ultimate objective, the destruction of Czechoslovakia. The Czech government obviously rejected these demands and the French and British governments attempted to mediate the conflict. When—under international pressure—the Czechoslovak President, Edvard Benes, finally conceded autonomy to the Sudeten Germans, the Nazi government demanded the complete transfer of the Sudetenland to Germany. This led to the infamous Munich Agreements of September 1938. Czechoslovakia's final destruction occurred with the German army's occupation the following spring. Bohemia and Moravia became protectorates of the Third Reich, while Slovakia became an independent Republic and ally of Nazi Germany after having its southern regions ceded to Hungary.

One of the leading British mediators was Lord Runciman, who made a report on this conflict to the British Prime Minister, prior to the Munich Agreements. While mostly sympathetic to the views of Henlein's German nationalists in Czechoslovakia, it also reflected some of the basic concerns of the entire German community.[14]

> It is a hard thing to be ruled by an alien race; and I have been left with the impression that Czechoslovak rule in the Sudeten areas for the last 'twenty years, though not actually oppressive and certainly not

"terroristic" has been marked by tactlessness, lack of understanding, petty intolerance and discrimination, to a point where the resentment of the German population was inevitably moving in the direction of revolt. The Sudeten Germans felt, too, that in the past they had been given many promises by the Czechoslovak Government, but that little or no action had followed these promises. This experience had induced an attitude of unveiled mistrust of the leading Czech statesmen. I cannot say how far this mistrust is merited or unmerited; but it certainly exists, with the result that, however conciliatory their statements, they inspire no confidence in the minds of the Sudeten population. Moreover, in the last elections of 1935 the Sudeten German party polled more votes than any other single party; and they actually formed the second largest party in the State Parliament. They then commanded some 44 votes in a total Parliament of 300. With subsequent accessions, they are now the largest party, but they can always be outvoted; and consequently some of them, feel that constitutional action is useless for them.

Quoted from: *Documents on the Expulsion of the Sudeten Germans*: Dr. Wilhelm K. Turnwald.

Evacuation and Flight of the Sudeten Germans from the War

Slovakia

The end of the Nazi regime in Czechoslovakia began with the Slovak uprising in August of 1944 aimed at over-throwing the pro-Nazi Slovak government led by Dr. Jozef Tiso. Prior to that development, this area was considered sheltered from the worst impacts of the war. In general, the male German population was not drafted into the Slovak Army. The militarized SS, the Waffen-SS, however, was actively recruiting among younger, ethnic Germans. They were assisted in this by the Volksdeutsche Mittelstelle in Berlin, the Nazi Party's organization, under the supervision of the SS, for political coordination and control of the German ethnic communities in East Europe. Initially, this was a volunteer effort, but by June of 1944, military service became compulsory. The German community in Slovakia greatly resisted this conscription and many men did not show up for induction. They were then hunted down by the SS for desertion. Those ethnic Germans serving in the Slovak army were transferred automatically to the Waffen-SS.[15]

In late August 1944, with the Red Army approaching, elements of the Slovak Army and guerillas trained by the Soviets were able to occupy most of the territory of Eastern and Central Slovakia. The uprising was under the overall command of the Slovak National Council, which comprised both communist and noncommunist parties. The uprising counted on support from the Soviet Armies, which, however, was not forthcoming. In fact, many of the arms sent by the Allies ended up in the hands of the communist units, who did not share them with the noncommunist combatants. The battles lasted about two months before German SS and police units suppressed the main uprising with a great deal of brutality. They were never able, however, to fully overcome the guerrilla movements, which continued their war in the Carpathian Mountains until the arrival of the Soviet Army the following January.

When the uprising began, the German communities in Central Slovakia were partially evacuated to the General Government in Poland and to Hungary. Most returned to their homes, however, after the fighting ceased. But because of the continuing guerrilla war, and as the Russian Armies approached Eastern Slovakia, the German communities there were evacuated to Western Slovakia. Subsequently, Berlin ordered the general evacuation of Eastern and Central Slovakia, the destination being Bohemia or Austria.

In general, the evacuations were orderly and well planned. Many inhabitants could take personal possessions with them and were brought out by trains. All in all, the evacuation of Germans from Slovakia went more smoothly than from other Eastern European regions. This was ascribed to the actions of organizations of the German ethnic groups, such as the German Protestant Church in Slovakia, independent from the Nazi Party. In the winter of 1944/1945, about 120,000 of the estimated population of 140,000 were able to be taken out of Slovakia ahead of the Soviet Armies.[16] Many of the refugees, however, found themselves in Bohemia and Moravia at the end of the war.

Bohemia and Moravia

During the war, the Protectorate of Bohemia and Moravia was known as the "air raid shelter" and "arsenal" of the Third Reich due to its distance from the fighting fronts, both East and West.[17] It effectively remained under German domination until the end of the war. Because of its sheltered location, it became a refuge for Germans fleeing from the Russian Army. About 1.6 million fled there from Silesia and another 100,000, approximately, from Slovakia. With the Soviet advance into Moravia, Bohemia became one huge refugee camp at the time of the armistice. It is estimated that the German population there at that time grew to 4.5 million.[18]

No. 1

Report of the experiences (letter) of Franz Kuhn, farmer and civil engineer, of Jägerndorf. Original, dated 11 January 1956, handwritten, 5 pages.

The passing of refugee treks from Poland and Upper Silesia; the evacuation of the town of Jägerndorf in March 1945; the flight of a family to the district Mährisch Schönberg and their return after the armistice had been concluded.

The first part of the report contains personal matters.

After the continuous withdrawal of the front from Russia, my home town came into direct proximity to the front during the last months of the war. The dissolution of the defense forces on the eastern front was heralded by endless treks of refugees from Poland and Galicia. It was a terrible sight to us, who had all our lives been settled and had never thought of leaving our homes. These German evacuees were billeted in our farms for a few hours only, mostly just for the night. Depression and bitterness was prevalent everywhere. Some of their carts, being overloaded, had to be abandoned when snow started to fall during this winter of 1944/45. The withdrawal of the police troops from Polish territory presented a specially disconsolate sight. Endless columns of the familiar "panje" carts came along the main road from Troppau towards the west, which is the direct connection to Galicia via Oderberg-Tetschen-Krakau. This prelude made it clear to all of us that our own district would soon be involved in front events. After the turn of the year, the evacuation of Upper Silesia started. We in Jägerndorf, whilst seeing little of the fleeing population, watched the transports of herds of cattle from the rich provinces of Upper and Lower Silesia passing our homes. The animals, being used more or less exclusively to being kept in stables, died in great numbers during this march over a distance of more than 100 kilometers, where feeding was sporadic and water often missing. The trail of their march and the adjoining fields were full of carcasses. Whether these transports had any aim at all, and whether they ever reached it, one never got to know. One can only guess at the wealth which was being destroyed in this way.

From the beginning of March onwards, the front had come so near that the thunder of guns could be heard continuously. The leadership of the Party was preparing for evacuation. Women and children made the start, and a special plan was worked out for the evacuation of the rural population of Jägerndorf and the neighboring villages... I had been called up to the Volkssturm (People's defense) since the autumn of 1944. The unit I had been attached to remained in Jägerndorf to guard factories important for the war effort. This unit got directly involved in the fighting during the last stages, when the town had become part of the front for the last eight weeks of the war. At the beginning, I still had the opportunity to go and see that everything was in order at the farm, and I prepared three carts for two pairs of horses, and a tractor which had been left to me, for the inevitable evacuation. The tractor and its trailer mainly accommodated my family, whilst the rest of the vehicles were to be used for the Ukrainian laborers who still worked for me. We had selected the loads with great care and left everything behind which was not absolutely essential. As much as possible we took clothing, food, feeding stuff for the horses, and petrol. Several things we tried to conceal in safe hideouts, or we buried them in the hope of making them thereby secure for the time of our return. We did find hardly anything again, it was mainly stolen by Germans who managed to avoid the evacuation.

On 23 March 1945, the order came for the evacuation of the farms. Around midnight, the trek assembled in Krotendorf, a part of Jägerndorf. The general direction to be taken was via Benisch, on the other side of the Gesenke, towards Moravia.

On the day following the evacuation of the farms, a clearance unit of the army appeared, drove all the animals away and collected the grain and other things. I myself remained to the end of the war with the Volkssturm and was sent with my unit to guard a factory some 2 kilometers outside Jägerndorf. We were engaged there in the usual routine jobs – digging trenches, erecting road blocks, etc. During patrol duties, from the hills surrounding Jägernorf, we saw the burning villages on the plains of the Oder valley. Our town was repeatedly under fire and ruins could soon be seen in nearly every street. On Good Friday, in the second half of April, a heavy bombardment by Russian airplanes took place. Troppau was almost wholly destroyed by incendiary bombs, and the Russians succeeded to the west of Ostrau in breaking through to Moravia. Jägerndorf could no longer be defended. During the night from 7 to 8 May, our Volkssturm detachment left the town which soon afterwards was occupied by the Russians. We arrived in Freudenthal, where all the units dispersed in spite of orders to the contrary. As I knew the whereabouts of my family, it was not difficult to reach Ullersdorf from Freudenthal via Römerstadt and the Berggeist. Two days later, the Russian advance caught up with us there.

My family's journey to this district had met with many difficulties. My wife had had all the worries about the children (still very young at this time, i.e. 7 and 10); about the horses, whose stabling and feeding was not easy, but who were extremely important for the continuation of the journey; and about the Ukrainians, whose attitude under the prevailing circumstances was always uncertain and unpredictable. But she had found understanding and helpfulness everywhere, so that she arrived in Mährisch Schönberg without having lost anything...

The subsequent move to Ullersdorf was made mainly because of the animals that could be better accommodated there.

When the advance guard of the Russians reached Ullersdorf, they distributed amongst the population all the discovered stores of food and spinning materials. This blessing did not last long, however, because the following detachments took it all back and everything in addition which they found desirable. The treatment of women by the Russians has been the same everywhere. To escape the worst, we ourselves spent several days hidden in the woods around Ullersdorf. My parents-in-law, who had come with the same trek, suggested that we should leave Ullersdorf again, because here, directly on the main road, we were bound to lose all our possessions to the looting Russians... If our tractor and our last pair of horses were not to be lost as well, we would have to go back and try to find shelter in some isolated village. And this is how we came to Marschendorf, where we stayed for about three weeks. All sorts of rumors circulated at that time, one to the effect that everyone would lose all his possessions who did not return to his parish at a given date. The trek therefore assembled again. We started our return journey on little-used side roads, and we chose a route via Rotherberg, Gabel, Würbental and Kronsdorf. Here we stopped again and rested for a few days, trying to get into contact with Jägerndorf, which is not far away. There, a German Communist administration had been set up in the meantime. A former coachman of my mother's had become mayor and I found it therefore relatively easy to return to the town. It was dangerous, at that time, to have any hostile relationships, especially to foreign workers. They often led to revengeful acts and ended many times with deportation to Russia. In Jägerndorf, a thin soup was handed out to the population, at several places, by the Communist town administration, together with a meager bread ration provided by a few bakers' shops. We found our farm completely empty and looted. Of all the stores, only some half-empty potato pits were left, and the rest of those provisions, which we had taken on the trek. We tried to get the farm going again.

Here follows a short description of the experiences up to the expulsion in April 1946.

Most of the Sudetenland was occupied by the Soviet Armies without combat. Only in the eastern districts of Moravia, the Soviet Fourth Ukranian Army Group succeeded in capturing several industrial towns in April 1945. The capital of Moravia, Brünn (Brno), was only lost to the Red Army late in April against fierce German resistance. The intent of the German armies was a slow, controlled retreat to the American lines, in order to avoid captivity in Russia. At the time of the

German collapse, there were still about one million German troops in Czechoslovakia. They were ultimately not successful, however, in avoiding the Soviets, as the U.S. Army generally refused to take them prisoner.[19]

Meanwhile, the U.S. Third Army under General Patton penetrated the Bohemian Forest and began to occupy Western Bohemia. It met with no serious resistance. The Soviets, however, saw this advance as a threat to their zone of influence, and negotiated with the Allied High Command for the U.S. Army to only advance to the line of Karlsbad (Karlovy Vary), Pilsen (Plzen), and Budweis (Ceske Budejovice). Actually Patton wanted to liberate all of Bohemia but was prohibited from doing so. The last American troops were withdrawn from Czechoslovakia in December 1945.

The evacuation of Eastern Sudetenland was initially more orderly than that from Eastern Germany. Nevertheless, the population was seized with panic with the Soviet offensive in Upper Silesia and with advance Russian units penetrating Northern Moravia in January 1945. This caused much of the population of Upper Silesia to flee into Eastern Moravia. Many of the refugees were transported to emergency shelters in inner Bohemia. When the front temporarily stabilized in February 1945, these transports ceased. Once the Soviet offensive resumed in March and April 1945, penetrating deeply into Northern Moravia, streams of refugees, mainly Silesians but Sudetendeutsche as well, headed for Bohemia. But at this point in the war, the local peasant population saw further evacuation as pointless and preferred to await the Russian occupation in their homes. Local officers of the Nazi Party and civil administration had to use threats to force people to leave. By this time, however, all roads were so jammed with refugees and retreating German soldiers that a planned evacuation was no longer possible. High Nazi Party officials and bureaucrats made arrangements to flee to the West in private transport.[20]

After the armistice was declared, much of the population of Moravia, especially the peasants, returned to their homes. In fact, in some cases they were ordered to return under threat of property confiscation by the newly formed Czech administration. Those who returned home often found their farms, as far as they had not been destroyed in the fighting, either looted or confiscated by Czechs. On the way home, some were interned, already at this point in time, in Czech labor camps.[21]

No. 18

Report of the experiences of Rudolf Grisnig, Swiss citizen. Original, dated 10 September 1955, typewritten, 8 pages. This report is based on notes from a diary.

Experiences of the author in northern Sudetenland during the German capitulation and after the entry of the Red Army; his flight to Saxony and his return to the Sudetenland.

I left Reichenau in German Silesia amidst the approaching rumbling of battles. Here had been my sphere of activities for many long years. In one of the very last trains going westwards, I reached the nearest district capital, Zittau, in the evening. All I had been able to take with me, I sent from Zittau as registered luggage to Komotau, to Klein Priesen. With a feeling of anxiety I crossed the frontier between Saxony and the Sudetenland at Grottau, traveling in the direction of Reichenberg. The same night, I went on from Reichenberg to Teplitz... The train had to proceed very slowly, on account of air activity; nevertheless, we passed through Aussig and Teplitz without any trouble... At about 6 o'clock in the morning, a few kilometers from Komotau, the journey came to an end as a result of a low-level bombing attack. Fortunately, there was no loss of life, but the engine and the tracks were badly hit. Like many others, I landed on my stomach in some nearby bushes.

All my thoughts were concentrated on the village of Zuscha and on my fiancée there. I had had no news from her for many weeks. Walking for two hours, I reached this purely German village, which lies a good 12 kilometers east of Komotau in the triangle Komotau-Potscherad-Saaz. To my great relief, I found my fiancée and all her relatives in good health. We are now in the middle of April 1945; everybody knows that the war is lost for Germany, and only the hopeless optimists still believe in a miracle...

At the end of April, I suggested that we should load two carts with all our moveable possessions and head westwards, i.e. homewards to Switzerland. There were still four horses in the stable—but father Linhart does not want to hear of the idea and other farmers laugh at me. They felt that it would only be possible to allocate one commissar to each village, and in any case, it would always be easy to get round the Czechs. Well, I had to give in...

On the day of the unconditional surrender of Germany, a motorized supply detachment arrived in our village. These were the last German soldiers I saw in an organized unit. In our courtyard, they burned a heap of military documents, and they distributed various machines and implements of bakery and butchery installations amongst the population. They also left standing in our courtyard the complete equipment for generating electric power. And then they left, saying that they were going to surrender to the approaching Americans, who at that time were in the neighborhood of Saaz. But towards evening, they returned in a great hurry and confusion. They had just managed to escape from the Russians. The Russians in Saaz! This was the first frightening news of their impending arrival. The German soldiers left again at once in the direction of Komotau...

The son of our farm laborer spent the afternoon in Komotau. He returned greatly excited with the news that the Americans had been seen 10 kilometers to the west of Komotau, coming from the direction of Karlsbad. But the columns of refugees had brought all movement to a standstill. The Sudetenland, after all, was the great reception area for the millions of refugees from Silesia. Even East Prussians had been billeted with us for a time. Our hopes were nevertheless greatly increased, maybe the Americans would reach us yet...

Meanwhile, we heard the increasing roar of the battle, the rumbling of guns and the unmistakable bark of Russian machine-guns coming from the area of Brüx. If the rumors about the Americans were true, it seemed beyond doubt that the two fighting powers would meet here in our region.

Although the war was officially over, guns could be heard all the time and the machine-guns had not been silenced, it seemed that at this last hour people were still dying on both sides. At 9 o'clock that night, we suddenly heard the roar of heavy engines and the grinding of steel chains on a hard road. Relatives of my fiancée's turned up unexpectedly from Holtschitz. They thought that they would find better protection with us through my presence as a Swiss citizen. Furthermore, in their village a large number of Czechs were present, some of them belonging there, and others who had arrived as laborers, either voluntarily or having been conscripted. On the previous day, they had already staged riots against the German population. They also brought the news of the approach of the Russians.

All of a sudden, people started running about the village in all directions... "The Russians are coming! The Russians are coming!" Everything stopped dead then—the Russians had actually arrived.

Heavily armored cars of the "Stalin" type were carrying 20 to 30 soldiers each, uniformed in the color of the earth. The armored vehicles form a square and the infantry which they carried swarm at once in all directions...

The tanks with their loads of infantry drive on without stopping, as they need not fear any resistance. They appear harmless and disappear as quickly as they came. My watch shows 10 p.m. An hour later, another unit arrives. They start at once to search all houses for watches, clocks, rings and other easily removable valuable objects. Within five minutes, in all haste, they take whatever they find and threaten to shoot in case that not all watches are handed over... Our

Polish farm laborer turns up with two workers from the east, who are strangers to us and look extremely dangerous. Without the slightest restraint he goes about the house with them—looting... After this looting, we venture into the cellar (used for storing potatoes), but we do not stay long, this place of refuge seems too eerie. So we creep from there (my fiancée and three of the people from Holtschitz) into the garden and hide amongst the shrubs...

At daybreak, we return home, where the Russians meanwhile had left their visiting card. The place looks like a pigsty. Our aged father, who had gone to bed as usual, had been thrown out of it by force, and two Russians—in full uniform and with their boots on—had slept in it. Under the bed, big heaps of bread were lying; whilst the oven, in which just this morning bread had been baked for the next fortnight, had obviously been mistaken by the Russians for the lavatory...

The village becomes a temporary resting place for troops of the Red Army, which enter from three different sides. Some come from Komotau, others from Dresden via Brüx, and a third lot from the direction of Kaaden-Postelberg. In general, their destination is Prague, where a certain Schörner does not seem to have surrendered 1). Peace and quietness have gone from the village of Zuscha. The workers from the east, who had been "settled" in he village for some time, particularly the Poles, have organized unrestrained looting and have incited the otherwise mostly quite peaceful Russians against the German population. In time, everything the "looting commandos" could lay their hands on was being tossed about, carried away or wantonly destroyed.

Whilst my fiancée with the other girls of our village is in hiding on one of the neighboring farms, we in the house have not a peaceful moment. The house of our neighbor, the public house and grocery store of the village is being looted systematically since early morning. The owners, a couple named Karras, who were quite well-to-do, have been reduced to beggars. People are running up and down the stairs in their house. Soldiers of the Red Army and workers from the east are carrying armfuls of linen, clothing, even furniture and sacks of food away...

In the afternoon (9 May), I call for my fiancée in her rather insecure hidingplace. We take a walk in the open field, some 2 kilometers from the farm. The Russians have received their ration of vodka and they intend to celebrate their victory at 4 P.M. We want to be on our guard and are hiding far away in the high clover.

We fear the worst. Since the previous night, troops have passed almost uninterruptedly along the road, traveling at high speed. Whilst we hide in great anxiety about our fate, looting goes on all afternoon in our house under the leadership of the Poles. I wonder whether our expensive trousseau has gone too? During the day, the horses had been taken away—the farmer has been robbed of his best helpers. All the newly baked loaves of bread have disappeared, and so have most of the stores of meat and flour. We are all terribly depressed and filled with anxiety. On top of everything, there is the continuous worry about my fiancée and the womenfolk in general. At dusk, I return with my fiancée to the farm, firmly determined to make a get-away. In my home country, we can start a new life in peace and freedom.

Father not only shares our views now, he urges us on to disappear as quickly as possible. He is old and not much would happen to him, and the same applies to the aunt: he hopes, on account of her age, that she will not be bothered. We want to depart dressed as we are, and to take only very few belongings…It is now 10 P.M. Some 200 meters from our house we spend the night behind a heap of straw… Suddenly we get a fright. In the distance we can hear the anxious screams of two or even more women. We feel no longer safe where we are and creep further into a field of high clover.

It is 3 a.m. on 10 May 1945. We continue our flight. At first we follow a ditch leading us between the villages of Klein Priesen and Trupschitz, and along the eastern outskirts of Wurzmes in the direction of Görkau. On the crest of a hill, Russian or Czech guards can be seen lying in wait. We pass them by making a detour and reach undetected a little rivulet. There, in the shelter of a wood, we meet a family of refugees from Kaitz. They tell us frightful stories. The hour of the Czech mob has come. From the nearby village we hear continuous shooting and wild screams. We withdraw through wet clover and fields in the direction of Wurzmes; we meet fellow sufferers and turn to the right towards Görkau accompanied by those three men. One of our companions turns out to be a former concentration camp prisoner. He tells us later of frightful details, but he maintains that by far the majority of his former fellow sufferers had not been persecuted for their political convictions, but had been criminals. At that time, we did not know much about these atrocities in concentration camps and we could hardly believe what he was telling us. But soon our other companion taught us otherwise. He turned out to be a former Baltic diplomat and his passport was made out in the name of Baron von Sass. He had had to flee from Dresden, had then arrived in Brüx in the middle of a skirmish (which we had heard on 8 May), had lost his wife and son, and was now continuing the flight on his own…

During the ascent of the mountains, we take a rest. Our three companions, just like the two of us, are very hungry. But they have nothing left to eat. So we divide our bread with them and open our only tin of meat for everybody's benefit. At about 10 A.M., we arrive via Hannersdorf at a point to the west of Göttersdorf where we quench our thirst at a little brook on the wayside and bathe our hot and tired feet…We move on and pass a lonely house. Suddenly the door is being thrown open, a young woman steps out. She has a wild look in her eyes and her hair is disheveled, and she leads a girl of about ten years of age, who looks absolutely bewildered. The young woman screams without stopping: "They have raped my child! They have raped my child!" Soon afterwards, a Red Army soldier leaves, a sub-machine-gun under his arm and grinning devilishly at the tormented woman… The woman with her violated child disappears into the adjoining forest from where her plaintive cries can still be heard. We force ourselves to walk slowly, but we go faster and faster, until we reach the edge of the forest, when we start to run as fast as we can…

We are avoiding the road, which leads from Saxony across the Erzgebirge into the plains of Northern Bohemia. We can hear the noise of armored cars racing along this road. Whenever we get near enough, we see sights in the open camions, which I would prefer not to describe. Agonizing screams indicate that German women are being dragged along. We move deeper into the forest, always anxious to proceed in the direction of Germany. In the evening, we pass a lonely sawmill. It seems that the Russians are there, enjoying themselves by tormenting the women in their usual manner…So we make a wide circle around this place of terror, and at dusk we reach a dense part of the forest. There we lie down, close together, wrap ourselves into a blanket and try to sleep. Searchlights and voices shouting in a foreign language soon convince us that some Czechs with their Russian "liberators" are at work, combing the forests for women who may be hiding in order to escape them. We seem to be near a village, and we are keeping as quiet as mice. The night seems endless and at crack of dawn we move on, hungry and tired. We eat our last piece of bread. Unexpectedly, we reach a bend in the road—it is too late to avoid a Russian standing there guarding a vehicle which is lying on its side. He calls sharply to us and we approach him with our hands up. There is one officer, one non-commissioned officer and a private. They search us immediately and find a fairly new Swiss watch on me. They allege that my fiancée had been a member of the armed forces of Germany and want to arrest her for it. I present my Swiss passport and they look at it—upside down. Baron von Sass explains to them that I am a Swiss citizen, that my fiancée is my wife, and that we are on our way home. After some negotiations, we are allowed to proceed. We have been relieved of watches, some jewelry—but also of the great threat of being separated. Once more, we spend a night in the safe shelter of the Sudeten German forests of the Erzgebirge. Next day, we cross the frontier into Saxony at a small hamlet called Rübenau. The nightmare is disappearing, we know we have escaped from the clutches of the Czech mob and its devilish hatred.

Some hours later, we reach Thalheim in the Saxonian part of the Erzgebirge. I have friends here, a Swiss family owning a textile mill and considerable landed property. Our little group separates here, the former concentration camp prisoner, having proved an excellent fellow, and the highly educated Baron continue the journey by themselves...

Three weeks later, the two of us went on to Chemnitz where I had been as a student at the State school for dyers. I hardly recognized the ravaged town. At nightfall, just as we were passing, the Schillerpost was being looted. With great difficulty, picking our way over the huge heaps of debris, we find the house of my former landlady. She has left, but her neighbor receives us with great kindness. Next day, we creep along hidden paths away from the chain of Russian guards and manage to reach towards the evening an American reception camp some 15 kilometers to the west of Chemnitz, in Burgstädt. Together with citizens of many other nations, who are on their way home, we are crowded into a roofless building. Two weeks we waited in vain to be moved, then we escaped and managed to reach a friend's family somewhat closer to Chemnitz...

Day by day, strange figures passed by. Old men accompanied by young girls, old women, children big and small. They carried an assortment of household stuff in their rucksacks, or had filled them with all sorts of things which were dear to them. Sometimes they pushed barrows or the strangest contraptions loaded to the brim with possessions of all kinds. They always replied, when being asked, that they were Sudeten Germans and that they had been forced to leave the country of their fathers, their beloved homeland. So it was true after all what we had been told some days ago—that the Allies had agreed to "purge" the Sudetenland of its original inhabitants...

The sight of these robbed and broken down refugees, and the terrible stories they related to us, combined to make it quite impossible for me to continue waiting any longer. I left my fiancée in the charge of my friends in Limbach and went back on my own, re-crossing the frontier near Weipert. Already my first impression in a once purely German village in the Erzgebirge, brought home to me the fundamental changes which had taken place during the short time since our departure. Not a single German sign-post could be found in the village and not a single German street name was to be seen. Even all shop signs in German had been removed and replaced by Czech inscriptions... In Komotau, where I had known my way about fairly well as long as I had been able to rely on the German street signs, I felt so lost that I first had to sit down on a bench. Suddenly the town was called Chomutov. I could not see a single familiar face anywhere, and everybody spoke in a terribly alien-sounding language. Russians paraded the streets, proud as peacocks...

On my way, I met an old acquaintance. He was furtively leaving another village and was wearing, on his right arm, a white armlet with the letter "N" inscribed. in big black letters. In answer to my question what this strange "uniform" meant, he told me that all Germans had now to wear it... This man, more than 70 years old, had once been the wealthiest farmer in the German village Zuschau. He had been expelled from his property and had found refuge with friends in a distant village. He was uncertain as to how long he would be able to stay there. (He was afterwards allowed to return home and await there the time of his expulsion.)...

Eventually we reached Zuschau. On the parental farm I found father and aunt as well as the farm laborer's family. A lad, some twenty years of age, asked me brusquely in Czech about my business. He turned out to be the "new and lawful owner of this Czech farm" ... A former circus rider from Prague tried to act the part of a qualified "Czech administrator" of this German model farm. He made me understand, in broken German, that "all German farms, everything German" had been nationalized, and he urgently advised me to disappear as quickly as possible. I told him that I had no intention to do this that I would instead go to Prague in order to start proceedings for the return of all our property, and that I would then come back with my wife. This had the effect of a bombshell, and I was arrested within the next quarter of an hour. Six men, armed to the teeth, took me to the town hall. There, they tried to find out all about my intentions, who I was, where I had come from etc. etc. I made no bones about my firm intention to go to Prague in order to demand the return of our farm and of all the things which had been stolen or confiscated from us. They appeared puzzled and discussed amongst themselves in Czech, which naturally I could not understand. Then, a very crafty one demanded once more to see my passport and declared it to be false. So I was informed that I was under arrest and was made a prisoner...Suddenly, I had a good idea.

I knocked firmly on the door. They were gracious enough to open and to ask what I wanted. I made them understand that an immediate search would start for me in case I did not turn up on the following morning at the Swiss legation in Prague (at that time a Consulate general). The people from there would look first of all whether I was in Zuschau, because that had been my last address and because I had announced to them from Komotau that I was coming here. After some hurried negotiations, I was released, but given strict instructions to leave the village before the morning. I did this, but not in the direction I had led them to expect—instead, I went as fast as I could across the Erzgebirge to fetch my fiancée. A week later, we both were together in Zuschau.

In a further report, the author describes the events and experiences in Czechoslovakia up to the time of his departure for Switzerland in April 1946.

1.   Field Marshall Ferdinand Schörner, Commander of Army Group Center

The Prague Uprising

The Prague uprising came on May 5, 1945, with riots in the inner city, the elimination of all German street and shop signs and the display of Czech and Allied flags. German patrols and individual troops were killed by the Revolutionary Guards if they offered resistance. The radio stations were the first to be occupied by the insurgents who then broadcast proclamations to support the insurrection and exhortations to kill the German occupiers. In no time at all the greater part of Prague was in the hands of the insurgents except for the government quarters. The insurgents were under the command of General Kutlvasr of the Czech National Council, which was established by the provisional Kaschau (Kosice) Czech government. The Czech National Council was formed at the beginning of 1945 by the Council of the Three (the largest Czech underground organization at the last stage of the War, the illegal trade unions and the underground Communist Party).[22]

German troops were called in to suppress the uprising from the surrounding towns, including the Waffen-SS, but they made slow headway against the resistance, which in the meantime had erected barricades around their critical positions, particularly the radio stations. The SS attempted to crush this uprising with their characteristic brutality, driving people from their homes, setting the buildings on fire, and shooting Czech women and children. It was reported that almost 2,000 Czech civilians were killed in the Prague uprising.[23]

The following is an excerpt from a Czech police report on the Prague uprising:

> In Pankrac and Krc members of the S.S. began maltreating the Czech population as early as May 6th, when they succeeded in penetrating into this quarter of the city from the south, supported by armed German civilians. Their violence reached its height on May 8th at 6:30 P.M., when a mass advance was begun on Krc...The worst acts of violence were committed by young men between 17 and 20 years of age. The doors of houses and flats were burst in, houses and shops were plundered, dwellings were demolished, furniture shot to pieces and set fire to. The inhabitants were driven from their homes, forced

to form a living wall with their bodies to protect the German patrols, and constantly threatened with automatic pistols. Many Czechs lay dead in the streets...A great many dead bodies of Czech civilians were later found in a little church. They included men, women and even children from one to three years of age, all killed in a terrible way. Their heads and ears had been cut off, their eyes gouged out and their bodies run through and through with bayonets. There were some pregnant women among them whose bodies had been ripped open. Twenty-three men from an estate were shot in the courtyard after being tortured for a long time. The state of affairs in Krc is best shown by the fates of the inhabitants of two of the many houses broken into. In house No. 295 alone, 37 persons were murdered, ten of them being children between the ages of 6 and 15, 13 women, two of them pregnant, and 14 men.

Quoted from: *Hitler's Spearhead*, London, 1945, Vincent Urban.

But as matters became more difficult for the insurgents, they called on the U.S. Army in Western Bohemia for support. The Soviets objected, however, to their advance past Pilsen. At this point, relief for the insurgency came in the form of General Vlassov's "Russian Liberation Army" (This armed group was formed by the German Army from Russian prisoners of war, to combat the Soviets. General Vlassov was a Soviet war hero from the battle of Moscow who was captured by the Wehrmacht and formed an anti-Stalin resistance army. After the war, he was expelled by the Western Allies to the Soviet Union and executed.) On May 8, when there was no further point in resisting, the German commander, General Toussaint, surrendered to the Czech National Council. German troops were permitted free withdrawal and German women and children were placed under the protection of the International Red Cross (IRC). The withdrawing troops attempted to take as many civilians as possible with them, but their efforts were frustrated by the arrival of Soviet forces on May 9 who then occupied Prague.

Please refer to: http://www.forgottenvoices.net, for a photograph (#12) of German civilian residents of Prague being rounded up for forced labor, May 1945.

The uprising in Prague came as a complete surprise to the German inhabitants. Most were taken from their homes and interned in schools, prisons, barracks, and other public buildings. They had insufficient food and many were subject to harsh interrogation by the Revolutionary Guards, even though many had no political affiliation. Suffering was widespread, especially for the children. The IRC, which had assumed the protection of women and children, was helpless to prevent the worst abuses. The barricades, which had been erected during the insurrections, had to be removed, for which German prison labor was used. German civilian prisoners on the way to the clearing work were frequently assaulted by the mobs, mistreated, and many were killed. Subsequently, the temporary prisons were cleared, and the Germans were sent to internment camps where conditions did not improve. The concentration camp of Theresienstadt, used by the Nazi regime as a way station principally for Jews en route to the extermination camps, was one such facility. The "purge" of all Germans from Prague began at this time with the population either going to forced labor in agriculture or to the internment camps. They stayed in these camps or on the farms until they were expelled from Czechoslovakia.[24]

Please refer to: http://www.forgottenvoices.net, for a photograph (#13) of German civilian residents of Prague forced to remove barricades after the liberation of Prague. A number of the prisoners have a swastika painted on their backs. May 1945.

No. 27

Report of the experiences of Dr. Korkisch, university lecturer, of Prague. Original, dated 2 March 1947, handwritten, 8 pages.

Experiences of a German of Prague during the days of the Rising and his internment in the police prison; transport of the internees to Tynice near Böhmisch Brod; conditions and events in this camp.

The report starts with some personal remarks concerning the question of the expulsion of the Sudeten Germans, and continues as follows:

On 8 May 1945, my wife and I escaped death by a mere coincidence.

Together with the other German inhabitants of our house, we were staying in the air-raid shelter. We had often spent many hours there, and had always felt quite safe. On this particular day, for some inexplicable reason, I felt very restive and tried to persuade everyone present to return to their flats. I failed, and everyone seemed to have the impression that I had lost my nerves. In order to get rid of me and my troublesome attempts of persuasion, the others eventually helped at least us to return to our flat, together with our belongings which we used to bring with us during an air raid. A quarter of an hour later, guerillas penetrated from a neighboring cellar into our air-raid shelter and killed every German present—two men, four women and a child of 4. The only sense in it being that at that time Germans could be killed without fear of punishment.

On the following morning, two guerrillas fetched us from our flat. They were not rough with us, not even rude, apart from the fact that they continuously pointed their revolvers at us. They told us that lorries were waiting in the street, which were going to take us to Austria. I suppose, they just told us this in order to be spared our moans and groans and to make their unpleasant task somewhat easier. They said that we could take whatever money we possessed, and whatever we would be able to carry in the way of clothing and linen. As that did not amount to much—considering that I was 67 and my wife 60, they asked whether we knew anyone who would be willing to carry a larger suitcase for us. We answered that the son of our caretaker had often helped us on similar occasions. They fetched him, and he was quite willing to carry a large leather suitcase with some of our clothing, underwear and shoes outside to the lorries. In the street, an excited crowd was waiting for us. As soon as they spotted the man carrying our suitcase, the cry went up that Czechs should not be porters for Germans. My ears were boxed, the man with the suitcase returned quickly to the house. I have never again seen anything of this suitcase and its contents, nor of our flat of four large rooms. Its furniture had been comfortable; according to our circumstances we had put a great deal of our savings, accumulated in a long life of work and worries, into this flat. But we could take nothing with us, apart from two small bags with the utmost necessities and, fortunately, two blankets. The curses of the people, flanking both sides of the streets, accompanied us all the way to the police prison. And I had my ears boxed once more, this time really without any apparent reason.

Inside the prison, our hand luggage was searched. When my wallet was handed back to me, 10,000 of the 30,000 Czech crowns which it had contained, were missing. So was most of the jewelry which had been in our bags. Silver, however, was not being confiscated at that time. But everything vanished during later checks—they were becoming progressively stiffer the poorer our remaining belongings became. Then, even a second suit or a third shirt were considered forbidden luxuries, and they were confiscated at a time when we had nothing else left. There had been no German workers in Prague—but the German intelligentsia of Prague was to be turned into proletarians.

In the overcrowded prison we spent days and nights sitting on narrow benches. It was here, that we began for the first time to get an inkling of what was in store for us. It sank in only gradually and seemed incredible for a long time...

Desperation claimed its first victim. Soon after we had been brought here, a high-ranking Civil Servant (Oberregierungsrat) had been ordered to clean the house and been severely reprimanded. He jumped out of the window on the fourth floor. Just before he did it, he had helped us to compile a list of all the prisoners. Soon afterwards, a woman was found unconscious in the lavatory—she had cut her wrists. Her life was saved, just as that of all the attempted suicides during the following days and weeks. But the lavatory was closed as a result, and we had to use buckets in a room with glass doors, which was thereby under observation. These buckets had to be cleaned by us daily.

We were asked to volunteer for the job of clearing the streets, especially for the removal of barricades. Nobody under the age of 60 was allowed to stay behind. When these people returned from their work, they were always terribly excited and exhausted. Many had large swastikas painted on their backs, and the women's hair had been shorn off. The mob in the streets had been responsible for their sufferings. They related how they had been forced by onlookers to take off their shoes and to work bare-footed, that they had been cursed and beaten. In some cases, where the occasion had presented itself, they had been made to walk with bare feet over glass splinters. Even if the guards had wanted to prevent all this, they would have been unsuccessful. All this was told and confirmed by many of them, and their reports agreed with one another. We feared that at any moment the mob might break into our prison and cause a bloodbath amongst us. Several times a day we had to line up for a call of the rolls, the only reason we could find for this might have been to intimidate us by giving us threatening talks at every such occasion. And they succeeded. We were filled with such terror that we were no longer able to think clearly...

The food we received seemed to us neither good in quality, nor sufficient in quantity. But compared with what we received later, it seemed almost luxurious in our memories. This is probably also due to the fact that at that time many of us were still able to draw on the provisions, which we had brought with us.

After some days, the storm outside seemed to abate, and we also grew calmer. On the sixth day at noon, we had to line up with our luggage outside the prison. Nobody bothered to give us any reason for this. We were marched to some railway station and loaded into goods wagons. Two Russian soldiers first took away our watches, then the doors were closed. In the evening the train started to move, it traveled slowly, stopped several times, and sometimes even reversed again. This went on all night. Nobody had the least idea where we were going or where we were. Sometimes we stopped at lit-up stations. Around midnight, several people thought they had made out the notorious concentration camp Theresienstadt. When the whole train seemed to turn back after an hour, many thought that the whole journey had only been arranged in order to frighten us and that we were now returning to Prague and to freedom. Others, however, when we were passing a station at full speed, expressed the opinion that we were definitely on a line to the east and that we were being transported to Siberia. Towards 3 a.m., we stopped once more and we could hear our engine being uncoupled and moving away. It was terribly quiet and dark... Towards dawn, another engine arrived and pulled us for another half hour. At 6 a.m., the doors were opened and we had to disembark in an open field. Our position was some 30 kilometers from Prague. We shall never know the reason for being driven to and fro during a whole night in order to reach this destination...

Some 2,500 people, two-thirds of them women and children, camped in this meadow. Whoever had anything left to eat finished it now. Towards 9 a.m., we were marched off. We had to carry our luggage for 6 kilometers. Whoever had too much of it or was too weak, threw away one suitcase after another. When we arrived in Tynice near Cesky Brod, the property differences amongst us had been almost leveled out. Nobody now owned more than the bare necessities, but many did not even have that much. Especially those who had been arrested at their places of work, or in the streets, or in the homes of friends whom they had been visiting. Those people had nothing but what they were wearing. It was particularly disastrous for those who had neither coat nor blanket. And many women had just thin shoes, which very soon got completely torn. There was never any question of having them replaced, not even for those who were afterwards sent to work in the fields or on the farms...

Tynice was our camp. At first it was called concentration camp, then labor camp, then internment camp, and in the end just "camp." What it really was from beginning to end, at least as long as we were there, was a destruction camp. It consisted of a big, old, four-storied grain-silo belonging to a farm, and it had neither light, nor heating, nor lavatories or washing facilities, nor a kitchen. We were supposed to erect all these. We built a kitchen shed, two barracks as sick bays, and two latrines—one for men and one for women, the latter one at a distance of 300 meters from the camp. We had to wash ourselves at first in a small pond, which was also used for our laundry and for washing up the dishes. Its water was soon unbearably polluted from the dirt of those who suffered from dysentery. Water for the kitchen was brought by a tank cart from a farm, which only those were allowed to enter who worked there. Despite all warnings, this water was drunk by some. Later on we dug a well, the water of which was used for drinking, cooking and washing. It was never considered quite safe and it has never been proved whether this water has not been the cause of the cases of typhus which occurred sporadically.

Straw was the only material ever supplied to us, apart from the timber for the buildings and the barbed wire for the fence. It was spread on the floors of the ground floor, second and third stories of the silo, the first story remaining as a store for the farm. We lay on this straw like animals, day and night in our clothes, covering ourselves with coats or blankets if we were the lucky owners of these things. When I sat again on a chair at a table, after six months' time, I felt very strange. The openings in the walls of the silo were boarded up at night.

We were guarded, at first, by a small detachment of soldiers under the command of the gentleman farmer, who was himself a lieutenant of the reserve. Later on, this job was taken over by the police. We used to call them "the blacks," as they wore the black uniform of the German tank corps. Their commandant was a sergeant-major of the gendarmes. These guards carried the Russian whip. The farmer, whose farms we kept in order and whose fields we tilled, was a severe, hard and disdainful man. His wife was no better. She was of the opinion that Germans were even unworthy of the sunshine. Most of the guards were uncouth and did seldom show any human feelings. It was always the same—passionate hatred which no method was considered too base to satisfy. An exception were the sergeant-majors of the gendarmes, they tried to prevent at least the worst excesses and occasionally even punished them. It was continuously pointed out to us that the former Nazi concentration camps were used as a pattern for our treatment, and pictures of these camps were displayed at the gate. It would have been quite easy to take similar pictures in our camp.

The running and administration of our camp was in the hands of supervisors selected from our own ranks. Their behavior was by far the worst. There had been no question of electing them, and nobody knew who had nominated them. Probably the camp commandant whose attention they had attracted or whom they had impressed with their servility. The "Führer principle" had obviously been accepted as a pattern, i.e. some made themselves into Führers and later on co-opted others to their clique. These potentates, as we called them, were the only inmates who were well-fed and who managed to escape the dreadful diseases we others had to suffer as a result of malnutrition. It was one of their main tasks to provide labor for the farmer and others from the neighborhood, who every morning arrived with their demands as if coming to a slave market. It was alleged and generally believed that they sold these workers for money and food. At the beginning, the pretence was kept up that all these workers were volunteers: later on, when the only people left were the old and crippled, it just became a call-up.

Most of the workers who were selected for work outside the camp, stayed at their places of employment. But some went out to work every day, sometimes several hours away. Nobody received any payment and treatment was usually bad. Very seldom we heard reports of good treatment, and only occasionally of examples of humane behavior. It was regarded as good treatment, if the food was adequate and the workers were not abused. To be driven on to work harder was considered normal. These people, who were not used to hard physical labor, took it for granted that they had to work hard. They also accepted the fact that they had to sleep in stables or even in pigsties. But they were outraged when they were treated to curses which did not just express dissatisfaction with an individual, but reflected the general hatred roused by the sight of Germans. I learned some Czech words during this time, which I had never known before. The situation in this respect became somewhat better after a time, and it was even said that some farmers asked for a certificate that they had treated their workers well, when they returned them to the camp—for all eventualities, as they said. In the autumn, when work started in the potato and turnip fields, the clothes of most of us were torn to shreds and the shoes were beyond repair. The age limit up to which work was compulsory, was raised again and again until there was no limit left. Age had really become an unimportant factor since the young ones were in such a bad state of health that their working ability was no greater than that of the old. In spite of all this, the camp was continually squeezed for more and more workers, since the farmers accused our "squire" that he was merely looking after his own interests.

Quite a number lost their lives as a result of overstrain. Here is one example of many. As a result of the departure of workers, the number of camp inmates had dropped to 1,000 after a few weeks. Those left were almost wholly the old and the women with a total of some 400 children. One day a man arrived by car and told us that he owned a plantation of soft fruit some 30 kilometers from the camp. He needed workers to pick the fruit and described this as an easy job. We had had some experience with "easy" jobs, but this time the matter seemed plausible. It was tempting to hear that there would be no objection if people helped themselves a little whilst picking. Amongst those who volunteered was an old couple, the man 73, the woman 65, both of them still fairly strong. The man returned after a week, completely exhausted. They had not seen a single bush of berries, but had been told instead to do heavy gardening jobs. He had collapsed after three days. As he had been unable to walk the whole long way back to the camp, he had had to wait until more people were ready to leave and the sending of a car had been worth while. His wife had been kept behind. This man never recovered again and died soon afterwards.

Doctors from our midst looked after our health. But there was a shortage of everything and they could get no medicines. For every prescription they needed the signature of a Czech doctor from outside... Some doctors from outside occasionally inspected the camp and its sanitary arrangements, they pronounced them as insufficient—and left after a short time. Already a few weeks after our arrival, we were afflicted by diarrhea, which never stopped again.

Almost incessantly, all the men and most of the women suffered from it. There were also periods of cystitis, the contracting muscles of the rectum and the bladder seemed paralyzed so that we could not help being dirty. The women turned out to be more resistant. The result of these illnesses was a continuous stream of people between the camp and the latrines. The long way seemed endless, especially when rain had made the ground completely waterlogged. During the night, the passage over the steep, damaged and rarely lighted steps meant a risk to one's life. There were many bad falls here, some with fatal results. To make things worse still, a plague of lice descended on us, it spared nobody and got constantly worse. Facilities for decontamination were not available. It was one of the saddest sights in the camp to see the people crowding round the latrines, or to see men and women (as far as they were not out at work and had time) trying to get rid of their lice at a special place reserved in the camp for this purpose.

The daily food ration consisted of one-eighth, later one-quarter kilogram of bread, black coffee in the morning and evening, for lunch three to five medium-sized potatoes in a bowl, or mashed, or in a soup, prepared only rarely with some fat and usually without salt. The coffee was often sugared. During the first few weeks, we sometimes had some peas or beans for lunch. Starting in the autumn, we were sometimes given a slice of bread with margarine in the evening. This insufficient food was the cause of many cases of edema, of ulcers on the legs, of badly festering wounds even after slight injuries which affected especially the younger women. Only a very few were in the possession of a cup, or the remains of a cup, to use as a container for their food. Most people had to use old tins for eating and for washing themselves.

During the five-and-a-half month which I spent in this camp, 130 people died, 30 alone during the last three weeks. Considering that in late summer we had a total camp population of 300 to 400, it can be assumed that the average population had never been more than 600 to 700. The death rate for the year must therefore have amounted to 40 to 50 per cent. The main cause of death, apart from phlegm, had been the "camp disease," i. e. complete exhaustion made worse by lice and neglect. All died without pain and remorse. The so-called threshing floor on the ground level was used to accommodate those whose death was imminent and inevitable. Everybody knew what it implied if anyone was brought down from the upper floors. But nobody was frightened—the fact that it was now easier for them to reach the latrine during the night, weighed more than the fear of death. The last sacraments could not be given to the dying. Their bodies were buried outside the nearest cemetery and they were brought there in a coffin which had to be returned to the camp. On days when several cases of death had occurred, all bodies were placed into that one coffin... Nobody was allowed to accompany the hearse, except the grave-diggers from our midst. The holders of this office were continually changed, but not by any means because this job was not liked, on the contrary, it was highly desired. The gravediggers had a chance to smuggle food and other things from the village into the camp, using the empty coffin which was not checked on return. And they also generally managed to sell the clothes of the deceased.

Cases of serious illness were brought to the hospital in Böhmisch Brod, but not all the infectious cases. Those with diphtheria and scarlet fever were generally isolated in one of the barracks, but they had to use the same latrine as all the others. In the beginning, confinements took place inside the camp, Later on in the hospital, from where the babies came to the camp wrapped in paper.

We had to surrender our money beyond 1,000 Czech crowns per head, our savings books, securities and jewelry. Some did not comply and managed to retain what they had brought. As most had had large sums with them, as well as savings books, the collected amount was very substantial...In October 1945, the entire property of Germans was confiscated as an advance installment of reparation payments.

One of the particularly sad aspects of our life was the frighteningly rapid spread of moral decay. People with a long life of what seemed to be natural good manners, shed them quickly and thoroughly, as if these manners had just been a thin veneer. Curses and rude words came easily from their lips. Thefts in the camp assumed catastrophic dimensions. Everything was stolen, because everything had become of value. Borrowed things often were not returned...

I do not want to enlarge on these experiences. The memory still makes me shudder. Not all the incidents I have reported have I seen with my own eyes, but I have only mentioned those which have been related to me by trustworthy witnesses whose statements were confirmed by others, so that I trust them as much as I trust many historical or contemporary events which I have not witnessed personally either... Purely as an illustration, I just want to mention two cases.

One night, a gentleman of over 60, a former employee of a factory in a small Czech place in Moravia, in our camp with his wife, was called for interrogation. This took place in a sort of caravan which was used by the guards for living and office purposes. He had to walk a distance of some 100 paces. The man was accused of having had contact with members of the Gestapo, which he denied firmly and consistently. On his way to the interrogation, he was beaten up so as to force him to a confession. This was repeated during several nights. At last this stopped—it had become clear that the whole affair was a case of mistaken identity. But a few days later the gentleman died as a result of the blows he had received.

We were not allowed to speak German amongst ourselves if we knew Czech.

One night, I was speaking German in front of the camp to an acquaintance. A guard heard it. He whipped my back and my outstretched hands and remarked that the Nazis in the concentration camps had done exactly the same.

At last the camp disease got hold of me too. In complete apathy I was lying on the straw and my wife had the 'greatest difficulty in coaxing me to eat, I had become indifferent to everything, I felt quite content and wished for nothing more than to be left in peace. I wish I could die such a quiet death one day. At the twelfth hour, help arrived. An application by relatives living in Krönau, a German town in Northern Moravia (district Mährisch Trübau), to release us for the purpose of being expelled together, provided an opportunity for one of the sergeant majors to remove us from the camp. Similar applications had already been made several times but had always remained unanswered. This sergeant major of the gendarmes took us personally to our relatives on 20 October 1945. He told them that I would hardly have survived another week in the camp. I weighed 60 kilograms, compared to 95 in July 1939 and 80 in May 1945...

Krönau had once been a town with 800 inhabitants, all of them German. When we arrived, however, all the big and most of the small farms were in the hands of Czechs. Although the organized removal of the Germans had not yet started here, a certain part of the German population was missing. They were in internment camps or had been sent away on compulsory labor.

Those who were left crowded together in the poorer habitations, all the better flats and houses were occupied by newly arrived Czechs who had driven out the Germans, retaining all their furniture and fittings.

In conclusion, the author gives a short description of his expulsion into the American occupation zone of Germany, which took place at the beginning of August 1946.

Please refer to: http://www.forgottenvoices.net, for a photograph (#14)) of a German woman, who after beatings from the local population, must help remove Prague barricades in May 1945. Her fellow prisoner's (L) back has been painted with a swastika.

The Condition of the German Population in Bohemia and Moravia at War's End

As the German armies retreated before the Soviet advance, the Czech Revolutionary Militia and Communist action groups, sometimes joined by Soviet troops, moved into the Sudetenland, looted homes, and attacked the residents in their homes and on the streets. For example, on June 18, 1945, when a Czech military transport met a train carrying refugees back to Slovakia, the officials in charge seized the Germans from the train and executed 265 civilians.[25] In May 1945, the Czech Militia took control of the entire border region, encountering no resistance.

Other examples of violence and humiliation against civilians were the "blood courts" conducted by Czech partisans or militia and Soviet troops. In Landskron, east of Prague, on May 17 and 18, German men were assembled and forced to hold up their arms for hours. Victims were then selected to appear before a table where a partisan court handed out sentences: beatings of ten to one hundred blows each or execution by shooting or hanging. There was a similar occurrence in Komotau, northwest Bohemia. On June 9, Czech forces ordered the entire male population of approximately 5,000 to the town square. They then made one hundred men remove their clothing, sing the German anthem, and say, "We thank our Führer." At the end, twelve to sixteen men were beaten to death and the rest were driven to the border. The Soviets, however, did not let them into their zone of occupation.[26]

In general, the armed partisans and Czech Militia made no distinction between antifascist Germans, peasants, or Nazi sympathizers, although anti-Nazi Germans were to have been spared retribution. The Sudeten Germans were randomly killed, villages were set on fire, individuals were hung by their heels from trees, doused with gasoline, and set on fire. The Czech Militia rampaged through the towns and villages,shooting Germans at will.[27] Occasionally, Czechs came to the aid of German neighbors or friends. Once a Czech landlord attempted to report to the Czech police about an attack on a German woman. He was reprimanded by the police, leaving him and others of the same inclinations with the clear message that there was no penalty for violence against Germans,but there was one for attempting to prevent it.[28] The German population could not understand, at this time, why there was so much hatred against them. They felt that they were the innocent victims of arbitrary state action based on an ascribed collective guilt for the actions of the Nazi regime in Czechoslovakia.

One of the worst cases of violence against German civilians was what occurred at Aussig (Usti nad Labem) on July 31. Fires started by a series of explosions in the local munitions warehouse killed twenty-eight people and wounded many more, both Czech and German. The Czech authorities blamed the German "Werewolf," a guerrilla army ostensibly established by the defeated Nazi regime in order to kill and sabotage the occupying forces. There was never any proof that in fact such an organization ever existed. The Czech Militia and civilians accepted the rumors as true, even though there was no evidence of sabotage, and proceeded to massacre the German population. Women and children were thrown from a bridge into the Elbe River and were shot until they drowned. The Czech population rampaged through the town, beat, and killed any Germans they encountered. The police and military did not hinder this massacre, but took an active part in it. Afterwards, it was estimated that up to 2,700 German inhabitants of Aussig were murdered.[29]

No. 53

Report by a former official of the Czech Administrative Commission in Aussig. Reprinted from "Londynske Listy" (London Letters, Fortnightly Review), published by Joseph Belina - 1), vol. II, no. 14 (London, 15 July 1948), pp. 143 f. (Direct translation from the Czech)

The expulsion in the district of Aussig in the middle of June 1945; the massacre of the German population of Aussig on 31 July 1945.

The way in which it was done.

Just now we received an eyewitness account of the events in Aussig, Elbe, which is bound to fill every decent human being with shame. It says:

'Lidice lit a torch which roused the whole civilized world against the cruelest tyranny and the debased nature of a totalitarian regime. Truth and humanism were on our side in the world when it happened. It was our right and our duty as soon as the war was over, to deal with the criminals who sinned against humanity. But our attempts to settle accounts with these criminals have been overshadowed by even greater acts of inhumanity than were those committed by the Nazi gangsters. This applies, for instance, to the way in which the first evacuations, which were really a driving out with whips, were carried out on 11 June 1945. The local National Committees were given the task to compile a register of all persons of German nationality who were members of the Nazi Party, in preparation of their removal. Lists were compiled into the late hours of the night. In the early hours of the morning, military units made up of the Revolutionary Guard and of so-called guerrillas, arrived in the affected districts. When members of the local National Committee asked them to evacuate the Germans in accordance with the compiled lists, they received very rude answers from the generally drunk "officers"—"You can put these lists up your... "

They went into action. They entered flats and every family was told to report within half an hour at the assembly point of the district. Jewelry was confiscated, and to make quite sure that nothing was hidden there, girls had even their genitals searched. Then the "transports" were loaded into tramcars and taken to Tellnitz, from where they had to walk over the Erzgebirge to Germany. Even people aged 78 and 81 were not spared this Calvary.

The explosion in Schönpriesen.

There is also a need to give a proper description of the events of 31 July 1945, which one might call a counterpart to Lidice. This affair will sooner or later be discussed and we have to mention it unless we want to be condemned collectively like the Germans. Just now, when the third anniversary of this massacre is approaching, for which the Communist Party of Czechoslovakia bears the sole responsibility, I think it important as an eyewitness and an official of the Administrative Commission in those days, to describe the cause of the explosion which then occurred and the inhuman reprisals which followed.

In our district, the last phase of the battles of the German army led by General Schörner, ended on 9 May 1945. All streets and roads were blocked by convoys of cars, guns and ammunition transports. On the following day, 10 May, the clearing away started. Arms and ammunition were stored in the warehouses of the former sugar refinery of Schönpriesen, which had been transformed during the war into the German cable factory. Hundreds of new aircraft engines were stored there. Grenades, anti-tank guns and ammunition of all kinds had been brought there. Soldiers were on duty guarding and supervising; they had been able to procure plenty of spirits from the liquor distillery Eckelmann in the neighborhood, and no care was taken to store everything properly: on the contrary, everything was just thrown together. This was the cause of the catastrophe.

The first explosion occurred at 3.45 p.m. on 31 July 1945, shattering all windows within a radius of 3 kilometers. Nobody in the town had the slightest inkling at that moment that this was to be the signal for murder. Soldiers surrounded the bridge over the Elbe, and when Communist provocateurs arrived at 4.10 p.m., accompanied by people in Russian uniforms, the "executions" started, Germans returning from work and wearing their white armlets, became the first victims on the Benes Bridge. The soldiers had been asked by Mr. Vondra, the chairman of the local National Committee of Aussig/Elbe, to avoid any massacre: but they did not obey his order and joined in the murder. A mother wheeling her child in a pram across the bridge,

127

was killed with sticks and, together with the child, thrown over the railings into the Elbe whilst sub-machine-guns fired at her.

Another incident which stayed in my memory and which will haunt me all my life, was that of a German anti-Fascist who had returned after four years in a concentration camp and was now employed as a mechanic in the firm of Brönner. This German fighter against Fascism—his name was Brainl—had his hair torn from his head and was then shot through his stomach. He died instantly.

There were hundreds of similar incidents. On the bridge and in the main square, people were killed and thrown into the so-called air-raid water reservoirs. Within three hours, more than 2,000 people had been murdered 2).

The dead were robbed; interned Germans had to load them on lorries and drive them to the crematorium in Theresienstadt. Those who accompanied the dead never returned.

After this massacre, the Minister of the Interior, Nosek, and the Minister of National Defense, General Svoboda, visited the town. It came to a severe difference of opinion in the council of the Administrative Commission. But this did not alter the fact that the explosion had occurred as a result of negligence on the part of the military administration. This is no excuse, however, for Minister Nosek. Neither the soldiers nor the police did anything to re-establish law and order; on the contrary, they themselves enticed people to riot. The inefficiency and lack of discipline of the military officials cost the Czech population of Schönpriesen material damage to the value of 8 million Czech crowns, quite apart from the loss of a large number of homes. And the German population paid with the loss of an extraordinarily large number of lives of mostly innocent people simply because the mob wanted to enrich themselves and wanted to get hold of their property.

Lidice was a living monument to the fatal "furor teutonicus," and Aussig, Elbe was the rehabilitation of the German Nazi murderers. The number of victims in this case was almost four times as large. Is this crime not going to become part of history as "furor Czechoslovakia plebs"?

1. Joseph Belina, the editor and publisher of the duplicated bi-monthly "Londynske Listy" (published in London in the Czech language), was a trade union official in the First Czechoslovak Republic. During the war and up to his death in 1948, he lived as an émigré in England, where he continued to be politically active on behalf of the Czechoslovak Social Democratic Party.
2. Accurate figures of the dead and missing in connection with these events are impossible to compile. In several reports,

contained in the documentary archives, the number of persons killed or missing is estimated to be between 1,000 and more than 2,000. German sources quote a figure of more than 2,700 dead.

The new Czech administrative commissions, the National Committees, assumed control over all of the Sudetenland. The Czech communist party had undue influence in these committees due to their efficient underground organizations as well as the help from the Soviet occupation authorities. Because of their lack of experience, improvisation, and emphasis on retribution, conditions were chaotic. Klement Gottwald, the leader of the Czech Communist Party, said, "When it comes to the state administration and apparatus, we have a clean slate." He called National Committees "a thorn in the side" of the noncommunist parties and identified them as "the main arena for the political struggle."[30]

Czech sources subsequently admitted that many criminal elements from the interior of Czechoslovakia, taking advantage of this chaotic situation, went to the border regions to plunder, loot, and persecute the German inhabitants. Control measures established for the Germans by the Czechoslovakian authorities were extremely harsh. On May 17, the Germans were given smaller food rations. They had to wear white armbands and were not allowed to use telephones or other means of communication. They could shop only at certain hours. They were forbidden to change their residences or visit theaters, movie houses, and other places of public amusement. In June 1945, all German schools were closed. Compulsory labor conscription was introduced for the Sudeten Germans to clean up the destruction. Many were also sent to do forced labor on farms or in the mines.[31]

The program of the provisional Czech government at Kaschau (Kosice), established in April 1945, had already announced that those Germans guilty of war crimes or other acts against the Czechoslovak state or people would be punished. Former Czechoslovak citizens of German origin would be expelled and lose their property unless their loyalty to Czechoslovakia were proved. To this end, Extraordinary People's Courts were established to provide the legal basis for these trials. The Kosice program also called for radical economic, political, and social reforms, including nationalizing land and industry.[32] In its eighth chapter dealing with the problem of the German inhabitants of Czechoslovakia, it said:

The Republic has no wish to persecute its loyal German citizens and they, and above all those who proved their faithfulness even in times of great difficulty, will be unaffected. The culprits, however, will be severely and pitilessly punished.

Czechoslovak citizenship for Germans...who held it before Munich 1938 will be confirmed and the possibility of their return to the Republic will be assured only if they were anti-Nazis and anti-Fascists, if they fought against Henlein ... for the Czechoslovak Republic in the period before Munich and if, after 15 March, they were persecuted for their resistance, their struggle against the regime then in power and their loyalty to the Republic by the German...official authorities, were thrown into prisons and concentration camps or had to flee abroad from the German...terror, where they actively participated in the struggle for the restoration of Czechoslovakia.

Czechoslovak citizenship of other Czechoslovak citizens of German...nationality will be cancelled. Although they may again opt for Czechoslovakia, public authorities will retain the right of individual decision in the case of each application.[33]

Quoted from *The Transfer of the Sudeten Germans, A Study of Czech-German Relations, 1933-1962*, Radomir Luza.

It quickly became apparent to the revolutionary government, however, that the Kosice government program was too moderate and did not reflect the radicalization that occurred in Czechoslovakia at war's end. A series of harsh decrees were then issued, the so-called Benes decrees. Under the Great Decree of June 19, 1945, all members of the SS, Nazi Party, and Volunteer SS, or Sudetendeutsches Freikorps (SF) as well as their Czech collaborators would be prosecuted. In this respect, it must be said, this law was not very different from those made by the Western Allies after the War.

About 15,400 Germans were sentenced by the Extraordinary People's Courts to prison terms of various lengths. Four hundred and fifty-five Germans were sentenced to life imprisonment and four hundred and sixty-seven received the death sentence. The most important of the latter was Karl Hermann Frank, a Sudeten German who was the highest-ranking officer of the police and SS in the Protectorate, and Reich Minister for Bohemia and Moravia after the assassination of Reinhard Heydrich. He had the ultimate responsibility for the deportation of Czechs to the concentration camps as well as forced labor to Germany. The other was Heinrich Jöckel, the commander of the Theresienstadt concentration camp. Although these were trials of war criminals, the Czech government repeatedly made it clear that they demonstrated the collective criminality of the German minority in the Czech Republic, to condemn the Sudeten Germans as a whole.[34]

A further series of decrees were published effectively taking away Czechoslovak citizenship rights of those Germans who acquired German citizenship after the Sudetenland was absorbed by the Reich in 1938. (All ethnic Germans in Czechoslovakia had automatically become German citizens at the time of the occupation.) As a result of Presidential decrees of May 18, June 21, and October 25, 1945, all German property was confiscated without compensation. Only anti-Nazi Germans who fought for Czechoslovakia during the occupation were exempted. Practically all movable and immovable property belonging to the German State, ethnic Germans, and citizens of Germany were confiscated. This property was given to Czech nationals or kept by the Czech State. German industrial and financial properties were nationalized. The former were mostly textile and glass factories, an industrial specialization of Bohemia and Moravia. The confiscation of German farm properties without compensation and their distribution to Czech farmers was the last step in destroying the economic foundation of the German community.[35]

The Internment of the Sudeten Germans in Labor Camps

The systematic internment of the German population in labor camps began shortly after the Prague uprising. This started in the interior parts of Bohemia and Moravia and spread westwards with the appearance of the Revolutionary Militia and action groups, including the National Committees. In parts of the Eastern Sudetenland entire villages and towns were affected. Families were torn apart without any consideration and only came together again after their expulsion to Germany. In one of the most notorious camps, Theresienstadt (Terezin), the only change was the victims; previously they were Jewish prisoners of the SS, many on their way to the extermination camps in Poland. Now they were Germans. The food rations and maltreatment were similar, the difference being that the Germans were not destined for extermination but to do forced labor and then to be expelled from Czechoslovakia[36] (Refer to the history of the Theresienstadt [Terezin] Ghetto below.)

There were three different kinds of camps: internment camps, labor camps, and assembly camps. The last category were transit stations for those destined for immediate expulsion to Germany.[37] Compulsory labor was decreed not only for the internees of these camps but for all

Sudeten Germans. This covered all males between the ages of fourteen and sixty and all females between the ages of fifteen and fifty. Forced labor was mainly employed in mines, industrial plants, especially in heavy industry, and in agriculture. Treatment and food rations depended on the Soviet model of meeting production norms. Hunger and sickness were widespread as food rations were never sufficient and health conditions in the camps were deficient. Some camps were known for the excessive use of force and humiliation exercised on the prisoners by the Revolutionary Guards. This treatment only improved once it became apparent to the authorities that production targets could not be met under these conditions. Only when the organized expulsions in family groups started in 1946, were some prisoners allowed to leave in order to join their families.[38] In addition to these camps in Czechoslovakia, German sources estimate that an additional 30,000 Sudeten Germans were sent as forced labor to camps in the Soviet Union.[39]

No. 37

Report of experiences (letter) of Hubert Schützsen, businessman and former town councillor, of Jägerndorf. Certified copy (completed and confirmed by the author), dated 4 January 1947, typewritten, 4 pages.

Internment in Jägerndorf at the beginning of June 1945, and conditions in the internment camp; compulsory labor in the foundry of Witkowitz until the author's severe illness.

In the first part of his report, the author mentions that he had to leave Jägerndorf on 25 March 1945, when this town became a front area and was evacuated. He had to go to Mährisch Schönberg where he experienced the entry of Soviet troops with all its terrors. He then describes the methods used by the National Committee of Mährisch Schönberg to induce the evacuees to leave this town, and continues as follows:

On 4 June 1945, I organized a group of fellow sufferers from Jägerndorf and we marched via Berggeist, Römerstadt and Freudenthal, back to Jägerndorf, dragging heavily laden handcarts with us. Nobody, at that time, dared to travel individually for fear of attacks and robberies. Spending the nights in the woods, we reached our destination after three days.

On reaching Jägerndorf, we immediately sensed the completely changed atmosphere in our hometown. It was 5 June 1945[1]). Guerrillas roamed the streets, ransacked our luggage and threatened the homecoming inhabitants. Nobody dared to enter his own house, because most of them were by now occupied by Czechs. Many houses were burned out, others demolished, damaged during the fighting or looted. The poor intimidated members of our group were individually escorted to their homes. When I reached my house, I found a long queue of people waiting outside. When I asked what was happening, I was informed that the Czech food office was accommodated there, issuing 100 grams of bread per person and day. My wife and I pushed our handcart into the yard, and I had to go and ask the Czech official in charge of the food office for permission to enter my own flat. Admission was only allowed when I had produced all my papers and when witnesses had confirmed that I really belonged in this house. Even then entry was not at all easy because the locks of the door had been damaged. When we finally opened, the door by force, we saw what had happened. All the cupboards, the desk, the sideboards etc. had been broken into, many things had been stolen and the furniture damaged. In spite of this terrible sight, we were happy to be back home. We started to put everything in order and lived on our resources, not daring to show ourselves outside as we were everywhere terribly molested.

1) Must mean 7 June.

Six days later, on 13 June 1945, I had been to the post-office and was on my way home when I saw a whole crowd of guerrillas marching towards the town square. Friends who were running along the street shouted at me that they were just going to proclaim martial law for Jägerndorf from the town hall. We were in fear and anxiety, but still, we did not expect the worst because we somehow felt comparatively safe at home and amongst our own people. My main intention was to reach my home as quickly as possible and I started to run. Near the church street, the guerrillas caught up with me and took me to the parish church. Some 50 fellow sufferers were already waiting there, and new ones kept on arriving. It was said that we would be released again as soon as martial law had been proclaimed. In the meantime it was 12:30 p.m. Suddenly the door opened, seven guerrillas entered with rifles on their shoulders; they searched us, beat the women and sent them home. We men had to line up and were taken to the guardroom of the police in the town hall.

We expected some sort of interrogation and stood there, crowded in a corner, till 7:30 p.m. Eventually, one of us was called for some kind of mock interrogation, which lasted till 8 p.m. At that time, the interrogating official suddenly interrupted and told the guerrillas that he wished to go home for supper and that the people should be sent home as well. But the guerrillas protested and drove us all into the remand cells. When we reached the cellar, we were one after another attacked, beaten up and thrown into the cells. Four of us found themselves in one cell which was completely empty except for two bunks with a torn stair-carpet for a blanket.... We expected to have peace now, be able to sleep, and to be interrogated on the following day and then released. But we were very much mistaken. Every ten minutes two different guerillas entered our cell and taught us to know better. Every time they entered, we had to raise our arms and report (in Czech): "We thank our Führer Adolf Hitler, the Chachar, that we are here." ("Chachar" is a swear word used in Ostrau to define a scoundrel.) When anyone was beaten up, we had to say: "We thank you for the repayment." If somebody was unable to speak Czech fluently and therefore could not report quickly enough, he got another beating. This went on until 3 o'clock in the morning. At 7 o'clock, the same torture started all over again. At 11 o'clock two guerrillas arrived with a bucket of water and we were allowed to take a glass each for drinking and were given 30 grams of bread.

At 5 o'clock in the afternoon we were all called out, lined up in the courtyard and marched to the guardroom…Suddenly the order was given that we should collect our hats, braces and the contents of our pockets, which we had had to surrender… When everyone of us was ready the order was given to line up in a double row. With a guard in front and one in the rear, we had to turn right and to start the march… We marched in the direction of the Troppauer Street…Compatriots meeting us in the streets did not even dare look at us for fear of being attacked by the guerillas, but we heard the furtive remark of one passer-by: "into camp." For the first time it came to our knowledge that a camp existed. This camp had been erected in the so-called tank barracks in the Troppauer Street, opposite the public house "Sonne." First it was called a camp for political prisoners, then a labor camp for political prisoners, and finally an internment camp for Germans. The name was changed according to public opinion abroad.

On arrival we saw thousands of people from Jägerndorf already inside the camp and more transports kept arriving. Our group had to line up near the camp office, the guards did not move from our side, and thus we had to wait for a whole hour. All of a sudden we realized that the guerillas guarding us had disappeared and I gave the signal to the others to disperse as well, and so we mingled with our compatriots. An escape from the camp was out of the question, the gates and fences were manned by guerillas and anybody trying to escape would have been shot immediately. It could not possibly have been worse in a concentration camp. One after another we were driven into the office for registration where we had to hand over our watches, money, jewelry and knives, and where we were given a place allocation in the barracks. There were in general two men to one bunk. Those of us who had been Party officials or had belonged to the SA or SS, were put in special barracks behind bars and three times daily beaten with rubber truncheons on their bare backs, sometimes until they collapsed…

Disciplinary measures in the camp were worse than even in army barracks.

All day long one heard nothing but the yelling of the guerrillas and the harsh commands to fall in line. All day long one saw people bleeding from hits across the face, and blows with rifle butts. The place was full of room commanders, group commanders, labor commanders. These commanders were Germans and if they did not do as they were told by the guerrillas, they were beaten up or put behind bars. (In the cells behind bars the treatment was that of a capital criminal.)

I went to work with one of the labor commandos and had to clean all the schools and gymnasiums of Jägerndorf. It was hard work but we went willingly so as to escape the tortures inside the camp. During the first three days we got nothing to eat and went begging to our fellow sufferers. Some who had been taken directly from their homes and had arrived only lately, usually had brought some food with them. On the evening of the fourth day, we were given half a liter of potato soup. Later on the issue was half a liter of black coffee in the morning, half a liter of potato soup and 130 grams of bread in the evening. When one month had passed, those working in labor commandos were given 200 grams of bread.

It took a fortnight before my wife heard by accident what had happened to me. There were three camps in Jägerndorf. One in the Troppauer Street, one on the Burgberg (formerly a camp of the labor service), and one in the Leobschützer Street in the new blocks of flats of the non-commissioned officers of the tank corps. These camps were later on organized in such a way that the camp in the Troppauer Street became the labor as well as the penal camp, in the Leobschützer Street was the labor camp of the Social Democrats, and on the Burgberg the transit camp. The whole population of Jägerndorf was driven from their homes without exception.

Just as I was working outside the technical school and taking a rest in the park in front of it, my wife and daughter-in-law happened to pass, as if sent by God. This was how we met again for the first time. My wife suffered from heart trouble, and on doctor's orders she had been given permission to have treatment at home so that she had been able to remain in our flat. She brought me a blanket and a rucksack with some underwear, a bowl and a spoon. I was now able for the first time to cover myself in my sleep, to change my underwear for the first time, and to eat for the first time with my own utensils. Up till then I always had to wait until a good neighbor lent me his bowl and spoon. It was unbelievable, never being able for days and nights to take off one's clothes. We had to sleep in a very large garage for armored cars, the floor was of concrete and we were lying side by side on the straw, which had been spread on it. The women and children remained in the barracks.

Two months later, when we had lined up again in the evening—we had to line up daily so that working slaves could be selected as in a cattle market—the much-hated commander of the partisans shouted: "All teachers, clerks, businessmen—step forward!" Naturally, I had to step forward as well. We were registered and had to state our age. The nine oldest ones, amongst them, myself were put aside as we were supposed to be too old. By now the rumor had spread that those who had been chosen would be sent to the iron foundry in Witkowitz for heavy work. When it turned out next morning that of the required 100 men only 60 had been found amongst the group of clerks, teachers and businessmen, we nine as well, and in addition others who were somewhat less indispensable from other labor commandos, were quickly taken by lorries to the railway station, From there we were transported in open trucks to Witkowitz.

In Witkowitz the work's militia received us, took us into the work's barracks, divided us into working parties and, the following day, drove us to work under militia supervision. At 4 a.m. we had to get up, at 5 a.m. we were given half a liter of black coffee, at lunch time half a liter of soup, in the evening half a liter of soup, and in addition 300 grams of bread for the whole day. We marched to work at 5.30 a.m. and had to start at 6 a.m. The shift ended at 2 p.m. Then we marched back to the barracks where we had to wash ourselves, clean and tidy the rooms, wash our things etc., so that there was very little time to get our breath back. Once every fortnight we were allowed to write a postcard to our families, but it had to be in Czech. This postcard was censored and if anyone wrote something wrong he was beaten up. Something wrong also meant if one mentioned hunger or hard work or that one was not well.

Together with a second comrade I had to unload every day within the eight-hour shift twelve wagons of coal, gravel, chalk, coke or fire clay, or sometimes iron-ore (120,000 kilograms). It was terrible because, first of all, we were not accustomed to this kind of work and, secondly, the food was bad and we were very hungry. After one month I became seriously ill. I had swollen legs right up to my stomach, the skin of my legs could expand no further and burst. Water started running from the sores so that shoe-laces and socks rotted on my feet and ulcers and erysipelas formed around those sores. I was not allowed to see the doctor. When I could walk no longer, I did not turn up at work and reported sick. I had vastly swollen genitals and starvation edema (dropsy!). Two days later I was taken on a small handcart to the "Hospital for Germans" in Mährisch Ostrau, pushed by two colleagues and escorted by a guard from the militia with a rifle slung over his shoulder. This so-called hospital for Germans was a pigsty. It was a former German public house (Pichler), badly demolished, with straw in the hall where the sick and the dead lay pressed like sardines side by side. I was examined on arrival and apart from the symptoms mentioned before, I was found to be suffering from an inflammation of the kidneys. I was a wreck and reduced to a skeleton (formerly 270 lb, now only 120 lb).

As more people died daily, an investigation of the hospital was ordered and a commission arrived which included the medical officer of health from the police headquarters in Mährisch Ostrau. He declared that I was "incurable and permanently unfit for work" on account of the diseases mentioned above. I was to be released at once and sent home for treatment. I kept on running a high temperature and got continuously worse. I would also like to mention that already on the second day in the hospital I removed 186 lice from my underwear, they would have eaten me alive, if the doctor had not rubbed me with an ointment of mercury and if I had not made myself a bed on some chairs.

The news had widely spread that I had died already, and this had also reached my wife. A1 last I was sent home—four weeks after the medical officer of health Dr. Odersky had ordered it. When I arrived home, I suffered in addition to everything else from tonsillitis and, after a few days, from a cholera-type dysentery with colic and loss of blood. This condition lasted for three weeks. Dr. Kiesewetter who visited me secretly (no doctor was allowed to visit a German in his home), had given me up, but eventually his treatment, in spite of all the limitations he had to contend with, did help. The firm determination to recover and the good treatment at home helped me to overcome everything. I spent many months in bed. Then I recovered after all. Eventually, on 12 April 1946, I was removed to Bavaria with a transport of 1,200 persons. The author concludes his report by stating that he is prepared to confirm his statements on oath and by producing official documents.

The History of the Theresienstadt (Terezin) Ghetto

Theresienstadt was originally a garrison town and fortress, not far from Prague, founded in 1780 by Emperor Joseph II, who named it in honor of his mother the Empress Maria Theresa. In October 1941, it was designated as a collection point for Jews from Bohemia and Moravia as well as from Germany and lands occupied by the Nazi Regime. Only certain classes of German Jews were sent there—older people, veterans who had been decorated in World War I, and prominent people in the arts and sciences. It subsequently became a model concentration camp to disguise the Nazis' plans to exterminate the Jews.[40] Its purpose was to mislead the prisoners initially by less harsh conditions in the Theresienstadt Ghetto, after which, dispossessed of everything they owned, they were sent to their death in the killing camps in the East. The SS commanders of Theresienstadt referred to it as a "Schleuse," a channel, a transient camp to steer prisoners to the camps in Poland. (See map 15 of the Theresienstadt Ghetto)

An old fort near the main camp, and built at the same time, called the Little Fortress was re-opened by the Gestapo in June 1940 as a punishment block for inmates of Theresienstadt. (See map 15) In the time of the Dual Monarchy, during World War I, it held political prisoners including Gavrilo Princip, the assassin of the crown prince, Archduke Franz Ferdinand of Austria. Around 30,000 prisoners passed through the Little Fortress on the way to Auschwitz and other extermination camps in the East. Conditions were terrible, with many prisoners kept in solitary confinement. Executions of prisoners by the SS were common.[41]

Although the mortality rate was less than that of the camps in Poland, of the 140,000 people who were sent to Theresienstadt between November 1941 and April 1945, almost 90,000 were sent to their death in Auschwitz or Treblinka, and 33,000 died in the Ghetto from starvation and disease. These were mostly older people and children; only 16,382 survived.[42]

The historian, H. G. Adler, in his book, *Theresienstadt 1941-1945*, describes the relationship of the Ghetto to Auschwitz as follows:

> In Auschwitz, there was only the naked despair or the pitiless recognition of the game, and even if there existed a spark of an indestructible vitality, even if the soul managed to escape from time to time into a delusion, in the long run no one could deceive himself, everyone had to look reality in the face.
>
> It was different in Theresienstadt. Everything there could be pushed aside, illusion flourished wildly, and hope, only mildly dampened by anxiety would eclipse everything that was hidden under an impenetrable haze. Nowhere had the inmates of a camp pushed the true face of the period further into an unknown future than here ... Only occasionally would the truth arise from the depths, touch the inmates, and after a bit of fright, they would [go back] into their existence of masks.[43]

Theresienstadt was a veritable Potemkin village, to fool the world as to what really was occurring in the East to Jews and other Nazi enemies in the killing camps. Several beautification programs were carried out by the SS command in order to make it into a "model" ghetto and prepare it for inspections from the IRC. At one point 17,500 inmates were deported to Auschwitz to make the ghetto appear less crowded to the IRC inspectors.[44] It appears, from subsequent IRC reports, that they were completely misled by the benign outward appearance of the Ghetto. By May 5 1945, with the end of the War, the SS abandoned Theresienstadt, and it was placed under the protection of the IRC. The Soviets arrived on May 9 and took control of the camp.

The suffering, however, did not end with the liberation of the camp. Shortly thereafter, Czech authorities filled the Little Fortress prison with over 3,000 ethnic Germans and German refugees, whether or not they were guilty of war crimes. The same mistreatment of the prisoners continued as before. They were generally not killed, however, but eventually expelled from Czechoslovakia.[45]

The following eyewitness report on life in the Theresienstadt Ghetto by Charlotte Guthmann Opfermann, is taken from the book, *Life in the Ghettos during the Holocaust*, edited by Eric J. Sterling. (Syracuse University Press, Syracuse, NY, 2004). Printed with the permission of the publisher. The writer was a victim of the Nazi regime for twelve years while in concentration camps and ghettos. After the war, she taught Holocaust studies in Texas.

Beware of Answered Prayers

Ghetto-Concentration Camp Theresienstadt / Terezin

CHARLOTTE GUTHMANN OPFERMANN

...No other camp or ghetto has received so much false publicity—from perpetrators and from survivors—as Theresienstadt, the two-hundred-year-old garrison village some sixty kilometers to the north of Prague. Long before Steven Spielberg introduced the world to such a camp with his film Schindler's List, Adolf Eichmann and his colleagues of the Reichsicherheitshauptamt (RSHA) decided to demonstrate to the German movie-going public, with a Fox Tonende Wochenschau newsreel, just where all these Jews were supposedly sent and how they passed their time—at leisure, attending concerts and lectures, reading, knitting, gossiping, with little children playing happily in sandboxes or on swings in well-landscaped parks.

The intent of this newsreel was not to put anyone's conscience at ease (there was no objection of consequences to the Jews' fate), but to contrast the supposed comfortable Jewish life style in the midst of the war with the suffering and hardships endured by the German population. The film was intended to stimulate further anti-Jewish sentiment...

In truth, the Jewish inmates of Theresienstadt had only a portion of the old garrison at their disposal. When I arrived at this camp in

June 1943, there were many guarded barricades and wooden fences, with entire streets off limits everywhere. The garrison was originally designed to house two or three thousand soldiers in barracks, plus a small contingent of support personnel in some two hundred small, one- and two-story houses.

Most of the time, forty to fifty thousand inmates were crowded into only a portion of the garrison. We were assigned approximately six feet by one yard of space per person. Appropriately, this is about the size of a coffin...

I lived in the attic of the Hamburger Kaserne, sleeping on the dirty, naked stone floor, sharing this area with roughly six thousand women who had been brought here from the four corners of the Reich. Most of the inmates at that time (June 1943) were from the Protektorat Böhmen und Mähren, Czechoslovakia. Most were young and at work in the many production programs with which the internal camp administrators hoped to persuade the German masters that this camp could be useful to the German economy. The vain hope and intent of the various production programs (such as crates for use by the Wehrmacht and split mica for the Luftwaffe) was to persuade the Kommandantur that we should continue to live and not be deported to the dreaded East.

When elderly and infirm prisoners began to arrive from Germany in the summer and fall of 1942, this influx was perceived as a threat to the work camp concept, and thus the new prisoners were far from welcome for a number of reasons. There was no way to care for the sick or to accommodate elderly prisoners. To no one's surprise, fully two-thirds (more than twenty thousand) of the camp's inmates were prisoners from Germany. The German veterans from World War I, who were also a part of this German contingent, were considered too patriotic, too much like the enemy, so there was a great deal of friction within the camp's prisoner population. I countered this problem as best I could by learning to speak Czech. Most of my fellow inmates preferred to speak their native tongue and did not speak German very well or at all.

Word of the massacre of Jews at the hands of the Nazis had reached the outside world almost from the very beginning. We knew of the intended killing of the Polish and stateless Jews from Germany to Poland as early as October 27, 1938. Details had been broadcast to the free world over the years. But little was done with this knowledge.

The Red Cross inspection in June 1944 was made possible thanks to the initiative of the Danish king Christian X, the cooperation of the president of the German Red Cross (from the Schutzstaffel [SS], Brigadeführer Dr. Ernst Robert Grawitz, who was responsible for many of the medical experiments performed on concentration camp prisoners), Reichsführer Heinrich Himmler, Sturmbannführer Adolf Eichmann, and other major players. They all participated in the charade. Likewise, many inmates and internal leaders of the camp were forced to help.

In June 1944, Maurice Rossel, then working for the Geneva office of the International Red Cross, wrote a glowing report after a brief visit to the camp. The Red Cross archives did not release this report and Rossel's pictures until 1992, almost fifty years later. I am one of the children captured in several of his photographs. Quite possibly, the institution was embarrassed by its content. The Pamatnik Terezin (i.e., the Gedenkstätte Theresientadt Museum) and Yad Vashem, Jerusalem, have a copy of this report. Almost all of the seemingly happy children and their caregivers whom Rossel photographed in June were dead within weeks after his visit. He did not understand that they had been carefully clothed in special garments and coached at great length concerning what to do and what to say for this special occasion.

We were "issued" special clothes for the occasion that had to be returned to the Kleiderkammer after the visitors had left. For my use, I received a navy blue pleated skirt and a spiffy white blouse, plus a necktie of sorts....

Along the preplanned route, several buildings had been painted in cheerful colors, with flowers planted along the way. A special children's playground was constructed, and children who normally would have been at work were taught how to play. There was a music pavilion. Many of the internal walls, barricades, and confining fences were torn down. Most of the prisoners were under strictly enforced house arrest and had to keep away from windows in order to hide the pitifully overcrowded conditions. For many months, the visit was planned in every conceivable detail. It was over in a few minutes.

As a result, there was no improvement of the horrible conditions in Theresienstadt. On the contrary, when a second such inspection was taken under consideration, 18,406 prisoners were deported, with most of them being killed in preparation.

The documentary film Bericht aus der jüdischen Siedlung Theresien-stadt had been a work in progress since 1942. It was completed in 1944. Most of the film disappeared into Soviet archives when Soviet soldiers entered the camp in May 1945; its some twenty minutes of excerpts are available at various archives. The film is now known by its postwar title The Führer Makes the Jews the Gift of a City.

From June 1943 until mid-June 1945, even after our liberation by the Soviet army, I was a prisoner in this camp. Our normal daily life consisted of hard physical labor, very little food, many deliberate deprivations...

The Czech Government's Justification for the Expulsion of the Germans

In the spring of 1945, the Provisional Czech government implemented a comprehensive program of national cleansing of "foreign bodies" to right past wrongs and prevent future crimes. In this case the "foreign bodies" were more than three million Sudeten Germans. The concept of national cleansing was also a primary instrument in the radicalization of the Czech populace and a means for the subsequent Communist seizing of power in 1948. Klement Gottwald, the General Secretary of the Czech Communist Party, in April 1945 told Party leaders that[46]

> [A] tool, which we have today in the fight for leadership of the nation, is the struggle against traitors and collaborators—that is, against the physical leaders of the compromised Slovak and Czech bourgeoisie ... [The] law for the prosecution of traitors and collaborators is a very sharp weapon, with which we can cut so many limbs away from the bourgeoisie that only its trunk will remain. This is a matter of the class struggle against the bourgeoisie—a struggle waged under the banner of the state and the nation, under the banner of the republic. Not to use this weapon is to let it rust. With this weapon we can strike our enemy directly, physically.

Quoted from: *National Cleansing: Retribution against Nazi Collaborators in Postwar Czechoslovakia*, Benjamin Frommer.

According to the prominent Czech émigré and journalist Jan Stransky, "after the War, Communists controlled the Revolutionary Tribunals, the People's Courts, the police, the Ministry of the Interior and the Committees trying citizens accused of offenses against the nation's honor."[47]

The basic rationale for the ethnic cleansing of the Sudeten Germans was their collective guilt for the crimes committed against Czechoslovakia by Nazi Germany. For this reason, they received the collective punishment of expulsion from that country. According to the government, an independent Czechoslovakia could not survive with a treacherous minority.

The Czech government in exile in London, under the leadership of Edvard Benes, already decided early in the War that it was necessary to expel the German population in order to preserve the Czechoslovak state. It felt that after the Munich treaties, Czechs and Germans could never again share the same land. Benes affirmed that only by transferring the Germans can another Munich be avoided. In September of 1941, Benes stated, "I accept the principle of the transfer of populations...If the transfer is carefully considered...the transfer can be made amicably under decent human conditions, under international control and with international support."[48] The British government had previously agreed, in 1942, with this program, and subsequently Roosevelt also concurred. In 1943, Benes received the support of the Soviet Union for the expulsion of the Sudeten Germans when he committed Czechoslovakia to a military alliance as a guarantee against future German aggression.

The German occupation policy for Czechoslovakia was fairly consistent throughout the War. Above all its purpose was the economic exploitation of the Protectorate's heavy industry and arms factories. To this end, Nazi policy was relatively benign, initially at least. It granted workers considerable benefits such as free lunches in the factories, health and life insurance coverage, and promoted social events. In contrast to the occupation policy in Poland, Hitler said in 1939, "the German authorities are to avoid anything that is likely to provoke...mass actions."[49] These pragmatic policies were credited with preventing the growth of an armed resistance movement in the Protectorate. Throughout the occupation, the Czech Protectorate government repeatedly said that armed resistance threatened the survival of the country. Even Benes, from the exile government in Great Britain, said that the public should not provoke the Nazis into retaliation. Observe, he said, and forget nothing.[50] Nevertheless, in the early years of the Nazi occupation, there were displays of opposition. In October and November of 1939, in retaliation for student protests, the Nazi regime shot nine student leaders, sent 1,000 to the concentration camps, and closed all universities and technical high schools. The occupation policy was targeted repression and limited economic concessions.[51]

The frustration and resentment amongst the Czech people, generated by these German policies, are reflected in the following contemporary letter from an inhabitant of the Protectorate:

> Everything you look at has the hand of occupation upon it. You are ordered about by notices in the street, new notices and new orders, or perhaps just ridiculous and outrageous translations of your own notices continuously hit you in the face. Every time you pass these inscriptions you are forced to realize afresh that you are no longer master of your own country, no longer at home in your own home.

143

The changes penetrate into every detail of your daily life. You must see the names in your village written up in German, hear the names of the tram-stops shouted out in German ... Everyday brings something bad, and every new thing is always worse. You are permanently living in anxiety, permanently afraid of what the next day will bring...

You suffer personally. You cannot get proper food. It is not the rationing itself, which brings discomfort in every country, but rather the way your food is rationed and why ... Your restriction is not a necessary sacrifice which you are making for the sake of your own country, your army, your struggle. You are starving in order that the men you hate should be well fed...

It is the uncertainty—how long will it last, how much worse will it become and what will be the end of it all—which is so hard to bear. And always in the back of your mind, at the back of all these sufferings and uncertainties is the main trouble and biggest pain. You are absolutely helpless, there is nothing you can do...

The whole atmosphere is somehow unhealthy and all the details of normal life become abnormal. You are under permanent pathological tension.... Now [our people] live in a sort of organized madness.

Quoted from: *A German Protectorate: The Czechs under Nazi Rule*, Shiela Grant Duff.

Concerned, however, about the success of the Nazi policies and their demoralizing effect on the Czech people, the government in exile planned the assassination of SS Obergruppenführer Reinhard Heydrich, Deputy Protector of Bohemia and Moravia. The Czech underground opposed this measure, fearing retribution against civilians. They proposed instead that a leading Czech collaborator should be killed. The London exile government, however, sent several Czech agents who were able to ambush Heydrich, who subsequently died of his wounds. The German revenge was not long in coming. On June 10, 1942, the SS shot the entire male population of Lidice, burned the town to the ground, and sent the women to concentration camps where many perished. The children were sent to orphanages. The village of Lezaky was also destroyed on June 24, 1942, because a clandestine radio operated there. Thereafter, the Nazi regime arrested 3,188 Czechs, condemned 1,357 to death, and executed 679 for having supported the assassination.[52]

Please refer to: http://www.forgottenvoices.net for a photograph (#15) of Lidice after its destruction by the SS, June 1942.

Karl Hermann Frank, Heydrich's successor as head of the Nazi government in Bohemia/Moravia, issued the following order at that time: "All adult inhabitants are to be shot. All females are to be evacuated to a concentration camp. The children are to be collected together; those capable of Germanization are to be delivered to SS families in the Reich and the rest are to undergo a different education. The place (Lidice) is to be burnt and razed to the ground."[53]

Hitler originally wanted to shoot 10,000 Czechs but was dissuaded by the Protectorate government as it would adversely affect industrial production. Hitler agreed, saying that he believed "the Czechs to be industrious and intelligent workers." Martial law imposed after the assassination was lifted after only seven weeks. But by then the Nazi terror had destroyed the Czech underground and convinced the Czech population that armed resistance was futile.[54]

Although living conditions in Bohemia and Moravia were generally no less onerous than in the Reich, the loss of sovereignty was very galling to the Czech people. The Munich Agreement greatly embittered them. They lost a large part of their industrial base. Thus they were not only impoverished but robbed of their ability to sustain themselves economically. Their moral shock, however, was the greatest. They were abandoned, even felt betrayed by their allies. They were forced to accept concessions that, among others, destroyed their country's ability to militarily resist the Germans by having to abandon their frontier defenses.

Vaclav Havel, playwright, a leading dissident, author of the "Velvet Revolution" and first President of Czechoslovakia after the fall of the Communist Regime, summarized these feelings very succinctly:

> Even if they never speak of it, people have a very acute appreciation of the price they have paid for outward peace and quiet: the permanent humiliation of their human dignity. The less direct resistance they put up to it—comforting themselves by driving it from their mind and deceiving themselves with the thought that it is of no account, or else simply gritting their teeth—the deeper the experience etches itself in their emotional memory. The man who can resist humiliation can quickly forget it; but the man who can long tolerate it must long remember it. In actual fact, nothing remains forgotten. All the fear one has endured, the dissimulation one has been forced into, all the painful and degrading buffoonery, and worst of all, perhaps, the feeling of having displayed one's cowardice—all this settles and accumulates somewhere in the bottom of our social consciousness, quietly fermenting...

Left untreated the abscesses suppurate; the pus cannot escape from the body, and the malady spreads throughout the organism...

No wonder, then, when the crust cracks and the lava of life rolls out, there appear not only well-considered attempts to rectify old wrongs, not only searching for truth, and for reforms matching life's needs, but also symptoms of bilious hatred, vengeful wrath, and a feverish desire for immediate compensation for all the degradation endured.

Quoted from Dear Dr. Husak, in *Open Letters: Selected Writings, 1965–1990*, Vaclav Havel.

In February of 1943, all Czech men between the ages of sixteen and sixty-five and women between seventeen and forty-five were called up to do war work for and in the Reich. Less than 500,000 Czechs, however, were actually sent to Germany during the war as forced laborers.[55] Another form of abuse of the Nazi Germany regime was the seizure of 150,000 hectares of land belonging to Czechs and Jews which were then given to Sudeten Germans or to Volksdeutche from the East. There was not, however, a large resettlement of this latter population as in Poland.[56] Approximately 77,000 Czech Jews and 7,000 Roma died in the Holocaust. Some 36,000–55,000 non-Jewish Czechs were killed by the Nazis.[57]

The Expulsion of the Sudeten Germans Prior to the Potsdam Conference

The expulsions which took place prior to the Potsdam Conference, in August 1945, were centrally directed with expulsion orders issued as public proclamations by the local and district National Committees. The first wave of expulsions, the so-called "wild expulsions," were characterized by terrible cruelties against the German population, causing the death of tens of thousands of the inhabitants of the Sudetenland. Particularly affected were women, children, and old people. Men were generally absent as they were prisoners of war of the Allies. The Sudeten Germans were treated as an outlaw population. Their homes were seized or plundered, they were only allowed to be on the streets at a certain time, they had to wear white badges or armbands to distinguish themselves, they were forbidden to walk on the pavements and to use public transportation.[58] Czech statistics for this period, year 1945, report that there were 5,558 cases of suicide of Sudeten Germans.[59]

One of the worst cases of terror against the population was the "death" march of 20,000 German inhabitants from the city of Brünn (Brno), capital of Moravia, in the direction of Vienna. The German inhabitants of Brünn were often given only ten minutes to leave their homes. They were only allowed to take with them the clothes on their backs. On the march, they were subjected to many acts of violence and plunder. When they arrived on the frontier, the Austrian authorities prohibited them from entering that country. They therefore had to camp in open fields, grain silos, and other precarious shelters for weeks, some even for months. As elementary hygienic conditions were lacking, a typhus epidemic raged, claiming many lives. Many others died of hunger and exposure to the elements.[60]

No. 97

Report of the experiences of Frau Maria Zatschek, of Brünn. Original, undated, typewritten, 55 pages. Printed in part. The report is based on notes in a diary.

Temporary internment of the Germans of Brünn from 12 to 15 May 1945; expulsion by being made to march to the Austrian frontier on 31 May; conditions and events in the camp in Pohrlitz; removal of women and children to Austria via the camp Muschelberg near Nikolsburg, on 23 June 1945.

The author first describes her experiences before and after the entry of the Red Army into Brünn; the arrest of her husband by the Czechs; and the incidents when compulsory labor was introduced in Brünn. She then continues as follows:

The hours of the evening always bring the most bitter experiences. An order is being taken from house to house: "All Germans, including old people and babies, have to assemble in front of their houses, carrying provisions for three days."

This time we were all prepared for the worst. Divided up into men and women, we were accommodated in schools and it was midnight before it became quiet. We had to lie on the floor on the blankets which we had brought with us. Sleep was out of the question. Babies cried with hunger, their mother's milk had dried up because of the excitement; I saw one young mother trying to feed her tiny baby with bread soaked in water.

In the morning we heard that president Benes would pass through Brünn and that we had been locked up because we were not to be trusted.

During the morning all women had to line up in the yard, they were given numbers and were told: "Remember this, in case anything

147

should happen to the president, every tenth woman will be shot. And if anyone should dare to look out of the window, the sentence will be death."...

The days pass miserably, it would be better to have something to do. The children look unwell, hardly anybody has anything left to eat.... The school-mistress F. cries a great deal, and when I ask her what she is worried about, she points to her fourteen-year-old daughter—this pretty blond child had been raped several times... I feel so sorry for her that it is hard to bear, and I myself worry so much about the boys and Hans.

On the third day, we are being visited by Czech priests. They do not agree with our bad treatment. As there is a great shortage of food, everyone of us who has a little store left at home, is given permission to go and fetch it. It is done under heavy guard. The few things which we find will be used to provide one cooked meal per day. We are also to be given some light work. But suddenly everything changes again: we are released and sent home and can carry our potatoes back again... We are told all the time: "Just as you have treated the Jews." A great surprise was expecting us—a notice stuck to our front doors was welcoming us: "This house has been confiscated and expropriated."

We have ceased to be surprised, it is amazing how quickly one stops to care. Father has arrived before us, he—who has always taken pride in his appearance—looks wild like a robber...It should be mentioned, just by the way, that during our absence all the carpets have gone and many other things besides.

Frau Resi, who thrives on sensations, reports: "You had only just gone when two enormous lorries arrived. Two Russian women and two soldiers went into the flat and carried away whatever they could." She said that one of the Russian women had presented a comic sight, she dressed up with the leftovers from my wardrobe—an evening gown of brocade (which was too small for her), my Tyrolean hat and high rubber boots. How I would have loved to see this combination. Frau Resi behaves like a giggling girl, but when she has finished her story she suddenly exclaims: "1 had quite forgotten that we Czechs are not allowed any longer, under the threat of the death penalty, to talk to Germans." And she is gone.

In the porch, a Czech stranger is talking to the caretaker, who tells him: "I will call the mistress of the house." Having heard it, I go and say: "Here I am, what is the matter?" Without introducing himself, the stranger, a man of some 40 years of age, hands me a form from the housing office entitling him to a flat in our (former) house. He inspects both floors and decides in favor of the ground floor flat. I dare to ask humbly where I am supposed to live now. With great arrogance he tells me that this is of no interest to him... And he adds:

"You have another flat in the house, so what do you want?" He wants to move in tomorrow afternoon...

We are made to do heavy work. Always four women together have to load heavy cases with broken glass inside on lorries. The long way we have to carry them, the lifting and loading is much too strenuous for our weak physical condition. Having made a few journeys, one of my colleagues falls and injures her hand. We others try to work harder. I sprain the thumb of my right hand and also feel a pain in my groin. Getting permission from the foreman, I go to an ambulance. A young, very overworked doctor bandages my hand and, to my dismay, diagnoses a rupture. But this has its good side too, there is now a remark on my pass, that I am only fit for light work.

Sooner than usual we arrived at home, and this proves to be quite necessary. The new tenant is just arriving... He told me: "You can take personal things but nothing else. And I want to have good linen, first for two and later on for more beds, (whatever next?) because we have suffered bomb damage." I retort that we have been robbed by the "brothers."

Mr. Guerrilla helps to clear out cupboards with music scores and the library; we carry hundreds of music scores away, but in the middle of the work, the gentlemen from the Narodni Vybor (National Committee) arrive...

For two hours they make an inventory of our possessions. The gentlemen are surprised that so much is already missing. The built-in display cabinets cause remarks of delight... The Copenhagen land Goldscheid china and the rest of the Carlsbad set are being evaluated, their value is noted according to their market price...At last the big house has been thoroughly investigated, the committee has finished its job and I sign.

This commission consisted of a solicitor who was personally known to us, and three Civil Servants. They behaved very presumptuously and watched us closely. In spite of this, I was successful in hiding mother's jewelry, which I always carry on me in a small silver purse, below a window in the radiator of the central heating.

Late that evening, the guerrilla's father arrives to give his verdict on his son's new flat. With great arrogance he criticizes that the grand piano is out of tune...

In great baskets we carry volumes of song books, other books, Gerhard's cello music scores, the volumes of classics, dictionaries for several languages etc. into the entrance hall where we intend to store them. But all this, collected in many years with great care and enjoyment, was to be taken away from us. For what purpose? It does not matter to us, we only know that it was a great loss. Deliberately and consciously we are being tortured...

With several bundles we move into the upper floor. Father and my daughter have adapted themselves quite well to the new situation. But Mädi has one great regret—as she is so musical, it means a great loss to her to have no piano. But I am able to comfort her by saying: "If we ask the major nicely, he will allow you to play sometimes." I do not believe it.

Father is glad that he did take the trouble during the winter to deposit Hans' compositions in the safe of the savings bank. It would have been a great pity if these painstaking efforts had been lost. The score of one of his string quartets had got lost in the fire of the broadcasting studio when we had not been able to fetch it in time after its performance. Father's precautions helped us now to rescue the score of his hymn with orchestra, which had been given a prize in Vienna and was to have its first performance there. All the other works we had kept.

One piece of our existence after another is taken away from us...

Tonight we shall be able to sleep in peace. The "Major" is our protection.

No Russian will dare molest us.

The work outside the house has become somewhat easier, but it is still strenuous enough with my painful hand...We are very disturbed about the arrest, yesterday, of my friend Lise, who had been mistaken for a "Nazistin" (as the Czechs called it). Every day, something like this could happen to anyone of us.

When I return from work, father expects me already in the street. The old man is desperate. The upper floor has already been cleared out, bundles and suitcases with our possessions are lying in the entrance hall. We have to move nearer to heaven, and are now allowed only to live in the attic. A servant's room up there has running water and two beds; a larger room, used as a guest room, is quite homely with old furniture and has a comfortable bed and a built-in wardrobe. Father will be able to sleep here well. We shall be able to install an electric stove...

On the staircase we meet the new tenants. If we have to sacrifice our flat—then I am this time quite satisfied. Our plumber F. (a Czech), who has worked for us for many years, has moved in with his wife and two grown-up daughters. Due to the shortage of flats they have so far lived rather miserably. The woman is especially nice, the new home seems much too large to her and she would have been quite happy with two rooms. She is embarrassed by the whole idea of moving into our house...During the evening, several visitors come—people from the neighborhood who ask for "souvenirs." They are troublesome and grasping. In order to get rid of them, I give them some of the hidden things—and vases, bowls, cups changed their owner, it was sometimes like a market place. With great difficulty I salvage an electric heater and a thermos flask.

Today our nerves are very strained, too much has come over us.

When the major has finally installed himself, he starts to play the part of the grand gentleman. The beautiful flat may have gone to his head...

30/31 May 1945.

Today we had to wash a great amount of crockery in the hospital of the district health insurance, which has quite modern equipment. Then we had to clean the huge kitchen. Annemarie said she had never seen so much crockery in her life... We came home earlier today, and in the hall I met the major who again was studying our books... I remembered that in the attic we had hidden the electric railway of the children, and I presented it to him for his boy. I am worried about the chaos amongst our things. Together with father, I start to get some order into the documents which we have left. The children's school reports, Gerhard's certificate of the State examination in English, the doctor's degree of Hans, and my own testimonials I manage to find and I put them into the red case of our car documents.

For supper I boil some potatoes on the electric stove and add a tin of mussels which I happened to find. It makes a delicious meal. Poor father is nearly starving. We are very tired and looking forward to sleep. But it was to be quite different. We are roused by loud voices and a commission of seven men appear to tell us that we are to be expelled. We are asked to sign a form stating that we voluntarily surrender all our property to the Czech State. "Nepodepisi, nikdy" (I wlill not sign, never). I will never put my signature to a lie. Dr. V., a Czech lawyer, tells me ironically: "Aren't you determined," and adds: "You will have to walk. Don't take too much luggage—one dress, one pair of shoes, some underwear, one blanket, one cooking pot, that must be sufficient for you. And you are not allowed to take any Czech money, or any jewelry or objects of value." Whilst father fills in a number of forms, we others pack. The most essential things are put into rucksacks... One of the men supervises our packing... I am getting impatient because we have only half an hour left und have to be ready by then. Mädi is the first to be ready, she acts with great deliberation and I am astounded by her composure. Her toilet requisites have been packed nicely, and with them a book of stories and a tiny doll... With a little help on my part we are soon ready to go. But we have no money. All father has on him are 5 Czech crowns, somewhat too little for a long journey. I remind him that he has had 5,000 Reichsmark in the house and tell him: "Do look in the first-floor flat, the plumber is sure to let you in." We are successful in getting in, but poor father in all his excitement cannot find the key to the safe in the bedroom. So we have to leave this German money behind, which we would have been allowed to take. I am worried about the jewelry and do not know where to leave it. In the end I give it to the old mother of our housekeeper. She promises to keep it in safe custody. A golden pocket watch and an armlet I leave with the plumber. Now we are ready and are being called. The sight we face outside the house cannot be described. Nobody had been prepared for this march. Bundles are carried on backs, prams are overloaded, children's pushcarts are piled high with the most incredible things. The children are tired and crying—it is a dreadful sight.

As this last evening in our hometown is wonderfully warm, the Czechs do not want to miss the spectacle and have all come into the street. They sit on garden fences and they look as if they were enjoying themselves at a fair. We have to wait until the different groups start to move. One of the neighbors comes to us und says: "You see, that's what you have done to the Jews." I cannot hold back and say: "Mr.Counsellor, please don't make yourself ridiculous; for nearly twenty years we have talked normally to each other. Who was so pleased some years ago when the Jews were persecuted—you or I?" He disappears in shame.

A last look into the garden—the peonies are in full bloom. Farewell, nice house, farewell, beautiful garden. The housekeeper takes leave from us, the old snake in the grass. Yet wishing us all the best and giving Mädi something to drink. I feel how happy she is—she is crying with one eye and laughing with the other one. "You have given us very little, madam (look at this: suddenly she addresses me like this again), couldn't I have the fur stoles?" (She saw that I had packed three.) I hand her one but add maliciously: "Now you have more than I have, isn't that anything?" But she says: "Please, these are not real souvenirs, the old gentleman has a Toledo rug on top of his suitcase, you don't need that any more." Father tells me to give her the rug and not to speak to her any more. But she still imparts the information to me that we are being sent to Russia, that some of the leaders, however, are said to be in favor of our expulsion to Austria. We are being lined up in rows four abreast: children, women of all ages, a few men, but only old ones, and here and there a disabled young man. A young doctor with only one leg is being supported by a boy...

Our grocer had always been nice to us and we had also been good customers...He was one of the most peaceful persons and had now been put into uniform, which did not fit him at all. He has been made into one of our guards and he tells me: "Don't be too frightened. There will be shots, but if all behave they will be fired only into the air." One can see that he has not been born to do this kind of job...

My memories are rudely interrupted by shouts: "Jdeme, jdeme," this is the shout which is to drive us on—let's go, let's go, faster, faster! Slowly we seem to get into our stride. There is one unpleasant stop.

Russian soldiers set upon us to take away all the jewelry if any can be found.

Father groans under his load of two suitcases, and I must confess that for the first time I am not patient. I have warned him not to take so much. At the age of nearly 86 you have to husband your strength even if you are in good health. Unfortunately we cannot help him. Mädi is carrying her small overfull rucksack, coat and bag. I will rather not talk about myself, because I am laden like a camel: one rucksack on the back, one in front, a leather suitcase with documents, an eiderdown, cushions, electric cooker, and other things which in the haste of our departure had seemed essential…Walking so quickly, father trips over a loose shoelace, which had not been tied properly during the rush, he is immediately separated from us. In spite of all the revolver shooting, the desired order cannot be maintained, the old and sick cannot keep up, and we proceed slower than had been planned.

We have to stop in the Eichhorngasse. Our certificates of domicile are being controlled at the police station there, and our names and dates registered. This procedure lasts for hours. It is already dawn when we are ready to continue the march. In the meantime, some wicked scoundrels (I cannot express myself otherwise) have been robbing us. Father, whom we have found in the meantime, loses one suitcase. We lose our cutlery and a pair of scissors—all that is left to us now is a silver spoon with initials. Piece by piece, everything melts away from us.

"Mother, I am terribly hungry."—"Poor Mädi, I have so little; our sole provisions are a small loaf of bread. Please don't be sad."—We divide it carefully into three parts and father gets his scanty ration as well. We do not even know whether we shall remain together. Annemarie gets a spoonfull of malt extract in addition, to keep up her strength.

At last we are lined up again, this time in wider rows. And we have to run now, unless we want to risk being beaten with whips. Machine-guns go into action. Father falls behind after a short time, others lose their children. All the time the shout goes up "jdeme, jdeme." These shouts sound like gramophone records. The second record sounds: "Faster, you lazy good-for-nothing bunch. These are the 'great' Germans." In this way we reach the central cemetery outside the town. A break has to be made here because many old people and children can no longer keep it up… It is decided to transport the very old and the disabled on lorries. My father is also allowed to get on. That relieves us of one worry, but we are not told when and where we would meet him again.

By a special caprice of fate, as soon as father is seated on the lorry, he finds the key to the safe with 5,000 Reichsmarks. The old gentleman is

153

near to tears, but there is no time for sentimentalities, the overloaded vehicle starts already to move off.

I quickly repack the rucksacks. In the rush of our departure they have not been packed properly and they are very uncomfortable to carry. I also want to change my linen shoes with wooden soles, which have served me well during the working days, to the only pair of decent shoes I still have left. When I just want to put on the second shoe, it falls into the dirty ditch alongside the road, and whilst I look for it the order is given to move on. I receive a blow with a whip and have to continue .the march with one brown and one black shoe…

Greater marching speed is demanded now. "Look, Mummy, it is going quite well," my brave girl says to me and moves her legs which have got so very thin, faster and faster. Since we have shared so many sorrows, she has become a friend and means everything to me. In her solid, but nearly too tight boots, she marches on and even tries to comfort a still younger boy who quietly cries with hunger. His mother has no time to look after him, she pushes a wide pram with twin babies and leads a three-year-old girl with the other hand…

The roads are in a terrible condition. The last fight for Brünn had taken place here, the peaceful villages like Bohonitz and Gerspitz are hardly recognizable. The estate of my father-in-law lies alongside the Bohonitzer road. Although we did not pass it directly, we think we can see the house having remained intact. How much we would like to go there! But it is possible that they had to leave even before us. We have to go on without a pause. Many start now to get rid of their luggage and I, too, can no longer carry everything…

The fields start to look like a bazaar with nice clothes and linen, and a large selection of eiderdowns, cushions, suitcases, cookers and many other things, inviting the Czech population to come and choose. We march till noon, but no longer in rank and file, even the leaders have got tired. Some sickly women, especially if they have something wrong with their heart, just lie down in the ditches. They do not care any longer what is happening to them. A kick does not bother anybody any more, and quite a few have become so lethargic that they would not mind even being shot. Shortly before we reach Raigern, we have our first case of death.

In Raigern we are allowed to rest. I put Annemarie on my coat. All the children sleep, the babies whimper with hunger before they go to sleep. Some of the few mothers who are blessed in having milk in spite of their malnutrition, help mercifully to breast-feed strange children. Most of the grown-ups do not find any sleep although they are tired out and have spent a sleepless night…

Continuously we are being searched. Apart from money and jewelry, which is still being found here and there, the search is for cameras. The bad conscience of the Czechs in perpetrating such a crying shame against humanity, seems to occupy the leaders, especially in view of public opinion abroad. They therefore announce that the owner of any camera will be shot. No pictorial record shall be allowed to exist of the outrage of this expulsion...

Wrapped up in my thoughts I did not hear a well-known voice, until I look up and see my friend Lise. It is a sad meeting. She has experienced a hard fate in the dreaded College, which has been turned into a specially strict prison for political suspects... she had been arrested and had spent nearly four weeks in prison until her innocence had been proved. That had been yesterday. She had not even been allowed to go home, to prepare herself for our march. Exactly as she had left her home weeks ago, with two handkerchiefs and an almost empty shopping hag, she was now going into an unknown future... As an innocent woman, together with many others, she had to suffer inhuman physical torture. As if these sadists (I cannot call them anything else) had been shy of the light of day, they always tortured by night. The mothers of soldiers were in a specially bad position. They were made responsible for the fact that their sons had gone to war. Czech women who had married German soldiers were also tortured. Many had died of their injuries...

All this my poor friend had to suffer after fate had taken everything away from her, which she had valued. She had no tears left. She asks sympathetically after Hans and father; she likes them both very much. To divert her somehow from her sorrows, I tell her about us, we also have not been on a bed of roses. Strange as it may sound, she hopes that Hans will get into Russian captivity. "For heaven's sake, not with the Czechs!" she cries, and she had never known anything about national hatred, just as little as we ourselves...

To the left and right of me a great deal of cursing against the Hitler regime is going on. I do not want to waste energy on talk of this kind, my conviction has always been that the use of force and brutality is wrong... I am surprised about the inconsistency of so many former enthusiastic supporters of the regime. There really had been some completely blinded people who still expected victory during the winter. They had not wanted to admit the mistakes of this ruthless leadership, although they must have seen them. There are only two possible explanations for this—either these people, for opportunist reasons, pretended to be blind and deaf, or they were not quite right in their heads. And there had been many of those. Now, suddenly, everything had been bad, most former supporters of Hitler condemned him now. One has to judge this as the basest opportunism.

A good sleep has refreshed the children. Annemarie sacrifices her story book with a heavy heart, but it means that she has now to carry one piece less. With the rested children, we make better headway, which is necessary as we still have 30 kilometers to go...The road seems endless. During the afternoon a thunderstorm breaks and we take shelter in an empty barn. After this the roads are muddy; quite a few people have to walk barefoot now as their shoes are worn out. In spite of all the difficulties we are getting on...It is soon evening but we are still a considerable distance from Pohrlitz, the place we are aiming for.

The leaders are worn out too and their zeal has evaporated. Natural human sentiments appear—young Czechs carry children on their backs; they are helpful now and don't chase us any longer. The individual can be good, but the fanatical leadership in both camps leads all those astray who are unable to form their own opinions and to judge for themselves. One could feel sorry for such people if their actions did not cause so much harm...

The stronger ones amongst us, who, in addition, have not to carry children, might still manage to reach the goal of our wishes today. But the children—hungry, wet through, tired out—can go no further... The guard allows us, at our own responsibility, to camp in a little wood. Through the mist we can see the lights of Pohrlitz, it looks to me like an oasis. It is a small group that wants to spend the night here on the soggy ground. The leaves of the trees are so wet that they no longer protect us from the rain. Our greatest worry is the children. In spite of the darkness I find an earth hole. I spread out the fur coat, wrap it round my daughter and cover this bundle of misery with raincoat and blanket...Two women with babies in wickerwork prams are desperate. It has again started to rain and the babies are lying in puddles—they have no longer the strength to cry and just whimper quietly. There are some women amongst us whom I know personally; one of them, Frau Brand of Brünn, is very old and complains of cramps in her legs. As it gets very cold during the night, her pains increase, but nobody is able to help her. The other one is the young wife of the Moravian composer Willi Österreicher. She is extremely distressed, she does not know in which part of the world her husband is and fears for his life. She has salvaged his latest composition, a handwritten score, and has to see now that the wetness in her rucksack has made the notes illegible... During the previous year he had been conducting two great orchestral concerts. It gets bitterly cold and we are wet through...

When dawn comes the rain stops at last. Annemarie has woken up refreshed and warmed. The two babies, although obviously cold, look a bit happier. We all get ready to reach our destination as soon as possible. Our progress is made difficult by water, puddles and the heavy clay of the soil. During the morning we arrive in Pohrlitz. Father is waiting for us in the square, I notice how haggard he looks. He had been very worried about us and lives now in a badly damaged school, where it is cold because the windows are missing. He has no bread, neither have we...

Toward noon we are directed into barracks. We have to put our blankets on the dirty floor as no broom is available. There is no chance to wash. The whole atmosphere is depressing. As we are non-smokers, I can use some cigarettes to exchange for some bread from a baker, and we also manage to find an empty bottle with which we can fetch water from a well to wash ourselves. In one of the empty gardens we can hide behind a wooden fence in order to do this, my daughter has brought some soap. In spite of the miserable "bed," we sleep well in the feeling that we have again a roof over our heads.

When we left Brünn, I had managed to put into my coat pocket a little baptismal locket of silver, an heirloom from my great-grandmother. I barter it now for bread at the grocer's. Father sacrifices his wedding ring for some dripping. The worst is over. In the fields, we collect some old potatoes and roast them on hot bricks. But soon the nutritional deficiency has its effects, an epidemic of paratyphoid breaks out. Hundreds die during the first few days. We also caught this painful illness. We had to line up for hours to get washing water, and it became too dangerous to drink water at all. In this difficult situation, everyone became helpful.

A few days later the Russians started to ambush the women and to invade the camp by night. We heard shots and screams and cries of fear from another barrack. My heart beat wildly. The Russians pushed the Czech camp guards aside and a great deal of evil happened during this night. Old men who wanted to protect the women were knocked down. Annemarie covered me with a cushion, I was nearly smothered, but it protected me. A young woman had a hemorrhage and died in the morning.

During the following night, the guards had been strengthened and the Russians had to withdraw. There were more cases of illness. The old people were lying in apathy on their miserable beds—terribly hard although new straw had been brought. The death rate amongst the old increases daily, and the babies perish too. At last the camp is getting provisions so that a soup can be provided daily. We are so hungry that nobody hesitates to take old bread from someone who is dying. My father is also in a bad state, but Annemarie is worst of all.

There is only one nurse in the camp, Frau Schubert. She is overworked and has very few means to help. She gives me some medicinal carbon, but she thinks Annemarie is a hopeless case. I am unbelievably shocked and implore her urgently to help somehow, but she has nothing to give me, which might save my child. She thinks that it is useless to torture anyone who is so desperately ill and that it is better to let the poor weakened child go to sleep. My desperation reaches its limits, but I still manage to restrain myself so that father shall not realize the seriousness of the situation. I search in vain for some way out and have at last an idea which might bring salvation:

I want to seek help outside. In the meantime, evening has come and I am very worried because at this time of day, in spite of any pass, it is prohibited to leave the camp. But worry about my darling gives me another idea: I offer our last cigarettes to the camp commandant, whom I find full of understanding.

As the gate cannot be opened at this time of day, he allows me to climb over the wall and offers to wait for me at its lowest point so that I shall not be shot by the camp guards on my return. The adventure is successful and I hurry to the chemist who is nearby. Unfortunately he has closed already. I knock, ring the bell, but nobody comes. I start to shout and soon the chemist opens. He explains that he has to be careful because of the Russians and that he therefore had to let me wait. He is a German and expects his expulsion at any time. He is very willing to help. I ask for opium and he gives me a tiny bottle. "You cannot give anything better to the child in her condition." I thank him with all my heart and run back.

I arrive in our barrack without hindrance and find Annemarie with a high temperature. In the light of a candle I force some drops between her lips and nurse her under extremely difficult circumstances. I sacrifice my rubber coat as a bed sheet and give her once more drops during the night. An improvement can be recognized and the temperature goes down. I do not yet dare rejoice, but I begin to hope. During the next hours she improves considerably.

Women with sickly children were given permission to leave the camp and to live in the town. Together with my girl I am placed in a house that had formerly belonged to Jews. In the average-sized dining room, 22 persons had to be accommodated. Annemarie and I slept on a table, the other twenty persons on straw on the wooden floor. Father has to remain in the camp. We are given a pass so that we can visit the old man every day. My girl has still to rest a great deal although she has surprisingly quickly recovered from the attacks. Now father becomes seriously ill. A woman from Brünn, whom we knew very well, is looking after him. He has lost his spare set of underwear, there is no water to wash anything, the lavatories are in a terrible condition and we all become more and more neglected...

Father deteriorates visibly and there is not much we can do to be kind to him.

15 June 1945

Today I went to the priest and begged him to come and visit my father. He was very willing, but he asked me not to talk about it as he had not been given permission. He will also have to come in civilian clothes and without ministrants. At the appointed hour of the afternoon, we meet in the barrack. The hot sun makes the smell inside even more unpleasant. The doors are wide open and a field of large red poppies provides a background of shining color. The patients are lying on foul smelling straw.

Father is conscious but unable to talk. He receives the holy sacraments and pious as he had lived he prepares himself for his last hour. Annemarie acts as ministrant. Most of the patients find solace and thank the priest, who gladly performed his duty. On our knees we all pray with him. We shall always remember this solemn hour in the midst of all this misery.

16 June 1945.

Twenty persons die during the following night, amongst them my father.

"Gerhard's hand is bleeding... " were his last whispered words. I was not present when he died. He went to sleep peacefully. Only today were we allowed to see his body—nobody had bothered to close his eyes, and together with the others he is buried somewhere. I never manage to find his grave. We do not feel aggrieved, we are glad in the knowledge that the nearly 86-year-old man has found his peace. On one of the following days the priest celebrates mass for him and we are able to attend.

We have to do everything to strengthen our health. Annemarie is daily getting thinner. As the German farmers have not been expelled yet, we have a chance to earn a little by helping them. But we have to be careful with our food, our stomachs have become so unaccustomed to food that they revolt against any more substantial meal. We find some empty paper bags in a disused paper mill and use them as clean sheets on which to make noodles from flour that we have acquired, rolling out the dough with a bottle. Every one of us women brings something from somewhere. We are allowed to cook in the kitchen and to collect firewood ourselves. This is how we try to exist, waiting and waiting all the time for some solution...

There is less strictness now, we can leave the houses without permission.

On our short walks, we search in vain for the graves. We are much too weak to go further afield.

The author goes on to report a conversation with her child, describes the search for food in the neighborhood of Pohrlitz, and continues as follows: During the morning, whilst I am pegging up our few pieces of washing in the yard, the command is given: "Pack quickly in order to be transported away." Glad as we are, departure on washing day is not quite ideal. So I dare to ask humbly at what time we would have to report. The answer is a blow with the butt of a rifle into my face, which costs me the loss of some teeth. We stuff the wet washing into our rucksacks and then wait for three hours for the hay-carts which

159

are to take us away. In the boiling sun and in very uncomfortable positions we pile on to the carts, and departure is postponed even then. It seems luxurious to us to be able to ride. Our destination is to be the Muschelberg near Nikolsburg. The castle looks beautiful against to-day's steel-blue sky, and Nikolsburg, the little Southern-Moravian town, lies in front of us in all its charm, surrounded by vineyards on the hills...

Muschelberg was a women's prison. This camp to which we were directed was better equipped. 1t consisted of low houses furnished with bedsteads and boards—everything else was missing. The very efficient doctor of law, Frau Grete Schindler, and a finance official from Brünn took over the administration of the camp, working hand in hand with the Czechs. We all helped and organized a kindergarten, because we had to go out and work in the fields and vineyards. The younger women especially were regularly employed. In return, regular though simple meals were provided, prepared by the older women.

It is a shock to realize how few we are now, thousands died in Pohrlitz, and for the rest of our lives we shall always remember it as our death-camp. Here, too, many meet their end. We ourselves learn that my dear father-in-law died of heart failure whilst still in Brünn. We are deeply moved...

Nobody can fail to notice that the atmosphere seems to be changing—the Czech camp commandants are getting polite and behave like normal human beings. Orders must have come from above. Repatriation is being allowed if one has Czech relatives, but only if one gives up all claims to property and rights, and returns as a simple number on the labor market. Only a few are prepared to accept this solution. To my amazement I find amongst them a kindergarten teacher who for a long time had been working for us in the afternoons...We try to persuade her to stay with us. We are told that we shall be sent to Vienna and we have relatives there who will not leave us in the lurch. I seriously advise her not to return. But she wants to rely on a sister who is married to a Czech. With tears she takes leave of us. These obedient slaves are even being provided with transport. They want to get rid of us too. The camp is apparently needed for military purposes. So we are told that we must go to Austria, otherwise we would be sent to Russia. It is childish of them to even try and use this threat as a means of pressure—no pressure is needed, we are looking forward to Austria, to which we were always bound by many ties...

23 June 1945.

We pack in haste, the Muschelberg has to be cleared quickly. An unfriendly morning makes leave-taking easy. At a quick pace we reach the frontier station where we have to suffer another search of our miserable possessions. Whoever looks suspicious is being bodily searched so that the Czech State should not suffer the loss of a single piece of jewelry or of a few Czech crowns. My girl and I have to show so little that our search is soon over. The little girl sits so shyly and miserably on her rucksack that the Czech frontier guard calls to her: "Go on, run to Austria." This was the last sentence in Czech which we heard, it was our farewell to the Czech Republic.

The author ends her report with some remarks summing up her experiences and observations in the Czechoslovak Republic.

Please refer to: http://www.forgottenvoices.net, for a photograph (#16) of the transport of expelled Sudeten Germans from the Buchau Camp 1946.

The Czech government encouraged violence against the German minority in order to accelerate their immediate flight and reduce the numbers that would have to be deported subsequently. The Benes government fanned the fires of hatred in the early days after liberation. In May 1945, Benes himself called for the expulsion of the country's Germans. Another high government official, Prokop Dtrina, Czech Minister of Justice, said, "We must begin immediately, this very moment to expel the Germans from our lands. We must use all possible means—nothing can be allowed to cause us to stop or even to hesitate." The communist leaders were in the vanguard of encouraging wild retributions. Communist Party leader Klement Gottwald stated on the radio that local authorities should immediately commence the severe punishment of the Germans.[61] Although it is evident that the entire Czech nation appears to have supported these wild expulsions, the Communist Party strongly encouraged them, thus increasing the dominance of the Party in the immediate postwar Czechoslovakia.[62]

One of Czechoslovakia's leading liberals, Pavel Tigrid, subsequently commented on this state of affairs:

> The "revolutionary retaliation" did not become "unstoppable." It was carefully thought out, prepared, and imported from Moscow by the new postwar rulers. It was decreed from above by an unelected power elite that did not bother to ask anyone—certainly not the Czech people who at every step it invoked and praised—about anything. Until the people finally said to themselves: if the bosses are going to play that tune, why shouldn't we dance?

As quoted from *National Cleansing; Retribution against Nazi Collaborators in Postwar Czechoslovakia*, Benjamin Frommer. (Pavel

Tigrid was a renowned Czech journalist and writer in exile in London during the War broadcasting for the BBC. He returned to Czechoslovakia after the War but came into conflict with the Communist authorities. Forced into exile again, he broadcast for Radio Free Europe. He returned after the "Velvet Revolution," and became a close advisor to President Vaclav Havel.)

In the course of this first wave of expulsions, between 700,000 and 800,000 Sudeten Germans were removed from Czechoslovakia, mainly from the Eastern Sudetenland, the industrial parts of the north-east and from Southern Moravia, including the city of Brünn (Brno). Of these, 150,000 were sent to Austria. Many were sent to concentration camps to do compulsory labor, pending their subsequent expulsion. Living and working conditions were terrible in these camps. The highest death rate was amongst the young, small children and babies, and the old. The latter could not work outside the camps and thus could not supplement their rations. The climax of the "wild expulsions" was reached in June and July of 1945.[63]

The Expulsion of the Sudeten Germans after the Potsdam Conference

At the Potsdam Conference, the Allies confirmed their agreement for the expulsion of the Germans from Czechoslovakia but insisted that the "wild expulsions" had to cease. Proper preparations had to be made in the several Allied zones of occupation to receive these refugees. It had to be an orderly process. This meant that the Czech government had to interrupt their actions, which greatly concerned them, as they feared the Western Allies would renege on their promise to support these expulsions. The Czechs began to immediately expand their detention and holding camps for the German expellees, increasing them by seventy-five in Bohemia, twenty-nine in Moravia, and three in Slovakia.[64]

In August 1945, the Czechoslovak government advised the Allied Control Council that 2.5 million Germans remained to be expelled. The Allies then decided to accept 1,750,000 in the American zone of occupation, and 750,000 in the Soviet zone. About 10 percent of the total were to be transferred before the end of that year, but, as it turned out, the organized expulsions only started in January of 1946.

According to agreements reached between the Allies and the Czech government, all expellees were to have sufficient clothing for the trip. They were to be allowed to take with them luggage up to 50 kilos (about

110 lbs.) as well as 1,000 Reichsmarks (the official exchange rate was 4.2 to the 1 US$, but by this time the Reichsmark was greatly devalued). They were to be furnished with sufficient provisions for a three-day trip and to receive hot food throughout the journey. Transports were to be arranged in groups averaging 1,200 persons in forty railway carriages. Lastly, families were not to be separated.[65]

The earlier transports consisted of people already in the camps. By February, four trains were sent daily to Germany with 4,800 people. However, the plundering of expellees' possessions continued, though less intensely than previously, and many of the agreements for their well-being were not kept. Consequently, due to American intervention, a new agreement was made in April 1946 between the Czech authorities and the Allied Control Council to reinforce humanitarian transfer conditions. As a result of these measures, the conditions of the expulsion of the Sudeten Germans improved appreciably in May 1946.[66]

No. 99

Report of the experiences of Dr. Karl Grimm, doctor of medicine in Brüx. Original, dated 4 December 1950, typewritten, 60 pages. Printed in part.

Experiences and impressions of a doctor of medicine in the expulsion assembly camp in Nieder Georgenthal near Brüx.

In the first chapter of his report, the author describes his experiences and impressions during his employment as a police doctor with the Czech criminal police in Brüx from May to July 1945. He describes in detail the wave of suicides amongst the German population (1); the raids of the Svoboda army in the industrial areas of northern Bohemia; the rule of terror of the re-established Czech administration; and the arrest, internment, call-up to compulsory labor, expropriation, expulsion, and deportation of the Germans. This is followed by a description of the author's own arrest on 1 August 1945 and of the general conditions and his experiences as a camp doctor in several labor and concentration camps in the district of Brüx, especially in "KT 28" (punishment camp), "IT 27" (internment camp), in the youth and women's camp 17/18 near Maltheuern, and in "UT 25" (accommodation camp) near Nieder Georgenthal. The report ends with the following description of the expulsion measures in the district of Brüx:

In 1946, camp no. 22 near Nieder Georgenthal was turned into an evacuation camp, from which the first transports were dispatched in April 1946. I had been in camp no. 27 and, when this had been closed, in camp no. 28, from where I was now transferred as camp doctor to no. 22, in order to deal with these transports. I then spent several weeks in camp no. 22 and helped to dispatch several transports. Afterwards, I was sent back to camp no. 27. At the end of May, I was transferred to camp no. 25, and as this camp adjoined camp no. 22, I had from then onwards continuous contact with the evacuation camp. At the end of August, I was sent to the punishment camp in Striemitz to undergo my first interrogation by the examining judge—after one-and-a-quarter year of imprisonment. Its result was that I was immediately declared free for expulsion without any preliminary proceedings by the People's Court. At the end of my odyssey through various Czech camps, I now returned again to camp no. 22. Therefore I know this evacuation camp and the procedure connected with the evacuation from my own work as well as from repeated observations.

Camp no. 22 had been separated from camp no. 25 only in 1946, when it was set up as evacuation camp directly subordinated to the District National Committee (Okresni Narodni Vybor), whilst camp no. 25 was attached to the hydration factory. It was a camp consisting of the usual barracks, surrounded by a single barbed-wire fence and guarded by soldiers. The evacuees were placed under quarantine and had to have a pass to leave the camp. The inspector of the criminal police, Naprstek, acted as evacuation commissioner and was in charge of the evacuation of the whole district of Brüx. He was a die-hard Czech for whom the German only counted when he had been evacuated; he was credited with the saying: the only good German is the evacuated German. The Czech personnel consisted of soldiers, gendarmes, finance officers, administrators and stokers. The office staff consisted entirely of Germans who had been kept back from the transports and who were doing the whole work on their own. The kitchen staff consisted first of Czechs, but after these had committed too many frauds, they were replaced by Germans.

From all the towns, villages and camps in the district Brüx, the Germans were brought to the evacuation camp. From the settlements and camps of the coal fields, they came by lorries; from the peasant villages of the Erzgebirge and the Brüxer Land, they also came by horse and cart. Piled high with people, suitcases, boxes, sacks and bundles, the vehicles entered the camp. They first drove to the office, where the people had to get off and register. This registration was carried out in order of arrival of the vehicles in the camp, the personal data of everyone were taken down and numbers issued. During this procedure they were asked whether they had relatives still kept back in some other camp with whom they wished to be jointly evacuated. It was quite common that false relationships were stated, young girls in particular, claimed to be engaged to some relative or friend held in some punishment camp. If the person in question had not been detained for some particular reason, this kind of claim was generally successful and many a poor devil was able to leave the punishment camp through these acts of charity. There was always a moving reunion when these shabby and emaciated figures arrived from the punishment camps. Naprstek must have been aware of these practices, but in this respect he showed generosity, his only concern being the actual evacuation.

After registration the vehicles went on to a different barrack, where the luggage was unloaded and checked by finance officers. The people stood there with their last possessions salvaged from looting, raids, searches and confiscations. The Potsdam Agreement had stipulated 50 kilograms of luggage but with regard to the first transports, the finance officers had not been petty in cases where this limit was exceeded. So far as the evacuees had been inmates of camps, they did not have much left anyway and not much was taken away, but those coming straight from their homes, often had a surprising amount of luggage, which sometimes meant a rich booty. The finance officers mainly took money, cigarettes, objects of value and furs, and they undoubtedly lined their own pockets. Luggage control over, the vehicles went to another barrack where medical inspection was carried out. It consisted of a superficial search for lice, and for signs of skin diseases and venereal diseases. Everyone was dusted with the American disinfectant powder DDT. Those who suffered from lice or itch, had to be retained and were transferred to the camp at Rössel, from where they returned cured after ten to fourteen days, to be evacuated with the next transport. The order for someone to be retained was every time a difficult decision, since the evacuees protested strongly and insisted on being evacuated with their original transport. Yet we had to be very strict in this respect, as the Czechs were extremely worried lest the Americans refused to accept one of the transports on medical grounds. Examining the women proved to be more difficult, as many objected to mass examinations, felt shy and got excited. It was also quite a job to look for nits in their long hair. We preferred to leave these examinations to women. Eventually the people were detailed into barracks and allocated accommodation. This was again done in the order in which the families had finished their reception procedure.

Accommodation was very primitive, the rooms consisted of four bare walls and bunks with straw mattresses alongside which some of the luggage was dumped—in view of their short stay, people did not bother to unpack their few household belongings. The better barracks were those in front, they had quite friendly little rooms with a certain amount of comfort and were mainly used as living quarters for the German personnel of the camp. The barracks in the back had large rooms accommodating 40 to 50 people each. Filled with such a crowd and so many bunks, suitcases, boxes, sacks and bundles, they reminded one of emigration camps on the lower deck of overseas liners. There were two kitchens in the camp, one for the Czech and German personnel and the other for the evacuees. The kitchen for the evacuees was the worst I had ever seen in any camp, but the effect was not as disastrous as it might have been, since most people had money and could get food from outside the camp. Even so, the conditions in this kitchen became so intolerable that its Czech staff later had to be replaced by Germans.

Each railway train consisted of 40 wagons with 30 persons in each, all together 1,200 persons. We therefore had to get 1,200 people together for every transport. During the first weeks this took us four to five days. These 1,200 persons were then divided into 40 groups of 30 members each and given the number of their wagon. A leader was appointed for each wagon, and a transport leader for the whole party. After that everybody was personally paid 1,000 Reichsmarks, the transport leader was given the necessary documents, and everybody had to submit again to two searches, one of his luggage and the other a medical examination. All this took time and it therefore lasted ten to fourteen days during the first weeks before a transport was ready for dispatch. At last came the day for departure. In the morning of this day all the luggage was piled up on the road alongside the barbed wire fence—in piles according to wagons. For this purpose, the numbers of wagons had been hung up on the wire fence (each one with an appropriate wreath of leaves). In the course of the morning this luggage was fetched by lorries. In the afternoon the people had to assemble in groups according to their wagons and were lined up in formation. Then, all the 1,200 people started to move... The long procession was followed by a lorry, which picked up those who were unable to walk. The train was boarded at the goods station of Nieder Georgenthal, and the same afternoon the train left for Brüx, where it stopped, for unknown reasons, till late at night. In the darkness of the night the train left Brüx in the direction of Eger, and went from there over the Bavarian frontier into the American occupation zone of Germany...

Since the Czechs had discontinued their "wild evacuations" after the Potsdam Conference at the end of August 1945, they only started the "humane evacuations," according to the stipulations of the Potsdam Agreement during 1946 (2). During the wild evacuations of 1945, Negerdörfel near Brüx had been the evacuation camp; during the humane evacuations of 1946 camp no. 22 near Nieder Georgenthal became the evacuation camp. Only the first transport of the humane evacuation in January 1946 left already from camp no. 22. Evacuation took place for the entire district, taking towns, villages and camps in turn; within the towns, it was done in order of streets. On the day before evacuation, the individual families were handed their evacuation orders by the evacuation commission. On the day itself, they had to clear their homes within half-an-hour and were allowed to take 50 kilograms of luggage. The evacuation commission provided a lorry and a commissioner accompanied them to the evacuation camp...the transport traveled to Eger and over the Bavarian frontier into the American occupation zone of Germany. Up to the end of May, the transports went to the American zone—and up to that time, each person received 1,000 Reichsmarks. From the beginning of June, the transports went to the Russian zone and every person was then only given 500 Reichsmarks (3). Later on, when the staff of the camp had developed a certain routine, the different jobs were organized into one single process, and the setting-up and dispatch of a transport took only five days. From then onwards, every five days a transport ... traveled to Bodenbach and over the frontier to Saxony in the Russian occupation zone of Germany. In the district of Dux evacuation had been concluded by the end of August 1946 and the last Germans of this district had to be attached to a transport of the district of Brüx. Evacuation of the district of Brüx was concluded in October 1946; the last transport left camp no. 22 in the middle of October, whilst the transport which was to be dispatched at the end of October, was kept back in the camp and not evacuated. It is easy to work out, on the basis of this information, that during the year 1946, 34 transports left the district of Brüx, evacuating over 40,000 Germans in the process of the humane evacuation of 1946.

Human beings stood in front of me who had lost everything that had been dear and of value to them and had given purpose to their lives. Now, with empty hands, they went into an uncertain future. Many of them were personally known to me—doctors, lawyers, business people, farmers, artisans, laborers... Then I remembered some incidents with highly pregnant women. We were not really supposed to include them into transports, but either these women lied to us, wanting to go, or else we allowed ourselves to be persuaded because we did not want to be too hard on women in that condition. As a result, we always had women start their labor in the camp. It was amazing how smoothly and easily their babies were born under these primitive conditions. In their impatient excitement and expectation the women did their best and I was often called to premature deliveries, when I had to leave everything else and run... With regard to young people, it was not surprising, that amongst the boys the excitement of adventure surpassed their fears of an uncertain future, young girls dreamt of the chance to be able to dance and visit the cinema once again. Even the grown-ups were no exception; farmers considered that it might be an advantage for them to emigrate to Canada or the Argentine, as there would be little prospect for them to own land in Germany; townspeople reflected in which part of Germany they might find relatives or friends and where they would best be able to establish themselves again.

There could be no doubt, that these people wanted to leave at all cost and join the transport, fearing nothing more, than to be excluded from it. There were some who were quite prepared to give part of their possessions and even pay money in order to be included. This went so far that experts, given the choice by the Czechs between a well-paid job and evacuation chose to be evacuated; skilled workers, retained by Czech firms as irreplaceable were desperately unhappy about it. It annoyed the Czechs that the Germans did not leave with a heavy heart and that they made no attempt to conceal this. They therefore began to paint a black picture of Germany, saying that the country had been destroyed and will not recover for the next hundred years, that starvation ruled there and that the Germans in the Reich would not welcome the Sudeten Germans. But our people had had too many bad experiences and were glad to escape from the hell of Czechoslovakia. Whoever falls amongst robbers, is glad in the end, if he can escape with his bare life. They had nothing more to lose, everything had gone anyhow and they could only hope to gain. No matter what their life held in store for them, it could not be worse than what they had experienced here. They had suffered too much for the simple fact that they were Germans, therefore they wanted to hold on to this last possession, they did not want to become Czechs and Communists, they wanted to be Germans and be free...

1. This wave of suicides reached its climax during June and July. The author, who as a police doctor had to conduct the inquest, relates that at one time he saw 16 corpses, at another time 21 corpses of people who had committed suicide, lying in the mortuary of the municipal cemetery. On his instruction a German employee of the undertakers compiled a list of suicides during May and June. On the basis of the result, which shows 300 suicides in these two months, the author estimates that 600 to 700 suicides occurred in Brüx between May and August. Investigating the causes of these mass suicides, amongst them families who had been personally known to him, the author reaches the conclusion that the main cause had been the terror against the Germans and mainly the expulsion measures. Those who committed suicide had become victims of the wave of panic, fear, desperation and insanity which affected the Germans when faced with the fate which the Czechs had intended for them.

2. These acts of "wild expulsion" during July/August, took place two or three times per week in the town area of Brüx and each time affected whole roads or town districts. The author's family was also expelled in this way, and he describes it in the first part of his report as follows: "On 6 August, my wife was driven from our home within twenty minutes, and apart from her mother and the child in its pram, she could take

only two small suitcases. Four heavily armed Czech soldiers escorted her to the evacuation camp (Negerdörfel, a former anti-aircraft encampment on the road to Saaz). On 9 August, she was evacuated over the frontier to Germany, whilst I was at that time already in prison. The Czechs called these evacuations "odsun," i.e. removal, using a term usually reserved for the act of pushing undesirable vagrants over the border. The use of this term is characteristic for the Czech attitude towards evacuation. The composition of the evacuation commission proves that all Czech State and civil authorities were taking part in the evacuation, i.e. the National Committee, the army, the police and the housing office. A special position was occupied on the one hand by the army, which provided the escort for the transports and, on the other hand, by the Communist Party, which at every occasion tried to wrest the initiative in the fight against the Germans from the other political parties."

3. On 8 and 9 January 1946, during the first American-Czech negotiations concerning the procedure to be followed in transferring the expellees to the American occupation zone of Germany, the Czechs had declared that each expellee would be allowed to take 1,000 Reichsmarks. In practice some districts had only allowed amounts of 500 or as little as 200 Reichsmarks. In the middle of April, during the renewed American-Czech negotiations, it was therefore agreed that in future a uniform amount of 500 Reichsmarks would be permitted. The Czechs adhered to this agreement even after June, when the transports were directed to the Soviet occupation zone of Germany.

Please refer to: http://www.forgottenvoices.net, for a photograph (#17) of Sudeten German refugees arriving in Germany after having been expelled from Czechoslovakia, 1945.

By the end of November 1946 the expulsion of the Sudeten Germans virtually came to an end when the U.S. Military authorities refused to take any more transports from Czechoslovakia. By this time, ironically, the remaining Germans in the country were anxious to be expelled, principally to the U.S. zone of occupation, because life in Czechoslovakia had become unbearable. Nevertheless, by October 1946, about 750,000 Sudeten Germans had been shipped to the Soviet zone of occupation. After the Communist coup in February 1948, expulsions started again to the U.S. zone, without, however, the agreement of the U.S. military authorities. These Germans were specialized industrial workers who had been kept in the factories and mines as well as prisoners in the various labor and retention camps. About 30,500 Germans were expelled in the period 1947/1948.[67] At this point, anti-Nazi Germans and those Germans that had supported the Republic and who had been permitted to remain in Czechoslovakia, also left, preferably for the American zone, because they saw no future for themselves in Czechoslovakia. On October 12, 1947, the Czechoslovak government declared the "Odsun," the expulsion, completed. At that time the government stated that there were still about 200,000 Germans in the country,[68] mostly skilled workers or Germans married to Czechs. In the period 1950–1989, however, an additional 100,000 ethnic Germans left for West Germany.[69]

The final number of Sudeten Germans expelled to Germany was about 2.834 million, of which the vast majority went to the Western zones of occupation with 914,000 going to the Soviet Zone. About 140,000 went to Austria. An additional 30,000 went to other countries in Europe or overseas. Thus the total number of Sudeten Germans expelled came to about three million.[70] The German government sources state that about 300,000 Sudeten Germans lost their lives in the expulsion. But this figure may be overstated as it could include Sudeten German war casualties. Non-German sources state it was only 100,000.[71] This uncertainty is just a reflection of the chaos and horror reigning in the Sudeten German regions and the terror to which these people were subjected.

Notes

1.   Anthony Komjathy and Rebecca Stockwell, *German Minorities and the Third Reich* (New York, 1980), 17.

2.   Theodor Schieder, ed., *Documents on the Expulsion of the Germans from Eastern-Central Europe*, vol. IV (Bonn, 1960), 7.

3.   Ulrich March, *Die Deutsche Ostsiedlung* [The German Settlement of the East] (Bonn, 1998), 12.

4.   Dr. Wilhelm K. Turnwald, ed., *Documents on the Expulsion of the Sudeten Germans* (Munich, 1953), ix.

5.   March, *Die Deutsche Ostsiedlung*, 12.

6.   Stefan Wolff, ed. and Lucy P. Marcus, *The Carpathian Germans, German Minorities in Europe; Ethnic Identity and Cultural Belonging, German Minorities in Europe* (New York, 2000), 98.

7.   Ibid.

8.   Ibid., 100.

9.   Ibid., 97.

10.   Radomir Luza, *The Transfer of the Sudeten Germans, A Study of Czech-German Relations, 1933-1962* (New York, 1964), 4.

11.   March, *Die Deutsche Ostsiedlung*, 12.
12.   Komjathy and Stockwell, *German Minorities*, 21.
13.   Ibid., 21, 22.
14.   Turnwald, *Documents on the Expulsion of the Sudeten Germans*, xiii.
15.   Schieder, *Documents on the Expulsion of the Germans*, 148–50.
16.   Ibid., 163.
17.   Ortfried Kotzian, *Die Sudetendeutschen, Eine Volksgruppe im Herzens Europas* [The Sudeten Germans, A People in the Heart of Europe] (Bonn, 1998), 15.
18.   Schieder, *Documents on the Expulsion of the Germans*, 17.
19.   Christopher Duffy, *Red Storm on the Reich* (New York, 1991), 295.
20.   Schieder, *Documents on the Expulsion of the Germans*, 23, 25.
21.   Ibid., 25, 26.
22.   Luza, *Transfer of the Sudeten Germans*, 258.
23.   Ibid., 260.
24.   Schieder, *Documents on the Expulsion of the Germans*, 60.
25.   Benjamin Lieberman, *Terrible Fate, Ethnic Cleansing in the Making of Modern Europe* (Chicago, 2006), 230.
26.   Ibid., 231.
27.   Norman M. Naimark, *Fires of Hatred, Ethnic Cleansing in Twentieth Century Europe* (Cambridge, MA, 2001), 115.
28.   Benjamin Frommer, *National Cleansing; Retribution against Nazi Collaborators in Postwar Czechoslovakia* (Cambridge, 2005), 59.
29.   Naimark, *Fires of Hatred*, 116.
30.   Frommer, *National Cleansing*, 47.
31.   Luza, *Transfer of the Sudeten Germans*, 270.
32.   Elizabeth Wiskemann, *Germany's Eastern Neighbours; Problems Relating to the Oder-Neisse Line and the Czech Frontier Regions* (London, 1956), 100, 101.
33.   Luza, *Transfer of the Sudeten Germans*, 255, 256.
34.   Frommer, *National Cleansing*, 243.
35.   Luza, *Transfer of the Sudeten Germans*, 271.
36.   Schieder, *Documents on the Expulsion of the Germans*, 76.
37.   Luza, *Transfer of the Sudeten Germans*, 275.
38.   Schieder, *Documents on the Expulsion of the Germans*, 87.
39.   Tomas Stanek, *Verfolgung 1945* (Persecution 1945) (Vienna, 2002), 28.
40.   Philipp Manes, *As if it were Life; A W WII Diary from the Theresienstadt Ghetto* (New York, 2009), 3.
41.   Ruth Schwertfeger, *Women of Theresienstadt, Voices from a Concentration Camp* (Oxford, 1989), 11.
42.   Norbert Troller, *Theresienstadt, Hitler's Gift to the Jews* (Chapel Hill, NC, 1991), xxii.
43.   Ibid., xxiii, xxiv.
44.   Manes, *As if it were Life*, 4.
45.   H. G. Adler, *Theresienstadt, 1941-1945* (Tubingen, 1960), 219.
46.   Frommer, *National Cleansing*, 6.

47. Ibid., 7.
48. Wiskemann, *Germany's Eastern Neighbours*, 65.
49. Frommer, *National Cleansing*, 16.
50. Ibid., 19.
51. Ibid., 16.
52. Ibid., 20.
53. Terry Goldwater, *Valhalla's Warriors, A History of the Waffen SS on the Eastern Front 1941–1945* (Indianapolis, IN, 2007), 82.
54. Frommer, *National Cleansing*, 20.
55. Luza, *Transfer of the Sudeten Germans*, 198.
56. Wiskemann, *Germany's Eastern Neighbours*, 59.
57. Frommer, *National Cleansing*, 25.
58. Turnwald, *Documents on the Expulsion of the Sudeten Germans*, xxi.
59. Stanek, *Verfolgung 1945*, 70.
60. Schieder, *Documents on the Expulsion of the Germans*, 102.
61. Frommer, *National Cleansing*, 42.
62. Wiskermann, *Germany's Eastern Neighbours*, 101.
63. Schieder, *Documents on the Expulsion of the Germans*, 102.
64. Ibid., 111.
65. Ibid., 111, 112.
66. Ibid., 114.
67. Ibid., 118, 119.
68. Wiskemann, *Germany's Eastern Neighbours*, 129.
69. Claus Hofhansel, *Multilateralism, German Foreign Policy and Central Europe* (London, 2005), 80.
70. Schieder, *Documents on the Expulsion of the Germans*, 122.
71. Wiskemann, *Germany's Eastern Neighbours*, 130, 131.

IV

The Expulsion of the Ethnic German Population from Hungary

Message from the President of Hungary, Laszlo Solyom, on the occasion of the inauguration of the National Memorial Place and Monument in Budaörs, Hungary, in memory of the expulsion of Germans in Hungary.

June 18, 2006

Ladies and gentlemen!

Today's commemoration rehabilitates humanity in its rights. Expulsion of the Germans of Hungary has been a taboo subject for long. Then, after the political transformation it was immediately admitted that the Germans' removal from Hungary that started in 1944, then the internments and resettlements were a series of unjust and unlawful measures. The Swabishes (Germans) suffered innocently. Compensation was due also to the deportees and the Constitutional Court cancelled the laws of 1945 declaring collective punishment. Historical facts are being explored, thus, the events of that time are slowly becoming common knowledge.

Nevertheless, it has never been felt in Hungary's public opinion that the expulsion of Swabishes could be justified by the sufferings caused by the German army and the occupation. The expulsion had first of all, economic motives: on one side, to increase the state land fund for the redistribution, on the other side, to have place for the Hungarians who escaped or were resettled from the neighboring countries. However, that way of solving problems—as Istvan Bibó pointed out already at that time—generates great moral detriment.

Neither is it an excuse for the Swabishes' expulsion that the winning states saw the key of stability in ethnically homogeneous nations or, that other states of Central Europe wanted to take advantage of the situation to get rid of their minorities, the more there is still such state that considers even now the nationalities' expulsion and deprivation of rights just and lawful. Today we have to raise our words precisely against the mentality that directed people's fate as if they had been simple objects.

In our times, it is already a subject at schools to speak about the post-war great renaissance of human rights as a counter-effect provoked by Nazism and inhumanity of the war. No doubt, it is true in general but cannot make forget all what happened and what continued during the communists ruling in the years of 50's.

Today, by erecting a monument to the calumniated and expelled ones, we shall finally leave impersonality. Although parliamentary decisions, judgments of the Constitutional Court and condemnation of collective guilt are important, those arrange matters only in law. Still, they are not enough to create peace in the soul.

I think, this memorial place is such one where one can come to remember, to think about fate, to mourn but also to draw strength from. Many of my acquaintances and schoolmates' children have taken back their old German family names and it is very joyful. Therefore, while I apologize as Hungary's head of state to the expelled Swabishes I bow my head in front of the memorial in the hope that the Germans of Hungary are again at home.

Source: Office of the President of the Republic of Hungary, 2006.

Introduction

On December 5, 1945, Imre Kovacs, one of the leaders of the National Peasant Party, allied with the Hungarian Communist Party, demanded the expulsion of the ethnic Germans for being traitors to Hungary. He made them responsible for having brought Hungary into a disastrous alliance and war, allied with Nazi Germany, resulting in the destruction of the nation. He said,

> The Swabs (Germans) who came to this country with one bundle on their back, should leave the same way. They cut themselves off from the fatherland as they demonstrated with their actions that they sympathized with Hitler's Germany. Let them now share the fate of Germany.[1]

Source: Quoted in *Hungary from the Nazis to the Soviets*, Peter Kenez.

The History of the German Settlements in Hungary

As a whole, the German settlements in Hungary were not in homogeneous, clustered areas but spread throughout the country. There were districts, however, that contained a higher concentration of people of German origin. On the western frontier with Austria, the Austrian Province of Burgenland, the German colonists had already come in the twelfth and thirteenth centuries from Bavaria and Austria. These border settlements were principally in Ödenburg (Sopron), Güns (Köszeg), and Steinamanger (Szombathely). These towns opted to remain in Hungary, when the Burgenland was ceded to Austria by the Trianon Treaty of 1920. (See map 18 of German settlements in Hungary).

Please refer to: http://www.forgottenvoices.net for a photograph (#18) of the medieval town of Güns (Köszeg) in Western Transdanubia, on the border of Burgenland, Austria.

Please refer to: http://www.forgottenvoices.net for a photograph (#19) of the medieval city of Ödenburg (Sopron) in Western Transdanubia, on the border of Burgenland, Austria.

A further concentration of German colonists existed in the area of Southern Transdanubia (see map 19 of the regions of Hungary) between the Danube and the Drau (Drava) rivers in the counties (Comitates) of Branau (Baranya), with its capital, Fünfkirchen (Pecs), Tolnau (Tolna), and Schomodei (Somogy). After the Habsburg defeat of the Turks in 1718, resulting in the peace of Passarowitz, Emperor Charles VI, his daughter, the Empress Maria Theresa, and her son, the Emperor Joseph II, called for emigrants to populate an almost empty land ravaged by the wars with Turkey. Between 1722 and 1787 over 150,000 German peasants and artisans arrived in what was then called "Swabian Turkey," and the people were commonly called Danubian Swabians.[2]

Even though feudalism was still prevalent among the Hungarian peasants settled on the large estates of the Magyar nobles, the German colonists were free peasants, in contrast, owing allegiance only to the Austrian emperor. They had all the rights of citizens such as owning their own land and homes, and freedom to marry and choose their own professions.

On the old "military frontier" of the Habsburg monarchy between the rivers Danube, Theiss (Tisza), and Marosch (Maros) and the Transylvanian Alps, previously in southwestern Hungary and now in Romania, further German settlements were created in the same period. This area was known as the Banat and the German settlers as Banat Swabians. These were communities planned to develop an area destroyed by war and the plague, to be filled with peasant farms and infrastructure. The Habsburgs gave support in the form of crops and livestock. Most colonists came from Southern Germany, but some came from Austria, Alsace, and Bohemia as well.

Germans were heavily recruited because they were thought to have the most skills in farming and mining to impart to the local Hungarian, Romanian, and Serb population. Many veterans of the various Austrian wars were sent by the Habsburg monarchy, the only proviso being that, initially at least, they had to be Catholic, thus assuring their loyalty to the Austrian Empire. By the middle of the eighteenth century, there were about 200,000 Germans living in the Banat.[3] With the peace Treaty of Trianon, of 1920, however, most of the Banat and its inhabitants was ceded to Romania, in the province of Timisoara. The Hungarian province of Vojvodina went to the new Kingdom of Serbs, Croats, and Slovenes, which became Yugoslavia in 1929. Only the Banat Swabian settlements in the Comitat of North Batschka (Bacs-Bodrog) remained in Hungary. (See map 18)

Widely scattered German settlements also existed in the villages west of Budapest, and to the north, in the Comitats of Nograd, Hont, and Gran (Esztergom). Other colonies were found to the west in the Schildgebirge mountains (Vertes) and the adjoining Buchenwald (Bakony) forest, stretching southwest to the Platten-See (Lake Balaton) in the Comitats Komorn (Komarom), Weissenburg (Fejer), and Vesprim (Vezprem). In these areas, larger or smaller concentrations of German villagers were dispersed among the majority Hungarian population. (See map 18)

In the 1941 Hungarian census, about 450,000 people considered German their native language. This amounted to 5.2 percent of the total Hungarian population. Germans who normally spoke Hungarian were not counted as such by the terms of the census, but classified as Hungarian. This was due to the strong, historical magyarization process promoted by successive Hungarian governments. Their purpose was to minimize the ethnic minorities in Hungary. It must also be stated that many ethnic Germans did not consider themselves as such but as fully assimilated Hungarians. In fact many had changed their last names from German to Hungarian. Taking these factors into consideration, it has been estimated that the prewar ethnic German population of Hungary was between 500,000 and 600,000.[4]

The Germans in Hungary were considered a peaceful ethnic group not prosperous enough to generate jealousy or resentment by the majority Hungarian population. The purpose of the Habsburg colonization process was not the creation of German enclaves in Hungary and in the Balkans, but the economic development of the region. The colonists had their own schools where German was taught as a first language as well as ample rights of local self-government. In summary, the major objectives of the Habsburg monarchy in the eighteenth century were the reestablishment of the Catholic religion, defense against the Ottoman Turks, and the dissemination of Western Civilization in the Balkans.[5]

This all changed in Hungary with the Austrian–Hungarian compromise of 1867, when the Hungarian half of the Dual Monarchy gradually adopted nationalistic policies in line with the nationalist–centralist thinking in Western Europe. Although there were constitutional guarantees for linguistic equality in Hungary, nevertheless, there, as well as in the other areas of the Dual Monarchy, language became equated with nationality rather than just having a functional purpose. Hungarian became the state language used in government, courts, and higher education. A forced "magyarization" of the educational system followed in order to forge one united, integrated Hungarian nation and to prevent other non-Hungarian nationality groups from developing their own educated elites. This nationalism based on language spread to renaming Hungarian towns and villages, even station names on the state railways. It became the language of communication in the civil service, business, and among professionals. To advance in the Hungarian state, knowledge of the language was now indispensable. Between 1880 and 1910, it is reported that about one-half million Germans became Hungarian in speech and culture (in pre-Trianon Hungary).[6]

The many middle class and educated Germans living in Hungarian towns and cities, particularly in Budapest, most readily assimilated. Once having adopted Hungarian language and culture, including changing their last names from German to Hungarian, they found all doors open to them, having the same opportunities as native Hungarians.

A first attempt by ethnic Germans to counter Hungarian nationalism and preserve their language and culture was made in 1906 with the foundation of the Hungarian German Peoples' Party (Ungarländische Deutsche Volkspartei). It had very little support, however, among the German population. Those ethnic Germans that were elected to parliament in Budapest were members of the traditional Hungarian parties. Subsequently, the German minority in Hungary was substantially reduced by Hungary's important loss of territory resulting from the Trianon Treaty. This did not, however, reduce the pressure for the assimilation of those minorities remaining in Hungary, principally the Germans. After World War I, a movement entitled the People's Educational Society of the Germans in Hungary (Ungarnländisch-deutscher Volksbildungsverein—UDV) was formed to strengthen German cultural identity and particularly to promote German schools in predominantly German settlement areas as guaranteed by the Treaty of Trianon. Again, this movement had little success in achieving its aims due to the resistance of the Hungarian authorities who asserted a strong cultural nationalism.[7] Furthermore, German national feeling among the ethnic minority was weak and in constant conflict with their feeling of loyalty to the Hungarian nation.

With the advent of Nazi Germany in 1933, a fundamental shift occurred in the thinking and behavior of the German minority in Hungary, as well as in the rest of Eastern Europe, for that matter. With its emphasis on race, nationality, and intolerance of other ethnic groups considered inferior, such as Slavs and Jews, National Socialist ideology found favor among many ethnic Germans in Hungary, particularly in the younger generations. In 1938, they formed a new, nationalist, pan-German organization, the "People's League of Germans in Hungary" (Volksbund der Deutschen in Ungarn—VDU) under the control of the German National Socialist Party. Their demands were for an end to the forced magyarization of the ethnic minority, especially in the educational system, and, in general, for cultural autonomy for the Germans in Hungary. In these endeavors, they were sometimes assisted and sometimes constrained by the Nazi German government. As Hitler had greater strategic interest in Hungary and in the Balkans than supporting German minorities, they were warned not to come into conflict with the Hungarian government. On the other hand, the Nazi German government used the national aspirations of the German community to further their negotiations with the Hungarian government. In short, the German minority was used as a negotiating instrument to achieve the foreign policy objectives of the Nazi government.[8]

The VDU became the leading organization representing the Hungarian Germans. In 1938, the Hungarian government accepted the Reich as the official patron and representative of the German minority in Hungary. In return, Hungary received its reward. In the First Vienna Award, following the Munich agreement on the Sudetenland, Hitler gave Southern Slovakia to Hungary. In the Second Vienna Award of August 1940, the Reich government transferred Northern Transylvania from Romania to Hungary. The latter became an ally of the Axis in November of that year. The German government then guaranteed the German ethnic group's privileged status within Hungary, making it virtually an autonomous national entity.[9]

Hungary's German Minority in World War II, Including Service in the Waffen-SS

The authority of the VDU increased substantially during the war, as it became the principal instrument of the Nazi system to mobilize the ethnic German population in the war effort. The internal organization of the VDU came to represent more and more the structure of the Nazi Party in Germany. Despite this pressure on the ethnic group, however, only approximately 150,000 Germans, out of a population of about 450–475,000 Germans in Hungary joined the VDU.[10] The resistance to conform to the new political structure came mainly from the small peasants who were still loyal to the Hungarian nation. In fact, there was a Hungarian government-sponsored patriotic loyalty movement for those Germans who did not want to be associated with the VDU.

No. 2

Interrogational Report based on the statements of a farmer from the District of Mohacs in the Baranya Comitat. Original, dated 3 September 1953, typewritten, 5 pages. Printed in part.

Recruiting for the German Army in the District of Mohacs in October 1941.

In the introductory remarks about his home locality, where the author of the Report had a property of 26 cadastral yokes (a cadastral yoke is equivalent to about 1.44 acres), one of the facts mentioned by him is that only about 20 percent of the German inhabitants had joined the organization of the Volksbund. Amid a general political apathy on the part of the inhabitants, such isolated disputes as arose were merely of a personal nature and did not, as a rule, attract much attention.

When, in 1944, the influence of the German Reich increased in Hungary, (Hungary was occupied by German troops on 19 March 1944), the influence of the Volksbund grew with it and consequently political tension increased too. The Volksbund wanted more people to become members and also to join the German army. Up to 1944, not very many men had joined and those Germans, who felt themselves to be Magyars despite their German nationality, refused to join the German army.

In October, 1944, all Germans under 50 had to be mustered and enrolled in the German army. Many preferred to volunteer for the Hungarian army.

In this month of October 1944, I, together with many others, entered the Labor Service. We had applied to serve in the Hungarian army but, owing to the agreements concluded between the German Reich and Hungary, we were not accepted by the Hungarian authorities for the Hungarian army but were only allowed to join the Labor Service. (German-Hungarian Agreement of 14 April 1944).

One day, the Gestapo appeared at the place where we were working near Fünfkirchen. As we tried to run away, they called out to us, "Just come along now, come along!" There were 15 of us in all, mostly from our home district. We were kept in Fünfkirchen for three days under police arrest (rendörlaktanya; if I remember rightly we were lodged in the Malom utca) and then we were loaded into lorries and taken under German military escort to Darda (Comitat Baranya) where we were enrolled. Some of us entered the fighting services but the majority were returned to the Labor Service.

My brother also entered the fighting services and was immediately transferred to Essig (in Croatia) and from there to the front line. At the end of the war, my brother was taken prisoner at Marburg (in Slovenia). According to his account they were thoroughly beaten up and very badly treated by the partisans. As he was a Hungarian citizen, he was handed over to the Magyars at Maria-Theresiopol (Subotica, Szabadka). The Magyars took them to Budapest, imprisoned them there, and finally transported them to the Soviet Zone in Germany. Later on, his family was expelled thither too.

We on the other hand, who were found fit for the Labor Service, were transported by rail from Darda with Vienna as our destination. However, we only got as far as Steinamanger (Szombathely), where our train was attacked by Russian aircraft. We ran away in all directions, the train went on without us, and we returned home. I think there was scarcely one among us who rejoined the train and went on to Vienna. On my arrival at home I kept myself hidden for a fortnight, as we had German troops with us. Afterwards I went about my work in the fields and nobody bothered about me.

In conclusion the author gives an account of the Russian invasion and of events that occurred in September 1947 during the expulsion.

The recruitment of young men for military service in the Waffen-SS constituted a prime example of Nazi pressure on the ethnic German community in Hungary. At first, only moral compulsion was used, because service was considered voluntary. Young ethnic Germans were invited to Germany for sports courses and then pressured to volunteer for the Waffen-SS. As results of this recruitment were meager, an agreement was reached with the Hungarian government which allowed ethnic Germans to serve either in the Honved (Hungarian Army) or the German armed forces. Subsequently, by April 1944, ethnic Germans no longer had this choice but had to serve in the German military. This provided for the compulsory induction of Germans in Hungary, mostly into the Waffen-SS. At first, recruitment was confined to members of the VDU, but thereafter any ethnic German in Hungary was liable for service in the Waffen-SS.[11] About 32,000 soldiers from the German communities in Hungary were killed in the war, 20,000 of these from the Waffen-SS.[12]

In October of 1944, when Soviet armies were already approaching Hungary, after Romania changed sides in August 1944, the 31st Waffen-SS Division was formed. Its members consisted principally of conscripted ethnic Germans living in Trans Danubia and the province of Vojvodina, which at that time was a part of Hungary. The Division was also called the Batschka (Bacska) Division because many of the ethnic Germans were recruited from this western region of Vojvodina. This Division was formed from the remnants of the Bosnian Moslem SS Kama Division, which had been dissolved due to reportedly poor performance and lack of reliability among its Moslem soldiers.[13] The Batschka Division ended the war fighting in Silesia and retreating through Bohemia, where it surrendered to Czechoslovak partisans and Soviet forces.

This Division participated in a massacre in the village of Czervenka (Tscherwenka), Hungary (present-day Serbia), in late 1944. Hungarian guards in the Bor copper mines were relieved by elements of the 31st Waffen-SS Division. During the night of October 7, the SS men shot many hundreds of Hungarian Jews who were slave laborers in these mines and who were being evacuated to Hungary. They were buried in mass graves. The next day, on the forced march of the prisoners to Hungary, the SS men continued shooting at the Jews for target practice. It was said that the roadside was littered with corpses well into Hungarian territory.[14]

One of the survivors related these executions:

> The pit was about 40-50 meters long and 8-10 meters wide. Its depth was about 1 1/2 meters ... On either side of the pit four SS-men were standing. Two of them brought up the victims, and two shot them.

They would take 20 to one side and 20 to the other. ... They were firing from a range of three meters ... I saw all this. Then they did the same to me. He (the SS-man) came up to me, prepared me and then stepped aside. Thus I also received the present, the bullet ...

Source: Quoted in *The Politics of Genocide; The Holocaust in Hungary, Vol. I,* Randolph L. Braham.

In all, about 700–1,000 slave laborers were killed, mostly Jews, but a number of Seventh Day Adventists and Jehovah's Witnesses as well.[15]

No. 1

Dictated statement of D. T. from Mekenyes, District of Hegybiit in the Baranya Comitat. Original, dated 22 May 1954, typewritten, 5 pages.

Recruiting of ethnic Germans from the Comitat of Baranya for the Waffen SS in the summer of 1941 under the guise of an athletic training operation.

At the beginning of June 1941, I received from the district headquarters of the "Volksbund der Deutscben in Ungarn" (VDU) an invitation, which did not bear the official VDU stamp, to the effect that I should report on the following Sunday (it must have been the second Sunday in June) at the communal offices in Magocs, to have myself medically tested as to my athletic fitness. We were told that only leaders and reliable members of the German youth organization were to undergo this test. It was even said in the notice that it was quite a special distinction to be invited.

We were medically tested at the local group center of the Volksbund in Magocs. The test was carried out by doctors in civilian clothes whom we did not know. It reminded one of the usual sort of inspections which take place when one is enrolled for the army. Along with the test we had to answer a questionnaire about our most essential personal particulars. No political questions were mentioned at the time. When the test was over, we were told nothing about its aim or purpose, nor did they let us know whether we had passed or failed.

On 6 July 1941, I was verbally informed that I might report to the German House in Budapest, together with all the others who had passed. For the time being, we had to pay our railway fares ourselves but we were reimbursed for this later when we got to Budapest. H. K. and I were the two who went from the village of Mekenyes to Budapest in answer to this invitation.

At the appointed time, about 60 men in all met at the German House in Budapest. We were told that we could not leave the German

House or show ourselves in the town. Meanwhile the word went round among us that we were going to be smuggled into Germany and take part in some athletic training courses there, in order to be better equipped for our youth work at home later on. As dusk was approaching, we were put on some SS lorries and, without knowing where we were going, taken over the frontier. On 10 July, we arrived at what is called the Arsenal in Vienna and were quartered in one of its blocks of barracks, We were placed under the orders of a captain in the German army, got German army rations, and waited with great excitement to see how things would develop. Every now and then, we were given instruction in the rudiments of military service. We were also allowed to visit the town, but only in parties and with officers in charge.

A few days later, we were ordered to go to the SS Headquarters in Vienna, where they had already got our personal details. At the same time, we were submitted to another medical test and, on this occasion, I got into difficulties over my personal documents, as some of them were missing (perhaps none of my papers were there in fact), and so I was once more thoroughly examined and had to answer another questionnaire.

Here again, nobody let a word slip about the so-called "athletic training operation." I could not say for certain whether the commander of our transport unit himself was in the know, nor can it be said that any official representative of the leadership of the Ethnic Group put in an appearance during our stay at the German House in Budapest. Only a few students paid any attention to us and they did make some reference to our "athletic training operation."

We were sent back from Headquarters to the Arsenal and had to wait again. After a stay of about a week, we got our marching orders, or instructions, as the case may be, to proceed in a party to the North Station in Vienna. Then we went by normal passenger train to Brünn via Gänsendorf. There were some service troops of the Waffen SS waiting for us at Brünn station and they took us to the Waffen SS camp on the Kuhberg. We were taken past the guard into the vast camp and got the impression for the first time that we were probably going to receive our "athletic training" in this camp. Many of us had hardly been out of range of the church tower in our little ethnic German village. Owing to our long wait and our hanging about in uncertainty, we had been lately becoming rather sullen and anxious, It was natural that our first impression of the SS camp on the Kuhberg was a very depressing one.

We were quartered in some barracks, where we were gradually informed by some compatriots from the Tolnau area (Szárazd), that we were to regard ourselves as "soldiers of the Waffen SS." Just the same thing had happened to them. This theory was soon confirmed, by the

Waffen SS N.C.O.s, who treated us like recruits. We tried to make these gentlemen understand that we had come to Germany for a few weeks athletic training and that we must have got into this camp by mistake. We requested the senior officers to clear the matter up. At first they said they did not know. None of the SS leaders concerned wanted to hear anything about how or why we had come there, but, instead of drawing the proper conclusion and discharging us, they left us in our civilian clothes still uncertain what was in store for us. So we remained dressed as civilians for about 3 or 4 weeks, but we were already obliged to take part in the normal recruits' training (fatigues, etc.). In the meantime, they were, I suppose, making enquiries about the meaning and purpose of our presence there and, I imagine, asking the advice of the Ethnic German leadership in Hungary. An emissary from the leadership of the Ethnic Group was supposed to have put in an appearance, though I cannot say for certain whether he actually came. Presumably everyone was waiting for some such representative of the leadership of the Ethnic Group but, apart from hearing it rumored that one had been there, we never got to know of his arrival. One day, we were told by our company commander that those of us who did not wish to stay should put their names in to be transported home. We got the impression at the time that this gesture was only intended to distinguish the "willing ones" from the "cowards" and that this news was not to be taken really seriously...

After four weeks we were given our uniform, and this gave rise to the first scenes, for many of us refused to put it on. Gradually two groups formed themselves. The gnawing uncertainty was too much for one lot, who regarded the whole operation as a crude method of press-ganging farmers. The rest, however, who had already at home been the most loyal members of the youth movement, were able to bear even this complete surprise, as they did not want to betray the German cause, though they too found it hard to stomach the pretext on which they had been enticed to leave. It was not so much the stark reality of now belonging to the Waffen SS and of being due soon to go the front, but much more feeling of having been thoroughly swindled by the leadership of one's own ethnic group. This loyal element had now to act as mediators and appeal for discipline in a case where they themselves felt very injured at heart.

The Waffen SS N.C.O.s and officers could not properly understand these farmers' sons who had been so unfairly enticed away from their village. They therefore resorted to all the usual tricks to make these recalcitrant people feel small. We ethnic German farmers' sons felt that someone had unjustly gone behind our backs and handed us over in a roundabout way to the Waffen SS. The officers and N.C.O.s of the Waffen SS, however, regarded our attitude as treasonable and lacking in a sense of duty. There were, however, some officers who honestly tried to understand our point of view and to get the matter properly cleared up. They kept asking us in a friendly way how the whole of this "athletic training operation" had started and asserting that they had had nothing to do with it.

We were now put through a regular course of training and were due to take the oath on 11 August 1941. About a half, who could not solve the problem at all, did not want to take the oath and there was another mutiny. These latter were then taken out of the ranks and formed together into a special group. I and the rest of my comrades, however, took the "oath" on 11 August. While we were allowed out of the camp on the occasion of the oath-taking celebrations and had already been treated as "men" and accepted on equal terms with the rest, the "cowards" were confined to barracks. Relations between the two groups became cool, for, in our case, that quiet and modest loyalty, which is typical of the ethnic German abroad, eventually won the day. After this we went on with our training. The group of "unwilling" ones was kept apart, while we, along with many other ethnic German comrades, were posted to reserve companies. On 28 August 1941, our training was over. We went to Stettin. The "unwilling ones," after a few weeks of hard training, were sent back to Hungary...

Please refer to: http://www.forgottenvoices.net, for a photograph (#20) of German refugee treks in Hungary, July 1944.

The Flight and Evacuation from the Soviet Army

In August 1944, Romania changed sides and became an ally of the Soviet Union. This caused the first evacuation of ethnic Germans from that country, who began their trek through Hungary. In September, the Red Army advanced into Hungary. (See map 20) The Hungarian head of government, Admiral Horthy, sought an armistice with the Soviet Union in October 1944. Nazi Germany then deposed him, and the German Army, which had already occupied Hungary in March 1944, installed a "puppet" Hungarian government of the Arrow Cross Party, a Hungarian fascist party.

In coordination with the Volksdeutsche Mittelstelle (Ethnic German Coordination Bureau) in Berlin, the Nazi Party organization responsible for the ethnic German communities in the East (under the control of the SS), the evacuation of the German communities east of the Danube was planned and already partially carried out in September and early October 1944. With the advance of the Russian forces, the German communities west of the Danube were ordered to evacuate.

The evacuations continued into December when the Red Army broke into this area. The Germans from Budapest and villages around it were ordered out in early December, but this action was generally unsuccessful due to Soviet forces encircling and besieging Budapest.[16]

Generally, the evacuation of the German population was well planned and timely. Of those who fled before the arrival of the Russians, however, most were members of the VDU. The majority of the population refused to leave their homes as they still considered themselves loyal Hungarians. The Catholic Church also advised against flight. The local Hungarian population reportedly attempted to induce their German neighbors to stay, a reflection of the existing good relations between the two peoples. That tension which existed was within the German community, between the Volksbund which urged the Germans to flee and their opponents who wanted to stay in their homes in Hungary. About 60,000–70,000 Swabian Germans left with the retreating German Army,[17] which represented about 15 percent of the German Hungarian population.

No. 10

Interrogational Report based on the statements of X from Lókut, District of Zirc in the Veszprem Comitat. Original, dated 2 November 1953, typewritten, 8 pages. Printed in part.

The attitude adopted towards the evacuation by those Germans who did not belong to the organization of the "Volksbund"

My home locality of Lókut numbered about 2,000 inhabitants. We had a German Local Council, of which J. S. was the last Chairman before the Russians marched in. The Clerk of the Council was the senior notary, Schwarz, who had changed his name into Foldrary after the First World War. He spoke German, as did the other local officials, but liked to be spoken to in Hungarian.

Father A. P. was the Catholic priest in charge of the parish. While he would read the lessons in German, he would preach in the language of the State. In the State primary school of the village, of which R. P. was headmaster, lessons were only given in the Magyar language. Among the members of the school staff was the head of the State youth organization, the so-called Levente, (Levente = boy or youth, was the name given to the Hungarian State youth organization, to which only boys between the ages of twelve and eighteen could belong. They received a preliminary military training similar to that given in the German cadet training camps. Membership in the Levente was compulsory) L. K. by name, who, by the skillful way he had in dealing with the people and by his tactful exploitation of the political situation, succeeded in getting many active members for the Levente.

The Volksbund was not active in Lókut until the year 1942. It embraced only about 60 per cent of the population. After the defeat of Stalingrad about a third of its members gradually resigned and tried to win prominence by their pro-Magyar attitude. We had only two to four volunteers for the SS in our locality, and the stories they told made an unfavorable impression. When, in September 1944, the general enrolment in the SS took place, it was looked upon with dislike in Lókut, And yet the enrolment call was obeyed from a sense of discipline. In our locality there was no thought of desertion as there was in other places.

Many treks of refugees had been driving through Lókut since the autumn of 1944. This meant, of course, that we too were compelled to think of the possibility of evacuation. I personally was against such a solution from the very start as I was of the opinion that nothing could happen to me, having been an opponent of the Volksbund. This does not imply that I disowned my German nationality. Even at the census I did not do this. From an economic point of view as well, I thought that it would be more sensible to stay in one's home. There were members of my family in the German army and I did not want them to find themselves without home or property when they were discharged. There were many of my acquaintances and relatives who thought as I did.

I spoke about the question of evacuation with the refugees who were passing through. Refugees from the Batschka told me that, before fleeing, they had made over their possessions to acquaintances and, in many cases, to people of a different nationality, in order to safeguard their property. Moreover, these refugees were no longer all of the opinion that they had done the best thing in leaving their homes. Many thought that it would have been decidedly more advantageous to have remained behind. So I found that my views were confirmed by what I thus learnt. I informed my acquaintances of what I had observed; their own experience confirmed mine. I might also mention that the refugees were still always expecting to be home again soon.

It is consequently not to be wondered at that, when our local group leader G. expressed himself in favor of the evacuation, his attitude was violently contested. G. had neglected to call large meetings and to win support for the evacuation idea from prominent personalities. Instead, he relied on a whispering campaign and the power of his own personal influence. The arguments which had still been quite honest and fair in September and October 1944 degenerated, especially after Horthy's coup d'etat, into unpleasant disputes which greatly harmed our common interests. Those who did not share G's opinion were declared by the members of the local Volksbund to be enemies of the German cause. We, for our part, pointed to the ghastly effects of the bombardments and the not very gratifying supply position in Germany. Such incidents became a daily routine. It was understandable that, in these circumstances, the Volksbund was unable to carry out the evacuation.

The fighting kept drawing nearer and we came into more frequent contact with the German troops. This prevented the opponents of the Volksbund from going over completely to the Magyar cause. Many soldiers advised us to remain at home and gave reasons for our doing so, but the majority advised us to flee. Shortly before Christmas 1944, the German army started an inspired propaganda campaign, aiming at evacuating the whole locality, but no practical preparations were made for doing so. On the 28th December, a large motorized force suddenly arrived in the locality from the front. The soldiers said that we might reckon on the Soviet forces arriving at any moment. They called on the inhabitants to leave the locality without delay. This sudden turn of events had a very frightening effect on us all, as none of us wanted to see the Reds in control of the place. In the course of that day about 80 families left their homes. I personally did not want to be a witness of this sad occasion. My brother Jakob, whom I had been urging to stay at home, finally decided to flee after a long discussion with the soldiers, although he had previously shared my opinion.

However, the front was stabilized about 30 kilometers east of Lókut. In the period that followed, our locality became not only a bastion for the reserve services of the front line but also an assembly point for refugees. Many Magyars, who had been fleeing before the Russian advance from the Weissenburg area, wanted to stop with us and await further developments. There were regrets that the evacuation summons of the Hungarian authorities had been obeyed and a fear that, after the return home, their houses would be found already plundered or destroyed. I was once again dissuaded by conversations of this nature from taking advantage of the chance which presented itself to flee before the Russians marched in. I think that there was nobody else who escaped from the locality before this happened, although we were living in fear, going to church and praying that the disaster might not come upon us. In long conversations which took place at night we tried to cheer each other up. At 4 p. m. on 27 March 1945, the locality was occupied by the Russians.

The writer goes on to describe the measures taken by the Russians after they marched in and his own condemnation to three years imprisonment, because of his two sons having been members of the Waffen SS.

The Hungarian Government's Justification for the Expulsion of the German Community

The justification for the expulsion of the ethnic Germans was based on two arguments. First, they were traitors to Hungary who supported Hungary's alliance with Hitler, which brought Hungary into a disastrous war with the Soviet Union. The Germans were collectively guilty of disloyalty to Hungary. Second, the expropriation of land owned by the Swabians was the keystone for a successful land reform.

Hungarian nationalism was reflected in the feeling that foreigners, namely the Hungarian Germans, played too great a historical role in the leadership of the nation. The nationalists opined that the German mentality and German customs were alien to the Hungarian people, who had to be defended against German expansionism. They considered that people of German background had played too large a role in Hungarian political life including domination of the highest ranks of the military. They felt that Germans occupied positions that should have gone to genuine Hungarians.

This chauvinistic view was projected back to the time of the original German colonies in Hungary in the eighteenth century, after the land was liberated from the Turks. It held that the Habsburg monarchy gave the best lands to German nobility, German princes of the church, monasteries, and large German landowners, forgetting that this country was already settled by Hungarians: the new German settlements received more privileges than the already existing Hungarian villages.

The greatest enmity was directed against the Volksbund and its members. It was considered a fifth column, a spearhead of German imperialism to subjugate Hungary. It created among the German minority in Hungary, especially in the younger generations, a sense of racial and cultural superiority over the majority Hungarians. It betrayed the Hungarian nation because the Swabian Germans felt more loyalty to Nazi Germany than they did to Hungary. Because of the support from Nazi Germany, it became a veritable state within a state. Among its many treasonous activities, it was accused of recruiting ethnic Germans for the Waffen-SS,[18] when they should have gone into the Hungarian army.

Land reform was the most important social issue facing Hungary after World War II. Two-thirds of the population lived in villages, and 40 percent of the village population was either landless or had plots too small to support themselves. Hungary is reported to have had the most unequal distribution of lands in Eastern and Central Europe. There was an attempt at land reform after World War I, but due to the opposition of the large landholders, only about 8 percent of the available land was subject to the reform. Those individual plots that were distributed were so small and uneconomic that the poverty of the peasants was not alleviated.[19]

The National Peasant Party, a political party of poor peasants and an ally of the Hungarian Communist Party, was one of the most radical supporters of the expulsion of all German settlers in order to distribute their land widely among the landless peasantry. For this reason, they wanted to encompass as many ethnic Germans as possible in the expulsion, not limiting it to just members of the Volksbund as proposed by other noncommunist parties in the Hungarian postwar government.

The goal of the Hungarian Communist Party was, with the critical help of the Soviet Union, the acquisition of a monopoly of power and the creation of a dictatorship of the proletariat. Communist seizure of power, however, was carried out piecemeal in order to maintain the semblance of democracy as long as possible. Their principal ally in this endeavor to seize power was the National Peasant Party, and one of their principal instruments was the imposition of their land reform.[20]

As a means to gain power, the Communist Party linked the expulsion of the ethnic Germans to land reform. They used the National Peasant Party to lead the anti-German campaign and win support among the poor peasants. In this way they were also undermining the main opposition party, the Smallholder Party. Lastly, to burnish their nationalist image, they pressed for the expulsion of all Germans in order to appear as the principal defender of the Hungarian nation.[21]

A further argument for expropriating German landowners was to make land available for Hungarians resettled from Slovakia. After the war, the Czechoslovak government wished to also expel all Hungarians from Slovakia. This was violently opposed by the Hungarian government and became a very serious bone of contention between the Czechoslovak and Hungarian communist parties. Arbitration was sought from the Soviet Union. Ultimately, the population exchange was minimal as Hungary could hardly absorb 650,000 Slovakian Hungarians compared to sending only 105,000 Hungarian Slovakians to Czechoslovakia. Had this taken place, it would have been a great loss of prestige and influence for the Hungarian Communist Party.[22]

The total amount of land expropriated from the Germans was 448,223 hold (1 hold =1.42 acres). This was about one-eighth of the total 3.2 million hold expropriated and distributed. In the area of Transdanubia, where the Swabian Germans were concentrated, however, about 50.3 percent of the land expropriated belonged to ethnic Germans.

The General Secretary of the Hungarian Communist Party, Matyas Rakosi, said in 1945 that the promise of Swabian land for the peasants could help the Hungarian Communist Party because;

> In the Hungarian countryside, the Swabian question, of Swabian land, has absolutely to be referred to frequently, especially as others are not doing it. Anti-Swabian propaganda should be used to depict the Smallholders as a pro-German party. As it would not work in German areas, it should not be made in public, only in door-to-door propaganda, and only in Hungarian areas. It is good therefore, if in the small agitation we explain that there is enough land, but it is still with the Swabians, and the Smallholder Party defends them and only the Communist Party defends the interest of the Hungarian tiller of the soil. We should speak about this question not in the German, but in the Hungarian countryside.[23]

Source: Quoted in *Agent of Moscow; The Hungarian Communist Party and the Origins of Socialist Patriotism 1941-1953*, Martin Mervius.

The Soviet Occupation of Hungary and Forced Labor in the Soviet Union

The Soviet Union regarded Hungary as an enemy country which it had not liberated but occupied. In the course of the war, and especially in its last months in the battle for Budapest, it had lost 80,000 men and 240,000 wounded. The men of the Red Army took their revenge on the local population, more akin to their behavior in German lands than in those countries which were liberated by the Soviets, such as Poland, Czechoslovakia, Bulgaria, or Romania. Atrocities were committed against Hungarian civilians, prisoners of war were shot, and there was mass raping of Hungarian women, particularly in Budapest, by the Red Army. Marshall Malinowsky, Commander of the Second Ukrainian front, authorized his soldiers to do three days of looting in Budapest, after it fell to Soviet forces.[24]

As in occupied Germany, the Allies established an Allied Control Commission to govern the conquered land. Marshall Kliment Voroshilov, a close associate of Stalin was the first Chairman. Although he was considered a failure as a military leader, he was still a member of the Politburo. The main concern of the Soviet occupation authorities, at this point at the end of the war, was not the expulsion of the Swabian Germans but the procurement of German forced labor for the Soviet Union. Men between the ages of seventeen and forty-five and women between the ages of seventeen and thirty were eligible for deportation to the Soviet Union. With the Soviet occupation came special NKVD, (the Soviet secret police) troops who began to round up ethnic Germans as slave labor, mostly to work in the Donbass coal mining region or in the metallurgical industry in Southern Russia.[25] If there were not enough Germans to fill their quotas, then Hungarians were seized. It is estimated that 35,000 Hungarian Germans were deported to the Soviet Union.[26]

No. 20

Report of the experiences of Frau L. A. from Mucsfa, District of Volgyseg in the Tolna Comitat. Original, dated 28 December 1950, typewritten, 7 pages.

The deportation of the German community of Mucsfa to the Soviet Union at the beginning of January 1945; their experiences during their term of compulsory labor in Russia until their return to Hungary in the autumn of 1949; their stay in the camp of Debrecen and their subsequent removal to Germany at the end of 1950.

After the Russians had already been some months in control of our little home village of Mucsfa, I was deported. It was on the first of January 1945. At noon the drums were heard beating, and we were summoned to work for a fortnight, though no one had any idea where we were going. The departure took place the next morning, on 2 January.

We left our little home village with our bundles on our backs and we walked to Bonyhad. Some Russian soldiers were waiting for us there and we were lodged in a big building. We stayed there for 8 days and on 10 January we walked further as far as Bataszek on the bank of the Danube. There we were told, though we did not believe it, that we were going to Russia and, during the night, we were rowed over the Danube to Baja. It was bitterly cold. Our hands and feet were frozen stiff. We had already gone through a lot but the worst was still to come and we had no idea what it was to be like.

On the next day we went to the station under Russian escort. We were loaded into cattle wagons, doors and windows were made fast with nails, and the train left during the night. The doors were not opened again for 5 days and there we were on the edge of our homeland, in Temesvar. After a few minutes, the door was made fast again and we moved on. The train sped on for days on end...

After a fortnight's traveling, we arrived at the Russian frontier. There we were loaded onto another train and then went on into Russia. On 21 January, in the morning, our door was opened again and there before us was a big camp, surrounded by two high wire fences. This was where we were to live... Then we were made to get out and were deloused... And now we came into the camp, where the rooms were cold and we had little boards of wood to sleep on.

Tired out by the journey, we lay down and slept till next morning. When we woke up, we found that our appetites had woken up too. We had nothing left of what we had brought from home and we felt like despairing... After two days we got something to eat for the first time. It was Kukruz (maize) soup and about 4 ounces of bread but it was not enough to appease our hunger.

Several days passed in this way and then we had 'to go out to work. We had to clear away railway tracks which had been destroyed in the war, and it was an icy cold, bitter winter. It was not easy to reach the earth through the snow, but our longing for our homeland remained as strong as ever. By now it was springtime and the' sun was shining, but it was so bitterly cold that we got no warmth from its rays...

Six months went by in this way and, in April 1945, I left the camp with a few others to work on a Kolchoz (collective farm). We thought things would be better here but, unfortunately, they were worse. From sunrise to sunset we were in the fields. We suffered terribly from hunger during our hard work and we were growing steadily weaker. Thus the summer passed and autumn came. We grew hungrier and hungrier and because we were so badly in want of nourishment we had an outbreak of typhus of the stomach, which I caught very badly myself. Things got steadily worse; there was not a sign of medical attention. Our daily fare was cabbage soup in the morning, with half a pound of bread, soup at midday and soup in the evening. It got worse every day, so that we all fell sick. Then, in September 1945, we went back to the camp. Typhus was raging there, too, and I fell sick for three whole months. My sight and hearing were already getting quite weak and I lay unconscious for most of the time. We women had our hair cut short like men so that we did not look any different. The whole camp became a hospital. On many days there were from 10 to 15 deaths and the dead were loaded onto a cart, driven out to the cemetery and there a hole was dug, the cart turned round and the dead were tipped out into it and covered with a little earth... The spring of 1946 came round, and this sickness decreased thanks to the warm sun. Yet we lost over 400 people as a result of it, so that there were now a thousand of us left in the camp.

1 became well again and went to work on the Kolchoz once more in the spring of 1946. Things were already going a little better for us, yet the rainy weather brought with it a new illness, malaria, which I also caught. Luckily, I got over this one too. Autumn came again and, one day, they took me back to camp, where I was detailed for work in the coal mines. The first time that I went down the pit-shaft I thought would be the last. I had quite heavy work to do, removing stones and delivering coal. Yet the hard life I had to lead made me grow tougher, and my hope of getting home kept me going. The years went by and 1947 arrived. Nobody knew what was happening at home and it was only in the autumn of 1947 that we got our first letters. It was a great joy for us all, but in many letters it was already being said that people had taken everything away from the family and they were now quite without a home. So great was our longing for home, however, that this did not shake us. If only one could get to one's dear ones, it would not matter how things stood. This year passed too and 1948 arrived. Month after month we were promised that we would be sent home.

Summer was now with us again. There were so many of our comrades who died in the grim coal pit. I myself got ill again from the hard work and poor fare and, one day, the Russian doctor wrote me out a paper exempting me from the coal mine. I got some quite light work which lasted for a whole 5 months.

Then came 1949. I recovered a little and went to work in the coal mine again, but things got steadily better, the post started arriving and conditions in the camp kept on improving. On Sundays, we had musical entertainments. German prisoners of war would visit the camp and entertain us with music and concerts. Hungarian prisoners of war came to visit us too, now and then, and now we were promised that we should go home in October. This month arrived after all the long time we had been waiting and yearning and, on the seventeenth, we went to work for the last time. In our joy, we could scarcely wait for the time of our departure to arrive and, 10 days later, on 27 October 1949, we were loaded onto the train and left for home in the evening.

For days on end our train sped on towards home and, on 2 November, we arrived in Maramarossziget (Maramarossziget lies on the Romanian-Slovak frontier). We were put out there and deloused. We had a good meal and went to sleep and traveled on homeward next day. At 5 'a. m., on 3 November, we crossed the Hungarian border. How glad we were to be home again after 5 years. On 4 November, we arrived in Debrecen at the camp for home comers. We got a kind reception, had something to eat, were deloused and many of us were discharged.

However, I remained behind with some others, because our parents had been expelled and wanted us to come to them in Germany.

We too were promised that we would be home by Christmas; yet Christmas came and there was no sign of making the journey home. We celebrated Christmas under a tiny little Christmas tree for the first time for five years. Now, again, we were told each month that we would be going home the next. Spring came and one transport after another arrived from Russia but there were always a few who remained behind with us in the camp. There were already over 500 of us and one day a transport left our place for the Russian zone. We were left behind, however, and could only hope that we would go home soon. In June, the camp was broken up and each one of us went off to find somewhere else to stay until we were allowed to go home.

Then I too returned once more to our little home village. Alas, I did not find it as it was when I left and had to say with the poet: "New faces look out of the windows. It was once my parents' house," I stayed there for two whole months with people that I knew until, one day, the joyful news came for which we had been longing for almost six years. We would have to wait till 5 September and then our transport would leave for our new home.

The time went by and we went to Budapest on 4 September, reported our presence and all went into a big building. There the doors were closed on us at once and we were all searched, from the smallest bundle to the biggest and from head to foot. They took everything that was new or pretty away from us. Clothes, money, wine, spirits, meat, flour, lard, even practically everything to eat which we had taken with us for the journey was taken away. Some people were left with only an empty trunk and the things that were taken away were worth 6,000 florins We left at 5 a. m. and traveled through Czechoslovakia to the Russian Zone and on to Hof-Moschendorf. There we were made to feel at home, got a kind reception and had a good meal. On 12 September, we were all discharged. Each one of us went to find their new home. It was a happy reunion after nearly six years.

The Expulsion of the Ethnic Germans

At war's end, the Hungarian government had not yet decided how to treat its ethnic Germans. Opinions were divided with the Hungarian Communist Party and its ally, the National Peasant Party, calling for the expulsion of all Germans, whereas the major democratic party, the Smallholder Party, favored only deporting former Volksbund and Waffen-SS members. In May 1944, the government announced that there was no Swabian question but only a question of German fascists. They then resolved to deport former Waffen-SS soldiers and confiscate the lands of the members of the Volksbund. Shortly thereafter, however, they did ask authorization from Moscow to deport 200,000–250,000 ethnic Germans to the Soviet occupation zone of Germany.[27] As this figure clearly was much greater than the number of Volksbund adherents, the issue really became one of eliminating an unwanted ethnic group rater than one of eliminating only German fascists. The German population in Hungary, however, was never subject to the same brutal persecution and excesses as in Poland, Czechoslovakia, or the former Yugoslavia.

The initiative for including the expulsion of ethnic Germans from Hungary in the Potsdam ""Big Three" Conference, in August 1945, (the Potsdam Agreements) came from the Soviet Union. They together with the Hungarian Communist Party wanted to use the argument of the collective guilt of the Swabians to cover their real purpose for a radical land reform. In the spring of 1945, Marshall Voroshilov demanded from the Hungarian government the complete expulsion of Germans from Hungary. All those ethnic Germans who declared German as their native language were considered eligible for transfer. The Hungarian government estimated the number to be removed from Hungary to be from 200,000 to 250,000.[28]

Certain categories of Hungarian Germans were exempted from deportation, most importantly those who had been active members of democratic parties or labor unions or had been persecuted by the Nazis for claiming Hungarian nationality. At a later date, in 1947, industrial workers in critical industries, miners, indispensable crafts-men, or agricultural workers were also exempted, unless they had been members of the Volksbund or Waffen-SS. Exemption Committees were established by the government, but in reality they were under the control of the Communist Party. Thus it occurred, on occasion, that wealthy Swabians who had not been members of the Volksbund were expelled whereas working class Germans, now members of the Hungarian Communist Party, were exempted, even though they were previously members of the Volksbund.[29]

Voices were raised in Hungary against these arbitrary expulsions. The liberal parties, particularly the Smallholder Party and the surviving democratic press, criticized the sweeping nature of classifying every ethnic German as a traitor. Cardinal Jozsef Mindszenty (he was of Swabian origin), as head of the Roman Catholic Church in Hungary and a fierce anticommunist, repeatedly protested the property confiscation and expulsion of all ethnic Germans. He addressed world public opinion, strongly condemning what was happening in Hungary. These protests had no effect, and with the increasing communist domination of the Hungarian government, the opposition was gradually eliminated. (In 1949 Mindszenty was tried for treason by the Communist government and given a life sentence. In the 1956 Hungarian revolution, he was given asylum in the U.S. Embassy in Budapest, from whence he was finally allowed to go into exile in 1971.)

No. 25

Interrogational Report based on the statements of Christian Pelzer, a farmer from Kunbaja, District of Bacsalmas in the Bacs-Bodrog Comitat. Original, dated May 1953, typewritten, 5 pages.

The evacuation of the German community from Kunbaja; the occupation of the place by Yugoslav partisans after the entry of the Soviet troops; the expropriation of the ethnic Germans' landed estates and its transfer by the Hungarian authorities to Magyar settlers.

My estate was situated on either side of the Yugoslav-Hungarian border. I lived alternately in Hungary and Yugoslavia.

Kunbaja was an almost purely German and Catholic parish. There were only between ten and twelve families which were Croat and they were Catholic too and, until the revolution, very pro-German.

Before the entry of the Russian troops (some time in October 1944), the main feature of the situation was the very lively and active propaganda carried out by the local leader of the Volksbund. In order to make a lasting impression on the people that evacuation was advisable, we were continually receiving descriptions of what would happen in Kunbaja if the Soviets and their accomplices once took over the reins. It was particularly pointed out to us that we would sooner or later be dispossessed of our property and deported for slave labor. It was true that our compatriots, as members of the Waffen SS, were greatly feared by the Soviets and their allies, but their families at home would have to bear the brunt of Russian vengeance.

This well conducted propaganda bore corresponding fruit. About 60 per cent of the German population allowed themselves to be evacuated. The evacuation was carried out by rail from Bacsalmas, Each refugee was allowed to take with him luggage weighing about 150 kilograms...

Those who voluntarily stayed behind had various reasons for doing so. My wife and I wanted to stay at home, because we assumed that nothing would happen to us on account of our advanced age. The rest assumed that they could save their property by staying. Some people gave political reasons for their decision, declaring that, as they had not been members of the Volksbund, they would be spared from the measures of persecution that were to be expected.

Immediately after the Russian entry, the exact date of which I cannot give any more (it was some time in October 1944), some partisans of Tito also arrived in Kunbaja. It must be realized that there had been no pro-Communist organizations in the place and that was what made it possible for this to happen. (The old Yugoslav frontier was not re-established until much later). The Yugoslav Communists infested us here in Kunbaja just as they did in the German villages of the Batschka and the Banat. These Tito units consisted almost exclusively of "Bunjewatzen" (that is to say, Serbs from the Upper Batschka—Bunjewatzen or Bunjewzen: Catholic Serbs living in the Batschka and numbering some 40,000. They had emigrated there from Herzogovina in the 17th Century to escape from Turkish oppression) and the majority came from the locality of Tavankut. They came in wagons and carts and took away everything which they could seize from the empty houses of the ethnic Germans.

The partisans also set up a provisional local administration, making use of the native Croat families for this purpose. The shoemaker Cubic and his relatives laid down the law. Though it was possible to present one's wishes at the local office in German, yet, on each occasion, one had the feeling that the Germans had no rights and the impression that they were regarded as citizens with third-class status. No one was prevented from going to church.

The partisans' headquarters was in the Yugoslav border town of Mariatheresiopol (Subotica). Prohaska, our former burgomaster, Ohlmann, a young farmer who was greatly respected, and a few other citizens, were taken there as hostages. Nothing was heard of them again.

The deportations to Russia were carried out at Christmas time, 1944. The new burgomaster, Cubic, behaved particularly unpleasantly on this occasion. About 30 people, including my neighbor Simon Arnold, were taken off to Russia. These unfortunate people first went to Bacsalmas, where there was a deportation assembly camp, and were taken on from there.

The confiscation of German property took place gradually (it ended in 1950). In 1945-46, the property of Volksbund men was taken away first. It was handed over to the new Magyar immigrants who had come to settle in the locality (the so-called Tschangonen). It should be remarked in passing that some of our richer, intelligent farmers were able to keep their heads above water. The richest of all, M. J. by name, managed, somehow to keep the office of Communal Treasurer until 1950. Despite the fact that he had an agricultural business of about 100 cadastral yokes—about 140 acres, he acted as though he were a Communist and avoided speaking German with his compatriots.

Everyone knew that he was no Communist at heart, but, on account of his specialist knowledge, the Communists had to keep him…

The new Magyar settlers did not all come together to Kunbaja. They came in groups of between 5 and 10 families from the neighborhood of Miskolcz and Debrezin. We were obliged on Cubic's order to fetch these people from the station and to show them into the German houses which had been allotted to them.

When the houses which stood empty had all been taken by the "Tschangonen," a gradual start was made on removing those who had remained behind out of their houses too. Those affected did not go to the camps because expulsions to Germany took place almost simultaneously.

At the beginning of 1947, I became very ill through overwork. I could not get a doctor to attend me and so I decided to have myself treated in a hospital as an in-patient. In the town hospital, I was told that I was already too old and, what was even worse, a "Swabian." I then decided, in August 1947, to leave Hungary by way of Strass-Somerein (Hegyeshalom), along with some other Germans from our neighborhood, and I succeeded in doing so.

I left my wife (I have been married twice) at home. She had brought up and provided for a Magyar orphan after the first world war and, consequently, she still enjoys comparative protection at the present time.

The first people to profit from the possessions of the ethnic Germans were, without doubt, the Bunjewatzen. They took away our movable belongings under the protection of Tito's partisans and enjoyed a privileged position up to the time of my departure. It was the Magyars, on the other hand, who profited from our immovable property, and their lust for booty was first aroused by the measures taken by the State.

The first transfer ordinance was published by the Hungarian government in December 1945. The decree ordered the expulsion of every Hungarian citizen who declared himself to be German in the last census or declared his native language to be German. Also included were ethnic Germans who had previously adopted Magyar last names but changed them back to their German family names. Members of the Volksbund and Waffen-SS were also to be expelled.

The expulsions occurred in two phases: The first phase lasted from January to June 1946. After a short interruption in the summer of 1946, they continued until December 1946. The refugees were sent to the American zone of occupation in Germany. The second phase started in August 1947, with the last transports leaving Hungary in late

1948. These transfers were directed to the Soviet zone of occupation in Germany.

For strategic and political reasons, the first transports were organized from Germans living in Budapest and the villages surrounding it. Then ethnic Germans were removed from the frontier region with Austria, in Western Transdanubia. The expulsion of Germans living in the rural areas was often delayed until after the harvest was collected, as they were required as agricultural laborers. In the course of 1946, there was disagreement with the U.S. authorities on the confiscation of the expellees' property, which the Hungarian government considered as war reparations. Because the United States did not accept this Hungarian claim, the transfers to the U.S. occupation zone were stopped. After agreement was reached with the U.S. occupation authorities, expulsion commenced again, terminating in late 1946. In this process about 170,000 ethnic Germans were transported to the State of Württemberg in the U.S. occupation zone.[30]

The transfer of ethnic Germans began again in August 1947. Because the U.S. government refused to take any more refugees into its zone, they were sent to the Soviet zone of occupation. About 50,000 Swabian Germans were transferred to camps in Saxony from which they were later dispersed to other areas in the Soviet Zone. But by this time the majority of the ethnic Germans that remained in Hungary were anxious to leave, as living conditions for them had become unbearable. Ironically, in this last expulsion, the most skilled and industrious German workers were driven out of Hungary. This had a long-term detrimental effect on the Hungarian economy.[31] The expulsions were completely discontinued in the autumn of 1948.

No. 30

Interrogational Report based on the statements of Heinrich Sziller, a farmer from Hegyhatmaroc, District of Hegyhat in the Baranya Comitat. Original, dated 2 June 1953, typewritten, 5 pages.

Classification of the German population of Hegyhatmaroc according to their political activities, carried out in the autumn of 1945; installation of Magyar immigrants from Czechoslovakia in the expropriated German farms in May-June 1947; transfer of the ethnic Germans to the Soviet Occupation Zone of Germany.

I was drafted into the Waffen SS in March 1944. On 10 February 1945 I got captured by the Russians near Budapest in a Magyar private's uniform, after having been badly wounded in the hand during a defensive action. I was in a military hospital for Hungarian prisoners of war, in

Budapest, under Russian supervision until early in April 1945. Here, I learnt by chance what in the meantime had happened to my wife: she had been deported to Russia. In the middle of April, I was taken with some of my Magyar comrades to a military hospital in Debrezin. We were handed over to the Hungarian authorities there and given specialist medical treatment. I do not' know whether there were any other ethnic Germans there who had disguised themselves as Magyars. Everyone had to be very careful at that time about speaking German, or there was no knowing what might happen to him. I was then let out of the hospital to go on leave for three months.

When I arrived home, Balazs (Baumgartner), the Clerk of the Council, told me that, as a former member of the Local Council, I should have to resume my office again at once... There were three other members of the Council left besides myself. We were indeed able to offer substantial help, particularly in dealing with the measures ordered by the Russian administration...

We were officially informed in the Autumn of 1945 that a so-called "Fact-Finding Commission" would be visiting the places in our area. The members of the Commission, qualified to pronounce a judgment, were: a public notary, one representative member of the Communist, and another of the Smallholder's Party, and, finally, the burgomaster of the locality. The Germans were to be graded in accordance with their political opinions. For determining this, the decisive factors were how they had professed themselves as to nationality at the previous census and whether they had behaved as friends or enemies of the Magyars. Our community was to be divided into six grades. The various consequences entailed for each individual, varying from expulsion, via transfer from one region to another, to the right to keep one's property, which affected only the last grade, depended on the category in which one was placed...

In our locality, the Commission was in session for more than ten days...The Germans were brought before the Commission in the order of the numbers of their houses and asked whether they had been members of the Volksbund, if so, for how long and what were their functions in it. These factors decided the length of their sentence of internment. It was also a matter of importance whether they had served in the German Army and the attitude which each individual had adopted towards the Magyars... I myself was later called in again. Dr. Szabó pronounced the verdict: Group VI. He emphasized the fact that, despite my membership of the Volksbund and of the Educational Committee, I had behaved well and never shown myself hostile to the Magyars. I had several further conversations with Dr. Szabó and Mathe, when we were off duty, and they told me that it was their wish, if possible, to keep the Germans in their homes and not to turn them out. They were in a difficult position, because the Commission was being accused by the Puszta Magyars of pro-German conduct. The Puszta Magyars were waiting to get hold of as much German land as possible for themselves. In our locality, a total of 11 families were placed in Class (I) which involved the gravest consequences (expulsion).

About a fortnight later, another Commission arrived, the so-called "Transfer Commission," which carried out the directions of its predecessor. This Commission took over the properties and lodged the Germans thus affected in houses to which they themselves had suggested they might go. They were allowed to take their furniture and linen with them. Until 1947, they were even allowed, with the exception of Stefan Weiser and Jakob Ruf, to keep their plots of land. Into their houses came the Puszta Magyars, who got their fields from the land belonging to the estate, each family receiving 14 cadastral yokes (about 20 acres).

There was comparative peace until May 1947. I was the village organist.

Farkasch (Wolf), our parish priest, once said to me, "The Germans are getting what they deserve. I should be glad to see them go off with their-packs on their backs to the station."

Then, in May 1947, another so-called "Transfer Commission" arrived with orders to provide dwelling space for the Magyars who had been removed from Czechoslovakia. Dwelling space was now requisitioned without any further regard for the previous classification. It did not matter whether a man had belonged to the Volksbund or not. Each Magyar from the CSR already had his allotment warrant when he arrived. Our fields, moreover, were taken away from us before the 1947 harvest. Each Magyar family from the CSR got its 14 yokes of land allotted by warrant in small plots. So we had to drive out to the fields with them and hand them over our agricultural property. This operation was over by June 1947. We Germans generally were living in one room of the house, which had formerly belonged to us, or with friends and relations.

The Local Council had already been dissolved in the autumn of 1946. We Council Members, who belonged to the German community, were asked to resign. We did so...

Teaching in the schools had been carried on in Hungarian since 1945. In the same way, all sermons since then had been preached in the language of the Magyars. It was only at the local office that, until 1947, people could officially express their wishes in German. Even after that, the new Clerk of the Council, Muhai, was prepared to hear wishes expressed in German, if the applicant was unable to speak Hungarian.

The expulsions to Germany started in our locality in May 1948. About 75 per cent, of the Germans were thus obliged to leave their home. The expulsion was not carried out in a brutal fashion. Our new masters, the Puszta and CSR Magyars, were very sorry to say goodbye to us. We were put on the train at Szasvar-Maza. Many of the Magyars put money into our pockets, though this was taken away from us on the journey by the Magyar police. There were even Magyars who drove after us to Dornbovar, where we stopped for a few days, bringing food for us with them. It was a very kindly parting gesture. I was personally glad that we were now delivered from our misery, but when we left our village and passed the cemetery I could not keep back my tears.

In conclusion, I might state that the sympathy which the Magyars showed towards us Germans increased in proportion to the oppression which we suffered.

On 25 May 1948, my transport went to Pirna (Saxony-Soviet zone of occupation) via Dornbovar and Budapest.

In total, 239,000 Swabian Germans were forced to leave Hungary. About 170,000 went to the US Zone in Germany, 54,000 to the Soviet Zone, and 15,000 to Austria. It is estimated that in these expulsions about 11,000 ethnic Germans civilians lost their lives.[32]

Those ethnic Germans who opted for Hungarian nationality in the 1941 census, who stated their native language as Hungarian and were completely integrated into Hungarian society, generally were able to avoid deportation. By 1948, with the communists dominating the Hungarian government, the issue of nationalism was replaced by class warfare. Communist Party leader Rakosy stated that the remaining Swabians, mostly skilled workers, should be reintegrated into the Hungarian State. In October 1949 a general amnesty of all Germans was announced. Six months later, in May 1950, the expulsions were officially stopped, and all Germans who remained were given Hungarian citizenship. This created its own crisis among the residual German community in Hungary, for now they could not leave because they were Hungarian citizens.[33]

Today the ethnic Germans remaining in Hungary have minority rights such as organizations (Verband der Ungarndeutschen), schools, and local councils. In the 1980s German gained the status of a minority language, thus having legal status within the Hungarian schools system. In the year 2001, about 62,000 persons declared themselves to be German, although the pressure to assimilate to the Hungarian culture continues to be very strong.

Please refer to: http://www.forgottenvoices.net, for a photograph (#21) of Emergency shelters for German–Hungarian refugees in Darmstadt-Hessen 1946.

Notes

1.	Peter Kenez, *Hungary from the Nazis to the Soviets: The Establishment of the Communist Regime in Hungary 1944-1948* (New York, 2006), 214.
2.	Zentrum gegen Vertreibung, ed., *Geschichte der deutschen Vertriebenen und ihrer Heimat* [The History of the German Deportees and their Homeland] (Bonn, 1995), 9, 10.
3.	Charles Ingrao and Franz A. J. Szabo, eds., *The Germans and the East* (West Lafayette, IN, 2008), 94.
4.	Theodor Schieder, ed., *The Fate of the Germans in Hungary, Dokumentation der Vertreibung der Deutschen aus Mitteleuropa* [Documentation of the Expulsion of Germans from Central Europe], vol. II (Bonn, 1961), 14.
5.	Ingrao and Szabo, eds., *Germans and the East*, 151.
6.	Ibid., 179.
7.	Schieder, ed., *Fate of the Germans in Hungary*, 22.
8.	Anthony Komjathy and Rebecca Stockwkell, *German Minorities and the Third Reich* (New York, 1980), 62, 63.
9.	Schieder, ed., *Fate of the Germans in Hungary*, 24, 25.
10.	Kenez, *Hungary from the Nazis to the Soviets*, 213.
11.	Schieder, *The Fate of the Germans in Hungary*, 36.
12.	Komjathy and Stockwell, *German Minorities*, 162.
13.	Carl Savich, *Vojvodina and the Batschka Division*, Elegance ed., Servianna.com (Michigan, 2008), 2.
14.	Ruth Bettina Birn, *Austrian Higher SS and Police Leaders and Their Participation in the Holocaust in the Balkans*, Holocaust and Genocide Studies, vol. 6, no. 4 (Oxford, GB: Pergamon Press, 1991), 359.
15.	Randolph L. Braham, *The Politics of Genocide, The Holocaust in Hungary*, vol. I (New York, 1994), 300.
16.	Schieder, ed., *Fate of the Germans in Hungary*, 38.
17.	Eric Roman, *Hungary and the Victor Powers 1945-1950* (New York, 1996), 63.
18.	Johann Weidlein, ed., *Geschichte der Ungarndeutschen in Dokumenten 1930-1950* [History of the Hungarian Germans in Documents 1930-1950] (Schorndorf, Württemberg, 1958), 334 .
19.	Kenez, *Hungary from the Nazis to the Soviets*, 107, 108.
20.	Laszlo Borhi, *Hungary in the Cold War, 1945-1956: Between the United States and the Soviet Union* (Budapest, 2004), 63.
21.	Martin Mevius, *Agents of Moscow, The Hungarian Communist Party and the Origins of Socialist Patriotism, 1941-1953* (Oxford, 2004), 113.
22.	Ibid., 155.
23.	Ibid., 117.
24.	Borhi, *Hungary in the Cold War, 1945-1956*, 39.
25.	Ibid., 55.

26. Kenez, *Hungary from the Nazis to the Soviets*, 213.
27. Roman, *Hungary and the Victor Powers 1945-1950*, 64.
28. Schieder, ed., *Fate of the Germans in Hungary*, 62.
29. Mevius, *Agents of Moscow*, 139.
30. Schieder, ed., *Fate of the Germans in Hungary*, 65.
31. Kenez, *Hungary from the Nazis to the Soviets*, 215.
32. Schieder, ed., *Fate of the Germans in Hungary*, 73.
33. Ibid., 70.

V

The Flight, Incarceration, and Expulsion of Ethnic Germans from the Former Republic of Yugoslavia

...The Hungarian population, as an indigenous population, shall enjoy all civic rights; only the criminals and servants of the Horthy occupation regime shall be punished. The ethnic German population which, collectively, stood in the service of German Fascism ... deserves no place in our country. However, those ethnic Germans who fought in the ranks of the partisans and the Yugoslav liberation army or supported in other ways the people's liberation battle, shall enjoy all civic rights ...
    —A declaration of the Supreme People's Liberation Committee of Vojvodina

Source: Genocide of the Ethnic Germans in Yugoslavia 1944-1948, Donauschwäbische Kulturstiftung, Herbert Prokle.

Summary

Much of the history of the German community in former Yugoslavia, during and just after World War II, can best be described as a set of mutual massacres between Germans and Yugoslavs. During the war, the Nazi German government raised the 7th Waffen-SS Volunteer Mountain Division, Prinz Eugen, from ethnic Germans living in the Serbian and Croatian regions of former Yugoslavia. Initially, the Germans were induced to volunteer, but as the war turned against Germany, they were conscripted, as occurred in other Eastern European German communities. This was one of the foremost German formations to fight Tito's Communist Partisans, who were mostly Serbs, though other Yugoslav ethnic groups were also represented

207

in its ranks. This unit had one of the worst records of human rights violations of any German formation, massacring civilians, particularly in the Bosnian and Dalmatian campaigns. For example, on September 16, 1941, the German Army High Command (OKW) issued an order that one hundred civilian hostages be executed for every German soldier killed, and fifty hostages executed for every German soldier wounded.[1]

At the end of the war, in retribution, Partisan bands engaged in massacres of ethnic Germans, primarily in the Province of Vojvodina in present-day Serbia. Villages were wiped out, with the inhabitants either killed or forced into concentration camps, where many died of hunger or disease. As justification for their actions to eliminate the German minority in Yugoslavia, the Partisans applied the principle of collective guilt to the German ethnic group for the atrocities of the Nazi regime. Although these acts of collective punishment could not be characterized as genocide, because "the intent to destroy in whole or in part, a national, ethnical, racial, or religious group, as such" (partial definition of genocide from the 1948 United Nations Convention on the Prevention of Genocide) would be difficult to substantiate. Nevertheless, some of their actions appeared to meet the definition of genocide. They were, in any event, clearly crimes against humanity according to the articles of the 1949 Fourth Geneva Convention, which defines collective punishment as a war crime.

The provisional government of Tito's Partisan movement was the AVNOJ (Anti-Fascist Council for the Liberation of Yugoslavia). In its meeting in Belgrade on November 21, 1944, it decreed that all property of ethnic Germans residing in Yugoslavia be confiscated. Their Yugoslav citizenship was revoked, they no longer had any civil rights, and they were declared enemies of the people. Exempted were those ethnic Germans who participated in the partisan national liberation movement, and those who were not members of German ethnic societies such as the "Schwäbisch–Deutsche Kulturbund," nor declared themselves to be members of the ethnic German community.[2]

Of the approximately 524,000 Germans living in prewar Yugoslavia, about 370,000 escaped to Austria and Germany in the last days of the War or were subsequently expelled by the Yugoslav government. Of this number, 30,000–40,000 escaped from Yugoslav concentration and work camps, often with the connivance of the authorities, most going either to Hungary or Romania. Those who went to Hungary subsequently fled or were expelled to Austria or Germany, whereas those who fled to Romania generally remained, at least provisionally, in the Swabian communities in the Romanian Banat. About 55,000 people died in the concentration camps, another 31,000 died serving in the German armed forces, and about 31,000 disappeared, most likely dead, with another 37,000 still unaccounted for. Thus the total victims of the war and subsequent ethnic cleansing and killings was about 30 percent of the prewar German population.[3] After the last important exodus from Yugoslavia ended in the 1960s, any remaining ethnic Germans, usually skilled workers in the mines and factories, made every effort to leave for the German Federal Republic. Today, therefore, no German community remains in the nations making up the former Yugoslavia.

The History of the German Settlements in Yugoslavia

As was the case in Hungary, the ethnic German communities lived in scattered villages and towns throughout Northern Serbia, the majority in the Province of Vojvodina, located on the southern borders of the Panonian Plain, and to a lesser extent, in Croatia and Slovenia. In Vojvodina, the communities were concentrated in the Banat, to the east of the Theiss River. This region was settled by the Banat Swabians who after World War I had their territory divided among Hungary, Romania, and Yugoslavia. To the west, between the Danube and the Theiss Rivers, also in the Province of Vojvodina, the ethnic Germans lived in the Batschka (Bacska) and Baranya regions. These German settlers were known as Danubian Swabians, related to their kinsmen in Hungary. Prior to World War I, the Vojvodina was a part of the Hungarian kingdom of the Dual Monarchy.

In Croatia, the main communities, also very scattered, were in Slavonia and Syrmia. In Slovenia, there were isolated settlements in the Gottschee and a concentration along the Austrian border in Lower Styria and South Carinthia. (See map 21 of German settlements in Yugoslavia)

The majority of the Germans were peasants and more than 80 percent lived in rural communities. They were fairly strongly organized in producers' agricultural cooperatives, financial institutions, and agro-production facilities such as flourmills. One of the largest agricultural cooperatives in Yugoslavia at that time was the German-owned "Agraria," established in 1922. In the Province of Vojvodina, although the Germans made up only one-fourth of the population, they reportedly controlled almost 50 percent of the economy before

World War II. Grain mills and construction firms, such as brick yards and cement plants, were under the control of the Germans, while 80 percent of the exports from Vojvodina originated from farms and companies owned by Germans.[4]

German settlers came into this area after the peace of Karlowitz (1699) and Passarowitz (1718) between the Ottoman and the Habsburg Empires. The Habsburgs found a devastated and almost empty land which they colonized with peasants and artisans from their German lands. Farmers were given many privileges, such as exemption from taxes and fees over a period of years. For craftsmen, the tax-free period was extended for another five years. Peasants in the Banat never had feudal lords, while those in the Batschka and Syrmia were subjects of the feudal regimes of Hungarian magnates.[5]

Please refer to: http://www.forgottenvoices.net, for a photograph (#22) of a typical baroque Catholic village church in the German settlements of Vojvodina.

The Empress Maria Theresa sent German colonists in large numbers to the Province of Vojvodina in the years 1765–1771. This continued under her son, Emperor Joseph II, during the years 1784–1787. As in the case of the German colonies in Hungary, the settlers had to be Catholic in order to ensure their loyalty to the Empire. In the Croatian territories, however, German colonists were brought in, almost exclusively, by aristocratic landowners. In the isolated German community of Gottschee in Slovenia, the Carinthian counts of Ortenburg settled Germans in this forested, sparsely populated region in the fourteenth century. The last wave of German immigration occurred in the nineteenth century, with the elimination of serfdom (1848); the permission for Protestants to settle in this area (1859); and the elimination of the old Austrian military frontier with the Ottoman Empire (1871).[6]

Please refer to: http://www.forgottenvoices.net, for a photograph (#23) of the Petrovaradin fortress, opposite Neusatz (Novi Sad) on the Danube. It was rebuilt by the Austrian Army in 1687 from a previous Turkish fortress. Near this site was one of the great victories in 1697 over the Ottoman Empire by Prinz Eugen of Savoy.

The privileged status of the German settlers came to an end with the Austro-Hungarian Compromise of 1867, when the Vojvodina and adjacent regions became a part of the Kingdom of Hungary. The enforced assimilation of the ethnic Germans into Hungarian society, or Magyarization, became the official policy, driven by the dominant Hungarian administration. This created hostility to the Hungarian

State, especially in the Vojvodina. With the collapse of the Hungarian Kingdom after World War I, the German communities hoped for an autonomous state joined to Romania. Based on President Wilson's Fourteen Point Program, they demanded self-determination in a state called the "Republic of Banat." But with Germany and Austria defeated, this proposal passed unnoticed.[7] The Banat, however, was divided between Romania and Yugoslavia, with a portion remaining in Hungary. In the new Kingdom of Serbs, Croats, and Slovenes, later the Kingdom of Yugoslavia, this region became the Province of Vojvodina.

The new Kingdom of Yugoslavia generally had a positive attitude to its German minority in Vojvodina, where the greatest number lived. Since the Serbian population, just as the German, had suffered from Hungarian assimilation pressures, their support of the ethnic Germans was an insurance against Hungarian irredentism. In those communities where they were a majority, Germans were permitted to have their own schools, newspapers, and cultural societies. At this time, they established a national cultural and educational organization called the "Schwäbisch-Deutsche Kulturbund," which over time came to represent the national and political aspirations of the German minority in Yugoslavia. Its main purpose was to maintain the sense of a separate German identity.

On the other hand, in the Provinces of Croatia and Slovenia, conditions differed appreciably. As these had previously been under the direct rule of the Austrian portion of the Dual Monarchy, the German communities were considered a remnant of the past. All German societies, institutions, and associations were eliminated and their property confiscated. In majority German districts, local German officials were replaced with Yugoslav functionaries and German civil servants were dismissed.

The Kulturbund did have its problems with the new Yugoslav government, which repeatedly closed it because of illegal political activity. Its authority was canceled and then reinstated a number of times, until 1934, when, with the German–Yugoslav trade agreement and political rapprochement between the two countries, it began to grow into a more important organization with the agreement of the Yugoslav authorities.

Just as in the other German Eastern European and Balkan communities, the advent of the National Socialist regime in Germany caused profound changes in the German community. Pan Germanism came to the fore, together with an evolution of the "Kulturbund" along Nazi ideological lines. An internal split developed in the German ethnic minority. Traditionalists wanted to maintain good relations with the host government, while a "renewal" movement sought greater autonomy for the ethnic group in the Yugoslav state. Nazi German foreign policy was ambivalent. The Nazi party wanted to support the German community and use it for its expansionist goals, whereas the official government position, as expressed by the foreign office, was to maintain good relations with the Yugoslav government for its trade and investment objectives, thereby discouraging a radicalization of demands by the ethnic Germans.

This dichotomy was reflected in relations between the German minority and the Yugoslav State, which swayed back and forth between more liberal and tighter regulations of the group. Yugoslav government difficulties with the Croats and Slovenes who were seeking a federalist state also influenced their relations with the German community. Good relations, however, came to an end on March 27, 1941, with the military coup against the then-existing Government of Prime Minister Dragisa Cvetkovic, which was considered too pro-German. The new military government, consisting of Serb nationalists, arrested the entire German ethnic leadership. Even before that date, the Serbian nationalist press had called for the expulsion of all ethnic Germans and warned that they were a fifth column within the State.[8]

The German Minority in World War II

The Wehrmacht attacked Yugoslavia on April 6, 1941, ostensibly to help its ally Italy—then involved in a losing conflict in the Balkans—but most probably to secure its southeastern flank in its planned attack on the Soviet Union. The Yugoslav government surrendered on April 17. On April 10, the nationalist Croats had declared an independent state of Croatia, led by Croatian fascists, called the Ustasha. Croatia then became an ally of the Axis. The Hungarians invaded on April 11 and re-incorporated the Western Vojvodina, namely the Batschka and Baranya, into the Hungarian state. The Eastern Vojvodina, or the Banat, remained under the German military government and was effectively turned over to the administration of the ethnic German minority. Their wish, however, of making a greater German community in South-Eastern Europe, a so-called Danubian State, was frustrated by the expansionist policies of the dominant nations of the region, plus the crucial fact that they did not receive any support from the Reich government. Although the majority of Danube Swabians were, in general, nonpolitical, they did welcome the German invasion because it would bring to an end the discrimination they felt as a minority in Yugoslavia and give them cultural autonomy.

As a result of the partitioning of Yugoslavia after its defeat, the ethnic Germans became subjects of independent nations. Germans living in Syrmia and Slavonia became citizens of Croatia. Those in the Batschka and Baranya regions of the Province of Vojvodina became Hungarians, and those living in the Banat were in German-occupied Serbia. The Germans of Lower Styria and South Carinthia, formerly a part of the Province of Slovenia, were annexed to the Reich (Austria). Because the Gottschee was given to Italy, the ethnic Germans were resettled in Lower Styria.

In the independent country of Croatia, the ethnic Germans were given legal status as a separate ethnic group. They enjoyed considerable cultural autonomy, such as equal rights in education. The central issue of cultural autonomy was schooling in the mother tongue, which was now permitted. After the Batschka and Baranya were incorporated into Hungary, the "Schwäbisch-Deutsche Kulturbund" became affiliated with the "Volksbund der Deutschen in Ungarn." (See Chapter IV on Hungary for details.) The German minority received the same privileged, legal status as in Hungary. For example, it could now have German schools and church services in the German language. In the Banat, the German military government permitted the ethnic Germans to establish an independent administration. In the case of Lower Styria and other adjacent areas that were incorporated into Germany, of those Yugoslavs who refused to be assimilated, about 10,000 were expelled to Serbia and 20,000 were sent to work in the Reich.[9]

The Yugoslav civil war began with the horrific massacres of Bosnian Serbs (Bosnia became a part of independent Croatia), as well as Gypsies and Jews, by the Croatian Ustasha. Their stated objective was to drive one-third of the Serbs out of Croatia, convert one-third to Catholicism, and kill the rest.[10] The massacre of Bosnian Serbs began in April 1941, shortly after the surrender of Yugoslavia. By the fall of 1941, over 120,000 Serbs had been forced out of Croatia into Serbia. It is estimated that 250,000 Serbs were converted to Catholicism, with the help of the Croatian Catholic church. In all, about 300,000–350,000 Serbs died at the hands of the fascist Croatian government in World War II.[11]

The genocidal Ustasha policy accelerated the build-up of two opposing Yugoslav resistance movements that ultimately came to blows. The first was the Serbian Chetnik movement under the royalist

Colonel Draza Mihailovic. The second was the all-Yugoslav Partisan army under the leadership of the Communist Party of Yugoslavia (CPY), which became active after the German attack on the Soviet Union. The Partisans fought the Germans and Ustasha all over the country, whereas the Chetniks limited themselves to resistance in Serbia. The CPY with Tito at its head fought a guerrilla war within the Communist popular front political framework. The Partisan approach was not to espouse revolutionary Communist ideology but to fight a war of national liberation. As such it was the only belligerent force in Yugoslavia that was multiethnic. In time, the Partisan movement became more effective in confronting the Axis forces than the Chetniks, so the Allies, particularly the British government, shifted their support from the Chetniks to Tito's armed struggle. By the end of 1942, the Partisan Army had grown to 100,000 men and was able to hold large swaths of liberated territory in Serbia, Montenegro, and Bosnia.[12] As a consequence, the Chetniks became more anti-Partisan than anti-German and increasingly cooperated with the Axis in their anti-Partisan campaigns.

Please refer to: http://www.forgottenvoices.net, for a photograph (#24) of Chetniks with German soldiers in a Serbian village.

The Ethnic German Participation in the Waffen-SS Division "Prinz Eugen"

To counteract the growing guerrilla activities, the ethnic German communities were recruited into the German war machine. At first, a number of Germans joined the local self-defense groups, called "Deutsche Mannschaft," which had already existed before the war in the form of sports clubs, "Deutsche Sportmannschaft." Despite later claims of the Tito government, these German self-defense groups did not materially help the German Army in their advance into Yugoslavia in April 1941, neither through sabotage nor other armed actions against Yugoslav government troops. They did serve, however, as a recruiting base for the Waffen-SS.

Beginning in 1940, the Waffen-SS began to recruit ethnic Germans aggressively because the professional army restricted it from doing so in Germany proper. Up to that point, the Waffen-SS was an all-volunteer army. For Himmler and the SS, the ethnic Germans were a fertile recruiting ground, unhindered by the prohibitions of the Wehrmacht. By the end of 1943, 25 percent of the Waffen-SS were ethnic Germans, with 310,000, serving in the various units.[13]

As early as 1938, SS recruitment of Danubian Swabian youths began in the guise of sport training in Germany. The goal of the SS was to establish a separate SS division from the Volksdeutsche in Yugoslavia for the purpose of protecting German communities and fighting the Partisans. There were problems in attracting sufficient volunteers to form the unit, so in the summer of 1942 unofficial conscription began using "public pressure" and stronger methods such as even beating recruits and carrying them away by force. The German Banat government stated that, "from this service nobody who is healthy can exempt himself." Ultimately, all males between the ages of seventeen and fifty were eligible for conscription in the Waffen-SS.[14] (See Chapter IV, Hungary, for an eyewitness description of this process.)

The majority of these recruits served in the 7th SS Volunteer Mountain Division "Prinz Eugen," which was formed in April 1942. The Division's name comes from François Eugene, Prince of Savoy (1663–1736). Born in Paris, France, he entered the service of Habsburg Emperor Leopold I, in 1683. He was made Field Marshall in 1693. One of the greatest European soldiers of the time, he led the military campaigns of the Holy Roman Empire against the Ottoman Turks that would lay the foundations for Habsburg power in central Europe.

The history of this Division is as follows:

> After a fairly long process of attempting to form an SS Division from the large Volksdeutsche community living outside of Germany, and not merely to incorporate them into other various Wehrmacht units, Gottlob Berger (As head of the SS recruiting office) managed to help create the 7th Division of the SS. The 7th Division of the SS was formed from the Volksdeutsche living in the Serbian and Croatian areas of Yugoslavia first by volunteers, and then through conscription. The Division was initially established in March of 1942 from an SS Selbstschutz (SS Protection Force) and the Einsatz-Staffel (Also called Prinz Eugen) from Croatia. In the early months..., it ...struggled to fill its ranks through the use of volunteers alone, and soon conscription was used to finish the Division, eventually gaining some 21,500 members.

> The 7th Division of the SS was designed for anti-partisan warfare in the Balkan region. It was during such operations in October, 1942, that the Division first saw action near the Serbian-Montenegro border.... Soon after, the Division was transferred to the Zagreb-Karlovac area and took part in Operation White with other German units. Operation White was one of many major anti-partisan operations in the Balkan Region aimed at destroying Tito's resistance movement.

This operation failed, however, as Tito's forces managed to evade the brunt of the German offensive.

Throughout the next few months, the Division was placed under Army Group E, and in May, 1942, took part in more anti-partisan operations, this time during Operation Black.

In the following years, the Division moved frequently, fighting in Bosnia, north of Sarrajevo, then Mostar on the border with Croatia. It then saw service in Dalmatia, disarming Italian troops in September 1943, after Italy left the war. In December of that year it was in action again against Tito's troops.

In January, 1944, the 7th SS Division was transferred to the Split, Dubrovnik area for more training and reorganizing. It returned to the Bosnian area in March, 1944, and continued its part in anti-partisan operations. In May, 1944, the 7th fought again against Tito's partisans near Drvar. Next, the Division was moved and fought against Russian and Bulgarian units in August, 1944. At this time, the Division suffered greatly and took many casualties.

In September, 1944, the Division saw action in what was probably its most important role so far. Prinz Eugen, along with elements of other Waffen SS units helped to hold a vital bridgehead in the Vardar Corridor in Macedonia in order to help 350,000 German soldiers escape from possible encirclement by the advancing Soviets. The 350,000 German soldiers were attempting to move north from occupation duties in the Aegean and Greek regions of the Balkans. Prinz Eugen was badly mauled, but the operation proved a success. After helping to hold the line in the Vardar Corridor, the Division subsequently took part in many rear-guard actions resulting in a long retreat from Cacak all the way to Brcko and over the Drina.

In January, 1945, the Division fought partisans near Otok, and later was sent to the area of Vukovar where it fought again against advancing Soviet forces and Tito's partisans. From February, 1945 to April, 1945, it was in action against Partisans and Soviets, finally surrendering in Slovenia and being taken prisoner by the Yugoslav government.

Source: Edited from *Axis History Fact Book.*

About 15,000 Germans from the Banat served in this Division and 17,500 from Croatia. Perhaps one of the worst atrocities committed by this Division occurred with the massacres in March/April 1944, when hundreds (other sources speak of some 3,000)[15] of Serbian and Croatian civilians were murdered, in reprisal actions, in the villages of

Ruda, Cornji, Dorfer, Otok, and Dalnji in Dalmatia. The Wehrmacht justified these actions as collective punishment for Partisan attacks on its soldiers.[16] The Partisans, on the other hand, deliberately used these German Army reprisal tactics by often provoking them and forcing local people to flee into the mountains to avoid the attacks, and then recruiting them into their ranks. Another example of collective punishment occurred in October 1941, when the German Army, Volksdeutsche units, and Serbian allies massacred, in retribution for German soldiers killed by Partisans, over 2,000 men and boys in the town of Kragujevac and nearly 1,800 men and women in the town of Kraljevo.[17] A further case of war crimes committed by the Prinz Eugen Division was in the summer of 1943, when it liquidated the inhabitants of Kosutica, because Einsatzkommando 2 (SS liquidation units whose members were often furnished by the Waffen-SS) reported that apparently its troops had been fired on from a church.[18]

One of the most graphic pieces of evidence against the Prinz Eugen Division was presented by the Yugoslav delegation at the Nuremberg war crimes trials. It was a photograph taken from a Waffen-SS prisoner showing a Yugoslav being decapitated with an axe while grinning Waffen-SS soldiers looked on.[19]

Please refer to: http://www.forgottenvoices.net, for a photograph (#25) of the execution of Serbian civilians. In one of the first German retribution actions, hostages were shot in the Serbian village of Panacevo, April 21, 1941, in retaliation for one German soldier killed and one wounded. One hundred civilians were rounded up at random, eighteen were shot, including those at a cemetery wall, pictured here, and eighteen civilians were hanged, including one woman.

A proclamation posted by SS-Sturmbannführer Breimeier, a Battalion Commander of the Prinz Eugen Division, illustrates their war crimes:

> On 3 November 1943, around 2000 hours, a German soldier on the Velika Street in Sinj was ambushed and killed. Since, despite all efforts, the culprit has not been found and the population has not supported us in this matter, 24 civilians will be shot and one hanged. The sentence will be carried out on 5 November 1943 at 0530 hours.

Source: The International Military Tribunal, 1946, vol. 20, 402.

Please see: http://www.forgottenvoices.net, for a photograph (#26) of a poster issued by the SS in January 1944 stating that as a result of the murder of German soldiers, the above thirty indicated individuals, "bandits," have been executed on January 19, 1944.

At the Nuremberg War Crimes Trials, the Yugoslav State Commission on War Crimes entered the following commentary on the war crimes committed in May 1943 by the Prinz Eugen Division in the Niksic area, at the time of its antipartisan operations known as Operation Black conducted in Montenegro and Bosnia.

> Immediately after its invasion, this formation, opening fire with all its arms, commenced to commit outrageous crimes on the peaceful villages for no reason at all. Everything they came across they burned down, murdered and pillaged. The officers and men of the SS Division Prinz Eugen committed crimes of an outrageous cruelty on this occasion. The victims were shot, slaughtered and tortured, or burned to death in burning houses. Where a victim was found not in his house but on the road or in the fields some distance away, he was murdered and burned there. Infants with their mothers, pregnant women and frail old people were also murdered. In short, every civilian met with by these troops in these villages was murdered.
>
> In many cases whole families who, not expecting such treatment or lacking the time for escape, had remained quietly in their homes, were annihilated and murdered. Whole families were thrown into burning houses in many cases and thus burned. It has been established from the investigations entered upon that 121 persons, mostly women, and including 30 persons aged 60-92 years and 29 children of ages ranging from six months to 14 years, were executed on this occasion in the horrible manner narrated above.

Source: The International Military Tribunal, 1946: vol. 20, 375.

It is estimated that about 93,450 Yugoslav Germans actively participated in World War II as soldiers either of the Waffen-SS or Wehrmacht. This represented 18.6 percent of the ethnic German population, according to the last prewar census of 1931.[20]

As a reaction to the Nazi German war crimes, the Yugoslav population, particularly the Serbs, developed a hatred of Germany and Germans which explains the harsh treatment of the ethnic group after the war. Despite the fact that the majority of the ethnic Germans were apolitical, many did side with Nazi Germany and some participated in the atrocities of the SS. Others, however, opposed this route. Some Swabians, especially among the Catholic and Protestant clergy, were against National Socialism. A small contingent of ethnic Germans even joined the Partisan movement.

Please refer to: http://www.forgottenvoices.net, for a photograph (#27) of German soldiers escorting Yugoslav civilians from Kragojevac to be executed.

The Evacuation and Flight of Ethnic Germans from Yugoslavia

Due to the advance of Soviet forces in the Balkans and the increasing success of Tito's Partisan Army, the German Army in October 1944 began a systematic evacuation of Danubian Swabians from Croatia. This was a difficult decision for the Nazi political leadership because it was tantamount to saying that Croatia and parts of Hungary were lost, thus putting in doubt the willingness of the Hungarian and Croatian governments to continue the war on Germany's side. Most of the Swabians were evacuated by train and wagon treks to Hungary, and from there to Austria. In this fashion about 225,000 Danube Swabians, from the Croatian regions of Slavonia and Syrmia, avoided Partisan captivity.[21]

In late 1944 the Red Army entered Vojvodina and the first persecution of Germans began, especially by the Soviet NKVD units. Local German authorities were immediately arrested as well as members of the Kulturbund. In this, the Soviets were assisted by the OZNA, the Partisan secret police (Department for the Protection of People). The German evacuation of the Vojvodina, the districts of Batschka, Baranya, and Banat, came too late to avoid Soviet occupation. In the Banat, less than 10 percent of the population escaped because the Nazi party authorities prohibited any preparations for flight. It is estimated that at this point, about 200,000 ethnic Germans came under the control of the Soviets and Tito's Partisans.[22]

Deportation to the Soviet Union

Following the Soviet Army's occupation of Vojvodina, and with assistance from the Partisans, mass arrests of ethnic Germans took place for the purpose of providing forced labor for Russia. From December 1944 to January 1945, it is estimated that between 27,000 and 37,000 Swabian Germans were rounded up by Soviet and Partisan forces. These were mostly women between the ages of eighteen and forty years.[23] They were deported to the Soviet Union to work on construction sites and mines in the Ukraine, initially for a period of three years, though some were forced to stay for five years. On their release, the survivors were sent to the Soviet occupation zone of Germany. There are different estimates of the death toll, but they run between 16 percent and 23 percent of those deported.[24]

219

The following report was recorded and published in *Leidensweg der Deutschen im kommunistischen Jugoslawien* taken from *Genocide of the Ethnic Germans in Yugoslavia 1944-1948*, Donauschwäbische Kulturstiftung, and forms part of the Central Government Archives in Bayreuth of the German Federal Republic.

The History of the Transports

It was during the Christmas days of 1944 that the ones selected by the local partisan/Communist functionaries had to leave all their loved ones, spouses, children, relatives and friends. They were forced to march with their baggage, often long distances and under strict military escort, to the collection camps. There, some of them were checked by Russian doctors, others were not, before chasing all of them to railway stations... During frigid temperatures the work slaves were shipped in cattle cars that were locked from the outside. There was no space for movement, ability to sleep only in a sitting position and running the risk of freezing to death while asleep. Food supplies were almost non-existent and people had to survive on what little they could bring along. The lack of water was particularly painful since it was often withheld for sheer sadistic reasons. In the crowded space and absence of all hygienic facilities, bodily functions could only be taken care of with greatest difficulties. In addition, they had to suffer the mental and emotional anxiety of not knowing where they were going and when this trip was going to end. The first casualties occurred already during the three-week trip.

Catastrophic Accommodations and Difficult Working Conditions

In Russia the tightly guarded billets initially often had neither windows nor doors. The premises were fenced in by barbed wire. Considering the notorious Russian winters, heating material was inadequate and often completely lacking, hygienic facilities insufficient, no warm water for washing and toilet facilities catastrophic. Epidemics and infestations started to erupt.

The food supply consisted almost entirely of lumpy, sour-tasting and hardly digestible bread as well as cabbage or flour soup without any meat or fat. The food had to be picked up from kitchens that were up to three kilometers away. The dishes consisted of rusty tin cans. Sometimes they were forced to exchange good clothing against torn and lice-infested military garb.

Extremely hard work had to be performed in all weather conditions. The work targets were usually set much too high. While bread rations were adjusted to the work requirement, they were still insufficient. In addition to the heavy work load, the long distance to the work stations entailed long arduous marches, even during snow storms. The women too had to perform hard labor, many of them below ground, down deep in the coal pits. Twelve hours and more daily, including Sundays, were mandatory, in winter at 40 degrees Celsius below zero in wet and torn clothing.

The High Mortality Rate

Even though Danube Swabian men and women were used to hard physical work, many could not endure the working conditions in the mines, at the railroad and construction sites. Undernourishment, humidity, rain, cold, excessive work hours and the excessively long distance marches led to the total exhaustion of many. Men in particular, who had to work the hardest, soon suffered from dystrophy...

The slave labor in the Soviet Union resulted in the loss of life of at least 2,000 Danube Swabians. That is about 17 percent, including 1,100 men and 900 women. For those who were able to survive, the term of the slave labor lasted up to five years.

The first repatriation of the very sick and unable to work started towards the end of 1945. At that time many had already died. One of the first repatriation trains went to Yugoslavia where the returnees were promptly put into camps, most of them into the death camps.

It was only during the last two years of their stay in Russia, 1948 and 1949, that the conditions improved. Food was adequate and working conditions more bearable. At the end of 1949 the Russians dissolved the camps and shipped the deported to Frankfurt an der Oder, in East Germany. The last to leave had spent five years of hardship in the "workers paradise."

The following eyewitness report was recorded and published in *Leidensweg der Deutschen im kommunistischen Jugoslawien*, taken from *Genocide of the Ethnic Germans in Yugoslavia 1944-1948*, Donauschwäbische Kulturstiftung, and forms part of the Central Government Archives in Bayreuth of the German Federal Republic.

4.2 "Life and Suffering in the Soviet Union"—An Eyewitness Report

In the Modoscher Heimatblätter no. 155, 156 and 157 Anna Bernauer nee Zettl gives an account on how her family was torn apart, on her forced labor in the Soviet Union, the ethnic re-education and suffering of her small son till he finally found his way back to his parents. Here are excerpts of this personal experience.

On the second Christmas holiday 1944, at six o'clock in the morning, the police drummer was already making his round and announced that all German women between 16 and 40 years of age have to report to the city hall at eight o'clock. At four in the afternoon they already took us away...

The writer reports further that they were chased to the provincial capital Betschkerek, via Stefansfeld, and there temporarily locked up. New Year's Eve we were again chased through the streets of Betschkerek to the railroad station. Along the way we were spit upon, yelled at, pushed and beaten. The train moved very slowly, and when it came to a halt I saw the church steeple of Modosch. At daybreak family members appeared: parents, grandparents and children. Word was passed around and they brought straw, clothing, bedding and food. First the Russian guards did not let them to the trains, but they pushed forward and finally, with the help of some packs of cigarettes, they let the cars containing the Modosch women be opened and the items passed over to them. But the children, that wanted to join their mothers, were not allowed to approach.

There were four trains with about 60 cars each and it was a blessing for the people locked inside that the Romanian engines still had not arrived and the trains remained at Modosch for several days. Thus most of the prisoners could obtain a few things for their long frigid trip into the unknown. The Serbian partisans tried to prevent the supply of the prisoners, however the Russians, who had already taken control of them, stopped them. Then we left the Modosch train station. There were heart-breaking scenes that I shall never forget; parents, grandparents and children clung to the railroad cars, crying and screaming. The partisans and Russians beat them with fists and rifle butts till they fell back and the trains could move forward...

The train moved very slowly through Romania. It stopped occasionally, but the doors were never opened. At Ploesti, we received, for the first and last time, some food for the 15 days trip. At the Russian border we were transferred since the Russian railroad was of a different gauge.

January 18th, 1945 we arrived at Kriwoi Rog in the Ukraine. It was terribly cold.

The five, six houses in the camp were all wet inside. The very next day after our arrival we had to start working. It was very hard, strenuous work; loading and unloading gravel, bricks, coal and carrying railroad tracks etc. Our Russian female guards, armed with rifles, constantly yelled at us to work faster...

We were often told we could go home, but these were always just lies. One evening we had to stand in formation in the courtyard. New officers arrived and inspected our hands and feet. They too said we could go home, but it wasn't true. The next day we were loaded on trains and taken to Dnjepropetrowsk...

During our stay in Russia we were never paid for our work. But our sleeping accommodations at Dnjepropetrowsk were good; we had plank beds. At Kriwoi Rog we had iron beds, but no mattresses and only wire and two women had to sleep in one bed; we always slipped on top of each other. A few days after our arrival we had to report for medical examination. We had to disrobe completely and, one at the time, enter a large room in which our 13 lieutenants were sitting. They were laughing and cracked suggestive jokes—only to degrade us.

The second day we were in Dnjepropetrowsk the Russians placed a large barrel with salted herring in each corner of the courtyard and told us we could eat as much as we wanted—and some did and died...

In 1946 I became so homesick that I had a breakdown. I was unconscious for two days and two nights. The nurse, from Transylvania, later told me that I wept a lot and always called for my child.

During the summer of 1946 they called for volunteers who were willing to work straight for twelve hours and then have 24 hours off. I noticed that the Russians sent those home that could no longer work. Therefore, I volunteered for the hard work in an iron mill. The first thing we did every evening, when we came home, was search for lice. Later I followed the advice of a Russian and used kerosene. While my head had a kerosene odor, I had no more lice.

In 1946 many of our deported men died; they often just keeled over and died.

1 don't know why, but women were able to endure better. Many inmates suffered from lack of vitamins, had large sores an their backs which were very painful- but they still had to go to work.

The winter of 1946 was very cold and many suffered from frostbite, as they did in other winters too .l was among them; my toes and heels in particular were affected. The water pipes were frozen and for six days we had no water. For cooking we brought water from the river Dnjepr, but there was no water for washing. Sometimes we had no bread for three to four days.

In January 1947 we were supposed to go to a medical examination, but who were the physicians? They were our 13 officers! We were told to listen carefully. They told us who was going home and therefore immediately relieved of work. We were supposed to recuperate and eat well. (I was one of them.) But the food became progressively worse and we always were fed last. The so-called soup was only hot water and I noticed I became worse day by day. I knew I could not survive on that food and I was getting weaker by the day. At the end of January a nurse told me to sell what jewelry I had left otherwise I would not be able to make the trip home. I still had two rings and a set of earrings and sold the latter. With that money I could buy oil, sugar and bread. Thereafter I felt better and the nurse saved my life with her advice.

In May 1947 we actually departed from Russia. For the entire trip through Poland all we had was one loaf of bread, nothing else. When we crossed the bridge to Frankfurt/Oder we fell onto our knees and thanked God that we had left the Soviet Union.

The Fate of the Ethnic German Minority in Tito's Partisan Government

The first action of the Partisans on taking over a community was to establish local "Peoples Liberation Committees." They initiated the arbitrary arrests of members of the German ethnic groups, not only those in public administration, former members of the "Deutsche Mannschaft," and of the Waffen-SS and other Nazi organizations, but of nonpolitical ethnic Germans as well. All men between seventeen and sixty years and their wives and families were sent to improvised detention camps. Concurrently, the Partisans began the arbitrary revenge murder of Swabian German civilians that had the character of a mass liquidation of a targeted ethnic group. It is calculated that between 7,000 and 8,000 civilians from the German communities in Vojvodina were killed in this fashion in the late fall of 1944.[25]

In November of that year, all Germans living in towns were sent to concentration camps established in former depopulated German villages whose previous inhabitants had either escaped, or been expelled, killed, or imprisoned. Simultaneously, all Germans were required to work for the Partisan government. These concentration camps then became labor camps as well. The first concentration camps for those Germans who could not work, the old, the infirm, and children, were established in early December 1944. They were called "liquidation camps" as food was grossly insufficient and many starved to death. From then until the last remaining Germans were released from Yugoslav detention in 1954/1955, the lives of the Swabian Germans played themselves out principally in concentration and work camps.[26]

The following report was recorded and published in *Leidensweg der Deutschen im kommunistischen Jugoslawien*, taken from *Genocide of the Ethnic Germans in Yugoslavia 1944-1948*, Donauschwäbische Kulturstiftung, and forms part of the Central Government Archives in Bayreuth of the German Federal Republic.

Banat

The murders and massacres in the Banat were partly carried out in the respective localities and partly concentrated in regional camps of the district capitals.

The Soviet army conquered the western Banat (belonging to Serbia) beginning of October 1944 and ceded power to the Communist Tito-regime. In almost all places immediate sporadic revenge actions occurred. A few days later general persecutions started against the ethnic German population which obviously were predetermined as they all followed the same pattern. About 4,000 victims are registered by name, however, many more ethnic Germans of the Banat were murdered with unimaginable cruelty during this bloody autumn 1944. Since many families and kinships were completely exterminated from 1944 to 1948, there was nobody left who knew and could have registered all victims of those family circles.

About 90 percent of the bloody autumn victims were men and an obvious aim of the partisans was to liquidate the Danube Swabian males of the Banat. Since all those liable for military service were in combat at the front-lines, the partisans mainly seized very young and relatively old men. Youngsters of 14 years upwards and seniors up to over 70 years were murdered.

The first killing phase generally took place in their respective home places during first half of October 1944. Most of the victims were intellectuals, leading and respected persons as well as well-off farmers and tradesmen ("Action Intelligentsia"). Starting by the middle of October 1944, the second killing phase continued through December 1944 and to a lesser extent until spring of 1945. Now all ethnic German men (and some women) within the specified age limits were arrested and taken to regional liquidation camps, regardless of their economic situation or education. Many of them were tortured for days and then murdered. The most notorious regional liquidation camps were the "Milk Hall" in Kikinda for the northern region of the Banat; the "Old Mill" in Betschkerek for the central area of the Banat; and the "Stojkovic-Telep" in Werschetz for the southern Banat. To a smaller extent but nevertheless with bestial cruelty the local camps in Deutsch-Zerne, Pantschowa and Kubin also were used to liquidate ethnic Germans from other villages.

In the course of 1945 all ethnic Germans were expropriated and interned in camps. During this process the regional liquidation camps were gradually integrated in the system of local and central civilian labor camps.

The expulsion of the ethnic Germans from Yugoslavia was not decided at the Potsdam Victors' Conference in August 1945, unlike the fate of the German population of Poland, Czechoslovakia, and Hungary. Prior to the end of the war, Tito's Yugoslav government did not yet have a clear idea of how to rid themselves of their German population, just that they had to go. As previously discussed, the AVNOJ issued a decree in November 1944 canceling all the civil rights of German citizens, confiscating their lands, and declaring them "enemy of the people." Already, in the previous month, October of 1944, the Partisan government decided to intern all Germans in concentration or work camps. Only those Germans remaining in Slovenia were expelled to Austria between August 1945 and spring of 1946. Austria, however, refused to accept large numbers of expellees, so they ended up in Yugoslav concentration camps as well. The majority of the ethnic Germans living in Vojvodina, particularly in the Banat region, were all sent to concentration camps. At one point, in January 1946, the Yugoslav government requested the U.S. military authorities' permission to transfer these ethnic Germans to the U.S. occupation zone of Germany, but it was not granted.[27]

There were three types of camps: The first were central labor camps, mostly for men sufficiently healthy to work in the fields and in construction; able-bodied men and women were initially put to work cleaning up war damage and then on road and other construction jobs. Later they were placed in factories and on state and private farms. The latter work was much preferred, for although difficult, it permitted them to increase their food rations and thus the possibility of survival.

The second were the community camps, in effect transit camps, where the inhabitants of a particular town or village were kept, usually in other abandoned, former German villages, before deciding their fate. The last were the concentration camps for those unable to work, the elderly, and many women and children. The concentration camps were called liquidation camps by the Banat Germans, because that is where they were sent to die. Food was extremely scarce and below the daily minimum required to survive. In the winter of 1945/1946, for example, some concentration camps did not receive any food at all for five or six days, leaving the prisoners to starve.[28]

The mortality rate in the concentration camps was very high due to malnutrition and disease. For example, in the Rudolfsgnad camp, of the total 33,000 ethnic Germans that passed through between October 1945 and March 1948, over 10,000, that is about one-third, died.[29]

The following report on the history of a main concentration camp was recorded and published in *Leidensweg der Deutschen im kommunistischen Jugoslawien*, taken from *Genocide of the Ethnic Germans in Yugoslavia 1944-1948*, Donauschwäbische Kulturstiftung, and forms part of the Central Government Archives in Bayreuth of the German Federal Republic

Camp Rudolfsgnad/Knicanin (Banat)

Established October 10th, 1945 for ethnic Germans unfit for work, particularly of the Middle and South Banat.

Original size of the town of Rudolfsgnad: 3,200.

Number of internees, average: 17,200 average (maximum: 20,500).

Duration of camp: October 10th, 1945 to mid-March 1948 (29 months).

Casualties: about 11,000 (7,767 documented by name).

Main cause of death: starvation, typhus, malaria.

Overview

The large "special camp" Rudolfsgnad was located at the edge of the ethnic German settlement area of the Banat. Traffic-wise it was well-situated and easy to control since it was positioned at the point where the river Theiss flows into the Danube. Of the town's 3,200 inhabitants, 900 did not flee.

Before all the camps in Yugoslavia were officially dissolved in 1948, all their remaining inmates were transferred to Rudolfsgnad. There all remaining ethnic Germans were conscripted into three years "work contracts," mostly serving in areas outside their home territories, e. g. the mines of Serbia and Kosovo and the marsh areas of Baranja, Batschka and around Pantschowa. For about three years they were not allowed to leave the assigned places, i. e. as from 1948 to 1950 they still were not really free but banished people.

The health conditions, illnesses, treatments and mortality statistics were well documented by Dr. K. F. With 11,000 deaths Rudolfsgnad had the highest mortality rate of all the camps...

On December 27th, 1944, 47 girls and women as well as 20 men were deported to Russia as slave workers. On April 14th, after the village was completely ransacked, the Rudolfsgnad inhabitants had to leave their houses. Then all the women and children were concentrated in the school building and the men age 14 and up in the Kindergarten.

As of October 10th, 1945 the Tito-regime interned thousands of ethnic German civilians, predominantly senior citizens, women with children and children whose mothers were shipped to Russia and concentrated them in the now empty houses. The camp was guarded by about 80 armed militia.

The arrivals, dressed with only minimal clothing, were crammed into the empty houses, usually 20 to 30 to a room. They had no blankets and were forced to lie on the floor which was only barely covered with straw. During the entire period of the camp's existence and up to its dissolution in March 1948, the straw was never changed nor replaced.

227

Nourishment consisted of ground corn soup, polenta (maize) mash, corn bread and tea, no salt. Even babies and feeding mothers received nothing else or any additional rations. Initially, the usual camp soup was ladled out, but already in the winter 1945/46 it was given out scarcely and the inmates received only about two kilogram of raw ground corn per month...

Klara Deutsch, at that time only 13 years old, records: "People became blind or insane because of starvation, or they just lay down, went into a stupor for a few days until they fell asleep for good. The worst off were the ones that became insane. They screamed day and night; many walked around aimlessly, could not find their way home and died in the street." Stray cats and dogs were butchered; even dead ones were eaten. The sufferings from diarrhea are indescribable; they drained the last strength from their bodies and also led to other diseases. Once hit by diarrhea or dysentery, there was rarely a recovery. That winter thousands died.

These conditions forced people to desperate attempts to slip out of the camp and beg for food in the surrounding villages, inhabited by other nationalities. The Catholic priest Johann Nuspl, formerly priest at Tscheb in the Batschka, remembers that during one of these begging trips four women and five children were shot by the guards. The ones caught were usually locked into the cellar, called the "bunker," received almost no food but instead fierce beatings which some did not survive.

Cooking in the camp's kitchen resumed in spring 1946 and was considered a comfort not known for many months. The soup consisting of peas and barley was, for those that survived this terrible winter, the essence of delicacy. Beginning 1947 the food rations were somewhat improved; however, for the emaciated inmates hardly noticeable. As of May the restrictions on receiving packages was eased... Also, many who had Serbian relations or acquaintances, could occasionally benefit from these relaxed restrictions. The Care program and the International Red Cross relief actions were supplying some camps. Now even packages from America arrived, sent by relatives who learned of the misery at Rudolfsgnad, father Nuspl reports.

Beginning May 1946 a "softer touch" in the elimination started at Rudolfsgnad as in other camps as well, apparently directed by higher authorities and due to political considerations. Now parcels could be shipped directly into the camp. The larger aid program, initiated by Peter Max Wagner and his Danube Swabian Aid Society of Brooklyn, started towards the end of 1946. The first phase of large-scale parcel shipments from the USA probably reached the camp around Christmas 1946.

Starting spring 1946, Serbs and Hungarians in the surrounding area could "lease" camp inmates for work, at a rate of 50 Dinar per head. The Germans were often shamelessly taken advantage of by their employers. Nevertheless, the inmates eagerly competed for this slave work since they received at least some food whereas there was almost nothing to eat within the camp. For many this outside work opportunity was a lifesaver. Also, starting in spring 1946 and particularly in 1947 many inmate workers took this opportunity to escape. At an opportune moment they sneaked away, searching a way to cross the border into Hungary or Romania. It was always a life threatening undertaking.

The heroic endeavors of the camp physicians and nurses, who them-selves were internees, to fight against diseases and the epidemic were mostly in vain. The deplorable hygienic conditions, the meager rations, lacking salt and vitamins contributed to the spread of the epidemic. The physical and mental deterioration of the humans robbed them even of the strength to defend themselves against the infestations of lice, mice and rats that suddenly appeared in large numbers. Where the rats didn't find anything to eat they started to gnaw not only at the dead but also the defenseless living. The mortality rate reached its peak in February 1946.

Finally, the spread of the epidemic alarmed the authorities and a medical commission arrived to investigate. Quarantine was declared and the camp was sprayed with DDT powder. The group of physicians and nurses, risking infection themselves, worked selflessly to fight the epidemic and to save the humans. Nevertheless, many succumbed. In April 1946, after the epidemic was eradicated, the quarantine was lifted and the camp received a "clinic" for adults, a "children clinic" and a "children home." There the food was somewhat better than in the camp.

The "homes for the aged" were virtual dying places. Father Johann Nuspl, a camp inmate himself, was allowed to visit the homes in Molidorf as well as Rudolfsgnad twice a week. He writes about his visits: "The sick and dying were lying on the floor which was covered with a thin layer of straw, tightly crammed together and separated only by some loosely placed tiles. Dirty bowls with rotten food leftovers, pots serving as spittoons, unwashed bed pans, dirty rags etc. were scattered among the sick and dying; many in their own feces. This was the last chapter of our people's tragedy. I had never seen our people in such misery and downcast as here, however, at the same time so heroic. Most of them died composed and god-devoted. I remember with awe and reverence the people in these homes."

The partisans' treatment of the ethnic German children is one of the saddest chapters in the chronicle of the Yugoslav liquidation and slave labor camps. One has to keep in mind that the initial occupants of the dying camps consisted of boys and girls under 14 years of age.

Lorenz Baron, assistant to electrician Weissmann who had to install electric lighting in the so-called "children home," writes: "Upon entering the home one could hear a monotonous hum. It was the song of the children dying. Every room of the large building was full of defenseless, dying children. Not able to express any feelings myself, I climbed up the ladder and installed the fixtures. Some of the skeletons below me were still able to move somewhat and followed every move I made. Some then fell back, their gaze still focused on me ~ and were dead. Nobody showed any compassion, knowing that we ourselves could be the next to die."

The same author writes also: "We went daily to the pump well to drink water.

There the children were sitting and catching each other's lice. Almost all had the scabies, pussy corners of the mouth and the cheeks of some were already rotted off, the teeth exposed like on a skeleton. Most were quietly weeping and listless, yet, the groaning of the poor children could also be heard outside the house."

During the summer of 1946 the authorities then began to allocate groups of children to government children homes in order to assimilate them as "good citizens" into the national fold...

Leaving the camp was strictly forbidden. Dr. K. F. recorded eleven executions in 1946 and three in 1947. In spring 1947 two men cutting down a tree were caught by a policeman and shot. Out of desperation eleven inmates committed suicide. Every death and cause was recorded. The month of February had the highest mortality: 1,346. February 4th had the highest daily number: 72. Total deaths during the existence of the camp (October 10th, 1945 to March 1948) were over 11,000.

The first mass graves were dug at the village cemetery. Due to the floods in spring 1946 no more dead could be buried there, but had to be moved to the Teletschka hill, about two kilometers south of Rudolfsgnad.

The following history of the labor camps was recorded and published in *Leidensweg der Deutschen im kommunistischen Jugoslawien*, taken from *Genocide of the Ethnic Germans in Yugoslavia 1944-1948*, Donauschwäbische Kulturstiftung, and forms part of the Central Government Archives in Bayreuth of the German Federal Republic.

Central Civilian Internment and Labor Camps

Overview

The internment of the Danube Swabians in Yugoslavia in central civilian labor camps began October 1944; the internment of the Gottscheer and German Untersteirer (German residents of the Gottschee and Untersteiermark - Lower Styria (see map 21) took place at the end of the war. By August 1945 all communities of Yugoslavia were "cleansed" of their ethnic German inhabitants. Only Germans married to other nationalities or the few that had joined the partisans were spared from confiscation of property and internment.

The Communists established three types of camps: work camps, central civilian camps and "special camps." The latter served as liquidation camps for those unable to work.

In July and August 1945 the central camps and work camps reached their maximum capacity of about 120,000 civilian internees, of which over 100,000 came from the Banat and Batschka. They consisted mainly of marginally able-bodied men and women.

There were ten central camps in the Banat, nine in the Batschka and one in Syrmia, and about 200 work camps under the jurisdiction of the central camps. Each community with more than 200 to 300 German inhabitants maintained a work camp, consisting mostly of empty, pillaged German houses.

The central camps were set up primarily in existing barracks or former factories.

Some were filled with several thousand internees in cramped facilities. These camps served, particularly in the Banat, during the "bloody autumn 1944" as the partisans' torture and execution stations.

The central camps allocated laborers for its work camps. The food provided for the forced laborers was usually completely insufficient. Starting in spring 1946 Slavs and Magyars could "buy" laborers for a day, month or longer periods (payable to the camp's commander; the prisoners did not receive any remuneration). For those lucky ones, it was often a life-saving opportunity. The condition in the central camps often resembled those in the liquidation camps. This is borne out by the fact that about 12,000 men and women, mostly of able-bodied age, perished between the end of 1944 and the beginning of 1948.

The Treatment of Children

Young children were normally sent to the concentration camps as they could not work. However, once they reached thirteen or fourteen years they were required to work in the factories or farms. A great many were orphaned as their fathers were either killed or working in labor camps and the mothers deported to the Soviet Union, died of diseases, or simply disappeared.

In the spring of 1946 the Tito government organized child transports from the survivors of the concentration camps and sent them to camps in Macedonia, Montenegro, Slovenia, and Croatia for renationalization as Yugoslavs.[30] (This was a violation of Article II of the Convention on the Prevention and Punishment of the Crime of Genocide of December 9, 1948, Paragraph e: Forcibly transferring children of the group to another group.)

In 1950, due to worldwide pressure and with the assistance of the International Red Cross and the German Federal Republic, the Yugoslav government permitted family reunifications. This was a very difficult undertaking as most of the children could no longer speak German and had no idea of the whereabouts of their parents. In the period 1950–1959, about 2,300 children could be reunited with their families in Germany and Austria.[31] Exact figures are very difficult to find, and often contradictory, but another report states that there were still 28,000 German children in Yugoslavia in the spring of 1950 awaiting family reunification, when this repatriation movement began, with an estimated 6,000–8,000 German children remaining in Yugoslavia, thoroughly integrated into the local culture.[32]

The following are eyewitness accounts of the treatment of children in the concentration and childrens' camps in Yugoslavia as published in *Leidensweg der Deutschen im kommunistischen Jugoslawien*, taken from *Genocide of the Ethnic Germans in Yugoslavia 1944-1948*, Donauschwäbische Kulturstiftung, and form part of the Central Government Archives in Bayreuth of the Federal German Republic.

> David Gerstheimer, born 1936 at Kischker/Batschka. Within a few months after being interned at the Jarek liquidation camp his mother, six siblings and grandparents died of starvation. David, at that time eight years old, was the only survivor and sent to a government children home for re-education and "Slavinizing" (LW III, 647; VDJ 244).

> Father Wendelin Gruber S. J. (1914-2002), born in Filipowa/Batschka. He spent some time in the Gakowa death camp: "Afternoons I went to the children sections which were set up in the larger farm houses. There the children, between 20 to 30 in a room, were lying around, only on straw and scantily covered. Only skin and bones, sick, and with infected wounds. Nobody cared for them. The small ones cried and screamed pitifully—they were starving. Others were lying motionless; they didn't even have the strength anymore to cry. I went from room to room, always the same picture. A woman who took over as caretaker led me to the room in the back. Carefully she pulled the cover from a pile of children... These little ones, in a row on rags are almost naked; skin and bones only. They were gasping

for air with open mouths. The last thing the world can offer them. 'We pulled these out since they cannot digest food any more and are the first to die,' was the reply" (LW III, 623; VDJ, 244 ff.).

Suco, the almighty commander of the Gakowa camp, responding to the question what plans the Communists had for the surviving children tells father Wendelin Gruber: "Don't worry, comrade Pope! Everything will be in order! Our Socialist State will look after the children. They now will be adequately fed and then housed in government children homes. A progressive kindergarten teacher has already arrived. She will now take over the responsibility for a good education. These children will be Tito's pioneers and brave fighters for our liberation revolution.

You will see, these fascist, capitalist children will become model members of the liberated working class and enthusiastic supporters of a better future" (LW Ill, 624; VDJ, 245 f.).

This programmed re-education which was supposed to awaken the hatred for their "fascist" parents was reported by most of the children. At the time of the reunification process there were children who did not want to go home to their "criminal parents"...

At the Jarek camp, Friedrich Glas from Bulkes who saw two of his great-grandparents and two grandparents, as well as his two years old sister starve to death, was caught, together with his friend Peter Kendl slipping out of the camp to go begging. The two partisans took them to the guardroom. After a while they were led back to the place where they were caught and motioned to go away. After they made a few steps the guards then shot at them from behind. Fritz, who played dead, survived. The wounded Peter however screamed, after the guards had already started to go away. They returned and killed him with a bullet to the head (LW III, 566 ff.; VDJ, 247).

Suicides because of despair, fright and sense of shame after being raped also occurred. Not even children were spared from rape during the mass rapes at Deutsch-Zerne in October 1944. Eva Bischof, only nine years old, was cruelly raped by nine men. Her injuries were so severe that she lost consciousness and was unable to move. Thereupon her own mother, in desperation, hung her child and she hung herself (LW III, 238 ff.; VDJ, 248).

Juliane Wirag (1908) from Ridjitza strangled her twin daughters, born in 1944, because she could find no way to save them from slow starvation and then hung herself (LW III, 546; VDJ, 248)...

Karoline Bockmiiller (1905), Deutsch-Zerne, Banat, describes the condition of the children section in a part of the Rudolfsgnad liquidation camp. "I had to visit this children camp and happen to enter a room which contained 30 to 35 children (from babies to 16 months old) whose parents had died. None of them could stand, let alone walk. They were just lying there or slid around the room on their bellies. The room was reeking of excrements. The children were crying, were pale and starving. Their bodies were smeared with excrement, which was partially dried to the skin. I fled from the room, weeping and asked the women whether there was anybody to look after these poor abandoned children. They replied they could not help since they had no diapers, nor towels, water basins, water, soap, practically nothing. They continually asked the camp administration for just the basic requirements, however received nothing, only the comment: "'The children should kick the bucket.' They also tried repeatedly to take away my grandchild and put it into the children camp, but I did not give her up. After she died I escaped from the Rudolfsgnad camp and went to Molidorf to look for my mother. There I was told that my mother and aunt had died of starvation in the camp" (LW III, 508; VDJ, 245 f.).

Peter Wilpert (1938) from Palanka/Batschka about the conditions at the liquidation camp Jarek: "Both grandmothers died within a week. After that I was, six years old ... all by myself, terribly alone" (LW III, 654 f.; VDJ, 248 f.).

Katharina Weber nee Lauterer (1935) from Bulkes/Batschka, at that time ten years old, was together with six of her schoolmates at the Jarek liquidation camp. Five of them died between September 1945 and February 1946. The sixth girlfriend died in October 1947 at the Subotica camp. The surviving Katharina was shipped to a government home (LW III, 572; VDJ, 247)...

The Flight and Eviction of the Yugoslav German Minority

In the spring of 1946 more and more opportunities presented themselves for the German inmates of the various camps to flee individually or in groups to neighboring Hungary and Romania despite rigorous government control of the camps. Particularly those Swabian Germans working outside the camps in agriculture or clean-up work had the best opportunities to escape. The still existent German communities in Romania and Hungary came to the aid of these refugees and facilitated their onward journey to Austria or Germany.

In early 1947 conditions in the camps improved slightly, with an increase in food rations, and above all with the delivery of food parcels from the Swabian immigrant communities in the United States. The application of the insecticide DDT to the prisoners and their living quarters helped to suppress the typhoid epidemics previously raging in the camps. The guards were also changed from Partisans to regular army or militia units that reduced the most blatant arbitrariness.[33]

Despite flight and deaths from executions, over-work, and starvation, by the beginning of 1947 it is estimated that there were still 100,000 ethnic Germans in the various Yugoslav concentration and labor camps. At this point, the decision was taken by the authorities to facilitate the eviction of the Germans by permitting them to flee the camps, against bribes to the camp commanders and guards, to Hungary and Romania. They occasionally even provided guides for the border crossings. For example, there were mass flights from the large concentration camp at Gakovo, when between December 1946 and March/April 1947 over 3,000 prisoners fled to Hungary. This would not have been possible without the connivance of the authorities. It is estimated that between 30,000 and 40,000 ethnic Germans escaped in this fashion in 1947.[34]

The following are eyewitness accounts of flight from the camps in Yugoslavia as published in *Leidensweg der Deutschen im kommunistischen Jugoslawien*, taken from *Genocide of the Ethnic Germans in Yugoslavia 1944-1948*, Donauschwäbische Kulturstiftung, and form part of the Central Government Archives in Bayreuth of the German Federal Republic.

> Johann Hebel of Gakova, an eyewitness who served as a gravedigger during his internment reports: "Whenever people were captured during an escape, the partisans finished them off right at the border. We picked up many such bodies and brought them back for burial at the camp cemetery. Once we had a husband, wife and their eight to ten years old son. The parents were beaten to death and the boy's stomach slit open with a bayonet from top to bottom with his intestines hanging out."

> Ernst Lung from Hetin, district of Modosch/Banat, reports: "During the autumn 1945 maize harvest, several ethnic German women and girls succeeded in escaping through the dense maize fields to Romania. These escapes disturbed the partisans.

> As a retaliation, two internees, arbitrarily selected, had to gather their bundles, were chased across the railroad tracks and shot to death 'trying to escape.'

> Despite further reprisals, threatened by the camp commander Kuljic, more and more inmates risked their flight. Thus, about 30 more Germans from the Deutsch-Zerne camp and others from Hetin managed to flee to Rumania. One night in January 1946, several Germans from the camp Deutsch-Zerne, among them Mathias Kaiser and Johann Hockl from Hetin, risked their escape. During this attempt one man and two women were stopped by a partisan

patrol near the border. These three, including Mrs. Retzler from Stefansfeld, were initially badly maltreated, then shot to death and buried at the knacker's yard.

The internees, in addition to their desperation, suffered from hopelessness since at the beginning of 1946 the daily food rations were reduced to three watery soups, in spite of the imposed heavy work load. The enslaved internees preferred risking death during the escape rather than languishing in the claws of the partisans."

Johann Pudel tells about his escape from Kruschiwl/Batschka in 1947: "Our first attempt failed. We sold everything we had. There was an order, stating that all persons left behind in a room or house out of which inmates escaped, were to be executed for 'aiding the escapees.' In order not to endanger anybody and not to be betrayed out of fear, we began to move out during the night into a house where finally all 30 persons who wanted to escape were the only ones in the house. One night we sneaked out of the village, following a guide, past the guards and across the fields. We had to cross a brook, over a narrow, rickety bridge. We have a painful and sad memory of this bridge. There, a mother lost her three to four years old child. Not to give us away, she could not call out for the child. In addition, she had to look after her own mother and had hoped her child was with some other person in the group; however, it could not be found and presumably slid into the brook and silently drowned."

Magdalena Brenner from Filipowa/Batschka describes how she was taken to the Gakowa liquidation camp, together with her two youngest daughters (out of a total of seven) Viktoria (12) and Katharina (9) as well as two grandchildren and also the starvation, maltreatments, typhoid epidemic and the mass dying in that camp...

Magdalena's husband Georg Brenner was a discharged soldier in Hungary and learned that a large part of his family was at the Gakowa camp. Together with a young man who had crossed the border several times as a guide for escapees and whose family was also at Gakowa, he went there to steal his family out of the camp.

During the mentioned snowstorm both men sneaked into the camp and Georg found his family, totally weakened by starvation and sickness. Sadly- he had to realize that they were not fit enough to undertake the escape and initially wanted to return alone to Hungary. However, his daughter Maria was not to be deterred. In order to escape the terrible camp life and certain starvation, she insisted in accompanying her father, together with her five years old son, even though she had not yet fully recovered from her typhoid disease. They also took along the daughter Viktoria.

Magdalena Brenner now relates the escape of part of her family: "The evening of January 16th my husband, daughters Viktoria and

Maria with her child Martin sneaked out of the camp. Their guide, a young man from Brestowatz, also took his family along. He was an experienced 'border crosser.' During the snowstorm it was easy to leave the camp unseen—but the route was very problematic. Once out of the camp they had to move through the high snow and storm towards the Hungarian border. For the weak camp inmates the going was terribly difficult... First the mother-in-law of the guide, then his wife died in the open field, about one kilometer from the Hungarian border...The guide had enough problems of his own. He pointed out to my husband the direction to go and told him to keep moving.

My husband could no longer find the way he came from Hungary. The children stopped to rest for a while and he went to search for the right way. When he returned Maria was getting worse. My husband took her to a stack of maize stalks, about one kilometer from the border. Here they found shelter. Maria became progressively weaker and could no longer walk... She died in the arms of her father... Outside the stack the snowstorm continued mercilessly and snow covered the maize shelter in which they endured their greatest misery and total loneliness.

My husband then got up again and resumed his search for the right way (when being sure about the route, he intended to pick up the children and flee across the border with his dead daughter), but was captured by a border guard. The guard wanted to take him along, however my husband told him that there were his children waiting for him. The guard went with him to the stalk pile. There my husband told him that he also had a dead daughter. Unmoved the guard replied 'we'll bury her' and forced everybody to go with him...

Three human beings out of a small group died in their desperate attempt to save their naked life. Nobody knows what ever happened to their beloved deceased. My husband, Viktoria and little Martin were chased to the headquarters at Rigitza.

There they were terribly maltreated...After a few days they were interrogated and the verdict pronounced: execution by firing squad. When my husband asked why execution, the partisan said because he took his family out of the camp.

They were chased into the street in front of the headquarters and had to sit down into the snow. A partisan opened the window and aimed his rifle at them. At the last moment another partisan pushed him aside and closed the window. Then they were chased into the Kruschiwl camp. The trip to the camp was terrible, through the snow, cold and torture. After several months they were able to escape from Kruschiwl and came back to the Gakowa camp; unfortunately without the daughter Maria."

The Closing of the Camps, Forced Labor, and Emigration to the German Federal Republic

Early in 1948, the Yugoslav government's strategy for dealing with its ethnic German minority changed again. The officially sanctioned flights to Hungary and Romania were stopped by increasing border controls. All the camps were closed, and those Germans capable of working were sent to the state-owned factories, mines, and collective farms. They were required to sign three-year work contracts, which did not give them, however, the status of free citizens. They were sent to live in barracks and emergency housing attached to coal and copper mines, factories, and farms and were not allowed to leave their place of work. Although the workers did receive some wages, at the end of the day, with government deductions for lodging and food, very little was left for their own use. Undoubtedly, this was a form of forced labor, but living conditions were a great improvement over life at the camps. Generally, they were allowed to take their families with them.[35]

Old people and those unable to work were eventually sent to old-age homes and clinics where there was a marked improvement in food rations, and medical and sanitary conditions, and overall, more humane treatment.[36] German orphan children went to state orphanages and schools where they underwent re-education in order to make them into loyal Yugoslav citizens.

At the end of the three-year forced labor period, the surviving Germans not only received their civil rights back, but ironically, their Yugoslav citizenship, even though most did not want it at this point, because their homes and villages were destroyed, and their families had either fled or were dead. If they did not accept Yugoslav citizenship willingly, however, they were then threatened with the withholding of housing and a return to the camps. Young Swabian German men were now even required to do their military service in the Yugoslav Army.[37]

In the early 1950s the West German government opened its borders to the Swabian Germans still living in Yugoslavia. With the assistance of the International Red Cross and the German and Yugoslav Red Cross organizations, a repatriation program first began for family reunification. This was later expanded to cover all ethnic Germans. As these Germans were now Yugoslav citizens again, however, they had to receive official authorization to emigrate. Initially, the Yugoslav government was unwilling to permit this as they needed the workers, especially the skilled workers, in their mines and factories. Permission was finally granted, however, against payment of a substantial exit tax of up to 15,000 Dinars, which was the equivalent of three or four month's wages.[38] Eventually all Germans were able to gather these funds, quite often with foreign assistance, and left in organized transports for West Germany. In the years 1950–1960, about 53,300 Germans emigrated[39] although some sources indicate that the total number was higher, 70,000–75,000.[40] In any event, this last exodus represented the end of 250 years of German colonization and settlements in the former Yugoslavia.

Notes

1. Theodor Schieder, ed., *Das Schicksal der Deutschen in Jugoslawien, Volume V, Dokumentation der Vertreibung der Deutschen aus Ost-Mitteleuropa* [The Fate of the Germans in Yugoslavia, Volume V, The Expulsion of the Germans from East-Central Europe] (Bonn, 1961), 60.
2. Ibid., 102, 103.
3. Johann Wuescht, *Jugoslawien und das Dritte Reich* [Yugoslavia and the Third Reich] (Stuttgart, 1969), 282.
4. Stefan Wolff, *German Minorities in Europe* (New York, 2000), 150.
5. Ibid., 145.
6. Schieder, ed., *Das Schicksal der Deutschen in Jugoslawien*, 7.
7. Wolff, *German Minorities in Europe*, 140.
8. Anthony Komjathy and Rebecca Stockwell, *German Minorities and the Third Reich* (New York, 1980), 140.
9. Herbert Prokle, ed., *Genocide of the Ethnic Germans in Yugoslavia 1944-1948* (Munich, 2006), 33.
10. Philip B. Minehan, *Civil War and World War in Europe, Spain, Yugoslavia, and Greece, 1936-1949* (New York, 2006), 104.
11. Ibid.
12. Ibid., 187.
13. Heinz Höhne, *The Order of the Death's Head* (New York, 1971), 517, 518.
14. Komjathy and Stockwell, *German Minorities*, 144.
15. Terry Goldsworthy, *Valhalla's Warriors* (Indianapolis, IN, 2007), 97.
16. Charles Ingrao and Franz A. J. Szabo, eds., *The Germans and the East* (West Lafayette, IN, 2008), 354.
17. Minehan, *Civil War and World War in Europe*, 142.
18. Höhne, *Order of the Death's Head*, 530.
19. George H. Stein, *The Waffen SS, Hitler's Elite Guard at War* (New York, 1966), 274.
20. Wolff, *German Minorities in Europe*, 152.
21. Schieder, *Das Schicksal der Deutschen in Jugoslawien*, 87.
22. Ibid., 89.
23. Ingrao and Szabo, eds., *Germans and the East*, 357.
24. Wuescht, *Jugoslawien und das Dritte Reich*, 282.

25. Prokle, ed. *Genocide of the Ethnic Germans in Yugoslavia 1944-1948*, 51.
26. Schieder, *Das Schicksal der Deutschen in Jugoslavia*, 93.
27. Ibid., 99.
28. Ibid., 109.
29. Ibid.
30. Ibid., 111.
31. Prokle, ed., *Genocide of the Ethnic Germans in Yugoslavia 1944-1948*, 139.
32. Wuescht, *Jugoslawien und das Dritte Reich*, 280.
33. Schieder, *Das Schicksal der Deutschen in Jugoslawien*, 112.
34. Ibid., 114.
35. Herbert Prokle, *Der Weg der Deutschen Minderheit Jugoslawiens nach Auflösung der Lager* [The Way of the German Minority in Yugoslavia after the Liquidation of the Camps] (Munich, 2008), 14.
36. Schieder, *Das Schicksal der Deutschen in Jugoslawia*, 115.
37. Ibid., 116.
38. Ibid., 117.
39. Ibid., 118.
40. Prokle, *Der Weg der Deutschen Minderheit Jugoslawiens nach Auflösung der Lager*, 19.

VI

The Fate of the Ethnic German Minority in Romania

Romanian Land Reform Law of 1945

Chapter II Expropriation.

Art. 3. For the purpose of realizing the program of agrarian reform, the following agricultural estates, together with the livestock and equipment belonging to them, shall pass into the hands of the State to be distributed to peasants entitled to acquire allotments and to form the reserves of land for which provision was made in Art. 2, points c) and d);

    a.   areas of land and agricultural property of any kind belonging to German citizens and to Rumanian citizens of German nationality (ethnic descent), whether they are natural persons or bodies corporate, who collaborated with Hitlerite Germany;

    b.   areas of land and other agricultural property of war criminals and of those responsible for the country's disaster;

    c.   areas of land of those who have fled to countries with which Rumania is at war and who fled the country after 23 August 1944;

Excerpt from the Romanian Land Reform Law of 1945.

Source: Documents on the Expulsion of the Germans from Eastern-Central Europe, vol. III, Theodor Schieder, ed.

The Historical Ethnic German Settlements in Romania

The Transylvanian Saxons

In 1224 the Hungarian King, Andras II (1205–1235), granted territorial, political, and religious autonomy to the Saxons in his "Golden Charter" (Goldener Brief, Andreanum). He granted privileges to "our faithful German guest settlers in the lands beyond the forests" (fideles hospites nostris Theuthonici Ultrasilvani). The translation from the Latin, "Transylvania," means the land beyond the forest. The names Ultrasilvani and Transylvania were used interchangeably for many years. They both mean "beyond the forest." Germans referred to it as "Siebenbürgen," for the seven original towns that were established by the colonists: Bistritz (Bistritsa), Hermannstadt (Sibiu), Sächsisch Regen (Reghin), Mediasch (Medias), Mühlbach (Sebes), Kronstadt (Brasov), and Schässburg (Sighisoara). (See map 22 of German settlements in Romania)

The Saxons were first called to colonize a depopulated and neglected region (terra deserta et inhabitata) by Hungarian King Geza II (1141–1162) as guests (hospites) to defend the southeastern frontier from incursions by Mongols and other eastern war-like tribes and to develop agriculture on the so-called "Königsboden," the king's grant. The Germans came mostly from South-Western Germany, the Rhineland, and what is today Lower Saxony, hence their name. German colonists also came to northeastern Transylvania, near Bistriz (Bistritsa) and Sächsisch Regen (Reghin). Because this land was not previously settled, the Saxons were able to create large territorial blocks almost exclusively inhabited by themselves.

As a result of the "Golden Charter," the Saxons now formed the third privileged ethnic ruling group in Transylvania, together with the Hungarians and the Szeklers, the latter a Hungarian-speaking ethnic group of nomadic herders that came from Eastern Europe.

In 1486 the privileges granted in the Andreanum were confirmed and extended to the other Saxon settlements by Hungarian King Mathias Corvinus (1458–1490). This second grant established a Saxon assembly, called University of the Saxon Nation, "Sächsische Nation-universität," in which all Saxon communities were represented. This institution represented the entire Saxon "Nation" over the centuries. Its authority included the administration of justice, management of the economy, and internal regulations and laws. The University was headed by the freely elected Count of the Saxons. It was an advisory as well as executive body. The capital was Hermannstadt (Sibiu).[1]

Please refer to: http://www.forgottenvoices.net, for a photograph (#28) of the Lutheran Cathedral of Hermannstadt (Sibiu, Romania).

Continuing conflicts with an expanding Ottoman Empire and strife within the Hungarian ruling class characterized the history of the Transylvanian Saxons in the fifteenth, sixteenth, and seventeenth centuries. The Turks defeated the Hungarians in the battle of Mohacs in 1526 and Central and Southern Hungary became an Ottoman province in 1541. Siebenbürgen maintained its autonomy, but became a vassal state of the Ottoman Empire. The Habsburgs inherited the Hungarian Crown with the death of the last Jagollonian King in 1526.

After the Ottoman invasion of Austria failed in 1683, the Habsburg armies went on the offensive against the Turks, led principally by Prince Eugene of Savoy. By the end of the seventeenth century, the historical Kingdom of Hungary including Transylvania was liberated from the Turks.[2] Transylvania became an Austrian crown colony (1687) ruled from Hermannstadt (Sibiu). Although the autonomous constitution of Transylvania was maintained by treaty, there was a decrease in its significance as all important decisions were now made in Vienna.

Saxon national autonomy—and Ottoman indifference—permitted the introduction of Luther's teaching at the time of the Reformation in 1540, despite the strong support the Habsburg emperors later gave to the Catholic Counter-Reformation. The autonomy of the Transylvania Saxons was temporarily abolished by the reforms of the Habsburg Emperor Joseph II (1780–1790) but was restored by his brother and successor Leopold II (1790–1792). In 1876, after the Hungarian Compromise of 1867 made Transylvania a part again of the Hungarian Kingdom of the Dual Monarchy, many of the Saxon privileges were eliminated. These affected primarily the territorial autonomy of the "Königsboden." The Saxon assembly, the University of the Saxon Nation, remained.[3]

The Swabians of the Banat

German colonists came from the Rhineland, and South-Western Germany (Swabians) in response to an appeal by the Habsburg Monarchy to settle an area devastated by the wars with Turkey. As was the case in the Saxon communities in Transylvania, the Swabians were able to create large blocks of land almost exclusively settled by themselves due to the depopulation resulting from the Turkish wars. The only condition imposed on the colonists was that they be Catholic in order to ensure their loyalty to the Monarchy. After the treaty of Passarowitz (1718) with the Ottoman Empire, Germans came in the course of the eighteenth century in several waves, from 1718 to 1739 and from 1756 to 1766.[4] In a marshy area located between the Danube and the Mieresch (Mures) rivers in Western Romania (see map 22), the Swabians created a highly productive agriculture. At the time, it was considered the bread basket of the Habsburg empire. An urban, middle-class culture of merchants, artisans, and professionals also developed. The Banat in today's Romania was part of a larger Swabian settlement area of ethnic Germans which was divided among Hungary, Yugoslavia, and Romania after World War I by the treaty of Trianon with Hungary. Romania received the eastern portion, with its capital at Temeschburg (Timisoara).

As with the German ethnic group in "Siebenbürgen," Transylvania, the Banat became a part of the Hungarian Kingdom of the Dual Monarchy as a result of the 1867 Hungarian Compromise. A Hungarian national administrative system was imposed on the minority which then became subject to very strong magyarization pressures on their German language and customs. Although the Hungarian Nationality Law of 1868 guaranteed the equality of all nationalities in the nation, it was never respected by the political leadership. Because the national institutions of the Banat Swabians were not as developed as those of the Transylvanian Germans, they were not able to resist this pressure and many became assimilated Hungarians.[5]

Please refer to: http://www.forgottenvoices.net, for a photograph (#29) of St. George's Cathedral, Temeschburg (Timisoara), built in 1774 by the Banat Swabians in the Austrian baroque style.

The Inter-War Years

After the collapse of the Austro-Hungarian Monarchy at the end of World War I, the Romanian parliament declared Transylvania a part of Romania. This was confirmed by the 1920 peace treaty of Trianon with Hungary. The annexation of Transylvania and the Eastern Banat had been previously agreed to by the Allies in exchange for Romania's August 1916 declaration of war on the Central Powers. (Although Romania adhered to the Central Powers' pact prior to World War I, it never declared war on the Allies). Because cultural autonomy of the nationalities in Romania was promised in the declaration of Karlsburg (Alba Julia), of November 1918, the Transylvanian Saxons, and later the Banat Swabians joined the Romanians in a declaration of union.[6]

> The Karlsburg Resolutions (printed in part)
>
> The Resolutions of the Rumanian National Assembly in Karlsburg (Alba Julia) of 18 November 1918.
>
> I. The National Assembly of all Rumanians from Transylvania, the Banat and Hungary, who in the persons of their authorized representatives assembled in Karlsburg on 18 November (1 December) 1918, has resolved that these Rumanians and all the lands which they inhabit shall be united with Rumania. The National Assembly proclaims in particular the inalienable right of the Rumanian nation to the whole of the Banat as enclosed by the rivers Mures, Tisza and Danube.

II. The National Assembly reserves to all the aforesaid territories the right to provisional autonomy, until the constituent body, elected on the basis of universal franchise, has met.

III. As regards this autonomy, which is to be the basic principle of the new Rumanian State, the National Assembly proclaims the following:

1. Full national freedom for all peoples living together in the State. Each people will be educated, administered and judged in its own language by persons from its own ranks and will have the right to be represented in the legislative bodies and in the Government in proportion to the number of its members.

2. Equal rights and full autonomous freedom of belief for all denominations in the State.

3. A truly democratic regime to be realized in full in all spheres of public life. A franchise that shall be universal, equal, secret, based on the localities and on the principle of proportional representation. The suffrage shall be extended to members of both sexes, from the age of 25 and over, for the election of representatives to the communal and regional councils and to Parliament.

4. Complete freedom of the press, of association and of assembly; complete freedom of thought.

5. A thorough land reform: The setting up of a land register to control all landed property and especially the large estates. By virtue of this land register it is to be made possible, by breaking up estates entailed on the eldest child and by the right to reduce as needs be the larger ones in size; for the peasants to acquire as much land (arable, pasture and forest) as they and their family can cultivate. The guiding principle in this agrarian policy is greater social equality combined with increased production.

6. The safeguarding of the same rights and advantages for industrial workers as have been secured for them by legislation in the majority of progressive Western states.

IV. The National Assembly expresses the wish that the Peace Conference may bring into being a community of free nations in such a way that justice and peace will be safeguarded for all nations, great and small, in the same way and that, in future, war be excluded as a means of determining relations between them.

V.   The Rumanians assembled in the National Assembly send greetings to their brothers in the Bukovina who have been freed from the Austro-Hungarian yoke and united with their Rumanian motherland.

VI. For the further conduct of the affairs of the Rumanian nation as regards Transylvania, the Banat and Hungary, the National Assembly resolves that a Greater Rumanian National Council be established which will be fully entitled to represent the Rumanian nation on all occasions and in all places before all nations of the world and to take all steps that it considers necessary in the interests of the nation.

Source: Documents on the Expulsion of the Germans from Eastern-Central Europe, Volume III, Theodor Schieder, ed.

In 1920 the German population in Romania totaled some 716,000, or about 4.5 percent of the population. Because of its long history of autonomous administration, it was probably the best-organized and best-led German minority group in Eastern Europe. In exchange for their loyalty to the new Romanian nation, the authorities granted a great deal of freedom to the German community, particularly in forming national organizations. The Deutsche Partei was formed in 1920 by German members of the Romanian Parliament, and an umbrella organization of the entire ethnic group, called the "Verband der Deutschen in Rumänien" (Association of Germans in Romania), was created in 1921. Their purpose was to maintain the cultural autonomy, language, and identity of the German ethnic group.[7] In general, the Romanian authorities favored the German minority over the Hungarian, as they were always concerned about Hungarian irredentism.

Even though minority rights were protected, Romanian nationalists continuously attempted to limit them by promoting a privileged status for Romanians in all parts of the society. For example, laws were made restricting the reach of national minority schools and churches. Additionally, the agrarian reform carried out between 1921 and 1924, affected especially the properties of German ecclesiastical and cultural institutions. Romania's minorities increasingly appealed to the League of Nations for redress. Between the years 1920 and 1940, forty-seven complaints were lodged by the Hungarian minority.[8] Nevertheless, the majority of the ethnic Germans reciprocated the freedoms they enjoyed in their community with loyalty to Romania.

With the advent of the Nazi regime in Germany in the early 1930s, there was a significant change in the political life of the German ethnic group. This also occurred in other Central and Eastern European lands having a German minority. A struggle for the control of the community erupted between local Nazis, supported by the Reich government, and the more traditional sectors of German society in Romania, particularly the Evangelical (Lutheran) Church and, to a lesser extent, the Catholic Church. But by the end of the 1930s, the overwhelming political influence from Berlin overcame all resistance, and a "Volksgruppenführer" (community leader) was appointed who, although a member of the German ethnic group, belonged to the SS. His principal task was to maintain the unity of the German community and subordinate it to the goals of the German Reich.

Due to internal and external political and military pressures in Romania, parliamentary democracy was eliminated in 1938. A new constitution was written and a royal dictatorship instituted under King Carol II. All existing political parties were banned. The Transylvanian Saxons also lost their centuries-old rights when their Nationuniversität was abolished. Nevertheless, Romania began to align itself with Nazi Germany due to its political and expansionist successes. A turning point came in the two state relations with the signing of a bilateral economic treaty in March 1939.

In June/July of 1940 the Soviet Union annexed the Romanian provinces of Bessarabia and Northern Bukovina, after giving the government only twenty-four hours to begin withdrawal. At the same time, Bulgaria realized its long-standing claim against Romania by occupying Southern Dobruja. (Please refer to map 22) Tensions increased between Romania and Hungary over Transylvania, but as Hitler could not afford a war between these two countries, he issued an ultimatum to them insisting that they arbitrate their conflict. This resulted in the Second Vienna Award of August 1940, which effectively divided Transylvania into two parts. The northern portion was awarded to Hungary, leaving Southern Transylvania in the possession of Romania. This fed into Nazi Germany's balance of power strategy in the Balkans by playing Hungary and Romania against each other. It permitted Germany to exert increasing control over both countries, including, most importantly, the control of Romania's oil fields.

These territorial losses undoubtedly led to the fall of the Romanian government on September 5, and the beginning of the dictatorship of the pro-German general Ion Antonescu (1882–1946), backed by his paramilitary unit, the Iron Guard. King Carol III was forced to resign shortly thereafter. The Antonescu government proclaimed a "National Legionary State" and adopted very nationalistic, anti-Semitic, and anti-Hungarian policies. The regime supported the Axis powers and, in November 1940, joined the German, Italian, and Japanese alliance.

The Nazi German orientation of the Romanian government had a beneficial effect on the German minority. A German–Romanian agreement was signed in August 1940 giving complete legal equality to the German community in Romania. It was followed shortly thereafter by a further agreement with the Antonescu government giving legal recognition to the German ethnic group in Romania, placing it under the protection of the Nazi German government.[9] This measure had the effect of making the German community a virtual state within a state. It also substantially improved their economic condition as well as expanding their cultural and educational rights.

The German Minority in Romania in World War II

In September 1940, Nazi Germany and the Soviet Union signed an agreement to transfer Germans living in Bessarabia and Northern Bukovina to the Reich. Germans settled in Bessarabia when it was a part of the Russian Empire, invited initially by Empress Catherine the Great, whereas Bukovina, before World War I, was a part of the province of Galicia, later Moldavia, of Austro-Hungary. This resettlement was later extended to Germans living in the Dobruja, principally under Bulgarian occupation at the time. All in all, this transfer encompassed about 166,000 German settlers.[10] (See map 22)

This treaty to resettle established Romanian German communities came as a great shock to the German population in Romania, as it had expected the Hitler government to protect and maintain their settlements. They were rightly afraid that the Nazi government would abandon them. They were particularly concerned about turning over Northern Transylavnia to Hungary and petitioned the Reich government not to subject them to Hungarian rule. As it turned out, both in Hungary and in Romania, the German minority became a privileged ethnic community as a result of German government pressure.

Romania entered Hitler's war on the Soviet Union in June 1941. Bessarabia and Bukovina were retaken and incorporated again into Romania. However, tensions with Hungary persisted, and both countries kept some of their best units facing each other, rather than sending them to fight in Russia. Hungarian–Romanian tensions decreased, however, with the approach of the Red Army in early 1944. Both countries hoped for an Anglo-American military intervention to forestall the Red Army, which, of course, was impossible without Soviet agreement.[11]

The main task of the Nazi leadership in Romania during the war was to fulfill the needs of the Reich, and by the 1940s this meant recruiting young Germans for the Wehrmacht and the Waffen-SS. Recruitment of German men into the SS already started in 1940 by sending volunteers to Germany, ostensibly as farm laborers, in order not to violate the laws of Romania. In April of 1943, Marshal Antonescu agreed to a large-scale recruitment campaign of Romanian ethnic Germans. This decree allowed ethnic Germans serving in the armed forces of Germany to keep their Romanian citizenship. But after Hitler gave German citizenship in 1943 to all ethnic Germans serving in Germany's armed forces, the Antonescu decree was annulled. Ethnic German soldiers were considered deserters and lost their Romanian citizenship when the Romanian regime changed sides in August 1944.

General conscription of all men between the ages of eighteen and thirty-six was proclaimed in May 1943. The Transylvanian Saxons mostly volunteered for the Waffen-SS, but in the case of the Banat Swabians, strong-arm methods often had to be used. (Some who resisted had their houses burned to the ground.) Not surprisingly, the Banat Swabians deserted from the SS more than any other German ethnic group. Desertions took place particularly in Serbia, where as members of the SS Mountain Division Prince Eugen, they were fighting Tito's partisans in bloody battles. In all, about 50,000 ethnic Germans from Transylvania and the Banat served in the Waffen-SS. Of these, an estimated 8,000–9,000 were killed,[12] about an 18 percent casualty rate. Very few of the survivors were able to return to their homes in Romania after the war.

The Collapse of the Romanian Government and Soviet Occupation

In early April 1944, the Soviet Army reached the border of Romania. (See map 23) The Romanian leadership quickly came to the conclusion that Germany could no longer win the war and surrendered to the Soviets on August 23. King Michael made a "coup d'etat" with several of the traditional parties and arrested Marshal Antonescu. The Red Army rapidly occupied most of Romania, and on August 25, Romania declared war on the Axis. Similar to what occurred in World War I, the Soviet government had promised to return Northern Transylvania to Romania in compensation for the loss of Bessarabia and Northern Bukovina and for Romania's entry into the war on the Soviet side.[13]

The collapse of the German Balkan front led to a rapid Soviet advance to the Hungarian frontier in Northern Transylvania. The German ethnic group in Soviet-occupied Romania was completely surprised by these sudden events and there were no plans for its evacuation. The Romanian government quickly took security measures against them. Their organizations were immediately dissolved and their leaders interned in concentration camps. About two to three thousand were arrested, but it is reported that they were treated correctly by the Romanian authorities. Most were subsequently sent to Soviet labor camps. All in all, the Romanians did not mistreat or harass the Germans, as occurred in other East European countries. There were generally no signs of hatred, which was a reflection of historically good relations between the two peoples.

Nr. 17

Report of the experiences of R. P. from Hermannstadt (Sibiu] in Southern Transylvania. Original, dated 5 March 1952, typewritten, 16 pages. Printed in part.

Events in Hermannstadt after 23 August 1944; internment of all ethnic Germans prominent in the political, economic and cultural fields; billeting and treatment of the internees in the camp of Targu-Jiu.

The writer begins by describing the effect of Rumania's capitulation on his professional activity and goes on to say: The population as well as the Rumanian officials were governed, during the days that immediately followed 23 August, by the conviction that the German troops would again advance and reoccupy at any rate Transylvania. The officials therefore, while they followed instructions from Bucharest, refrained from showing any signs of unfriendliness towards the ethnic Germans, on account of their fear of German reprisals and also of the terror and hatred which the majority felt for the Russians.

I was told by Rumanian officers that the principal military centers in Hermannstadt, with General Macici at their head, were hesitating as to whether to play the Soviet game or to take the side of the Germans. General Macici had to reckon with being made responsible for the massacre of the Jews, which the Rumanians had carried out in Jassy. His conviction, however, that the Germans could now no longer win the war, decided him. He therefore played the role of the general who was loyal to his King, while he allowed the German troops on the spot to withdraw without interference.

The German troops in Hermannstadt, together with those members of the German Wehrmacht and Waffen SS who were on leave, formed a hedgehog defensive position round their garrison headquarters. The senior officer of the garrison, a cavalry colonel, told me that he had no means of communication with his superiors. On 25 August, some hours before the expiration of the time limit for evacuation granted by the Rumanians, he received the order to evacuate and as I was later informed in Hermannstadt, crossed the Hungarian frontier that same night with his marching column and all his arms and equipment.

The behavior of the Rumanian officers towards the Germans, who had up till then been their comrades, varied considerably. Whereas, in the oilfields, Rumanian troops had surrounded, attacked and disarmed the Germans, there was no clash of any kind in Hermannstadt. The officers of the specialist cavalry school gave a farewell party to the German officers on the eve of their departure...

The senior officer of the Wehrmacht garrison had approached the District Leader of the German Ethnic Group in Hermannstadt with the request that the Community's local defense guard, which in any case was unarmed, should be used for the defense of the Wehrmacht's positions. The District Leader declined. In a conversation which he had with me, his excuse for doing so was that he expected the German troops to withdraw and did not wish to expose such ethnic Germans as stayed behind to still heavier reprisals than those which in any case were to be feared. He, moreover, took the view that the leading officials of the Ethnic Group should not be allowed to take refuge in flight, as that would throw the burden of responsibility onto the lesser officials and the broad mass of the German Community itself.

The mood of the members of the Community as a whole was one of anxiety without any change in their patriotic attitude or any trace of approval of the pro-Soviet course which the new regime was evidently steering.

About a week after August 23, the officials of the Ethnic Group, from the rank of Local Group Leader upwards (there were 16 local groups in Hermannstadt), as well as the officials of the Reich German NSDAP, were arrested without exception. The system of arrest varied in the other towns with a German population... In some localities in the old kingdom of Rumania and in the oilfields, the arrests affected even ethnic Germans who had never engaged in any kind of political activity, especially when they lived in isolation among Rumanians. This period was marked, too, by the beginnings of a system, which was later developed to its very perfection by the Rumanian police, of temporarily arresting well-to-do members of the Community and of then setting them temporarily at liberty after they had paid a bribe; in spite of this, they were soon arrested again on some new pretext.

I remained unaffected by the first wave of arrests, but I held myself in readiness all the same. I did not wish to flee, for fear of exposing my family to reprisals, though, as it later turned out, there were no cases of threats to arrest relatives being issued until the Communists took over the entire machinery of government.

On about September 5th, it was my turn to be arrested. The writer mentions the man whom he believes to have denounced him and then proceeds: My arrest was undertaken by a young and courteous police inspector, who had clearly been instructed by the Prefect of Police in Hermannstadt to show me special consideration... It is possible that the Prefect wanted to give me a chance to escape. He, like all other police officials still in service, was in a prejudiced position on account of the measures that they had previously taken against the Communists. They were counting on an, at any rate temporary, return of the Wehrmacht and clearly did not wish to prejudice their position by ill-treating the German Community. No trial followed any of the arrests nor was any arrested person subsequently interrogated or searched up to the time when we were transported to Russia...

The people arrested in Hermannstadt (about 50 in all), including one woman (Fräulein K. the official responsible at district headquarters in Hermannstadt for women's affairs) were taken by a Rumanian infantry detachment under the command of an anti-German and hostile-mannered reserve lieutenant and housed in the so-called Diaspora Home of the Evangelical Church. The lieutenant did not abuse his authority. Direct control over the prisoners was exercised by a police inspector, who was clearly anxious to offer us all kinds of facilities, to encourage our families to visit us and not to forbid the introduction of comforts and alcoholic drinks. The German women's organization in Hermannstadt set up a kitchen in the next building and fed us excellently. We were sometimes detailed under escort to carry beds into Russian military hospitals. The male German population was also daily employed by the police to work for Russian military projects, such as the construction of an airfield. The women of the German Community were subsequently used regularly for cleaning up, cooking and other such tasks in Russian hospitals.

On 10 September or thereabouts, the Russian troops marched into Hermannstadt. Their columns rolled day and night along the main road which passed within view of us...

The Russians never visited our camp. On the other hand, we heard tales of acts of violence and rape in the outer districts of the town. In the central districts discipline was to a certain extent maintained. The excesses of the Russians usually took place when they were drunk and, for this reason, it was forbidden to sell alcohol in the town...

We, who had been arrested, expected to be handed over to the Russians and then perhaps shot. On the other hand we were expecting, on the strength of the news which penetrated to us, a German counter-offensive. The mood of the German population in the town was as patriotic as ever. We were told of various signs which showed that a great many of the Rumanians were still hoping to be saved by the Germans...

On about September 17, we were unexpectedly transported to the assembly camp of Targu-Jiu. We were conducted on foot by Rumanian policemen to the station of Hermannstadt past some Russian armored columns. Here some Rumanian Communists called upon the Russians, whose leading vehicles were halted in the station, to fire into our ranks. The Russians paid no attention...

On the journey to Targu-Jiu we were given plenty of opportunities to escape. We declined to make use of them for the sake of our families, but we were on terms of such close understanding with the police that, on one occasion for example in Craiova, where we stopped for several hours, they went off to a neighboring restaurant with the tips which we had given them and relied on us to look after their weapons. We did not allow this to happen a second time, as some Russians, eager for booty, were prowling around us. We arrived at the camp of Targu-Jiu after a journey which lasted three days.

In the camp, which had formerly housed those condemned by Marshal Antonescu to a concentration camp, the old team of prison guards was still to be found, under the command of a punctilious colonel and the rules of the old camp were still in force. The colonel received us in a most courteous manner. As was the case in Antonescu's time, there was a first, second and third class among the prisoners. Those who, of their own free choice, joined the first class could eat together, (at midday there were three courses) and pay for the meals out of their own pocket. The officers of the camp had the same fare. There were Rumanian soldiers acting as waiters during the meal. Members of the first class were quartered in barrack rooms with 4 military beds in each. The second and third classes were in mass dormitories, fitted with two-storied bunks. The second class paid a modest sum for their food but, like the first class, did not have to do any work. The third class did not have to pay anything for the food but was obliged to work. In fact, the labor which was demanded even of them was not heavy and consisted mainly of maintenance work in the camp itself (cutting wood, keeping the paths tidy, etc.). The food of the second and third class, which was of the same standard in each case, was, in contrast to that of the first class, insufficient and had to be supplemented by family parcels.

The inmates of the camp numbered about 7000[1]). The whole town of Targu-Jiu had business dealings with the camp... Members of the

German Community who had been arrested and Germans from the Reich who had been interned had been sent to the camp from all parts of the country but, above all, the Reich Germans from Bucharest were there, with the exception of those who had been sent to the special camp for members of the Legation. It was only from October onwards, when Targu-jiu began to be overcrowded, that other camps like Slobozia were started up.

The officers adopted a neutral and not unfriendly attitude, with the exception of one detachment commander of Polish origin. Intercourse between the various sections of the camp was prohibited in principle, but in practice there were no restrictions except in the case of the barracks which came under his command...

Visitors from Bucharest, who came to visit Germans from the Reich in the camp, told us of two typical incidents. In Bucharest, the Russians had conducted several thousands of German prisoners of war through the streets of the capital in a demonstration march but had never repeated such victory demonstrations, because cigarettes and flowers had been thrown to the Germans from the windows 2). In Craiova, a Rumanian baker distributed his whole supply of bread to German prisoners who had been led past his shop, whereupon he had been promptly arrested by the Russians.

Whereas in the early days old and invalid Germans from the Reich had not been put into the camp, soon all of them, literally all, including the old people, invalids and children of both sexes, were interned. The Rumanian officers declared that this had been done in response to a Russian order. We often helped carry in crippled old women, who were incapable of walking themselves, from the gate... Their barracks were dirty and crowded, the food, unless relatives sent parcels, insufficient and the hygienic arrangements were enough to break anyone's spirit.

Letters to relatives were censored but, up to a point, one could say what one liked in them. They could be written in. German, though from time to time the announcement was made that it was our duty to use the Rumanian language. Whereas the Rumanian Communist papers and the yellow-press, which had been banned under Antonescu, made violent attacks on the German Ethnic Group, the national-royalist press was obviously striving to play down the importance of its role in past years, while at the same time making fun of its officials and their behavior...

Towards the end of 1944, Russian commissions appeared in the camp, on one occasion only in order to requisition with extreme politeness the private cars of the Rumanians which had been hidden in the camp, but on others to inspect the camp as a whole. They had a most courteous reception from the Rumanian officers and their chief interest was to find out whether we were working and what kind of work was being done... Some of us were afraid that we were to be deported to Russia and we secretly began to intensify our studies of the Russian language.

Attempts to escape were seldom made, although there would have been some prospects of success. On the contrary, German soldiers smuggled themselves into the camp. Even civilians felt that to stay there was safer than in the country which was overflowing with Russians. For ethnic Germans were continually being arrested by the Russian secret police on the suspicion that they were engaged in espionage.

The Report closes with a description of the compulsory deportation to the Soviet Union.

1. According to figures given in other reports of this collection, the camp at Targu-Jiu comprised only 3000 people, of whom barely a half were ethnic Germans.

2. Scenes of this kind are not verified by other reports and are highly improbable because of the German bombing raid on the Rumanian capital.

The Evacuation of Ethnic German Civilians

In view of the precarious military situation, the order was given to evacuate German civilians from Northern Transylvania. In contrast to the usual situation where the local Nazi party prohibited flight, the order to begin the evacuation was given by the Waffen-SS. Consequently, most of the Saxon villagers obeyed these instructions and began their trek through Hungary, eventually reaching Austria. In some cases, where the inhabitants refused to leave, they were forcibly evacuated by the Wehrmacht or Waffen-SS. These units also undertook the care and feeding of the refugees.

No. 31

Report of the experiences of Thomas Henning, a district notary from Heidendorf, Plasa Sieu (Grossschogen), Judet Nasaud (Nassod) in Northern Transylvania. Original, dated 7 February 1956, typewritten, 5 pages.

Evacuation of the community of Heidendorf; flight of the "security detachment," left behind to defend the place, on the approach of the battle front; care of the refugees in the District of Nikolsburg and second flight to Upper Bavaria.

When the Rumanian army capitulated on 24 August 1944. and Rumania became Russia's ally, the frontiers of Transylvania could not be defended any longer. To prevent the people falling under

Communist domination, instructions were issued for the evacuation of Northern Transylvania, which at that time belonged to Hungary. Preparations were started immediately after the capitulation. From then on, all orders relating to the evacuation were part of a well conceived plan. The evacuation was to take place by rail, treks and with the help of German military units... At the same time, steps were taken to ensure the maintenance of public order until the evacuation had been completed. An instruction was issued to all local headquarters to the following effect. Local headquarters should retain the services of 30 to 40 young men for the maintenance of public order until the evacuation had been completed. This group should be armed and have as its most important task the protection from assaults of such Saxons as had remained behind and, in general, should maintain order on the assumption that the evacuation would be of short duration. At the same time, the administration issued instructions for the evacuation of the local officials and for their transfer to a place in the territory beyond the Danube, with the express proviso that the official in charge of the local administration should not leave his post unless expressly ordered to do so. This order never reached me.

In the meantime, the numbers of German troop columns engaged in the withdrawal as well as the large bodies of refugees from Southern Transylvania and the frontier districts of Northern Transylvania were steadily increasing. The town of Bistritz and its surrounding villages were becoming one vast military and refugee camp. The battle area was continually drawing nearer and, on 11 September 1944, the supply units, which had been stationed in Heidendorf for a considerable period, began to withdraw. The first of our women, among them my wife, left Heidendorf with these troops for the west, though their exact destination was not fixed. At the same time women with small children, old people and invalids, were removed to the west by rail. Shortly afterwards, the main body of Saxon inhabitants of the villages left by trek with their wagons fully loaded and in many cases a milk cow tethered behind 1)...

The continuous discharge of our duties became more difficult every day. Admittedly, the retreating troops had received an order not to occupy any billets on their own initiative but only to act on the instructions of military headquarters in Bistritz and in agreement with local headquarters. Marauding acts against the population that had stayed behind, however, grew more and more frequent and it seemed that ours was a forlorn post and that we were serving no useful purpose any more. Before, however, finally deciding to leave the village, I made one more appeal for assistance to military headquarters in Bistritz. One military police sergeant was placed at our disposal and this sufficed to restore order and put a stop to the marauding, etc. With the help of this sergeant, we were able to maintain peace and discipline up to the very last day...

The departure, during the night of 9-10 October 1944, of the field kitchen of a battle unit, which had been stationed in Heidendorf for a considerable time, caused us to break up our headquarters on the morning of 11 October and to set off on our bicycles, which we had ready, in a westerly direction on the track of the wagon convoy which had gone on ahead of us. 2) ... We rode at a great speed in the direction of Des (Dej). That was our first day's goal, but as the town was already under shell fire, we rode on towards Szatmar.

We continued to ride at great speed with short intervals for rest, as there was always the fear that we might be cut off by the enemy coming up from the south. We had originally been given the route Debrecen-Szolnok-Budapest, but this had to be changed and we made instead for Tokay, as Debrecen had in the meantime been occupied and, I think, Szolnok as well. We crossed the Theiss at Tokay on 15 October and then rode on in the direction of Budapest... From here we proceeded first to Ödenburg and then to the neighboring village of Wandorf. We remained here till 8 January 1945, when we were transferred to the market town of Wartenberg in Upper Bavaria.

We had hardly settled down in Wartenberg, when I received orders to take charge of refugees settled in the Nikolsburg District (then in Lower Austria). I traveled via Munich and Vienna to Nikolsburg at the end of January and took up the post which had been assigned to me. In the meantime, several communities from the Nösnergau, including those of Heidendorf and Baierdorf which belonged to the district in which I officiated, had been settled here. I obtained further information here about their journeying up to that date. The whole journey had been accomplished in very good order without any incidents of particular importance. The Nikolsburg District had always been regarded as their final destination and the last station in the course of the evacuation and it was from here they were all to return home again at the end of the war. The problem now was to procure satisfactory lodging for men and beasts, to help those who were entitled to benefits to obtain them, and to get them their food ration cards and clothing vouchers. I was able with the help of the district and local officials to overcome all difficulties and solve all problems in a satisfactory manner. Those men and women who were fit to work were incorporated into the labor scheme. Our peasant farmers found satisfactory work to do in agriculture and vine growing and the relations between the refugees and their hosts, which had at first often been strained, began to settle down to normal.

Once again, however, things did not work out as we had thought and planned. The battle front drew nearer as the war moved on towards its tragic conclusion. A second evacuation had to be carried out and, in some of the areas in our district, this took place as early as the beginning of April. People often left their place of domicile only when the enemy had come within attacking distance. The district authorities left Nikolsburg on 23 April and I accompanied them. The Russians entered the town on the following day. We stopped immediately behind the front within artillery range of the enemy and hung on there till the capitulation, pushing forward with the evacuation of the villages behind the front line. The capitulation took place on May 8 and what followed was a flight in the true sense of the word, a flight far more tragic , and not to be compared with, the orderly evacuation of our homeland. Soldiers of the Wehrmacht and refugees marched in endless columns westwards, all struggling to reach the American lines, so as not to be taken prisoner by the Russians. The roads were often blocked and then people cursed each other. At the end of a few days, the Russians had overtaken us. The Wehrmacht had to turn about and march into Russian captivity. Some of the refugees turned about also, with a view to getting back to their homes. I proceeded on my way westwards and was now on foot, as the Russians had taken away my bicycle. I reached the American lines between Kaplitz and Freistadt and marched on via Passau as far as Wartenburg where I arrived ill and starving. Between 8 May and my arrival in Wartenburg there had been nothing for me to eat except some potatoes and a little dry bread.

The Report ends with some observations about what happened to people of the writer's home village and to his family in the post-war years.

1. Martin Broser from Heidendorf reports that the evacuation order issued by Generaloberst Phleps became known in Heidendorf on 10 September. Some of the women and children were able to leave the place during the night of 12 September with a German Tank Salvage unit temporarily stationed in Heidendorf. The trek, consisting of about 70 wagons and in the charge of an SS Corporal. who happened to be on leave, left the place at 8 a. m. on 19 September. (Report of the experiences of Martin Broser, original, dated 13 April 1956, typewritten, 10 pages.)

2. Dr. Gotthold Rhode, who was stationed at Sangeorz-Bai near Bistritz with a Wehrmacht unit from September 1944 onwards, was able to state from his diary notes that Corps Headquarters at Nassod issued an order, on 8 October, to commence the withdrawal to Maramaros-Sziget, but its execution was delayed until 12 October. The Soviet troops thereupon advanced into Northern Transylvania between 12 and 15 October.

An effort was made to also evacuate the population from the Banat. But this was more difficult due to the confused situation caused by the incursion of Tito's Partisans from Yugoslavia and the retreat of the Hungarian and German armies. Evacuation of the Swabians from the Northern Banat was more successful, with a number of towns evacuated in October 1944. It is difficult to arrive at precise figures, but it is estimated that almost 100,000 ethnic Germans from Transylvania and the Banat were evacuated. The majority of the German population, however, remained.[14]

Please refer to: http://www.forgottenvoices.net, for a photograph (#30) of German peasants and Romanian soldiers fleeing the Soviet advance in the direction of Hungary, summer 1944.

The Banat

No. 37

Interrogational Report based on the statements of B. N. from Reschitza (Resita), Judet Caras (Karasch) in the Banat. Original, dated 3 February 1953, typewritten, 6 pages. Printed in part.

The course of events in Reschitza and Steierdorf-Anina after 23 August 1944; occupation of Steierdorf by German troops and evacuation of its German community; their transfer to Western Hungary and subsequently to Germany.

The author begins by describing in detail the general situation and particularly the political attitude of the German population of Reschitza, the majority of whom were employed in the iron and steel industry. In the course of this he mentions the fact that a Communist cell had been formed among the German workers who, in general, held social-democratic views.

On the day after Rumania's capitulation (24 August 1945), I was driving in a car from Steierdorf, where I was domiciled, to Reschitza. Life was going on as usual. Just before 9 a.m. a German airplane appeared over the town. The Rumanian police gave orders that the population was to make for the air raid shelters without delay. We Germans thought that this precaution was absurd, but the police officer, who was Rumanian, said: "If the Germans are not prepared to go to the air raid shelters, we shall open fire on them!"...My driver came into the office and said that no German was now being allowed to leave the town.

Rumania had capitulated. The "Siguranta" (the Rumanian police) however, gave me permission to do so. On my arrival at home (in Steierdorf), I learnt that the drum had been beaten to inform everyone that their wireless sets and bicycles were to be handed in.

The local group leader, Karl Sch. and other politically prominent personalities of the German Ethnic Group were arrested in the afternoon and shut up in Frank's Hotel in Anina. These Germans who were arrested, about 23 in number, arrived some days later in Craiova and were deported from there to Russia...

Nothing of importance occurred until 14 September. It was no longer possible to get to Reschitza as the army had barred all access to the town. One could go however to places in the neighborhood, such as Anina, without a permit. We were requested by a police notice at the beginning of September to receive the Russians with flowers, should they appear, and give them the most cordial welcome. A Rumanian Commissar was put in charge of the communal offices. All power was exclusively in the hands of the Gendarmerie.

On 14 September 1944, a long Rumanian column marched through the place. The Rumanian authorities were leaving Orawitza where the Prefecture of Police was situated and withdrawing into the mountains. I heard a Rumanian Colonel reply to a query as to what was the matter: "The Germans have crossed the frontier and are at the gates of Orawitza."

On the next day (15 September 1944) there was a short exchange of fire in the morning, followed by a Rumanian withdrawal. The place was then occupied by German troops under the command of a major. We entertained the Rumanian soldiers who were taking part in the battle very nicely. One of them said to me that it was really silly that the Rumanian army should be fighting against the Germans, after the two nations had been allies and had achieved so much when fighting Communism together...

That evening the major had it proclaimed in the streets of the village that the German population should prepare for a three days' evacuation into Yugoslavia. The transport was due to start at 8 next morning (16 September 1944). Force would be used against anybody who refused to go. We assembled at the church in the market place, which was the point from which the transport was due to leave. By the evening of that day, 4,000 people had been taken by heavy lorries to Orawitza. A further 2,500 covered the distance on foot. A few hundred or so remained behind in Steierdorf-Anina.

We were driven from Orawitza next day to Alibunar in the Yugoslavian Banat. At Werschetz we were put into various goods wagons, some of which were uncovered, taken to Hungary and distributed among different localities in the Comitat of Veszprern. Here, too, we were constantly told that we should soon be returning home.

A fortnight later, however, we were put into wagons and taken to Germany. The transport from the Hungarian frontier onwards was a mixed one, our numbers including even some Russian émigrés.

I should say that we refugees from Steierdorf had between 20 and 25 deaths to lament in the course of our journey. I believe that I was the only German from Reschitza who succeeded in leaving the town in September 1944.

Please refer to: http://www.forgottenvoices.net, for a photograph (#31) of a poster in Northern Transylvania exhorting Germans to stand firm against the Soviet Army, August 1944.

The Fate of the German Minority after the War

In contrast to the other countries containing large German minorities, the postwar Romanian government did not expel them. Not even the Communist Party, which came to power in December 1947 with the proclamation of a Romanian People's Republic, ever seriously considered the elimination of the ethnic group. There were several reasons for this policy. First, Germany/Austria was not a neighbor of Romania and thus Romania never felt itself directly threatened. Second, the ethnic Germans, having been a part of the nation for so many centuries, generally had good relations with their Romanian neighbors. Last, Romania's traditional conflict was always with Hungary, and its much larger Hungarian minority, in the endless contest for possession of Transylvania. The German minority was often used as a counter-balance against Hungarian demands. Nevertheless, by a decree of October 1944, the privileges granted in 1940 by the pro-German Romanian government to the German ethnic minority (Deutsche Volksgruppe in Rumänien) were cancelled. In August 1945, a considerable number lost their Romanian citizenship if they were considered war collaborators, sympathizers of the Nazi regime, or members of the German armed forces.[15]

The Deportation of Romanian Germans to the Soviet Union

Soviet forces arrived in Romania as friends and allies and the troops were relatively disciplined. Russian commanding officers tried to ensure peace and order, particularly in the towns, by prohibiting alcohol and enforcing strict discipline with threats of punishment. Although Romania was not considered enemy territory, the government was forced to comply with Soviet demand for forced labor to rebuild the Soviet Union, as a part of its reparations payment contained in the Armistice Agreement of September 12, 1944, with the Soviet Union. In this the German minority was selected for forced labor in the Soviet

Union because they were considered collectively guilty for the war and thus subject to collective punishment.

No. 54

Report of the experiences of S. T., a girl living in Kronstadt (Brasov) in Southern Transylvania. Original, dated 27 April 1956, handwritten, 25 pages. Printed in part.

The entry of the Red Army into Kronstadt; levy of ethnic Germans and their deportation to the Soviet Union; the work on which they were employed and their living conditions in the camp of Lubovka; sick persons being collected and repatriated to Germany in the late summer of 1946.

The Report begins with some sentences of a general introductory nature. After the Rumanian coup d'etat of the night of 23-24 August 1944, which gave rise to a great outburst of joy on the part of the majority of the Rumanian people, who felt that the longed for 'pace' (peace) had come, life began to change in my home town of Kronstadt. Among other changes was the purely visual one, that the field gray of the German uniforms had just vanished like the wind from the scenery of the town; the German troops had withdrawn in close column...

It is true that, at first, some of "our people" claimed to have seen leaflets of the "Prince Eugen" Division with the text: "Hold out, we are coming!" But I suppose these were just rumors. It was not Prince Eugene who came, but the Russians instead. On the strength of reports passed from mouth to mouth, we followed their daily progress towards us from Bucharest and, finally, they were in Kronstadt.

Those who had expected something very sensational were disappointed. As far as I know, nothing very monstrous happened in Kronstadt itself. Admittedly, reports of acts of violence of the most varied kinds came in from the surrounding villages, What was fact and what was rumor in them is, I suppose, hard to determine. But the dark cloud of the threatened deportations grew denser every week and brooded heavily over the town.

That the Rumanian State, faced with the demand to supply manpower to Russia, would snatch first at the ethnic Germans, belonging to the age groups in question, was indeed very easy to foresee...11 January arrived like a lightning flash in a sky from which the clouds had already seemed to be withdrawing. This was the first day of the levy for the Germans in Kronstadt. Girls and women between 17 and 35 and men between 17 and 45 were affected. Two further levies took place in Kronstadt after that date in addition to many more throughout the country.

Then began a period of unspeakable suffering for our small Transylvanian Community, though I imagine that the scales of suffering were weighted more heavily against those who remained at home, particularly our parents, than against those who were actually affected. On 12 January 1945, after spending the previous night in a reception camp near Kronstadt, we were "loaded" into cattle trucks, a motley throng of little men and little women of every calling and class all mixed up together. Our relations, on the other hand, were left standing outside the train on the platforms.

Then we set off eastwards.

The journey to the temporary central camp at Lubovka lasted a fortnight... The outward spectacle, which is easy to reconstruct, was as follows: a long train of cattle trucks, each of them barred, bolted and crammed full of young people, numbering anything between 40 and 60...

Opportunities for sleeping were few and far between, as there were, only a few boards at our disposal as sleeping bunks and even some of these were used in many of the wagons as fuel for a small iron stove, for it was very cold. So one could only sleep in shifts, each person getting about 4 hours each day. We each of us had with us the prescribed amount of food for a fortnight and warm clothes, except for those who had been "picked up" in the street; these last were helped out of their difficulty by their neighbors in general.

The most primitive requirements of a civilized society which, in normal civilian every-day life are just taken unconsciously for granted, had to be gradually reduced and cut down to a minimum: c'est aussi la guerre. The problem of getting water was a complicated one, for our field flasks, in so far as we had any, were soon empty. Some of us,...succeeded, it is true, in getting hold of icicles, which were hanging from the roof of the wagon, by pulling them through the bars of the window, but these were only drops in the ocean....

Now and then, when our train stopped and we were allowed to get out of our trucks for a short time, water would be fetched from the wells but even that did not occur until after we had passed the frontier...After a fortnight's journey, we arrived, as dusk was falling, at our first camp at Lubovka, in the district of Voroshilovgrad in the Donetz region (coal basin) and entered the big stone and wooden huts, of which it was comprised, through the usual barbed wire fence, by which it was surrounded.

The only dominant impression which I still have of that first night is one of chaos. Everybody looked for somewhere to go to bed, whether it was on suitcases, blankets or, in the case of the really clever ones, on mattresses which they had brought with them. We were all dead-tired.

The camp during the first days presented a scene of tremendous activity. The men were fashioning bunks or putting in doors and windows which had previously not existed, while the women and girls melted snow on stoves of a primitive kind in the saucepans which they had brought with them for washing and cooking purposes; for the camp kitchen only came into action gradually, as did the bath, while water had at first to be fetched in tiresomely small quantities from a distant but very lovely reservoir.

And now a list was drawn up of our names and there was a roll call every morning. Men and women were lodged in separate huts, most of them in big rooms containing 50 to 100 inmates with a "senior person" in charge of each. The interpreters (pirivotschiks) did not emerge from our ranks until a later date, to become the real masters of the camp (though some deserved, while others did not, to be recognised as such).

The kitchen was now in action with a Russian woman in charge as head cook. The cooking was done in huge tureens, for the camp of Lubovka contained about 1,500 people. There was soup with very little variations, the most common form being the national Capusta (cabbage, soup). Our civilized stomachs took a long time to get accustomed to the bread; it is a heavy sort of bread made of bruised grains which sticks to one's throat. Apart from that, there were some homoeopathic-sized doses of Kascha (pearl barley mash) and tinned meat...Many of us especially the men, suffered severely from hunger (this was especially true during the first few months—later on the fare became better and is said to have become really good in the 4th and 5th years) and this often gave rise to moral lapses.

Some weeks after our arrival, first the men were sent to work outside the camp and, shortly afterwards, the women. Many of us went to shovel away snow on the railway tracks, a hard and, during the frequent heavy snowstorms, somewhat thankless task. Others again went to the coal mines which are densely spread over this part of the country; or they worked outside the pits, loading up coal on the "Atkatka" (slide). Work below the surface is sometimes, from a purely physical point of view, not so hard as it is outside the mines, but there are other factors at play which make it less desirable.

I myself first came into contact with the interior of a Russian coal mine in shaft no. 31 at Lubovka. Here I stood for three whole shifts (each of which normally lasts 8 hours, though on Stakhanov days they are extended to periods of 12-16 hours) by a water pump, but was subsequently transferred to the "Stanzia" (railway station) to work on the rails...

Round about March, 1946, the first cards and letters from home arrived... Soon after this, we were allowed to write ourselves, though our letters were strictly censored. We had long been allowed to roam about as we pleased, that is to say we could leave and enter the camp without restrictions.

Sometimes we were joined by transports of internees from East Prussia who had been in parts of Siberia and were now billeted in our camp. These East Prussians, who were almost exclusively women and girls, had had a far harder time of it than we Transylvanians. They told us how many people had died on the transport which took them to Siberia. The girls and women had had some bitter experiences as a kind of daily routine which was certainly not true of our camp. As far as I know, there was not a single genuine case of rape.

A whole year had already passed since the end of the war and the rumor "Skoro domoi" Russian for "going home soon" kept cropping up first in one place and then in another... So we had begun to grow skeptical. Incidentally, "Skoro domoi" was not the only current phrase. We equally frequently heard "skoro budjet" ("you will soon be having this or that") whether it referred to pay, soap, working clothes or other such things. "Skoro budjet" became one of our slogans, and it was often really amusing to see how, on occasions, a Russian would grin in self-mockery when he used it.

All this was not really very surprising when one realizes that everyone had been impoverished by the war, that reconstruction had been held up for several reasons and that many of the Russians, who worked alongside us, were themselves as poor as beggars and had almost as few possessions as ourselves. Politics did not affect us much, though we encountered it in the enigmatic form of the Party officials.

Within our own ranks inside the camp, the A. F. O. (Anti-Fascist Organization) used to hold meetings, but did not exert great influence on us, all the less so as our own "functionaries" were people of very modest intellectual capacity. Besides we kept guessing as to the political tendencies of that organization.

Then came the summer of 1946 and a hot, burning summer it was.

The scene in our camp courtyard during the night was often a colorful one, as many people took refuge after dark with their palliasses outside the stifling huts, in order to escape the heat and the noxious insects. In the midst of this summer heat wave, in August 1946, came the news that a medical commission was expected in Almasna, the largest of our branch camps, for the purpose of making up a sick transport.

As a member of Lubovka's "cripple brigade," I was among the invalids put onto a lorry... Then we drove over bumpy roads to Almasna. I was, however, to experience a dramatic intermezzo before my medical interview.

This was the only occasion of significance when I myself was either a witness or a victim of corporal punishment. The "Combat" (Camp

Commandant) of Almasna, a curious kind of individual, was in a state of violent intoxication and, for some inexplicable reason, had fixed his eye on me. Crying out: "Ah, bleath sirnulant, idi suda ia tibi dam!" (Come here, you infernal malingerer, I'll teach you!) he rushed at our interpreter, who had just lifted me down from the lorry, (it was just at that time that I was having difficulty in walking) and started to drive me on ahead of him with savage blows from his stick,... when one of the other officers dragged me to safety inside a camp hut.

About three hours later, the raging berserk which the "Combat" had been, had changed into a sober, benevolent, friendly human being, who was sitting among the doctors at the interviewing table and asking me: "Na, dewutschka, kak tibi ghela?" ("Well, little girl, how are you?") He clearly remembered nothing of the "intermezzo"...

On 15 September 1946, a party of sick and very sick patients left the camp of Almasna. Some of the farewells were profoundly touching, especially in cases where husband and wife were to be separated from one another. Among the patients there were some young mothers whose infants were not yet weaned and others whose babies had still to be born.

There we stood then, all of us shabby and emaciated in varying degrees.

And now, after they had checked our numbers, came the first decisive step, the step that was to take us outside the barbed wire...

The cattle trucks were standing there again, but with wide open doors this time, and then the journey started...

This time we saw the country through the open doors, the steppe, which has its own peculiar melancholy charm and which to me seemed to keep on melting away in a harmonious blend with the music of Russia.

We saw too that we were not going to Rumania where our families were, but to Eastern Germany. At the beginning of October, we arrived at the discharge camp in Frankfurt on the Oder and were then finally discharged by the Russians...

A few of those who had real initiative went off on their own and arrived home safely. The great majority, however, went into quarantine in the Ziethen barracks at Torgau on Elbe. We lived there for 5 months in definitely worse conditions than in Lubovka. The organization, apparently, just could not cope with the problems.

Then we were scattered to the four winds and, armed with the Russian discharge ticket, one could now take charge of one's own destiny.

This was what I, like many others, did. I took a chance and wrote to my brother at a Stuttgart address, as he had already been studying there before the war started. And, lo and behold, an echo came back to me!

The Report closes with an account of the authoress' reunion with her brother and her fiancé.

The round-up and deportation began without warning in January 1945. It affected men between the ages of seventeen and forty-five and women between the ages of eighteen and thirty-five.[16] In contrast to the wild deportations of Germans in other Eastern European and Balkan countries, the deportations in Romania took place according to a well-prepared plan of the government.

The names were selected from the National Register prepared by the Romanian German minority in 1940. Under guard by Soviet soldiers they were loaded into cattle trucks and after a several weeks journey arrived at the labor camps principally in the Donets basin, around Stalino and Voroshilovgrad. They worked mostly in the coal mines, forestry, and infrastructure projects. In 1946 and 1947 the first train loads of invalids, who were not able to work anymore, were sent to the Soviet zone of occupation in Germany. They were not allowed to go back to Romania. The bulk of the slave laborers were returned to Germany and Romania in 1948/1949 though some were not released until 1951.[17] In all about 80,000–100,000 people were deported to the Soviet Union. It is estimated that 20 percent never returned.[18]

No. 58

Report of the experiences of U. R. from Ulmbach [Peciul-Nou], Piasa Ciacova (Tschakova), Judet Timis-Torontal in the Banat. Original, dated 26 March 1956, handwritten, 5 pages.

Labor conscription at Ulmbach, deportation of ethnic German laborers; the author's experiences up to his repatriation in April 1947.

On 11 January 1945, which was a Sunday, all men, aged between 15 and 45, and women and girls, aged between 17 and 33 were summoned by the communal drummer to report at a given spot. We knew very well what was up; we had been prepared for days for the whole able-bodied labor force to be assembled for a transport. What made us so sure was a long row of cattle trucks standing in our station, cleaned out and fitted with wooden bunks of a kind and stoves. We were told to comfort us that they were wagons which were to be used for transporting the wounded. We had every reason to be suspicious, as this operation had already been carried out in the neighboring Serbian Banat at Christmas time.

I was 17 at the time and bowed to my fate as did all my compatriots.

We were allowed time to pack our clothes and food. We were made to march in silence from the assembly point to the main town of our district, where we were joined by people from several other places. About 400 people from our locality were affected out of a total pre-war population of 2,500. In the main town, a strict guard was kept over us by Rumanian soldiers. No one thought of trying to escape for they had threatened to take a member of our family in our place...We remained for three days in this assembly camp. A commission of Russian officers and a woman interpreter carried out a fairly superficial medical inspection. Cripples, people who were really ill and mothers with a child less than a year old were set at liberty; no account was taken of women who were pregnant.

Then our detachment of Rumanian guards was relieved by a Russian one of picked troops belonging to the Stalin Guard...The Russian sentries with fixed bayonets led us in column of march to the station...There were thirty people to each wagon. When everybody was on, the doors were bolted on the outside and the train moved off slowly...

We stopped in Temesvar. From there we traveled fast in the direction of Transylvania. There a second transport was coupled on to us. The Russian sentries were not unfriendly. They allowed us regularly to have water. We were also allowed to collect fuel. This was very necessary, as we could feel the Russian wind when we got beyond the Carpathians. For our other needs we had sawn a hole in the floor of the wagon, thereby making ourselves "independent!" Though we were not in the best of moods, we kept our spirits up by making jokes and singing songs. There were over 30 people to each wagon and we used to sleep in shifts. Nobody knew to what destination we were going... After ten days there was something hot to eat; we had always been able to get something cold. On and on we traveled into the Russian winter; the landscape became more and more dreary as we could see through our barred windows, until, after our journey had lasted three weeks, we were ordered to get out. We were told by our guards that we were just outside Stalino.

We went to our quarters; emergency quarters they might well be called. Preparation had been made for 500 and the transport consisted of 1,300 people in all. We were billeted in semi-ruins and the wind whistled through every cranny. Many people could not stand up to the iniquitous weather conditions and fell ill and we were soon to mourn our first deaths.

We were then formed into working gangs. There were some large brickworks there, and this was the work to which the majority were allotted. Skilled workers were sent to the workshops. Another group was given work on the collective farms, and I went with this one. In winter we transported manure, cut up firewood and stocked vast icehouses. Our group was reinforced in the spring and we were billeted on the collective farm outside the town, the camp and the barbed wire. Food was scanty, the stores which we had brought from home were soon finished, and our stomachs began to cry out for more. We had a hot meal three times a day, cabbage soup in the morning, cabbage soup with "Kasch" (pearl barley with a few bits of meat) at midday and cabbage soup again in the evening with some occasional tea. Our main form of nourishment was bread. The daily ration for those doing the heaviest work was 1,000 grams (nearly 2 lbs.), for heavy work 750 g., and for lighter work 500 g. The bread was bad, as it contained a great deal of oatmeal and was never properly baked. Our rates of pay varied but nobody was able to get very far with them; so we used to sell our surplus clothing which the Russians coveted very much at first. In the early days, the civil population was very unpleasant to us; sometimes stones were thrown at us when we marched in file to the kitchen which was outside the camp. The vermin too gave us a lot of trouble as bugs, fleas and lice took their turns on us according to the season. We were regularly deloused but this did not do any good. Washing facilities were also very poor.

Camp administration became somewhat better later on, and we received new billets and pelisses; we had previously had to sleep on bare boards. Our death-roll increased steadily. The majority succumbed to dropsy brought on by under-nourishment and there were a few cases of typhus as well. We were injected for this later on. After we had been there a year, a sick transport was made up; and this enabled our families to find out where we were. Later on we were allowed to write to them.

I went on working on the collective farm. I stayed on there over the winter, looking after the cattle with other comrades. I was not well but was not really ill either. We could at least eat as much as we wanted a few times a week. There was a great shortage of food in the camp and so the heavy manual workers were exchanged, and I was affected by this. I was put into a working gang which could be described as a penal squad. I received a kilogram of bread each day but the work was very hard. We were moreover given work targets which could not be attained in the normal eight hour shifts and so we had to work overtime every day. The food was wretched and, in camp, there were the bugs which kept one from resting. We had to do work inside the camp in addition. I had soon lost all my superfluous flesh and I was growing feebler day by day. A new sick transport was made up and those who were completely undernourished, of which I was now one, were registered.

It was Christmas 1946 and bitterly cold. It was then decided to take all those who were totally under-nourished out of the working shifts, but they at once deprived us of our special bread ration and we had to be content with half of it. We were hoping soon to be discharged as we had been promised but this did not happen for three months and in the meantime a catastrophe occurred and a plague of deaths broke out. Every morning a few corpses were carried off. The older age groups were the most heavily hit while the women held out the best. I too was feeling very weak. The thought occurred to me that I must get away to the collective farms, where the older Russians, who knew me, would help me. We had been strictly forbidden to leave the camp and it was taking a risk to set off on a 7½ miles walk in the snow and in 22 degrees of frost. I looked upon it as my last chance however, so I slipped out one morning with a working party and struck out for my destination. When I was outside the town, I realized for the first time how horribly cold it was and was intending to turn back. Just then someone came along in a sleigh and gave me a lift. When I arrived, nobody recognized me any more, I had grown so thin. I was given something to eat at once and exchanged a few trifles for some food. I drove back to town by lorry that evening but was caught at the camp gate and put in the cooler. I had resigned myself to spending the night there but presently the door opened and one of those gun women led me off to see the man in charge of the guard, a rough sort of fellow of whom everyone was afraid. He questioned me but I had no good excuse to offer. He then fell into a fit of rage and started hitting out at me like a horse; he belabored me with his fists and feet and did not let up until I had collapsed unconscious. Then he sent me off to my billet.

I hobbled away groaning and that made him think. He probably thought I was going to the camp doctor, who used to give strict instructions to go easy with the sick and the weak. He soon came after me and asked me in an undertone how I was. He let me fetch some food from the kitchen and then told me that I could work outside more often, provided that I asked him first. That too is what happened. The weather became milder and I took the opportunity to go out several times. Thus I kept going and the incident turned out to my advantage. I would add that the blows were not so painful as my feeling of hunger.

On 10 April, we were actually discharged. That day, they kept back all our food rations. We were thrust into cattle trucks and our feelings of joy were soon stifled by our hunger. We did not get anything to eat till next day and that was too late for many of us. Sixteen dead were taken off the train; they were left lying beside the railway track and the train went on through Poland, until we arrived at Frankfurt on the Oder on 20 April. I weighed myself there and found that my weight was 93 lbs. Four months later, I found that I had put on another 88 pounds!

The Confiscation of German Farms

The agrarian reform of March 1945 targeted, initially at least, the German minority in Romania. It stated that, "Rumanian citizens of German nationality (descent) who were members of the German Ethnic Group and all those who engaged in Hitlerite propaganda by fighting against democratic principles or contributing in any way to the support of Hitlerite Germany, either politically, economically, culturally or in the field of sports," should have their property confiscated without compensation. As the 1940 Romanian decree relative to the German "Volksdeutsche" declared all Romanian citizens of German extraction to be legally members of the German Ethnic Group in Romania, this resulted in the complete expropriation of all German peasants, no matter the size of their properties.[19]

The land and buildings were redistributed to landless Romanian peasants as well as to Romanian refugees from Bessarabia, Moldavia, and Bukovina, which had been reabsorbed by the Soviet Union. The Romanian state kept 350,000 hectares of the 1.4 million hectares seized to create state farms. As such, it was one of the first actions by an increasingly aggressive Romanian Communist government to implement its policies of nationalization of productive enterprises. Actually, there was no need for a land reform as all large landed estates had been broken up after World War I. Although this agrarian reform also targeted large- and medium-sized property owned by the other ethnic groups, when the first phase halted in 1947, 97 percent of the expropriated owners were Germans and 49 percent of the seized land came from the German ethnic group.[20] The result was the impoverishment of German peasants, as they not only lost their land and buildings but their farm implements and animals as well. Some moved to the cities to work in factories, but a large number became landless farm laborers, many working in the newly established state farms.[21]

No. 64

Report of S. R. from Kronstadt {Brasov] in Southern Transylvania. Original, dated 20 September 1952, typewritten, 21 pages. Printed in part.

The confiscation of German agricultural property in Southern Transylvania and the position of the German peasant farmers during the years 1945-1947.

The first part of the Report describes what happened within the leadership of the Ethnic Group after 23 August 1944, and the situation in Southern Transylvania during the winter of 1944-45.

I now had occasion, from 1945 till August 1947, to witness at first hand how the confiscation of farming land was carried out. The governments of Sanatescu and Radescu had already prepared the way for the first "Agrarian Reforms." The latter were promulgated in the form of a law on 23 March 1945 . Every big landed estate of over 50 hectares in area was confiscated and, in addition, the property of all those owners who did not farm their own land as well as of all those whose main source of income was not agricultural. Exceptions were made in the case of model farms, church property and a number of religious foundations and convents. In the summer and autumn of 1945, our farmers of the German Community were still able to work and harvest their own soil independently and dispose of the greater part of their harvest themselves, provided that the local committees had not already, under Communist influence, proceeded with the confiscation of farming property belonging to the ethnic Germans.

After the autumn elections of 1945 had ended in a victory for the "Popular Front," the Executive Ordinance to the Agrarian Law was published, in accordance with the terms of which the large majority of the ethnic German farmers were expropriated without compensation even in those places where the Agrarian Law had not been carried out. Those farmers (from 5 % to 10 % of the total number) formed exceptions, who had "fought" in the Rumanian army after 23 August 1944. They were the people who happened to be in advanced battle units and had not been affected by the deportation levy which had extended to members of the age-groups concerned who were serving in Rumanian military units. This favored treatment was also received by those few ethnic Germans, enrolled in the ranks of the Rumanian army, who were over 45 years of age and had therefore not been deported. At the same time, all large Rumanian landed estates were confiscated.

The confiscation was carried out by the local committees which had already been formed earlier. These committees went to the fields lying within the boundaries of each village and, in an amateur fashion, measured out plots of land about 3 to 4 yokes (one yoke equals 1.44 acres) in area for the new owners. None of those who benefited from the distribution received more than 5 yokes, which meant that wretched little dwarf farms were being created, most of which did not provide a livelihood for their owners. It proved later that, for lack of expert training and corresponding hard work on the part of the majority of the "Colonists," what was happening was nothing less than the creation of a country proletariat, which the regime was intending to use as a means for bringing about the complete collectivization of agriculture.

Among the applicants for land it was mainly landless shepherds, handicraftsmen and casual laborers who were taken into consideration; there were not many small farmers among them. In some villages, claimants were selected only from among the villagers themselves and the inhabitants of neighboring places. In others, refugees from Bessarabia, Moldavia etc. also received an allotment...

The years 1946 and 1947 were very bad ones for the ethnic German farmers. Scarcely one of them had any property left and all their reserves were used up. I heard cases of Saxon farmers' wives who had actually been driven away, when they were collecting stray ears of corn from fields which had already been reaped. The former owners of farms kept themselves alive by offering themselves as casual laborers to the new owners, many of whom were glad to be able to have recourse to "technical advisers"...

The housing conditions of the Saxon farmers varied considerably. Many were driven completely out of their former property, while others lived together on the farm with the new settler. This was generally the case when the farm had two dwelling houses on its premises.

I was told in the spring of 1947 by a Transylvanian Saxon farmer from Northern Transylvania, who came begging to the neighborhood of Hermannstadt, that the new owners of land, which had belonged to the ethnic Germans, had held a meeting in Lechnitz or Tekendorf at which the demand was made that the soil should be given back to the Saxons, as the colonists had been better off before than they were now. The truth was becoming apparent there, as in Southern Transylvania, that the dwarf farms were already not paying their way at all, because most of them had less than the minimum area of 5 yokes required to keep a farmer's family in our homeland in existence. Quite apart from the fact that the new owner was not able to produce enough, there was the additional consideration that a great part of his harvested products had to be handed over to the State.

I was still able to see for myself, in the summer of 1947, how the first severe measures were taken against the new colonists, when they were deprived of their plots of land again in order to start co-operative farming. At the same time, propaganda in favor of the formation of collective farms (Kolchoses) was intensified, though admittedly this expression was always avoided and the term "agricultural co-operatives" used instead.

Attempts made by one or other of the ethnic German Communists (of whom there were only a handful) to obtain some alleviation of the lot of their fellow-countrymen in the form of equality of rights were everywhere unsuccessful. I once had occasion to talk to Rudolf Mayer, the Social Democrat, in Hermannstadt. He had held seats on the corporations of the German Community as a workmen's representative for many years. After the first World War, he had commanded an international brigade in Soviet Russia, where he happened to be a prisoner of war. He now tried, on the strength of this past record, to set up an anti-Fascist democratic organization among the Transylvanian Saxons. It held frequent meetings, in 1945 and 1946 and was really nothing but a bourgeois association with a red label. It was dissolved in December 1946. Mayer's children were deported to Russia just like those of the other ethnic Germans. In the villages, it was still more impossible than in the towns to conceal the fact that our farmers were thoroughly hostile to Communism.

At the beginning of September 1947, I escaped clandestinely over the Hungarian frontier to Austria.

The Forced Resettlement of Banat Germans

As the expropriation and the collectivization action of the Communist government intensified, the agrarian population of the Banat, mostly ethnic Germans, rebelled against the government's policies in the winter of 1950/1951. Their action may have also been influenced by Tito's defiance of the Soviet Union. The Romanian government reacted immediately and removed this unreliable population from the borders of the Banat with Yugoslavia. They were sent to the Baragan steppes (see map 22), a marshy area in the Danube Delta. It is estimated that between 30,000 and 40,000 Banat Swabians were deported in this police action. It was, however, not exclusively limited to the German ethnic group. They were forced to labor on cotton and wheat collective farms. Some were able to return in 1955 to the Banat, but found their houses and possessions taken by strangers.[22]

The Compulsory Resettlement from the Banat to the Baragan Steppe in the summer of 1951.

No. 87

Interrogational Report based on the Statements of T.T., a farmer from Hatzfeld (Jimbolia), Plasa Jimbolia, Judet Timis Torontal in the Banat. Original, 30 October 1952, typewritten, 19 pages. Printed in part.

How the resettlement operation was carried out in Hatzfeld; transport of the settlers to Dudesti in the Baragan region; conditions in the new settlement till the autumn of 1951.

The first part of the Report describes the experiences of the author in Temesvar where he was serving with the Rumanian army, after

Rumania had capitulated and while the Russians were entering the town. There follows an account of how the situation developed in Hatzfeld up to the autumn of 1951.

At the beginning of June 1951, we could observe an unusual number of closed goods wagons at the railway station. The significance of this remarkable phenomenon was interpreted in different ways. We believed that it was connected with the Rumanian refugees from. Bessarabia and the Bukovina who had continually been called upon by the Russians to return home ever since 1945; the Russians had finally threatened that they would bring the "refugiati" back by force. We now assumed that the wagons had been got ready to help in carrying out some measure of this kind. The "refugiati" believed, on the other, hand, that we Swabians were going to be deported. Thus, both we and the Bessarabians and Bukovinians (who were feeling wonderfully at home in our farms) were surprised at being carried off as we all were...

Things began to move during the night of 17-18 June. There was a banging on the door of my room at 2 a.m. I opened it to find a group of security troops facing me. There was an officer in charge of them. The latter asked for my papers, glanced at a list and said "That is correct." He took away my identity card and all my personal papers. Then he ordered me to get ready and be at the station within two hours at the latest. When I asked him where I was being sent and why I was being deported, he just shrugged his shoulders. I felt as though I had been struck in the face. As he turned to go, I asked what I could take with me. "Don't take too much," he called out, as he walked away. "You'll find everything you need in the place where you're going to." It was only later that we found out that it had been expressly laid down that the compulsory settlers might take all their belongings with them. Furniture, food, pigs and poultry and even horses, wagons and cows, in so far as those affected still possessed them, could be brought along. There were sufficient wagons available for this purpose. It was the fault of the executive authorities (who made out that it would be an unnecessary burden to take all one's movable property with one, as the settler's families would find "all the necessities of life" provided for at their place of destination), that only some of the evacuees took advantage of this clause. The reason for this deliberate deceit on their part may well have been that they wanted, at this last moment, to wrest all our very last belongings from us poor devils and divide them up among themselves.

At first I allowed myself to be misled and only packed two suitcases with my most urgent belongings. Then I noticed that my neighbors were loading their furniture and their entire food-stores on to horse wagons—the colonists, who were staying behind, had been officially ordered to provide these vehicles—and were taking all their belongings with them. I changed my mind and also started to collect together all that I possessed. My colonist, who was Hungarian, allowed me to have his cart and I loaded everything on to it. Above all, I laid in a store of flour, bread, fat and bacon. This was good luck for me, as I was to find out later.

Alas, many of my companions in misfortune were less suspicious than I was. They let themselves be persuaded by the people entrusted with conducting the levy to leave their cattle and their furniture. The value of what was left behind was assessed, and its departing owner paid in full, though the prices given were ridiculously low. They later bitterly regretted having done so.

I was ready within two hours and carted my belongings to the station. After receiving the summons to get ready, each evacuee family had a sentry standing over them with a loaded rifle to see that nobody tried to escape. I, too, was escorted by a soldier. Nobody was beaten. I heard later that, in the village of Lerchenfeld, one Swabian was shot dead...

The columns of evacuees were assembling at the station. They consisted mainly of Swabians but there were many from Bessarabia and the Bukovina as well... Those who had brought their heavy cattle with them, found special wagons to take them. The smaller livestock was put in with the passengers. Large-sized families had single wagons for themselves, furniture and stores, while those of smaller size had to share wagons with others. The station was surrounded and nobody would have had a chance of slipping through the cordon of sentries...

I was put into the first transport train. This left Hatzfeld in the afternoon of 18 June. It consisted of 65 wagons. Three further transports followed, also of 60 to 65 wagons. A fifth transport, which was due to be the last, was got together but then broken up and its evacuees sent back to Hatzfeld. I do not know why it never left. Nor can I give the exact numbers of Hatzfeld inhabitants who were deported in the four transports which did leave. I should guess, however, that there were between 800 and 1000. It is said that the total number of human beings (Swabians, Rumanians, Serbs and Hungarians), evacuated from the Banat, was 50,000.

We traveled for two days... From Ploesti we went southeastwards into the broad treeless plain of Baragan. At last we stopped at a small station. It was called Dudesti and lay, so our railway staff told us, 62 miles south of Galatz. The village behind the station was a wretched sort of hole. Was this our destination?

When we got out of our wagons, a number of horse-drawn vehicles were assembling at the station. They were driven by Rumanian farmers and they were miserable carts with lanky old horses. They had been ordered for us. We obtained some idea of the company we were in, as soon as the unloading from the train and the loading up of the luggage carts had started. The drivers were stealing like birds of prey. Despite our poverty, we were still inviting objects of spoil to the rabble.

I threw my stuff on to one of the carts and sat down beside the driver. Even he did not know where we were going. Our column clattered through the wretched place and out into the steppe. The crops were already yellow and a hot wind was blowing in our face. We had been driving thus for what must have been a good hour, when my driver suddenly stopped and pointed away from the road into a field. There in the midst of an enormous tableland of wheat, the cart driving ahead of us was seen to stop. "I think," said the Rumanian, "that that is where you are going."

He was right. We were set down in the middle of the steppe, right among the wheat which was being trampled down by the wheels and the hooves of the horses. Officers were bellowing out orders. Each family was being allotted an area of seven to eight thousand square klafters. The furniture and other belongings were thrown out of the wagons. There was soon the strange and shattering spectacle to be seen of piles of chests of drawers, beds, mattresses, tables and bundles dumped in the middle of the wheat steppe, with people standing helplessly round them, gazing at the carts as they drove away...The militia announced that each family would be given boards to build a roof over its head. We were taken to a wood depot, which was half an hour's walk away, and each head of family was given, believe it or not, 8 boards of a meter's length. These were to be used, we were told, for building a roof!

There was no fuel. As far as one could see, the steppe did not contain a single tree. We had no idea how we were going to cook our food. No oil was distributed to us. We were just being abandoned to our fate and, if we had not had the food which we had brought with us, we should have starved in a few days.

The first night passed and then the second day, followed by other days and nights. We dug out "bunkers" for ourselves, holes in the earth into which we put our furniture and over which we made a covering with the help of our 8 boards and some bundles of straw. When some days later it began to rain, these holes in the earth were filled with water and mud. People lie down on their beds and put up their umbrellas, if they had any. We were soon wet through to the skin and our clothes began to rot. The children, who crouched coughing and shivering in the corners, suffered most. At last the sun came out again and dried us.

Our troop of security police had left us. They were relieved by sentries posted at the nearest militia headquarters. We were told that we were not to enter the neighboring villages and that the Rumanian farmers in the vicinity had been forbidden to have any contact with us. This meant that we could not do any shopping. On the third day, some officials appeared from the neighboring state farm, which had once been a Boyar's estate, and called out that anyone, who was looking for work, could find employment by helping with the threshing on their farm. I at once offered my services, hoping thereby to be sure of getting enough food to live on for the next few weeks. I was wrong for, after working very hard for three weeks, I was given just enough pay to buy half a cubic meter of wheat. I did not go to the farm any more after that.

In the meantime the sentries in our "field camp" had been urging people on to start casting bricks. At first this was done collectively, but later everybody produced the bricks which he needed for himself. Anybody who refused to do this was taken away by the militia in the night and beaten till the blood ran. There had been some refusals on the score that: "The State has taken away my house in Hatzfeld and must now provide me with another one." This refractory behavior ceased, once the militia had shown with what brutality they could crush any resistance.

I joined up with two girls, who had no relatives, and began casting bricks. Both of them had come back from Russia and had only been discharged in 1949. They worked diligently in silence and we were soon able to start with the building.

Two types of houses had been prescribed: the "big" house and the "small" one. The former consisted of two rooms, kitchen and passage and the latter of one room, kitchen and passage. The "big" class of house was meant for the larger families and the "small" class for single persons. The settlement grew up at an astounding speed. The houses stood in a straight line and were dressed to the nearest centimeter, while the space for the garden in front was made to keep to the prescribed measurements. We worked feverishly to be ahead of the approaching autumn. Commissions from Bucharest and our militia authorities kept urging us on with the words: "Don't think any more of your Banat. You will never go back there any more! See that you make a lovely new Banat here!"

Besides building the house we had to do compulsory work without payment. There was a school, the local administration office, the police station, a hospital and other communal buildings to erect. As the food supplies, which we had brought with us, were coming to an end, we demanded that we should be given, if not money, or reserves of food, at least our daily fare. Thereupon a public kitchen was installed, which provided meals for those who did compulsory work. It was done away with, however, three weeks later on the grounds that there was no money to pay for the food. Now everybody tried to shirk the fatigues and to steal the crops from the fields instead, so as not to starve. The Rumanians and Hungarians were the most daring in this respect. They just drove off into the fields belonging to the state farm with their hand-carts or horse-carts; this either resulted in a brawl or they, succeeded in bribing the guards...

One day, 100 people from our settlement were herded together and taken off to a cotton farm 6 miles away. I was among them. We had to help with the cotton crop, a tiring, exhausting kind of work, as one had to spend the entire day bent almost double. We were paid 70 leis for our work, just enough to cover our daily meals. Being on my own, I got off lightly but it was very bad for fathers of families who earned far too little to be able to feed their children.

After a fortnight, even this wretched source of subsistence came to an end. The problem of how to get food arose again. We were able, occasionally to work in the neighborhood in sort of convict gangs for a daily wage and our food; yet this was not sufficient to ensure the livelihood of 450 families, of which about 300 were Swabian ones. What would it be like in winter?

All these worries lay heavy on us like ghosts. For me personally, a chance of escaping from this hell seemed to be sorting itself out. On one of the first days of October, I received news from Bucharest that my application to be allowed to emigrate and join my family, which was living in Germany, had been favorably considered. When this joyful news arrived, I did not know whether I was standing on my head or my feet. I did all that I could, just to get away at last.

At the end of his account, the author describes his attempts to obtain an emigration permit, his successful escape from the deportation area to Grosswardein, the station from which the emigration transport was to set out, and the departure of the transport on 1 November 1951.

Developments after 1949

After 1949, the harsh measures against the German minority were gradually lifted. German language schools were opened again in those areas where the ethnic group formed a majority, German cultural associations were also re-established, and a German language newspaper was even allowed to publish again. In 1949, the Communist government formed an "Anti-Fascist Committee of German Workers in Romania" for the purpose of organizing the German workers in support of the regime. In 1950 the ethnic group received the right to vote, and in 1956 they were recognized again as a national minority. In this difficult period the German Evangelical (Lutheran) Church was allowed to continue to function. It effectively became the bearer of the

Transylvanian Saxon traditions and culture as well as the spokesman for the German community.

In 1952, a new constitution was enacted which guaranteed the civil rights of all the inhabitants of the country, but it did so in a form that subordinated them to the goal of building socialism. The subsequent constitution of August 1965, entitled the Constitution of the Romanian Socialist Republic, guaranteed "equal rights for all citizens of the Socialist Republic of Romania in every sphere of economic, political, juridical, social and cultural life." Fundamental rights were guaranteed irrespective of nationality, race, sex, or religion. These rights, however, regulated relations between the state and individuals. It did not guarantee the collective rights of the minorities. All in all, this period reflected one of forced assimilation of the national minorities to the dominant Romanian culture, a radical homogenization of the society. Measures included, for example, destroying national minority libraries and archives which could still be used as a source of national awareness.[23]

In the Romanian census of February 1956, the German minority stood at 382,400, about 2.2 percent of the national population.[24] In 1978, the Secretary General of the Romanian Communist Party and dictator, Nicolae Ceaucescu, signed an agreement with the German Federal Republic to permit the annual emigration of 12,200 ethnic Germans in return for a payment of DM8,000 (US$4,000) for each one. The rapid deterioration of economic and political conditions, the increasing shortages of all goods, and the elimination by Ceaucescu's policies of Romania's traditional rural and agricultural society motivated more and more Germans to leave the country. In the year 1990, the first after the fall of the Ceaucescu communist government, about 110,000 Germans left Romania for the Federal Republic. This emigration continues to this date, though at a slower rate, and only about 60,000 ethnic Germans remain in Romania today.[25]

Notes

1. Elemer Illyes, *National Minorities in Romania, Change in Transylvania* (Boulder, CO, 1982), 12, 13.
2. Dr. Konrad Gündisch, *Die Siebenbürger Sachsen* [The Saxons of Transylvania] (Bonn, 1994), 9.
3. Illyes, *National Minorities in Romania*, 13.
4. Ibid., 18.
5. Ibid., 19.
6. Ibid., 73.

7.   Charles Ingrao and Franz A. J. Szabo, eds., *The Germans and the East* (West Lafayette, IN, 2008), 351.
8.   Illyes, *National Minorities in Romania*, 75.
9.   Ibid., 79.
10.   Theodor Schieder, ed., *Documents on the Expulsion of the Germans from Eastern-Central Europe*, vol. III (Bonn, 1961), 45.
11.   Illyes, *National Minorities in Romania*, 81, 82.
12.   Schieder, *Documents on the Expulsion of the Germans*, 62.
13.   Illyes, *National Minorities in Romania*, 95.
14.   Schieder, *Documents on the Expulsion of the Germans*, 77.
15.   Illyes, *National Minorities in Romania*, 100, 101.
16.   Ibid., 101.
17.   Schieder, *Documents on the Expulsion of the Germans*, 82.
18.   Illyes, *National Minorities in Romania*, 101.
19.   Schieder, *Documents on the Expulsion of the Germans*, 89.
20.   Ibid., 91.
21.   Ibid., 92.
22.   Illyes, *National Minorities in Romania*, 119.
23.   Ibid., 134, 135.
24.   Schieder, *Documents on the Expulsion of the Germans*, 122.
25.   Stefan Wolff, *German Minorities in Europe: Ethnic Identity and Cultural Belonging* (New York, 2000), 135.

VII

Conclusion: Integration and Reconciliation

> To impose the guilt of some Germans upon the entire German nation means absolving those particular individuals of their guilt and, with a pessimistic fatalism, submerging them in an irresponsible anonymity. And to take any kind of hope away from ourselves. It would be the same if someone were to call us Stalinists, as a nation. Suffering obliges one to practice justice, not injustice. Those who have really suffered usually know that.
>
> The gift of forgiveness, and thus freedom from one's own anger, can flourish only on the terrain of justice.

From the speech of Czechoslovak President Vaclav Havel on March 15, 1990, welcoming German President Richard von Weizsäcker to Prague.

Integration of Refugees and Expellees into German Society

The majority of the ethnic Germans expelled from Central and Eastern Europe landed in West Germany. The task of feeding, clothing, and sheltering these twelve million destitute people fell primarily to the United States, British, and French occupation authorities. Approximately eight million people went to West Germany, subsequently the Federal Republic, and four million settled, initially at least, in the Soviet zone of occupation, which later became the German Democratic Republic. Of these, a great many subsequently fled to West Germany, before the construction of the Berlin wall in 1961.

(According to a West German government census, of the approximate 2.7 million Germans who fled the GDR prior to 1961, 839,000 were expellees.) Of the total expellees and refugees, about 15 million, 500,000 went to Austria and over 2 million were killed or died.

At the time, the expellees represented more than 16 percent of the West German and over 20 percent of the East German population.[1]

The integration of these refugees into a destroyed, conquered nation, occupied by foreign powers, was a formidable task for which there was no comparable historical precedent. The fact that it was accomplished successfully within a period of two decades in the face of such adversity was one of the great achievements of the German Federal Republic. For the refugees the hard part was, and continues to be, coming to terms with their expulsion and a lost homeland.

Economic and Social Integration in West Germany

The refugee problem was one of the principal challenges faced by the postwar West German government. Expellees and refugees living in precarious conditions, mostly in refugee camps, comprised about one-sixth of the population. In the first decade after the war, substantial antagonism existed between the residents and the new arrivals from the East. Acute housing and chronic food shortages, plus a general dearth of employment, made this quite understandable. A disproportionate concentration of refugees in rural areas led to a particular prevalence of conflict with the local residents. Stated in another way, there was an acute competition for scarce resources.

In the summer of 1948, the Western Allies told the German government to take steps to alleviate the hardship of the expellees as this could destabilize the nascent German democracy. Parliament approved the Immediate Aid Law (Soforthilfegesetz) in August 1949. It provided monthly payments to refugees plus financial assistance for housing, education, and establishing businesses.[2]

The most comprehensive measure to assist the expellees in their new home was the Equalization of Burden Law (Lastenausgleichsgesetz) of May 1952. The moral premise was to share the total loss of many with those who suffered little or no loss. A tax on the assets of all German citizens funded compensation to the refugees for lost homes, lands, businesses, and other assets. The tax was payable over a thirty-year period in order to lessen the impact on those, normally the better off, who had to pay it.[3] Although the loss verification process often took years, causing many expellees to complain that they received only a fraction of the value of their former properties, this law significantly contributed to their material and moral integration. The feeling of solidarity with a large destitute population helped to integrate them into a national endeavor of reconstruction, resulting in Germany's postwar economic success.

The emphasis now was on work and consumption rather than yearning for lost lands. Economic growth and their pride in it was the most important factor. The large masses of workers and artisans seeking work undoubtedly also helped fuel Germany's postwar recovery. Although the expellees were considerably poorer than the native population, by the mid-1950s they began to share in the general prosperity. By the mid-1960s the refugees were no longer considered a separate social group requiring government support. Therefore, the government ministry dealing with expellee issues and problems disbanded in 1969, and the Ministry of the Interior absorbed its remaining functions.[4]

After German Chancellor Willy Brandt signed a bilateral treaty with Poland in the early 1960s (during a period of relative political liberalization in the Eastern-Bloc countries), exit permits were granted to ethnic Germans still living there in exchange for economic assistance from the German Federal Republic. In the period 1950–1987, about two million ethnic Germans emigrated to West Germany, of which 62 percent came from Poland (these were the Germans who considered themselves Polish by language and custom or members of autochthonous communities; see Chapter II) and 15 percent came from Romania. They were known as "aussiedler" (resettlers). With the collapse of the communist system in 1989, another 2.3 million "spätaussiedler" (late resettlers) came between the years 1988 and 1996, but this time they were mostly from the former Soviet Union, followed by settlers from Poland and Romania.[5]

In contrast to the immediate postwar period, the Federal Republic had no difficulties integrating the returning Germans into a flourishing economy. The immigration policies of the German government did change, however. During the Cold War, it was the government's policy to foster ethnic German immigration from the Eastern satellite countries, as these immigrants were considered German nationals and victims of the Cold War. (According to the German constitution, German nationality is determined by ethnicity, the principle of "jus sanguinis.") With the collapse of communism, however, the policy changed to promote minority rights and the welfare, including financial assistance, for those ethnic Germans still residing in Central and Eastern European countries, so that they would not emigrate to Germany.

Please refer to: http://www.forgottenvoices.net, for a photograph (#32) of German refugee children in a West German camp, 1945.

Political Integration

A principal political objective of the Western Allies at war's end was the integration of the expellees into the new German democratic order. The Allies initially prohibited the expellees from forming political parties, as they felt that this could have a destabilizing effect, and hoped they would join existing parties. The ban was later lifted, and a political party of ethnic Germans did arise which had limited success in the elections of 1950, particularly in the North, in the province of Schleswig-Holstein, where they were numerous. In time, however, with increasing prosperity and integration into German society, the expellees joined the traditional German political parties, especially the Christian Democratic Party (CDU). The CDU appeared more supportive of the expellees' aims, but the then-Chancellor, Konrad Adenauer, took no concrete steps to promote their claims of lost lands in the East, as his priority was the integration of West Germany into Europe and the North Atlantic community.

Regional associations (Landsmannschaften) promoted the objectives of the refugees. Based on national origins, they provided the organizational structure to press for social assistance needs as well as to preserve cultural origins and keep alive memories of the old homeland.

As integration into German society progressed, the political work of the Landsmannschaften changed to one of emphasizing social and cultural aspects of the refugees' former homes. Their previous demand of a right to a homeland, "Recht auf Heimat," which meant their right to go back and live in their old homes in Central and Eastern Europe (a right based in international law), became increasingly irrelevant vis-à-vis the treaties the West German government was signing with Poland, Czechoslovakia, and other Eastern European countries which recognized the territorial status quo.

The main work of the regional associations was now to keep alive the memory of the former homelands, as well as the general history of the German "Ostsiedlung," that is the German settlement of Eastern Europe and the Balkans of which these people were such a vital part. These historic settlements functioned as a bridge to Western European culture and a conduit of European civilization during the Middle Ages and up to the eighteenth century, culminating in the reconquest of lands from the Ottoman Empire. In this the Landsmannschaften were assisted by the West German government, which established archives, libraries, and research institutes dedicated to the preservation and study of the history of the German settlements in Central and Eastern Europe.[6] One of the most important achievements of the Government Ministry for Expellees and Refugees was the publication of the history of the expulsions. Written by a group of prominent German scholars, it recorded eyewitness accounts of flight and expulsion, not only from the German territories that became Polish, but from Czechoslovakia, Hungary, Romania, and Yugoslavia as well. Although criticized by some for not also recounting Nazi war crimes, its primary purpose was to tell the story of what happened and not why it happened.[7]

Integration in the Soviet Zone of Occupation

The history of the integration of the expellees in the Soviet zone of occupation, later the German Democratic Republic, was the opposite of what occurred in West Germany. This reflected a totally different frame of reference on the overthrow of Nazi Germany. For the Communist regime, the war in the East was a war of liberation of Germany from fascism. The Soviet army did not destroy the German homeland but National Socialism. The soldiers of the Red Army were not war criminals but rather socialist heroes. Therefore, the term "expellee" or "refugee" was not used, as it implied criticism of allied, communist states. The term "umsiedler," or repatriate, was used to denote that there was no going back to their homes in the East. Also of great importance, the East German State recognized the Oder-Neisse border in a treaty with Poland already in July 1950.[8] This caused great consternation and opposition among the expellees, the majority of whom came from Eastern Germany, now Poland. Further, organizations formed by the expellees to promote their interests were not permitted, and labeled "revanchist" by the communist government. This prohibition extended even to complaints about problems of integration, criticism of the new German–Polish border, or even any reference to their previous homes. All of these actions were considered crimes in violation of the East German constitution.

Expellee policy had some initial success, in that the Soviet Zone was able to dissolve most of the refugee camps by 1950 and place their occupants into requisitioned homes and apartments. There was also a modest attempt to redistribute income to the refugees—of minimal effect due to the general poverty of the Russian occupation zone, exacerbated by the economic policies of the Soviet system. Some redistribution occurred in the socialization of resources, specifically through land reform. But its limited nature based on smallholdings ownership of land did not greatly assist the refugee peasants from the East. By 1953, the GDR phased out the last of its programs to help the expellees, and in fact, no longer officially used the term "umsiedler."[9] Their ultimate integration occurred through the communist industrialization and urbanization of the German Democratic Republic.

Reconciliation with East European Nations

In its early years, the West German government was slow to normalize relations with the East European countries. The Federal Republic was preoccupied with other issues, both domestic and international. Domestically, it faced the challenge of rebuilding the country and integrating millions of refugees. Internationally, Chancellor Konrad Adenauer's main objective was to anchor the new, democratic German state firmly in the Western Alliance, NATO, and the European Common Market.

Normal diplomatic relations with East European states, with the exception of the Soviet Union, were nonexistent until the 1960s, and then only with the two maverick states, Romania (1967) and Yugoslavia (first in1951 and then again in 1968). There were several reasons for this. One was the Hallstein Doctrine of 1955, whose purpose was the diplomatic isolation of East Germany. It stated that the Federal government would not have international relations with any government, except the Soviet Union, that maintained relations with the GDR.

A further reason was the Polish suspicion of the West German political class concerning territorial revisionism in Eastern Europe. The Federal Republic government and major political parties rejected the Oder-Neisse frontier with Poland, claiming that Germany existed within its 1937 boundaries and that any final settlement of the Eastern boundary would have to be decided by a peace treaty, as stipulated in the Potsdam Agreements between the United States, Great Britain, and the Soviet Union.

In the mid-1950s the Federal Republic adopted the principle that it was the sole representative of the German people, "Alleinvertretungsanspruch," because it was the only legitimate German government resulting from free and fair elections. This had as a consequence a commitment to a foreign policy of promoting humanitarian assistance to the ethnic Germans still living in Eastern Europe and negotiating their eventual migration to West Germany. To begin this process, a Soviet–German treaty was signed in 1955, which, among other conditions, permitted the repatriation of German nationals from the Soviet

Union who had been German citizens prior to June 1941—the date of Nazi Germany's attack.[10]

Reconciliation with Poland

The Polish fear of Germany's revision of the Oder-Neisse border, and the pressure of exile groups for the recuperation of their lost lands, played directly into the hands of the Communist party in facilitating and maintaining its control over the nation. They promoted a nationalist, anti-German ideology to rally public support for the alliance with the Soviet Union, including the integration of the Polish Army into the Warsaw Pact.

The first significant thawing of relations occurred in October 1965, when the German Evangelical (Lutheran) Church published a letter to the West German government advocating the formal renunciation of the eastern territories and the beginning of a dialogue between Germans and Poles to overcome their differences. Polish bishops responded with a conciliatory letter stating, "Let us try to forget! No polemics, no more Cold War... We forgive and we ask you also to forgive." The German Catholic bishops then replied, "We too ask to forget, yes, we ask to forgive."[11] (Copies of both letters are given in the "Appendix." The Polish document is also an interesting recount of 1,000 years of German–Polish history.) This exchange of letters had a profound effect on German public opinion, which now began to favor a normalization of relations with Poland by accepting the Oder-Neisse line as Germany's eastern border.

Although the West German government and Poland had signed a trade agreement in 1963, the Polish government advised the Germans that normalization of relations was not possible until the Federal Republic recognized Poland's western borders.

The relations between the two countries changed fundamentally in the late 1960s with the emergence of "détente" between the West and the Soviet Union, characterized by agreements on arms control and confidence-building measures. (One of the major achievements of détente was the Conference on Security and Cooperation in Europe—CSCE. A treaty signed in Helsinki on August 1, 1975, called for a multilateral renunciation of use of force and embrace of East–West cooperation. Both German governments were represented.) In 1969, the German Chancellor Willy Brandt introduced a new "Ostpolitik" whose purpose was to seek more contacts with the East German government and to arrive at a modus vivendi with the Soviet bloc.

In effect, it accepted the post-Yalta status quo. It aimed to improve German security and prepare for the eventual reunification of the country by building economic and cultural ties to the GDR. As Chancellor Brandt said in his government's 1969 declaration, "We want to be a nation of good neighbors."[12]

A first step toward that end came with the signing of a treaty with the Soviet Union in August 1970. The Federal government believed that improved relations with the Eastern European countries could only come about based on a prior normalization of relations with the Soviet Union. Having achieved this, the German government then signed the Warsaw Treaty of December 1970 and subsequently a treaty between the German Federal government and Czechoslovakia in December 1973. All these treaties contained a statement of renunciation of force in settling disputes and the inviolability of national frontiers. In the case of the Polish treaty, the Federal Republic recognized the Oder-Neisse frontier line.(However, the Bundestag and Constitutional Court later said that this recognition was provisional, that final determination would have to be made by the government of a united Germany.)[13]

The most dramatic example of this new policy occurred at the time of Brandt's official visit to Poland in December 1970. During a commemoration at the monument for the Jewish victims of the Warsaw Ghetto uprising, he fell to his knees. This was an unequivocal apology to Poland for Nazi German war crimes and a personal statement of contrition. The gesture had a profoundly positive effect on Polish perception of Germany.

Please refer to: http://www.forgottenvoices.net, for a photograph (#33) of German Chancellor Brandt on his knees before the monument to the Warsaw Ghetto uprising, Warsaw, December 1970.

As a practical consequence of this policy of reconciliation, by 1973 the Federal Republic of Germany became Poland's most important trade partner, after the Soviet Union. In 1972 the two governments agreed on German compensation for certain Polish war victims, and in August 1975, Brandt and the Polish Premier Edward Gierek signed an agreement to permit 120,000–125,000 ethnic Germans still living in Poland to emigrate to West Germany in exchange for loans totaling one billion marks (US$410 million).[14] The Soviet invasion of Afghanistan in 1979 marked the collapse of the period of detente, but the close German–Polish relationship was maintained. The bilateral trade agreement of 1974 was renewed, and West Germany became Poland's largest foreign trade creditor.

With German reunification, the Polish government was concerned that a unified Germany would challenge its postwar eastern boundary, especially as the Federal Republic had accepted the Oder-Neisse line only with reservations in its 1970 treaty. The Polish position received sympathetic support from the United States, France, and Great Britain, all of whom insisted that the reunification of Germany had to be predicated on the acceptance by a united German government of the Oder-Neisse frontier as its eastern border. France's President Mitterrand went even further by predicating approval for Germany's unification on the country's continuing participation in NATO and the European Union.

German Chancellor Helmut Kohl accepted these conditions and signed a treaty with Poland in November 1990, confirming existing borders and obligating both countries to respect each other's sovereignty and territorial integrity. This was followed in June 1991 by a treaty of Good Neighborly Relations and Friendly Cooperation (in economic, commercial, cultural, and environmental fields), which was based on the German/French 1963 Elysée treaty of cooperation and reconciliation. Germany then became Poland's strongest supporter for the latter's membership in NATO and the European Union.

The demands of the expellees, on the other hand, for restitution of their lost properties or compensation were not accepted by the Polish government. Now that Poland is a member of the European Union, however, and once the transitional period expires in 2016, Germans may settle and work in Poland, like any other citizen of the Union.

In April 1995, the Polish Foreign Minister, Wladyslaw Bartoszewski, made a speech before both houses of the German Parliament on the fiftieth anniversary of the end of World War II. As the first Polish Foreign Minister to speak before the German Parliament, he apologized on behalf of the Polish people for having exiled Germans, and for making them suffer terribly after the war. (Please refer to the introduction of Chapter II.)

In 1998, the German government and German industry came to an agreement to compensate former foreign slave workers with a $5.1 billion fund. The largest national group, among the twenty-five countries to receive compensation, was 500,000 former Polish workers.[15] (All in all, the West German government—and after 1990, the German government—paid between 1953 and 1997 roughly $58 billion to victims of National Socialism who survived the war. The communist regime of the GDR did not make any compensation payments, as it did not accept any responsibility for the crimes of the Third Reich.)[16]

Reconciliation with Czechoslovakia

During the Cold War, German–Czech reconciliation presented a greater problem than reconciliation between West Germany and Poland. This was due in great part to the reluctance of the West German government to abrogate the 1938 Munich Treaty which gave Sudetenland to Germany and led to the destruction of the Czechoslovak Republic. The Germans argued that they could not do it unilaterally as it was an agreement which also included Italy, France, and Great Britain. The underlying reason, however, could have been a fear that a cancellation of this treaty would deny refugees from the Sudetenland all right to compensation from Czechoslovakia for confiscated lands and property.

This was complicated by the expellees' demands for a right of return to their homeland—"Recht auf Heimat"—and the parallel demand for the right of self-determination. This meant for the Czechs, in effect, the restitution of German properties in the Sudetenland by Czechoslovakia, followed by the right of the ethnic Germans to then determine their own government, which could have resulted, conceivably, in either autonomy within Czechoslovakia or perhaps, even, annexation again to Germany. Needless to say, these ideas were totally rejected by the Czechs and led to many years of poisoned relationship with Germany. The expellees also demanded the annulment of the Benes Decrees which formed the basis for the seizure of their properties without compensation and, in general, legalized their expulsion from Czechoslovakia. Again, the Czech government agreed neither to the annulment of the Decrees nor to any form of compensation.

Although contacts to improve relations with the Czechoslovak government were initiated by the West German government in 1963, a number of factors prevented full diplomatic recognition. On the German side, the Hallstein Doctrine impeded recognition of Czechoslovakia as it had diplomatic relations with the East German government. On the Czech side was the problem of Germany's reluctance to formally annul the Munich Treaty, even though West Germany publicly stated that it had no territorial claims against Czechoslovakia. Meanwhile, the hardline communists within Czechoslovakia's government continued their promotion of fear of German aggression to maintain their control of the country.

When the first Eastern-Bloc country, Romania, established diplomatic relations with West Germany in January 1967, it meant the effective end of the Hallstein Doctrine, as Romania already had diplomatic relations with the GDR). This was followed in August 1967 by a trade agreement with Czechoslovakia, which did not involve full diplomatic recognition. It did commit, however, to the establishment of trade missions.

After Chancellor Brandt signed normalization treaties, first with the Soviet Union and then with Poland, negotiations started in 1970 to conclude a similar agreement with Czechoslovakia. It was not until 1973, however, that sufficient progress was made to achieve a treaty. The basic problem again was the validity of the Munich Treaty. In December 1973, the heads of the two governments finally signed a state agreement: regarding the validity of the Munich Treaty, Article I stated, "The Federal Republic of Germany and the Czechoslovak Socialist Republic regard the Munich Agreement of September 29, 1938 as void in regard to their bilateral relations under the terms of this treaty." Under Article II, Czechoslovak material claims against Germany for reparations based on this treaty are not allowed.[17]

Despite this progress in normalizing relations, there were still many important unresolved issues, including the Czech government's refusal to invalidate the Benes Decrees, which were the legal basis for the expropriation of Sudeten German property without compensation, forced labor, and the final expulsion of the Germans from the country. The Germans wanted the Czech government to formally disassociate itself from the excesses caused by these expulsions in the form of an official apology. Related to this issue was the expellees' demand that the Czechs compensate them for their loss. On the other hand was the question of compensation for Czech victims of the Nazi regime. The Czechoslovak government also insisted on assurance from the Federal government that it would not support Sudeten German claims for the restitution of their property.

Relations improved with the collapse of the communist regimes and the establishment of a democratic government in Czechoslovakia. In March 1990, President Havel welcomed German President Richard von Weizsäcker to Prague on the fifty-first anniversary of the German invasion of Czechoslovakia. He stated,

> ...Six years of Nazi rule was enough, for example, for us to allow ourselves to be infected with the germ of evil. We informed on one another, both during and after the war; we accepted in just, as well as exaggerated, indignation the principle of collective guilt. Instead of giving all those who betrayed this state a proper trial, we drove them out of the country and punished them with the kind of retribution

that went beyond the rule of law. This was not punishment. It was revenge.

Moreover, we did not expel these people on the basis of demonstrable individual guilt, but simply because they belonged to a certain nation. And thus, on the assumption that we were clearing the way for historical justice, we hurt many innocent people, most of all women and children. And, as is usually the case in history, we hurt ourselves even more: We settled accounts with totalitarianism in a way that allowed totalitarianism into our own activities and thus into our own souls. Shortly afterward, it returned to us cruelly in the form of our inability to resist a new totalitarianism imported from elsewhere. And what is more, many of us actively helped it into the world....

Source: The Art of the Impossible; Politics and Morality in Practice Speeches and Writings 1990-1996 by Vaclav Havel, Published by Alfred A. Knopf, New York, 1997.

In a speech at Charles University in February 1995, President Havel echoed the same theme. Havel was criticized severely by his fellow Czechs, in both instances, for having expressed regret for the treatment of the Sudeten Germans after World War II, but he courageously maintained his position (Please refer to the introduction of chapter III.)

Please refer to: http://www.forgottenvoices.net, for a photograph (#34) of German President Richard von Weizsäcker being welcomed by Czech President Vaclav Havel at the time of the first visit by a German President to the Czech Republic on March 15, 1990.

In 1991, negotiations began on a treaty of Good Neighborly Relations and Friendly Cooperation, similar to the treaty the Federal Republic signed with Poland. Work was completed in February 1992, when both parties signed the treaty. Although many portions of this treaty paralleled the Polish treaty, such as that neither side had any claim to the territory of the other, the respect for each other's sovereignty and territorial integrity, plus the commitment of the Federal Republic to support Czechoslovakia in its efforts to join the European Union, many of the issues dividing the two countries were not addressed. This applied particularly to the question of restitution of property rights or compensation for the Sudeten Germans by Czechoslovakia.

Thus, further negotiations were held, resulting in a joint German/Czech Declaration of Reconciliation of January 1997, meant to address these open questions. Its basic statement was:

The German side acknowledges Germany's responsibility for its role in a historical development which led to the 1938 Munich

Agreement, the flight and forcible expulsion of people from the Czech border area and the forcible breakup and occupation of the Czechoslovak Republic.

It regrets the suffering and injustice inflicted upon the Czech people through National Socialist crimes committed by Germans ...

The German side is also conscious of the fact that the National Socialist policy of violence towards the Czech people helped to prepare the ground for post-war flight, forcible expulsion and forced resettlement.

The Czech side regrets that, by the forcible expulsion and forced resettlement of Sudeten Germans from the former Czechoslovakia after the war as well as by the expropriation and deprivation of citizenship, much suffering and injustice was inflicted upon innocent people, also in view of the fact that guilt was attributed collectively ...

Both sides agree that injustice inflicted in the past belongs in the past, and will therefore orient their relations toward the future ... Both sides therefore declare that they will not burden their relations with political and legal issues which stem from the past.

Source: Auswärtiges Amt, German Federal Republic.

In another part of the Declaration's text, the Czechoslovak government stated that it is willing to accept applications from Germans to live and work in the Republic (in any event, this would be a right that any European Union citizen, including German, would have as soon as the Czech Republic joined the EU). For Czechoslovakia, the most important clause of the Declaration was the last, meaning that the German Federal Republic would not support legal claims against Czechoslovakia by the Sudeten German expellees. Additionally, the Czech and German governments would establish a "Fund for the Future" to be used for the benefit of Czech victims of Nazi persecution. The German government would contribute DM140 million (US$88.2 million) and the Czech government DM25 million (US$15.8 million).[18]

The German Chancellor, in March 1999, confirmed government policy stating that the Federal Republic would not press property claims against the Czech Republic. For its part, the Czech Prime Minister said that the laws dating from 1945 (the Benes Decrees) no longer had legal force, although he refused to repeal them, apparently afraid of a wave of individual legal demands by Sudeten Germans for property restitution. Political factions in Germany, Austria, and Hungary, however, insisted that the repeal of these Decrees be a condition for the Czech Republic to join the European Union, but neither the German government nor the European Commission supported this link to admission.[19] Ultimately, the Czech Republic was admitted without this condition.

The latest irritation occurred with the signing of the European Union's Lisbon Treaty. The Czech President, Vaclav Klaus, a leading euroskeptic, was the last head of state to sign it on November 3, 2009. He only did this after insisting on an opt-out clause to the European Union's Charter of Fundamental Rights, ostensibly to protect his country from property claims by the Sudeten Germans.

Nevertheless, despite occasional differences, the various treaties and declarations have clearly had a positive effect on German–Czech relations. What is more important, however, with both Germany and the Czech Republic now members of the European Union and NATO, their security is guaranteed, and their national interests coincide and are mutually reinforcing.

Finally, as an illustration of reconciliation, on June 3, 2010, a memorial service was held in Postelberg (Postoloprty) to commemorate the slaughter in May/June 1945 of about 2,200 ethnic German men, women, and children by Czech gendarmes and soldiers. A plaque was unveiled, dedicated to all innocent victims of the events in Postelberg in May and June of 1945. The plaque is written in Czech and German. The German ambassador to the Czech Republic was present at the dedication. This development represents a basic change in how the Czech public and nation view the postwar expulsions and violence against the ethnic Germans and reflects a fundamental reconciliation of the two peoples.

Reconciliation with Hungary

The process of reconciliation with Hungary was qualitatively different and easier than that with Poland and Czechoslovakia, as Hungary was a German ally in World War II. Additionally, Germany does not share any borders with Hungary, so the potential threat level from a nascent, aggressive Germany did not exist. Relations with Hungary, as with Romania and the former Yugoslavia, were conducted with minimum concern for the claims and revindications of the ethnic German expellees from these regions.

Relations began to improve in May 1962, when the Hungarian government indicated an interest in the establishment of a West German trade mission in Hungary.[20] Full diplomatic relations with Budapest were restored in December 1973 under the aegis of Chancellor Brandt's Ostpolitik.

The West German President, Richard von Weizsäcker, made a state visit to Hungary in October 1986. Bilateral relations were further strengthened by an agreement signed by Hungary's foreign minister in Bremen in July 1987, resulting in a German financial credit to Hungary in excess of a billion marks (US$540 million). The agreement also established cultural exchange institutions in both countries. In March 1988, a West German cultural and information center opened in Budapest. With West Germany's support, Hungary was able to sign an economic agreement with the European Community in 1988, which permitted it a greatly expanded export access to Western Europe.[21] At this point, the German Federal Republic became Hungary's largest Western trading partner.

In the late 1970s and early 1980s, the Hungarian government began a reassessment of the postwar expulsion and, in general, the treatment of its ethnic Germans. There was a general moral rehabilitation of those unjustly treated, not only of those still living in Hungary but of those expelled as well. A compensation law was approved which paid compensation to those whose property was expropriated. They received the same compensation as did expropriated Hungarians. Although the amounts were small, the compensation weakened the expellees' pressures on the West German and Hungarian governments. Indeed, they were even permitted to return to Hungary and buy property there.[22]

On March 14, 1990, after the fall of communism, the Hungarian National Assembly pardoned all of Hungary's citizens who had been unjustly condemned by the courts during the Stalin era. Financial compensation was also considered for ethnic Germans who had suffered discrimination because of the government's accusation that they were collectively guilty for the crimes of the Nazi German government. The National Assembly stated "it asks for the nation's forgiveness and bows its head before all the victims of illegal acts, for the crimes in question were not committed by citizens of the state but by the Stalinist authorities."[23]

Hungary made a very significant contribution to German reunification and the political transformation of Central and Eastern Europe in September 1989 when it allowed tourists from the German Democratic Republic, who did not wish to return to their homeland, to freely cross its border into Austria. This led to the collapse of the Berlin wall and the subsequent demise of the Eastern German communist government. Hungary had previously announced that it would dismantle its security border with Austria, beginning that May, despite strong protests from East Germany, Czechoslovakia, Romania, and Bulgaria.[24]

German–Hungarian friendship increased and a cornerstone in bilateral relations was laid with the February 1992 treaty of Friendly Cooperation and Partnership in Europe, a treaty very similar to those signed at that time with Poland and Czechoslovakia. It covered territorial integrity, peaceful relations, national sovereignty, and cooperation in cultural, social, and economic affairs. It also committed the Federal Republic to support Hungary's accession to the European Union.[25] The Federal Republic also supported Hungary in its bid to join NATO in March 1999.

German–Hungarian reconciliation reached a high point with the inauguration on June 18, 2006, in Budaörs, of a memorial to the ethnic Germans expelled from Hungary. On that occasion, Hungarian President Laszlo Solyom said:

> ... I think, this memorial place is one where one can come to remember, to think about fate, to mourn but also to draw strength from. Many of my acquaintances and schoolmates' children have taken back their old German family names and it is very joyful. Therefore, while I apologize as Hungary's head of state to the expelled Swabishes I bow my head in front of the memorial in the hope that the Germans of Hungary are again at home.

Source: Office of the President of the Republic of Hungary, 2006.

Please refer to Chapter IV for the complete speech.

Please refer to: http://www.forgottenvoices.net, for a photograph (#35) of a monument to expelled Swabian Germans in Elek (Renndorf), Hungary.

Relations with Romania and the Former Yugoslavia

One cannot really speak of reconciliation between the Federal Republic of Germany and Romania and the former Yugoslavia, in the same terms as that with Poland, Czechoslovakia, and Hungary. The overriding demands of the Cold War and Western support for these two maverick states, as well as the need to lessen Soviet domination of Eastern Europe, required a different German foreign policy. Additionally, in the case of Romania, German policy was determined by the need to assist and ultimately to repatriate the Germans still living there.

Romania

Although it was a member of COMECON (the Soviet East-European trading pact) and the Warsaw Pact, Romania, under its First Secretary of the Communist Party, Gheorghe Gheorghiu-Dej, pursued an independent foreign policy. Particularly in the matter of trade relations, he promoted trade with the West as early as the 1950s. His primary purpose was to avoid dependency on the Soviet Union. On his death, his successor, Nicolae Ceausescu, continued this policy and Romania became the first Eastern-Bloc country, aside from the Soviet Union, to establish diplomatic relations with the German Federal Republic in January 1967.[26]

This relationship continued to develop when West Germany and Romania in December 1969 signed a long-term economic and technical cooperation agreement for the period 1970–1974. This was followed by a trade agreement in 1970.[27] In 1979, West Germany's Chancellor Helmut Schmidt visited Bucharest and extended export credit guarantees for approximately US$368 million in exchange for Romania permitting ethnic Germans to emigrate to West Germany. This agreement permitted 11,000–13,000 Romanian Germans to emigrate annually. The annual payment was subsequently increased from about $2,632 to $5,263 per individual. These payments remained in effect until the collapse of the communist regime in Romania.

In April 1992, the German Federal Republic signed a Treaty of Friendly Cooperation and Partnership in Europe with Romania. Its main clauses were similar to the treaties signed at that time with Poland, Czechoslovakia, and Hungary. As distinct from these treaties, however, this document strengthened the collective legal status of the German minority. It accords them general human rights and liberties and they can exercise these rights without discrimination, just as any other Romanian citizen. They can maintain, express, and develop their ethnic cultural, linguistic, and religious identity. The Romanian state agreed to refrain from all attempts at forceful assimilation of this minority.[28]

There is still a community of about 60,000 ethnic Germans living in Romania today. They are organized politically in the Democratic Forum of Germans in Romania with headquarters in Hermannstadt (Sibiu). They have elected a large number of representatives in the local assemblies of the Banat and Siebenbürgen (Transylvania) as well as mayors of the principal cities, such as Hermannstadt. They also have a deputy in the National Parliament. The German government remits yearly €2.4 million (US$3.2 million) to Romania to support Germans in Romania.[29]

Yugoslavia

A special session of the Soviet Cominform in June 1948, held in Bucharest, which Yugoslavia refused to attend, expelled that country for betraying the international communist movement. The Soviet Union called on Yugoslav communists to overthrow Tito. The West, particularly the United States, slowly began to support the Tito regime, first economically and then with military assistance, for the purpose of keeping Yugoslavia out of the Soviet orbit. As a result of the conflict with the Soviets, Yugoslavia became a founder and leader of the nonaligned movement, which held its first international conference in Belgrade in September 1961.

In 1951, Yugoslavia opened an embassy in Bonn, which was reciprocated in Belgrade by the Federal Republic in February 1952. It was the first communist government to recognize West Germany. The first economic agreement between the FRG and Yugoslavia was signed in 1951 when the West German government gave a DM 180 million loan (US$78 million) to the Tito government. In 1952, a trade agreement was signed, with four additional agreements made between 1952 and 1957. In this period, West Germany became one of the leading Western exporters to Yugoslavia.[30]

The most contentious issues confronting the two countries were Yugoslavia's request for indemnification for suffering and damages caused by the Nazi regime during World War II, and Germany's wish that their prisoners of war be released from the camps. They also requested that those ethnic Germans still living in Yugoslavia be allowed to emigrate to West Germany. In 1955, the Yugoslav government presented an indemnification demand for DM 2 billion (US$860 million) to the Bonn government. The Germans made a counter offer of DM 60 million (US$25.8 million) in cash and an interest-free 99-year reconstruction loan of DM 240 million (US$103.2 million).[31] This issue, however, was not resolved. On the other hand, by this time all German war prisoners held in Yugoslav camps had been repatriated and ethnic Germans were allowed to leave after renouncing their Yugoslav citizenship and paying an exit tax. (See Chapter V)

After Stalin's death in 1953, Yugoslavia's relations with the Soviet Union gradually improved and Tito wanted an accommodation with the Soviet Union. In October 1957, he recognized the East German government. He considered that the existence of two German states was indisputable and a logical consequence of World War II. The Federal Republic immediately broke relations, invoking the Hallstein Doctrine. From then until diplomatic ties were reestablished in 1968, relations were essentially in the field of trade and other economic sectors, such as the availability of the German government Hermes export guarantees.

By the time diplomatic relations resumed in January 1968, as a result of Chancellor Brandt's "Ostpolitik," fundamental changes had occurred between Germany and Yugoslavia. Beginning in the 1960s, there was a strong movement of Yugoslav guest workers to Germany. The income of more than 500,000 workers in Germany was an important source of foreign earnings for the Yugoslav government. Also, West German tourism in Yugoslavia became a major earner of foreign exchange. The main bilateral issue confronting the two governments was Yugoslavia's continuing demand for war reparations. Although the Bonn government refused this demand, the issue was finally resolved in 1973 by giving development loans totaling DM 1 billion (US$375 million) under very favorable conditions.[32]

With these improved relations, Germany became Yugoslavia's principal economic partner. For example, 11 percent of the country's foreign debt was owed to Germany, placing Germany third among the country's creditors, behind the United States and Italy.

Additionally, 32 percent of foreign tourists came from West Germany, the single-most important source of tourism, and in foreign trade it was first in terms of exports to Yugoslavia.[33] These favorable relations continued under subsequent West German governments until the break-up of the Yugoslav state in 1991.

Please refer to: http://www.forgottenvoices.net, for a photograph (#36) of President Tito of Yugoslavia on a private visit to German Chancellor Willy Brandt in Germany on October 11, 1970.

Concluding Remarks

It is quite evident that the criminal policies of the German National Socialist regime were the basic cause for the tragedy that befell the German people of Central and Eastern Europe, who became victims of terror, flight, and expulsion. That is not to say there was a moral equivalency between the crimes committed by the German Nazi regime and the crimes committed against the Germans. The former was genocide and the latter ethnic cleansing. The violations of human rights committed by the Nazi German regime far overshadowed those committed against the Germans. On the other hand, two wrongs do not make a right, and even horrendous Nazi crimes could not justify the expulsion of a people from their ancestral homes. Thus, the expellees were also victims of the Nazi regime, even though some of them, no doubt, had supported it. For the expellees and refugees, the expulsion was a deeply traumatic experience that certainly scarred many for life because of the brutalities that accompanied their flight and deportation. Many were victims of horrible atrocities. The enormity of their loss cannot be justified with any historical argument to the contrary. There is no moral justification for saying they were collectively guilty of the crimes of the Nazi regime and thus deserved to be punished collectively.

What can be honestly said was clearly stated in Chancellor Helmut Schmidt's speech in November 1977, when visiting the death camps at Auschwitz-Birkenau, summing up in the following manner Germany's responsibility for the crimes of the Nazi regime, "The crime of Nazi fascism and the guilt of the German Reich under Hitler's leadership are at the basis of our responsibility. We Germans of today are not guilty as individual persons, but we must bear the political legacy of those who were guilty. That is our responsibility."

Former President Richard von Weizsäcker said in his famous speech to the Bundestag on the fortieth anniversary of the end of the European War, "There is no such thing as the guilt or innocence of an entire nation. Guilt is, like innocence, not collective, but personal...The vast majority of today's population were either children then, or had not been born. They cannot profess a guilt of their own for crimes that they did not commit. No discerning person can expect them to wear a penitential robe simply because they are Germans. But their forefathers have left them a grave legacy. All of us, whether guilty or not, whether old or young, must accept the past. We are all affected by its consequences and liable for it...Precisely, for this reason we must understand that there can be no reconciliation without remembrance."

So what remains? A common cultural heritage resulting from centuries of interaction between Germans and Slavs, Hungarians, and Romanians. And despite the tragedies of the twentieth century, Germans in the East fulfilled a vital historical function of helping to bring the East into the orbit of West European civilization.

Appendix

Letters of the Polish Bishops of November 18, 1965 and the Reply from the German Bishops of December 5, 1965.
Polish Bishops Appeal to their German Colleagues

Most Reverend Council Brethren: Honored brethren, we permit ourselves, before the Council is ended, to share with you, our nearest western neighbors, the good tidings that next year—in the year of Our Lord 1966—the Christian church in Poland together with the entire Polish nation will celebrate the millennium of the birth of the church and the thousand-year anniversary celebration of Poland's existence as a nation and a state.

We wish to invite you, in a brotherly and also most solemn manner, to take part in the church's celebration of the Polish millennium. The high point of the Polish "Te Deum laudamus" is to take place in the beginning of May 1966 at Jasna Gora, Shrine of the Holy Mother of God, the Queen of Poland.

It may be that the following survey can serve as a historical and at the same time highly topical commentary on our millennium; and perhaps also, with the help of God, will bring our two peoples ever nearer in a reciprocal dialogue.

It is a historical fact established beyond question that in the year 966 the Polish Duke Mieszko I, influenced by his wife, the Czech princess Dombrovka, received, along with his court, the Holy Sacrament of Baptism, as the first Polish duke to do so.

From this moment, the work of Christian missionaries in Poland—a mission begun in our land generations earlier by Christian disciples—began spreading throughout the entire area in which the Poles resided. Mieszko's son and successor, Boleslav Chrobry (the Brave), continued the Christianization begun by his father. He obtained from the then Pope Sylvester II the establishment of Poland's own ecclesiastical hierarchy, with its first metropolitan in Gniezno (Gnesen), and three suffragan bishoprics: Krakow, Wroclaw, Kolobrzeg (Cracow, Breslau, Kolberg). Until 1821 Gniezno also remained the metropolitan of the bishopric of Breslau. In the year 1000, the then ruler of the Roman Empire, Emperor Otto III, together with Boleslav Chrobry, went as pilgrims to the shrine of the holy Wojciech-Adalbert, who some years before had died as a martyr while among the Baltic Prussians. Both rulers, the Roman emperor and the future Polish king (he was crowned king shortly before his death), went in bare feet a large part of the way to the holy relics in Gniezno, which they thereupon honored with great devotion and high emotion.

Here, then, were the beginnings of Christian Poland and also the foundations of its national and political unity. From these foundations—simultaneously Christian, religious, national and political—it was developed further, by rulers, kings and bishops and priests, generation to generation, for a thousand years. The symbiosis of Christianity, church, state has existed in Poland from the very beginning and has never really been destroyed. In time it molded the almost universal political attitude: Polish has come to mean Catholic. From this association there emerged, too, the Polish religious form, in which the churchly and the political have been woven closely together from the start, with all the positive as well as the negative aspects of this problem.

One of the main expressions of this religious style of life has also been the Polish Marian cult. The oldest Polish churches are dedicated to the Mother of God (among them the Metropolitan Cathedral in Gniezno); the oldest Polish song is a hymn to Mary which is sung even today: "Bogurodzica-dziewica, Bogiem Slawiona Maryja" ("Mother of God Virgin Mary"). Tradition links the creation of this song with Saint Adalbert, as legend does with the Polish white eagles in the nest of Gnesen. These and similar traditions and folk-legends, which are entwined like an ivy vine around historical facts, have woven together the common heritage of the people and of Christianity, creating a fabric that simply cannot be unraveled without damage. These concepts illuminate—yes, even to a considerable degree determine—all subsequent Polish national and cultural development.

The very newest German historical writing gives these beginnings of ours the following political and cultural significance: "In the encounter with the empire of Otto the Great, a thousand years ago, Poland completed her entry into Latin Christianity; and through the admirably adroit policy of Mieszko I, as well as that of Boleslav the Brave, the country became an equal member of the universally conceived Imperium Romanum, aimed at encompassing the entire non-Byzantine world, of Otto III. Thereby Poland has made a decisive contribution to the formation of eastern Europe."

Thus the foundations were laid and the form and prerequisites determined for the future fruitful German-Polish relations and for the dissemination of the culture of the Occident.

Unfortunately German-Polish relations have not always, in the later course of history, remained fruitful; and in recent centuries they have changed into a kind of "hereditary hostility" between neighbors. More about that later.

The inclusion of the new Polish kingdom within the Occident—done with the help of the Papacy, whom the Polish kings always served—resulted during the Middle Ages in an active and extremely enriching exchange between Poland and the western nations, especially with the south German countries, and also with Burgundy, Flanders, Italy, and later with France and Austria and the states of the Italian

Renaissance. In this exchange, it was natural that Poland as a younger community, as the youngest of the elder brothers of Christian Europe, at first played the role more of recipient than of donor.

Between Kalisz and Cracow, the Polish royal city of the Middle Ages, and between Bamberg, Speyer, Mainz, Prague, Paris, Cologne, Lyons, Clairvaux and Ghent more than goods were exchanged. From the west came the Benedictines, the Cistercians and later the mendicant orders; all achieved great gains in Poland, the new Christian country. During the Middle Ages the German Magdeburg Right contributed greatly to the foundation of Polish cities. German merchants, architects, artists and settlers also streamed to Poland and many were absorbed by the Polish nation. They retained their German family names and today, in the large Church of Saint Mary in Cracow, we still find epitaphs of numerous German families from the Middle Ages, families that in time all became Polish. It is from this fact that Hitler and others—of unholy memory—drew the simple conclusion that Cracow with all Poland was only a German settlement and should be treated accordingly.

A classical example of German-Polish cultural and artistic co-operation during the later Middle Ages is the world-famous Veit Stoss (Wit Stwosz) from Nuremberg, who worked through nearly his whole lifetime in Cracow. All his works were inspired by the spirit of the Polish environment. He founded his own school for artists in Cracow; it continued its work for generations and enriched the Polish country.

The Poles have greatly honored their brothers from the Christian west who came to them as the messengers of true culture; nor have the Poles ever denied the fact that these men were of other than Polish extraction. We truly have much for which to thank the Occidental—including the German—culture.

Apostles and saints also came to us from the west; and they are probably among the most valuable gifts that the Occident has given to us. In many places we still feel their blessed activities of community welfare today. Among the most well-known we count Saint Bruno of Querfurt, called the "Bishop of the Heathens," who by agreement with Boleslav Chrobry converted the Slavic and Lithuanian northeast. Notable, too, was Saint Hedwig (Jadwiga), Duchess of Silesia, a native of Andechs, wife of the Polish Prince Henry the Bearded (Brodaty) of Silesia and founder of the Cistercian cloister Trzebnica (Trebnitz), where she was buried. She was the greatest 13th-century benefactress of the Polish people in the then western region of the so-called Piasten Poland, in Silesia. It is quite certain that this Silesian duchess even learned Polish just to be able to serve the simple Polish people. After her death and her canonization throngs of people, both Polish and German, streamed to her grave in Trzebnica (Trebnitz).

They continue to do so today by thousands and thousands. Nobody is concerned that our great national saint was of German origin; on the contrary, she is generally regarded—except by some nationalistic fanatics—as the best example of the existence of a Christian act of bridge-building between Poland and Germany. We are happy to hear the same opinion quite often from the German side. Bridge-building between peoples can in fact be done best by holy persons, by those who have an honest mind and pure hands. They do not want to take anything away from the brother-nation, neither the language, nor the customs, nor the land, nor material goods. On the contrary, they take to the brother-nation the most valuable things they have, namely their culture and themselves. They thereby cast the seed of their own personality into the fruitful soil of the new neighboring mission country according to the words of the Lord. The seed will then bear fruit a hundredfold and for generations. That is how we in Poland look on Saint Hedwig of Silesia and all the other missionaries and martyrs who came from the west to work in Poland, led by the apostle and martyr Wojciech-Adalbert from Prague. Here one encounters what is most probably the profoundest difference between a genuine mission of Christian culture and the so-called colonialism which is justly in ill repute today.

After the year 1200, as the Polish state became constantly more Christian in regard to its population and its institutions, the country's Polish saints began to emerge.

It was as early as the 12th century that Bishop Stanislaus Szczepanowski of Cracow, confessor and martyr, was killed at the altar by King Boleslav the Brave. The king himself died as a pious penitent in exile in a monastery in northern Austria. At the grave of Saint Stanislaus in the royal church of Cracow a majestic song in his honor was created which today is sung throughout Poland in Latin: "Gaude mater Polonia, prole foecunde nobili ... "

Then appeared on the horizon the three holy members of the Odrowaz family (an old family line, whose members for long centuries made their home on the Oder in Upper Silesia). The greatest of them is Saint Hyacinth, also called Jacek. This Dominican apostle traveled throughout eastern Europe from Moravia to the Baltic countries, from Lithuania to Kiev. A relative, the Blessed Czeslaw, was also a Dominican. He defended the former city of Wroclaw against the Mongols. Today he rests in Wroclaw in the reconstructed church of Saint Wojciech (Saint Adalbert). He is honored by the pious populace as patron of the city resurrected from its ruins after 1945. The third member of the family, Blessed Bronislawa, said by tradition to be the sister of Blessed Czeslaw, rests in Cracow. She was a member of the Silesian order of Saint Norbert.

The stars in the firmament of saints become more and more numerous: In Sacz, it was the Blessed Cunegunda, in Gniezno, Bogumil and the Blessed Jolanta, in Masovia, Wladyslaw; in the royal castle of Cracow lies the saintly Queen Jadwiga, who has been called a new Polish Hedwig. She is awaiting her canonization. Later came new saints and martyrs: Saint Stanislaus Kostka, a novice in the Jesuit order in Rome, Saint John Cantius, a professor at the Jagiellonian University in Cracow; Saint Andreas Bobola, the east Polish martyr, canonized in 1938, and other saints down to the Franciscan Maximilian Kolbe. This friar, called the Martyr of the Auschwitz concentration camp, voluntarily gave his life for his brethren. Today some thirty Polish candidates are awaiting canonization or beatification in Rome. Poland honors its saints and considers them the most noble fruit a Christian country can produce.

The above-mentioned Polish University of Cracow was the first of its kind, besides that of Prague, in eastern Europe. Founded as early as 1363 by King Casimir the Great (Kazimierz Wielki), it was for centuries the center from which emanated in all directions not only Polish, but—in the best sense of the word—universal European cultural influences.

In the 15th and 16th centuries, when the Silesian Piast countries no longer belonged to the Polish kingdom, thousands of students and professors from Wroclaw (Breslau), Raciborz (Ratibor), Gliwice (Gleiwitz), Glogow (Glogau), Nysa (Neisse), Opole (Oppeln) and many other Silesian cities studied or taught in Cracow. Their names and the names of their birth-places, written in this Polish-Latin idiom, are inscribed in the old university registers. The great Nicolaus Kopernik (Copernicus) is also mentioned there. He studied astronomy in Cracow with Professor Martin Bylica. Hundreds of scholars of the highest levels of learning brought this university into being, men who have contributed greatly to European culture. Mathematicians, physicists, physicians, jurists, astronomers, historians and philosophers were among them. One of them was the famed Paulus Wlodkowicz, rector of the University of Cracow, who applied the highest scholarly authority in speaking out frankly and freely at the Council of Constance for a spirit of religious and human tolerance which, for those times, was most unusual. He defended his view with the greatest personal courage, stating that the heathen people of eastern Europe should not be converted by fire and sword and that they had natural human rights just as did Christians.

Wlodkowicz was, so to speak, the classical example of tolerance and liberal thought in Poland. He directed his arguments against the Teutonic Knights, the so-called "Knights of the Cross." These men were using fire and sword to battle the original dwellers in the Slavic north and the Prussian and Baltic areas. In the course of centuries, these knights became a terrible, a highly compromising burden for European Christendom and its symbol, the Cross, as well as for the church in the name of which they acted. Even today, after many generations and centuries, the term "Krzyzak" is an insult and a nightmare to every Pole and unfortunately is identified all too often with things German.

From the territory where the "Knights of the Cross" settled there emerged those Prussians who have discredited everything German in Polish areas. In the historical pattern they are represented by such names as Albrecht of Prussia, Frederick the so-called Great, Bismarck, and finally, at the end of the line, Hitler.

Frederick II has always been regarded—and doubtlessly not without justice—by the entire Polish people as the one responsible for Poland's partitions. For 150 years, the millions of Poles were divided among the three great powers of the day: Prussia, Russia and Austria. It was not until 1918, at the end of the first world war, that Poland was able to emerge from its grave. Utterly exhausted, living under vast difficulties, it began once more to create its own existence as a state.

After a short period of independence, about 20 years (1918 to 1939), the Polish people were overwhelmed, without guilt on their part, by what is euphemistically called the second world war, but which was intended to be the total annihilation and extermination of us Poles. A terrifyingly dark night fell over our poor fatherland, a darkness unlike anything that we had known for generations. The era is generally known to us as the "period of German occupation" and has entered Polish history under that name. All of us were defenseless and powerless. The country was strewn with concentration camps, and the chimneys of their crematoriums smoked all day and night. More than six million Polish citizens, the majority of Jewish background, had to pay for this occupation with their lives. The leading lights of Polish intellectual life were simply snuffed out. Two thousand Polish priests and five bishops (a quarter of the episcopate of the time) were killed in camps. At the outbreak of war, hundreds of priests and tens of thousands of civilians were shot on the spot (278 priests in the single diocese of Kulm). The diocese of Wloclawek alone lost 48 percent of its priests in the war; the diocese of Kulm 47 percent. Many others were deported. All secondary and university-level schools were closed. The seminaries for priests were abolished. Every German uniform, not only that of the SS, became for all Poles both a nightmare and a reason to hate all Germans. Every family in Poland had its dead to mourn. We recall Poland's terrible night not to reopen wounds which may not have yet healed, but only to point out that one should try to understand us and our present way of thinking. We are striving to forget. We hope that time—the great, divine Kairos—slowly will heal the spiritual wounds.

After all that has happened in the past—unfortunately in the most recent past—it is not surprising that the whole Polish people feels the pressure of a basic need for security, and continues to view its nearest neighbor to the west with distrust. This mental attitude is, so to speak,, the problem of our generation. God willing, and with goodwill, it will and must disappear.

During the most severe political and spiritual crises of the people, through their centuries-long partitioning, the Catholic Church and the Holy Virgin, along with the Polish family, have constantly remained the anchor of salvation and the symbol of national unity. In every battle for freedom during the time of suppression, the Poles, mounting the barricades, took with them this symbol: the white eagle on one side, the Mother of God on the other side of the freedom flag. The rallying-cry was always: "For your and our liberty."

That, sketched in broad terms, is the story of the thousand-year development of the history of Polish civilization, with particular reference to the Germans and Poles as neighbors.

The strain on our mutual relationship continues to be great, and is increased by the so-called "hot iron" of this neighborly relation. We well understand that the Polish western border on the Oder and Neisse is, for Germany, an extremely bitter fruit of the last war of mass extinction. Part of the bitterness is caused by the sufferings of millions of German refugees and expellees (expelled by an inter-Allied order of the victorious powers at Potsdam in 1945). A large part of the population of this region left from fear of the advancing Russians, and fled to the west.

Our fatherland emerged from the mass murder not as a victorious state, but extremely weakened. What is at stake for us is our existence (not a question of "more Lebensraum"). Without the western territories, it would mean that our more than 30 million people would be compressed into the narrow corridor of the "Government-General" of 1939-45—and also without the eastern territories from which millions of Poles have had to cross over since 1945 into the "Potsdam western territories." Where else were they to go at that time, when the area of the "Government-General" together with the capital, Warsaw, lay in rubble and ruins?

The waves of destruction typical of the last war have not engulfed the Polish nation only once, as they have Germany, but several times since 1914. Back and forth rolled the tide, like the horsemen of the Apocalypse. And each time the waves of destruction left in their wake rubble and ruins, poverty, illness, epidemics, tears, death; and growing complexes of vengefulness and hate.

Do not hold it against us, dear German brethren, that we have recounted what has happened in the last part of our millennium. It is less an accusation than our own justification! We know very well how large numbers of the German population bore up under

309

superhuman pressure exerted on their consciences, for years on end, by the National Socialists. We recognize the terrible inner distress to which righteously acting and highly responsible German bishops were subjected at that time—to name only three among them: Cardinals Faulhaber, von Galen, Preysing. We know of the martyrs of the White Rose , and of the resistance fighters of the 20th of July. We know that many laymen and priests sacrificed their lives (Lichtenberg, Metzger, Klausener and many others). Thousands of Germans, as Christians and as Communists, shared the lot of their Polish brethren in the concentration camps...

And despite everything, despite this situation that is almost hopelessly burdened with the past, we call on you, highly esteemed brothers, to come out and away from precisely that situation: let us try to forget! No polemics, no more Cold War, but rather the beginning of a dialogue, such as that which the Council and Pope Paul VI today are seeking to foster everywhere. If there is genuine goodwill on both sides—and that is surely not to be doubted—then a serious dialogue certainly must succeed and in time bear good fruit—in spite of everything, in spite of hot irons.

It seems to us that precisely here in this Council at the Vatican, a task of the hour is to begin this dialogue, at the pastoral level of the bishops, and without hesitation, so that we can come to know one another better, and to know our respective folk-customs, along with our approach to worship and our ways of living—all rooted in the past and indeed conditioned by this cultural past.

We have sought through the so-called great novena under the patronage of the most holy Virgin Mary to prepare ourselves and the entire Christian community of Poland for the thousand-year celebration.

Over the course of nine years (1957 through 1965) we have acted in the spirit of the concept "per Mariam ad Jesum," to dedicate' the pulpit in all Poland, along with the whole institutional body of our church, to our pastoral duties, including such duties in a contemporary sense. We have directed our pastoral activities to religious and to social tasks: guidance to youth, social progress in justice and love, confrontation with asocial dangers, national soul-searching, marriage and family life, catechetical duties and similar activities.

The entire Christian community, moreover, has taken an active part in the Ecumenical Council through prayer, sacrifice and deeds of repentance. During sessions of the Council each pastoral community held special devotional services. Meanwhile Tschenstochau with its holy picture of the Mother of God, its confession booths and its Communion benches has been besieged for weeks on end by delegations of pastoral communities from throughout Poland who wanted to aid the Council by personal sacrifice and prayer.

Finally, during this year, the last of the great novena, we have all consecrated ourselves to the Mother of God-bishops, priests, members of religious orders and all strata of our laity. From the tremendous moral and social dangers which threaten the soul of our people, but also its biological existence, we can be saved with the help and grace of our Redeemer. We ask His help, through the intercession of His Mother, the most Blessed Virgin. Full of child-like confidence, we throw ourselves into her arms. It is only in this way that we can become free internally as serving yet free children, even as "God's slaves," in Saint Paul's words.

We beg you, Catholic shepherds of the German people, to seek in your own way to join in our celebration of our Christian millennium—be it through prayer or be it through a special memorial day. For any gesture of this sort you will have our gratitude. Convey our greetings and thanks, too, we pray you, to the German Evangelical brothers, who are trying along with us and with you to find solutions for our difficulties.

In this all-Christian and at the same time quite human spirit we extend our hands to you across the benches of the Council that is drawing to an end; we grant forgiveness and we ask your forgiveness. And if you, German bishops and Council fathers, grasp our outstretched hands in brotherhood, only then can we celebrate our millennium in Poland with clear consciences and in a true Christian spirit. We invite you most cordially to come to Poland for this event.

May this be the will of our merciful Redeemer and the Virgin Mary, the Queen of Poland, Regina Mundi et Mater Ecclesiae.

Rome, November 18, 1965

Stefan Cardinalis Wyszynski Primas Poloniae

German Bishops' Reply to their Polish Colleagues

Most esteemed colleagues and brothers in the office of bishop: It is with deep emotion and joy that we have received your missive of November 18 of this year and your friendly invitation to the thousand-year celebration of the Christianization of the Polish people. That you have been able to address this message to us we consider as a precious fruit of our common work in the Council. We accept the message thankfully, and we hope the dialogue that has begun can be continued among us in Poland and Germany. With God's help this discussion will foster and confirm the brotherhood between the Polish and the German people.

We are aware of how hard it was and still is for many Christians in Europe, after the terror of the second World War, to hold fast with all their hearts to the fundamental truth of our faith: that we are

311

children of the Heavenly Father and brethren in Christ. The fact of this Christian brotherhood was strikingly expressed in the year 1948 on the occasion of the celebration of the anniversary of the Cologne cathedral, through a visit to the event by French and English cardinals and bishops. May the millennium of the conversion of Poland to Christianity, to be celebrated in the coming year, be a similar sign.

In your communication, honored brethren, you have called on us to remember how many links have united the Polish people with Christian Europe over the centuries, and to remember the role that Poland has played within this Christian Europe—and, as we hope, will continue to play. In doing this you were so generous as to recall first and above all, from the history of all these centuries, examples that do honor to your people as to ours—examples of common enterprise, honest respect, fruitful exchange and mutual support. You did this even though such aspects might have been overshadowed by the injustice and the pain that the Polish people have had to bear during the course of history.

It is an encouraging omen for that future which we hope for and are working towards with all our capabilities that you remind us of how the Polish church during the Middle Ages carried on a many-faceted interchange, regardless of borders, with German cities, communities and religious orders. It moves us deeply to realize that we and you are united in our homage to Saint Hedwig, who while of German blood was—as you write—the greatest 13th-century benefactor of the Polish people.

For this bright side of the Polish-German historical relationship there is no doubt that we have our common Christian faith to thank. We are convinced of the following point, honored brothers, and at one with you in regard to it: if we wish to be brethren in Christ despite all differences; if we bishops, as it became clear during this Council, first and above all want to be a comradeship of shepherds, serving one people under God; and if we are to lead our individual churches in this spirit, then the shadows must vanish that unfortunately still enshroud the people of both our countries.

Terrible things have been done to the Polish people by Germans and in the name of the German people. We know that we must bear the consequences of the war, consequences that for our land, too, are harsh. We understand that the time of the German occupation has left behind a burning wound that even with the best will is hard to heal. The more thankful are we, then, in view of these facts, for your recognition, with truly Christian generosity, that in the time of National Socialism a large part of the population of Germany was under extreme pressure of conscience.

We are grateful that in the face of the millions of Polish lives sacrificed in that era you also recall the Germans who resisted the evil and in some cases gave their lives in doing so. It is a consolation to us that in the night of hatred many of our priests and Christian believers stood up, in prayer and sacrifice, for the Polish people, and accepted imprisonment and death because of this Christian love. We are thankful that along with the immeasurable suffering of the Polish people you also think upon the hard lot of the millions of German expellees and refugees.

To present a bill for guilt and injustice—here you and we are of the same opinion—will certainly not help us. We are children of one Heavenly Father. All human injustice is first of all guilt towards God, and forgiveness must be asked for first of all from Him. It is first of all to Him that the Lord's Prayer addresses itself: forgive us our debts. Then with honest hearts we may seek forgiveness from our neighbors.

So it is that we too beg you to forget; yes, we ask you to forgive. Forgetting is an act within the realm of human beings. The request for forgiveness is an appeal to Him who suffered injustice to see this injustice with the merciful eye of God, and to permit a new beginning.

This beginning is burdened in particular by the bitter consequences of the war begun and lost by Germany. Millions of Poles have had to leave the east and resettle in an area to which they were ordered to go. Indeed we know what, as a result, this area signifies for the Poland of today. But millions of Germans, too, had to abandon the homes in which their fathers and their fore-fathers had lived. These people had not arrived in their homelands as conquerors, but were called there over the course of centuries by the local rulers.

That is why we must say to you in love and truth: When these Germans speak of "right to a home" they—aside from a few exceptions—have no aggressive intention. Our Silesians, Pomeranians and East Prussians are trying to say that they lived rightfully in their old homeland and that they retain their tie to this home. At the same time they are aware that now a new generation is growing there, of people who also consider this territory—to which their fathers were sent—as home.

Christian love seeks to feel for the cares and sorrows of other persons, and thus to overcome tensions and cross borders. Christian love wants to eradicate the evil of hate, of hostility and of revenge. This Christian spirit will contribute, therefore, to the reaching of a solution to all the unhappy consequences of the war, a solution satisfactory and fair to all sides. You may be sure that no German bishop wishes, or ever will call for, anything other than the brotherly relationship of our two peoples in a completely sincere and honest dialogue.

The experience of the Council can encourage us towards such a brotherhood of goodwill. For the Council, too, the way ahead was not always visible. The goal was not always crystal-clear, and often the church fathers stood hesitant at a cross-roads. But then through God's grace a way was shown to us, and sometimes an astonishing solution was presented to us. So we hope, together with you, that God will also show our two peoples solutions for their future, if we give Him evidence of our goodwill.

As an indication of our goodwill, honored brothers, we wish, in gratitude for your invitation, to come as pilgrims to your shrine of Mary in Czestochowa and share in your joy and that of all your people. We want to pray with you at the shrine where the Polish people have so often and especially in the present day prayed for strength and the blessing of God. We promise to call upon our faithful to join with us and you in prayer during the coming Marian month.

We want to do everything to keep this link from breaking ever again. In the year 1968 the German Catholic convention will be held in Essen. In the same year the bishopric of Meissen marks the thousand-year anniversary of its foundation. It would be a great pleasure for us and for our followers to be able to greet Polish bishops on these occasions. In issuing these invitations, we share with you the wish that the encounter of the bishops and the dialogue that has now begun will be emulated and continued by our two peoples in all walks of life.

We will welcome with full hearts all steps that can serve this goal. Therefore we are happy to fulfill your wish that we convey your special greeting to our Evangelical brethren in Germany. Furthermore, we may consider ourselves, in our efforts towards mutual understanding, to be united with all persons of goodwill.

Most esteemed brothers! The Council has brought us together in the Holy City to work and pray together. The grotto of Saint Peter shelters the little chapel of the Madonna of Czestochowa. There we found too the picture of Saint Hedwig, especially revered by your people, and whom you called "the best example of the existence of a Christian act of bridge-building between Poland and Germany." Let us learn from this great saint to meet one another in love and respect.

At the conclusion of your message stand the precious words that can augur a new future for our two peoples: "We extend our hands to you across the benches of the Council that is drawing to an end. We grant forgiveness and we ask your forgiveness." With brotherly respect we grasp the proffered hands. May the God of peace grant, through the intercession of Regina Pacis, that the unholy spirit of hatred never separate our clasped hands again!

Rome, December 5, 1965

Source: Embassy of the Republic of Poland in Berlin.

Notes

1. Pertti Ahonen, *After the Expulsion: West Germany and Eastern Europe, 1945-1990* (Oxford , 2003), 1; Andreas Kossert, *Kalte Heimat* [Cold Homeland] (Munich , 2008), 16.
2. David Rock and Stefan Wolff, eds., *Coming Home to Germany?* (New York, 2002), 25.
3. Ibid., 27.
4. Stefan Aust and Stephan Burgdorff, eds., *Die Flucht* [The Flight] (Munich, 2002), 226.
5. Rock and Wolff, eds., *Coming Home to Germany?* 20.
6. Ibid., 23.
7. Robert G. Moeller, *War Stories: The Search for a usable past in the Federal Republic of Germany* (Berkeley, 2001), 55.
8. Stefan Wolff, ed., *German Minorities in Europe: Ethnic Identity and Cultural Belonging* (New York, 2000), 189.
9. Rock and Wolff, eds., *Coming Home to Germany?* 73.
10. Wolff, ed., *German Minorities in Europe*, 190.
11. Yinan He, *The Search for Reconciliation* (New York, 2009), 77.
12. Ibid.,
13. Marcin Zaborowski, *Germany, Poland and Europe* (New York, 2004), 67.
14. He, *Search for Reconciliation*, 78, 79.
15. Ibid., 103.
16. Ann L. Phillips, *Power and Influence after the Cold War: Germany in East–Central Europe* (Lanham , MD, 2000), 74.
17. Claus Hofhansel, *Multilateralism, German Foreign Policy and Central Europe* (London, 2005), 37.
18. Ibid., 62.
19. Jürgen Tampke, *Czech-German Relations and the Politics of Central Europe* (New York, 2003), 153.
20. Hofhansel, *Multilateralism*, 26.
21. Jörg K. Hoensch, *A History of Modern Hungary, 1867-1994* (New York, 1996), 287.
22. Phillips, *Power and Influence after the Cold War*, 87.
23. Hoensch, *History of Modern Hungary 1867-1994*, 304.
24. Ibid., 295.
25. Phillips, *Power and Influence after the Cold War*, 66.
26. Ibid., 55.
27. Aurel Braun, *Romanian Foreign Policy Since 1965, The Political and Military Limits of Autonomy* (New York, 1978), 25.
28. Wolff, ed., *German Minorities in Europe*, 197, 198.
29. Auswärtiges Amt, [The Foreign Office], *Federal Republic of Germany*, October 2009.

30. Dirk Verheyen and Christian Søe, eds., *The Germans and Their Neighbors* (Boulder, CO, 1993), 318.
31. Ibid.
32. Carole Fink and Bernd Schaefer, eds., *Ostpolitik, 1969-1974* (Cambridge, 2009), 237.
33. Verheyen and Søe, eds., *Germans and Their Neighbors*, 323, 324.

Bibliography

Adler, H. G. *Theresienstadt, 1941-1945.* Tubingen: J.C.B. Mohr, 1955.

Ahonen, Pertti. *After the Expulsion: West Germany and Eastern Europe, 1945-1990.* Oxford: Oxford University Press, 2003.

Allen, Debra J. *The Oder-Neisse Line; The United States, Poland and Germany in the Cold War.* Westport, CT: Praeger Publishers, 2003.

Arndt, Werner. *Die Flucht und Vertreibung: Ostpreussen, Westpreussen, Pommern, Schlesien, Sudetenland: 1944-1945* [Flight and Expulsion: East Prussia, West Prussia, Pomerania, Silesia, Sudetentland: 1944-1945]. Wölfersheim-Berstadt: Podzun-Pallas, 2004.

Aust, Stefan, and Stephan Burgdorff, eds. *Die Flucht* [The Flight]. Munich: Deutscher Taschenbuch Verlag, 2002.

Bartlett, Roger, and Karin Schönwälder, eds. *The German Lands and Eastern Europe: Essays on the History of Their Social, Cultural and Political Relations.* London: Macmillan Press, 1999.

Benz, Wolfgang, ed. *Die Vertreibung der Deutschen aus dem Osten* [The Expulsion of the Germans from the East]. Frankfurt/Main: Fischer Taschenbuch Verlag, 1995.

Bessel, Richard. *Germany 1945.* New York: Harper Collins Publishers, 2009.

Birger, Trudy. *A Daughter's Gift of Love.* Philadelphia, PA: The Jewish Publication Society, 1992.

Birn, Ruth Bettina. *Austrian Higher SS and Police Leaders and Their Participation in the Holocaust in the Balkans.* Holocaust and Genocide Studies, vol. 6, no. 4. Oxford: Pergamon Press, 1991.

Blanke, Richard. *Orphans of Versailles, The Germans in Western Poland 1918-1939.* Lexington: University of Kentucky Press, 1993.

Boockmann, Hartmut. *Der Deutsche Orden in der deutschen Geschichte* [The Order of the Teutonic Knights in German History]. Bonn: Bund der Vertriebenen, 1998.

Borhi, Laszlo. *Hungary in the Cold War, 1945-1956: Between the United States and the Soviet Union.* Budapest: Central European University Press, 2004.

Bozo, Frederic, Marie-Pierre Rey, N. Piers Ludlow, and Leopoldo Nuti, eds. *Europe and the End of the Cold War.* New York: Routledge, 2008.

Braham, Randolph L. *The Politics of Genocide, The Holocaust in Hungary.* Vol. 1. New York: Columbia University Press, 1994.

Braun, Aurel. *Romanian Foreign Policy since 1965, the Political and Military Limits of Autonomy.* New York: Praeger Publishers, 1978.

Cadzow, John F. Andrew Ludanyi, and Louis J. Elteto, eds. *Transylvania; The Roots of Ethnic Conflict.* Kent, OH: Kent State University Press, 1983.

Casagrande, Thomas. *Die Volksdeutsche SS-Division "Prinz Eugen"* [The Ethnic German SS Division "Prinz Eugen"]. Frankfurt/Main: Campus Verlag, 2003.

Cohen-Pfister, Laurel, and Dagmar Wienroeder-Skinner, eds. *Victims and Perpetrators, 1933-1945.* Berlin: W. de Gruyter, 2006.

Cordell, Karl, and Stefan Wolff. *Germany's Foreign Policy towards Poland and the Czech Republic, Ostpolitik Revisited.* London: Routledge, 2005.

Curp, T. David. *A Clean Sweep? The Politics of Ethnic Cleansing in Western Poland, 1945-1960.* Rochester, NY: University of Rochester Press, 2006.

Davy, Richard, ed. *European Détente: A Reappraisal.* London: The Royal Institute of International Affairs, 1992.

De Zayas, Alfred M. *Nemesis at Potsdam.* London: University of Nebraska Press, 1977.

_____. *A Terrible Revenge.* New York: St. Martin's Press, 1993.

Deutsche Ost-und Siedlungsgebiete [Germany's Eastern Colonization Territories]. Edited by Bund der Vertriebenen, Bonn, 1998.

Dönhoff, Marion Countess. *Before the Storm.* New York: Alfred A. Knopf, 1990.

Duffy, Christopher. *Red Storm on the Reich.* New York: Castle Books/Scribner, 1991.

Erb, Scott. *German Foreign Policy, Navigating a New Era.* Boulder, CO: Lynne Rienner Publishers, 2003.

Fink, Carole, and Bernd Schaefer, eds. *Ostpolitik, 1969-1974, European and Global Responses.* Cambridge: Cambridge University Press, 2009.

Freeman, Michael. *Atlas of Nazi Germany.* New York: Macmillan Publishing, 1987.

Friedman, Saul S., ed. *Terezin Diary of Gonda Redlich.* Lexington: The University Press of Kentucky, 1992.

Frommer, Benjamin. *National Cleansing: Retribution against Nazi Collaborators in Postwar Czechoslovakia.* Cambridge: Cambridge University Press, 2005.

Gal, Kinga. *Bilateral Agreements in Central and Eastern Europe: A New Inter-State Framework for Minority Protection?* Flensburg, Germany: European Center for Minority Issues, 1999.

Gellately, Robert, and Ben Kiernan, eds. *The Specter of Genocide, Mass Murder in Historical Perspective.* Cambridge: Cambridge University Press, 2003.

Geschichte der deutschen Vertriebenen und ihrer Heimat [The History of German Expelees and their Homeland]. Edited by Zentrum gegen Vertreibungen, Bonn, 1998.

Giertych, Jedrzej. *Poland and Germany.* London: Jedrzej Giertych, 1958.

Goldsworthy, Terry. *Valhalla's Warriors, A History of the Waffen-SS on the Eastern Front 1941-1945.* Indianapolis, IN: Dog Ear Publishing, 2007.

Gollancz, Victor. *In Darkest Germany.* Hinsdale, IL: Henry Regnery, 1947.

Grant Duff, Shiela. *A German Protectorate: The Czechs under Nazi Rule.* London: Frank Cass, 1970.

Gruber, Wendelin. *In the Claws of the Red Dragon, Ten Years under Tito's Heel.* Toronto: St. Michaelswerk, 1988.

Gündisch, Konrad. *Die Siebenbürger Sachsen* [The Transylvanian Saxons]. Bonn: Bund der Vertriebenen, 1994.

Hastings, Max. *Armageddon, The Battle for Germany, 1944-1945.* New York: Alfred A. Knopf, 2004.

Havel, Vaclav. *The Art of the Impossible: Politics and Morality in Practice Speeches and Writings, 1990-1996.* New York: Knopf, 1997.

_____. *Dear Dr. Husak, in Open Letters, Selected Writings, 1965-1990.* New York: Knopf, 1991.

He, Yinan. *The Search for Reconciliation.* New York: Cambridge University Press, 2009.

Hillgruber, Andreas. *Hitler, König Carol und Marschall Antonescu.* Wiesbaden: Franz Steiner Verlag, 1965.

Hoensch, Jörg K. *A History of Modern Hungary, 1867-1994.* New York: Longman, 1996.

Hoffmann, Joachim. *Stalin's War of Extermination 1941-1945.* Capshaw, AL: Theses and Dissertation Press, 2001.

Hofhansel, Claus. *Multilateralism, German Foreign Policy and Central Europe.* London: Routledge, 2005.

Höhne, Heinz. *The Order of the Death's Head.* New York: Ballantine Books, 1971.

Huber, Gustl. *Der Weg der Donauschwaben* [The Way of the Danubian Swabians]. Bonn: Bund der Vertriebenen, 1997.

Illyes, Elemer. *National Minorities in Romania, Change in Transylvania.* Boulder, CO: East European Monographs, 1982.

Ingrao, Charles, and Franz A. J. Szabo, eds. *The Germans and the East*. West Lafayette, IN: Purdue University Press, 2008.

Kaltenegger, Roland. *Mountain Troops of the Waffen-SS, 1941-1945*. Atglen, PA: Schiffer Publishing, 1995.

Keesing's Contemporary Archives. *Germany and Eastern Europe since 1945, From the Potsdam Agreement to Chancellor Brandt's "Ostpolik."* New York: Charles Scribner's Sons, 1973.

Keil, Thomas J. *Romania's Tortured Road to Modernity*. Boulder, CO: East European Monographs, 2006.

Kenez, Peter. *Hungary from the Nazis to the Soviets, The Establishment of the Communist Regime in Hungary, 1944-1948*. New York: Cambridge University Press, 2006.

Kimminisch, Otto. *Das Recht auf die Heimat, Ein universelles Menschenrecht* [The Right to a Homeland; A Universal Human Right]. Bonn: Bund der Vertriebenen, 1996.

Kittel, Manfred. *Vertreibung der Vertriebenen?* [The Expulsion of the Expelees?]. Munich: R. Oldenbourg Verlag, 2007.

Knopp, Guido. *Die Wehrmacht, Eine Bilanz*. [The Wehrmacht; an Assessment]. Munich: C. Bertelsmann Verlag, 2007.

Koburger, Charles W., Jr. *Steel Ships, Iron Crosses, and Refugees, The German Navy in the Baltic, 1939-1945*. New York: Praeger Publishers, 1989.

Kokot, Jozef. *The Logic of the Oder-Neisse Frontier*. Warsaw: Wydawnictwo Zachodnie, 1959.

Komjathy, Anthony, and Rebecca Stockwell, *German Minorities and the Third Reich*. New York: Holmes and Meier Publishers, 1980.

Konschitzky, Walther. *Die Banater Schwaben* [The Banat Swabians]. Bonn: Bund der Vertriebenen, 1999.

Kopelev, Lev. *No Jail for Thought*. London: Secker and Warburg, 1975.

Kossert, Andreas. *Kalte Heimat* [Cold Homeland]. Munich: Siedler Verlag, 2008.

Kotzian, Ortfried. *Abschied von einer historischen "Brückenfunktion" im 20 Jahrhundert* [Farewell to a Historical Bridge Building Function in the 20th Century]. Augsburg: Bukowina Institut, 1991.

_____. *Deutsche Ost-und Siedlungsgebiete* [Germany's Eastern Colonization Territories]. Bonn: Bund der Vertriebenen, 1991.

_____. *Die Deutschen und ihre Nachtbarvölker* [The Germans and their Neighbors]. Augsburg: Bukowina-Institut, 1991.

_____. *Die Sudetendeutschen, Eine Volksgruppe im Herzen Europas* [The Sudeten Germans; A People in the Heart of Europe]. Bonn: Bund der Vertriebenen, 1998.

_____. *Motive deutscher Ostsiedlung* [Reasons for the German Settlement of the East]. Bonn: Bund der Vertriebenen, 1991.

Lieberman, Benjamin. *Terrible Fate; Ethnic Cleansing in the Making of Modern Europe.* Chicago, IL: Ivan R. Dee, 2006.

Liulevicius, Vejas Gabriel. *The German Myth of the East: 1800 to the Present.* New York: Oxford University Press, 2009.

Lukas, Richard C. *The Forgotten Holocaust, The Poles under German Occupation 1939-1944.* Lexington: The University Press of Kentucky, 1986.

Luza, Radomir. *The Transfer of the Sudeten Germans.* New York: New York University Press, 1964.

MacDonogh, Giles. *After the Reich.* New York: Basic Books, 2007.

Manes, Philipp. *As if it were Life; A WWII Diary from the Theresienstadt Ghetto.* New York: Palgrave Macmillan, 2009.

March, Ulrich. *Die Deutsche Ostsiedlung* [The German Settlement of the East]. Bonn: Bund der Vertriebenen, 1998.

Mast, Peter. *Kleine Geschichte West und Ostpreussens* [A Short History of West and East Prussia]. Bonn: Bund der Vertriebenen, 1997.

Merridale, Catherine. *Ivan's War.* New York: Henry Holt, 2006.

Mevius, Martin. *Agents of Moscow, The Hungarian Communist Party and the Origins of Socialist Patriotism, 1941-1953.* Oxford: Oxford University Press, 2004.

Minehan, Philip B. *Civil War and World War in Europe, Spain, Yugoslavia and Greece 1936-1949.* New York: Palgrave Macmillan, 2006.

Moeller, Robert G. *War Stories: The Search for a Usable Past in the Federal Republic of Germany.* Berkeley: University of California Press, 2001.

Muller, Jerry Z. "Us and Them, The Enduring Power of Ethnic Nationalism." *Foreign Affairs* 87, no. 2 (March/April 2008): 18–35.

Naimark, Norman M. *Fires of Hatred; Ethnic Cleansing in the Twentieth Century Europe.* Cambridge, MA: Harvard University Press, 2001.

_____. *The Russians in Germany: A History of the Soviet Zone of Occupation 1945-1949.* Cambridge, MA: Belknap Press of Harvard University Press, 1995.

Nawratil, Heinz. *Die Deutschen Nachkriegsverluste* [The German Post-War Losses]. Graz: Ares Verlag, 2008.

Nord, Lars. *Nonalignment and Socialism, Yugoslav Foreign Policy in Theory and Practice.* Stockholm: Raben & Sjögren, 1974.

Pencz, Rudolf. *For the Homeland; The History of the 31st Waffen SS Volunteer Grenadier Division.* West Midlands: Helion, 2002.

Phillips, Ann L. *Power and Influence after the Cold War, Germany in East-Central Europe.* Lanham, MD: Rowman & Littlefield Publishers, 2000.

Prokle, Herbert. *Der Weg der Deutschen Minderheit Jugoslawiens nach Auflösung der Lager* [The Fate of the German Minority in Yugoslavia after the Closing of the Camps]. Munich: Verlag der Donauschwäbischen Kulturstiftung, 2008.

Prokle, Herbert, Georg Wildmann, Karl Weber, and Hans Sonnleitner. *Genocide of the Ethnic Germans in Yugoslavia 1944-1948*. Munich: Documentation Project Committee, Verlag der Donauschwäbischen Kulturstiftung, 2006.

Rabinovici, Schoschana. *Thanks to My Mother*. New York: Dial Books, 1998.

Reichling, Gerhard. *Die deutschen Vertriebenen in Zahlen* [The German Expelees in Numbers]. Bonn: Kulturstiftung der Deutschen Vertriebenen, 1986.

Reinoss, Herbert, ed. *Letzte Tage in Ostpreussen* [Last Days in East Prussia]. Munich: Langen Müller, 2006.

Rikmenspoel, Marc J. *Waffen-SS Encyclopedia*. Bedford, PA: The Aberjona Press, 2004.

Rock, David, and Stefan Wolff, eds. *Coming Home to Germany?* New York: Berghahn Books, 2002.

Roman, Eric. *Hungary and the Victor Powers, 1945-1950*. New York: St. Martin's Press, 1996.

Savich, Carl. *Vojvodina and the Batschka Division*. Michigan: Serbianna.com, ELEGANCE Editions, 2008.

Schieder, Theodor, ed. *Das Schicksal der Deutschen in Jugoslawien* [The Fate of the Germans in Yugoslavia]. Vol. V. Bonn: Bundesministerium für Vertriebenen, Flüchtlinge und Kriegsgeschädigte, 1961.

_____. *Documents on the Expulsion of the Germans from Eastern-Central Europe*. Vols. I, II, III, IV. Bonn: Federal Ministry for Expellees, Refugees and War Victims, 1956–1961.

Schwertfeger, Ruth, ed. *Women of Theresienstadt: Voices From a Concentration Camp*. Oxford: Berg Publishers, 1989.

Stanek, Thomas. *Verfogung 1945* [Persecution 1945]. Vienna: Bölau Verlag, 2002.

Stein, George H. *The Waffen SS, Hitler's Elite Guard at War*. New York: Cornell University Press, 1966.

Sterling, Eric J., ed. *Life in the Ghettos during the Holocaust*. Syracuse, NY: Syracuse University Press, 2005.

Tampke, Jürgen. *Czech-German Relations and Politics of Central Europe; From Bohemia to the EU*. New York: Palgrave Macmillan, 2003.

The Hamburg Institute for Social Research. *The German Army and Genocide*. New York: The New Press, 1999.

Theile, Karl H. *Beyond "Monsters" and "Clowns", The Combat SS: Demythologizing Five Decades of German Elite Formations*. Lanham, MD: University Press of America, 1997.

Theisen, Alfred. *Die Vertreibung der Deutschen-unbewältigte Vergangenheit Europas* [The Expulsion of the Germans-Europe's Unresolved Past]. Bonn: Bund der Vertriebenen, 1995.

Thorwald, Jürgen. *Die Grosse Flucht* [The Great Flight]. Stuttgart: Steingrüben Verlag, 1949–1951.

Troller, Norbert. *Theresienstadt, Hitler's Gift to the Jews.* Chapel Hill, NC: The University of North Carolina Press, 1991.

Turnwald, Wilhelm K., ed. *Documents on the Expulsion of the Sudeten Germans.* Munich: Association for the Protection of Sudeten German Interests, 1953.

Urban, Vincent. *Hitler's Spearhead.* London: Trinity Press, 1945.

Verheyen, Dirk, and Christian Søe, eds. *The Germans and Their Neighbors.* Boulder, CO: Westview Press, 1993.

Vertreibung und Vertreibungsverbrechen 1945-1948 [Expulsion and Crimes of Expulsion 1945-1948]. Bonn: Kulturstiftung der Deutschen Vertriebenen, Bericht des Bundesarchivs, 1974.

Von Lehndorff, Hans, Count. *East Prussian Diary.* London: Oswald Wolff Publishers, 1963.

Von Normann, Käthe. *Tagebuch aus Pommern 1945/1946* [Diary from Pomerania 1945/1946]. Munich: Deutscher Taschenbuch Verlag, 1962.

Von zur Mühlen, Heinz. *Die baltischen Lande, Von der Aufsegelung bis zum Umsiedlung* [The Baltic Lands, from Arrival to the Transfer]. Bonn: Bund der Vertriebenen, 1997.

Weidlein, Johann, ed. *Geschichte der Ungarndeutschen in Dokumenten 1930-1950* [History of the Hungarian Germans in Documents 1930-1950]. Schorndorf: Württemberg, Adolf Haushan, 1958.

Wiskemann, Elizabeth. *Germany's Eastern Neighbours; Problems Relating to the Oder-Neisse Line and the Czech Frontier Regions.* London: Oxford University Press, 1956.

Wolff, Stefan, ed. *German Minorities in Europe: Ethnic Identity and Cultural Belonging.* New York: Berghahn Books, 2000.

Wuescht, Johann. *Jugoslawien und das Dritte Reich* [Yugoslavia and the Third Reich]. Stuttgart: Seewald Verlag, 1969.

Zaborowsky, Marcin. *Germany, Poland and Europe, Conflict, Co-operation and Europeanisation.* New York: Manchester University Press, 2004.

Zach, Krista, ed. *Migration im südöstlichen Mitteleuropa* [Migration in Southeastern Central Europe]. Munich: IKGS, 2005.

Ziemke, Earl F. *Stalingrad to Berlin, the German Defeat in the East.* Washington, DC: The U.S Army Center of Military History, 1968.

Index

Adenauer, Konrad (German Chancellor), 286, 288
Alba Julia
    See Declaration of Karlsburg
Allied Control Commission, 79, 191–192
Allied Control Council, 76, 162–163
Allied Zones of Occupation of Germany, xii, 10–11, 20, 162, 170
Allies, xiii
    Chetniks and Tito, 214
    Curzon Line, 4
    and acceptance of refugees, 10–11
    effects of bombing, 30
    expulsion of inhabitants of
        Sudetenland, 112, 146
    Polish frontier, 83
    postwar political objective, 286
    Potsdam Conference, 64, 162
Anti-Fascist Council for the Liberation of Yugoslavia
    See AVNOJ
Antonescu, Ion (General, 1882–1946), 247–249, 253–254
Äôs Courts
    See Czech Extraordinary People's Courts
Arrow Cross Party, 185
Association of German Friendship Circles in Poland, 80
Auschwitz-Birkenau, xiv, xx, 9, 65, 85–86, 138–139, 302, 307
Aussig (Usti nad Labem), Czechoslovakia, 107, 125–128
Austria, xii, 2–4
    assassination of Archduke Franz Ferdinand, 138
    cession of Burgenland to, 175

Austria (*continued*)
    expulsion of Germans from Hungary to, 199–200, 208
    German escapes to, 208
    German evacuation to, 102
    German expulsion to, 147, 152, 160–170
    Habsburg, 87
    1910 census, 95
Austro-Hungarian Compromise of 1867, 210
Austro-Hungarian Empire, 2, 95–98,
Autochthonous peoples, 76, 80, 285
    See also Kashubians in West Prussia and Pomerania
    Masurians in East Prussia
AVNOJ (Anti-Fascist Council for the Liberation of Yugoslavia), 208

Banat (Yugoslavia, Hungary and Romania), 2–3, 16, 175–176, 198, 209–219, 224–235, 259–261, 267, 299–300
    forced resettlement of Banat Germans, 274–279
    Swabians of, 243–246, 249
Banat Swabians, 175–176, 209, 244, 249, 274
Baragan steppes (Romania), 274–276
Baranya, 175, 179–182, 200, 209, 212–213, 219
Bartoszewski, Wladyslaw (Foreign Minister of Poland), 23, 291
Batschka (Bacska), 176, 187, 198, 209–210, 212–213, 219, 227–228, 231–232, 234, 236
Batschka Division
    See 31st Waffen SS Division
Bavaria, xii, 17, 137, 175, 255–257

Donets Basin (Ukraine), 58, 267
Draza, Mihailovic (Colonel), 214
  See also Chetnik

East Prussia
  creation of, 88–89
  deportations to Soviet Union, 61–62
  expulsion of Germans from, 20, n21,
    80
  flight of population from, 11–15,
    40–47
  political views of German residents,
    xiii
  and Potsdam Conference, 2
  return of German residents to,
    56–58
  Soviet attack on, 25–26
  treatment of Germans by Soviet Union
    in annexed portions of, 70–75
  treatment of German residents by
    Poland, 76
Ehrenburg, Ilya (Soviet writer), 24
Eichmann, Adolf (SS leader), 139, 141
Elbing (Elblag), 12, 41, 43–44, 47, 88
Elblag
  See Elbing
Equalization of Burden Law (Lastenausgleichsgesetz), 284
ethnic cleansing, 1–7, 81, 142, 209, 302
ethnic Germans
  See Volksdeutsche
expulsions, xi, xiii-xiv, xx, 2, 5, 7–11, 17,
  20, 70–91, 132, 146, 161–162, 169, 196,
  199–203, 287, 293, 296
Eugene (Prince of Savoy), 215, 243,
  262

Federal Republic of Germany
  See German Federal Republic
forced labor, 3, 26, 293
  Czechs in Germany, 130–137
  Germans in Czechoslovakia, 115–116,
    129
  Germans in Poland, 69, 78, 85, 131
  Germans in the Soviet Union, 58–64,
    70, 191–195, 219, 221–224
  Germans in Yugoslavia, 238
  Poles in Germany, 69, 78
  Romanians of German ethnicity in the
    Soviet Union, 261–270
  See also, slave labor.
Fourteen Points, 2, 5

Frank, Hans (Nazi Governor-General of
  Occupied Poland), 85
Frank, Karl Hermann (Reich Minister for
  Bohemia and Moravia), 130, 145
Frisches Haff (East Prussia), 42–44

Gdansk
  See Danzig
GDR
  See German Democratic Republic
Gdynia
  See Gotenhaven
German Democratic Republic, 283,
  287–288, 290
  Poland's decision to allow tourists
    from GDR to enter Austria, 297
German Federal Republic
  Central Government Archives of,
    220–221, 224, 226, 230, 235
  emigration of ethnic Germans from
    Romania, 6
  from Yugoslavia, 209, 232, 238–239
  integration of refugees, 284–285
  reconciliation with Czechoslovakia,
    292–295
  with Hungary, 296–298
  with Poland, 289–291
  with Romania, 280, 299–300
  with Yugoslavia, 300–301
Germany, Soviet Zone of Occupation of
  xii, 17, 56, 76, 80, 162, 169–170, 180,
  200–203, 267, 283, 287–288
Geza II, (King of Hungary, 1141–1162),
  2, 224
Gheorghiu-Dej, Gheorghe (First Secretary of the Communist Party of
  Romania), 299
Goebbels, Josef (Nazi Minster of Propaganda), 11
"Golden Charter" of the Saxons,
  241–242
Gomulka, Wladyslaw (Polish Communist
  leader), 6, 25, 81
Gorny Slask
  See Upper Silesia
Gotenhaven (Gdynia), 45, 48–49
Gottwald, Klement (General Secretary of
  the Communist Party of Czechoslova-
  kia), 129, 142, 161
Great Britain
  and cancelation of 1938 Munich
    Treaty